CANADIAN
POLITICS

CONCISE THIRD EDITION

RAND DYCK
Laurentian University

THOMSON
─ ✦ ─
NELSON

Australia   Canada   Mexico   Singapore   Spain   United Kingdom   United States

THOMSON

★

NELSON

Canadian Politics
Concise Third Edition

Rand Dyck

Associate Vice-President, Editorial Director:
Evelyn Veitch

Publisher:
Chris Carson

Senior Executive Marketing Manager:
Don Thompson

Senior Developmental Editor:
Rebecca Rea

Photo Researcher and Permissions Coordinator:
Terri Rothman

Production Editor:
Tammy Scherer

Copy Editor:
Eliza Marciniak

Proofreader:
Wendy Yano

Indexer:
Edwin Durbin

Senior Production Coordinator:
Helen Locsin

Design Director:
Ken Phipps

Interior Design Modifications:
Roxanna Bennett

Cover Design:
Liz Harasymczuk

Cover Image:
© Digital Vision/PictureQuest

Compositor:
Nelson Gonzalez

Printer:
Webcom

Library and Archives Canada Cataloguing in Publication

Dyck, Rand, 1943-

Canadian politics / Rand Dyck.— Concise 3rd ed.

Includes bibliographical references and index.
ISBN 0-17-641679-X

1. Canada—Politics and government—Textbooks. I. Title.

JL75.D93 2005   320.971
C2005-901594-2

To Emma, the sweetest granddaughter in the world

Contents in Brief

Contents

Preface

It is very gratifying to be writing a third edition of the concise version of *Canadian Politics* for those who want a briefer and less detailed version of *Canadian Politics: Critical Approaches*. As in previous editions, this book is most appropriate for first-year university courses and community college use.

This book addresses Canadian government and politics in two separate but equal parts, either of which can be studied first. Chapters 2 through 10 could be classified as "politics," and Chapters 11 to 16 could be called "government." In this way, the book remains a comprehensive treatment of the whole subject, although it is more factual and less analytical than *Critical Approaches*.

In Part 1, this edition continues to emphasize the societal setting in which most political activity originates, including regional economic cleavages and class cleavages; the French and Quebec questions; Aboriginal, other ethnic, and gender issues; and the ever-increasing importance of external forces. Part 2 turns to linking people to government, including political culture, socialization, and participation; the mass media and public opinion polls; elections and the electoral system; political parties; and pressure groups, social movements, and lobbying. Part 3 deals with the constitutional context, including the Constitution, the Charter of Rights and Freedoms, and federalism. Part 4, "Governing," comprises chapters on the executive, the bureaucracy, Parliament, and the courts.

The book is accompanied by its own website, at http://www.concise3e.nelson.com, and the two are intended to be used as an integral unit. On the website, you will find the following items:

1. Regular updates of material in the book that has changed
2. Constitutional documents, such as parts of the Constitution Act, 1867; the Constitution Act, 1982 (including the Charter of Rights and Freedoms); and the 1987 Meech Lake Accord
3. Relevant web links for each chapter
4. Additional discussion questions
5. Detailed citations for important Supreme Court decisions

It should be added that Thomson Nelson also maintains a more general Political Science site at http://polisci.nelson.com, which supplements the one for this specific book.

In addition, Thomson Nelson has prepared a study guide for students to accompany this book (ISBN 0-17-640671-9), and an instructor's resource manual is available for professors (ISBN 0-17-640672-7). The latter contains an instructor's manual, a test bank, and overhead transparency masters.

Once again, I extend my thanks to everyone who helped in the preparation of this book, including those who contributed to previous editions. Many individuals and organizations were generous in providing information, and I have a particular affection for the cartoonists who permitted their work to be used. I am especially grateful for the many constructive suggestions made by reviewers of the manuscript: Anne Charles at Conestoga College, Shauna Longmuir at Sir Sandford Fleming College, and Richard Sigurdson, now at the University of Manitoba.

As usual, it was a delight to work with the staff of Thomson Nelson. Over the years, Rebecca Rea, Chris Carson, and Murray Moman have become close friends. I also interacted regularly with Tammy Scherer, Eliza Marciniak, and Wendy Yano, but there were many others behind the scenes who also contributed their magical talents to this production. The manuscript bears little resemblance to the final product, and I thank them all most warmly. Finally, as usual, my wife, Joan, provided the most supportive home environment imaginable.

Rand Dyck

Chapter 1

Introduction

If you are reading this book, you are probably already open to the excitement and importance of the subject of politics and government in Canada. How a whole society makes collective, public decisions is a fascinating question. Political personalities are often as interesting as movie stars, and the conflicts between them and their respective teams are as hard-fought as any hockey game. Politics often brings out the worst in human nature—ambition, selfishness, greed, and the will to control—but it is sometimes characterized by the best—an altruistic desire to serve the public interest and to improve the lives of the less fortunate. Politics and government may be the only way to solve many societal problems, and may well be the best way to solve some of your own!

Chapter Objectives

After you have completed this chapter, you should be able to:

Identify the many ways in which government action affects your life

Draw a comprehensive model of the Canadian political system

Explain the main function of each of the major institutions of Canadian government, including the prime minister and cabinet, House of Commons, Senate, bureaucracy, and judiciary

Appreciate the concentration of power in the executive branch of the government of Canada

Outline the basic differences between the Canadian and American systems of government regarding the separation of powers, party discipline, and the framework of federalism

The Political System

Perhaps it is best to begin with the 31 million residents of Canada. All these individuals have an array of needs that they attempt to satisfy, ranging from water, food, and shelter through security and friendship to self-esteem and self-fulfillment. Some of these needs are felt personally and individually, while others are concerns that we share with people of similar position, in small or large groups. Most of us spend much of our time trying to satisfy such needs.

In the first instance, we do so by our own efforts, in pairs, in families, in organizations of all kinds, at work, and at play. By not automatically calling for government help, we are essentially operating in the **private sector**. At some point, however, we may begin to feel that the satisfaction of our needs is beyond personal, interpersonal, family, or group capacity, and we come to the conclusion that the government should step in to help us. When we express the opinion that the government should take some action, we are converting a "need" into a "demand" and crossing the threshold between the private sector and the **public sector**. We can therefore say that a demand is the expression of opinion that government take some action (or desist from an action that it is already taking).

The first fundamental question that arises in politics and government is therefore whether people should "solve their own problems" or whether they should ask the government or the state to intervene. Almost everyone agrees that the government should provide certain security measures, such as police services and armed forces. Most people also support public highways and a public education system. The population is more divided, however, on the extent to which the government should provide such programs as social assistance, social housing, public pensions, and universal health care. One of the main reasons for such divisions of opinion is that government intervention normally costs money and usually relies on taxes of one kind or another. People also disagree on which areas of life the state should regulate and on how much regulation is appropriate.

The largest group of people reading this book will be young students, some of whom have probably not yet given too much attention to the role of government in their lives. But if you do, you will note that many interesting questions come to mind. To what extent should you be expected to pay for your postsecondary education, and to what extent should it be financed by the state? Why do tuition fees keep increasing, and what form and level of student assistance is most appropriate? Should the state (provincial or municipal) provide a transit system and/or subsidize bus or subway fares for students travelling to school or work? Should the state (federal or provincial) intervene to regulate the price of gasoline? Should the housing needs of students living away from home be met by private landlords, should the province regulate the rental market, or should the municipality, university, or college provide public housing? For those who work, should there be a minimum wage, and if so, what is an appropriate rate? Should all colleges and universities be public institutions, or is private postsecondary education a good idea?

What Do You Think?

Is it fair to bar and restaurant owners to prohibit smoking by municipal bylaws? Is it fair to smokers? Whose interests should prevail: those of smokers, nonsmokers, employers, or employees?

Many of these and other questions go beyond one's status as a student. For example, should affluent people be able to get quicker medical attention because they can pay for such health care, or should Canada maintain a universal system where no one can jump the queue? Should the public health care system be extended to pharmaceutical drugs and dental care?

Should the state put more restrictions on gasoline exhaust and other environmental hazards, or should companies be unrestricted in pollution emissions in the interest of providing jobs? How far should the state go in prohibiting discrimination in the workplace? Should it engage in employment equity programs to enhance the employment prospects of those discriminated against in the past? Should the federal government enact a national daycare program? Should people be able to enjoy pornographic materials, or should these be censored by the state? Such a list barely scratches the surface of issues involving potential government action, but it serves to demonstrate the relevance of government to our daily lives.

Many demands arise from deep, persistent divisions within society that are sometimes called "cleavages." The cleavages in Canadian society that generally have the greatest political significance are those between the geographic regions; between English, French, Aboriginal, and other ethnic and linguistic groups; and between various socioeconomic classes. Other common cleavages are related to gender, religion, and age. The relative importance and nature of these cleavages changes over time, and they are the subject of Chapters 2, 3, and 4.

Linking People to Government

Both those who seek state intervention and those who prefer that the authorities leave them alone must transmit their demands to the government. In either case, of course, such action requires knowledge and other resources that may well exclude a large proportion of people on the margins of society.

Figure 1.1 shows that individuals can communicate their needs directly to the government. This can be done on a personal basis, such as by means of a letter, fax, telephone call, e-mail, or face-to-face encounter. Sometimes such directly transmitted demands achieve their desired result, but very often they do not. When they do not, it may be time to consider some kind of group action.

Canadian society contains many groups, and it is quite likely that a group already exists to articulate the demand that any individual decides to transmit to the government. If such a group is not already in existence, it may be worthwhile to create one, since, as a general rule, the authorities are more likely to respond to a demand coming from a group than from a single individual. Such groups are usually called **advocacy groups**, **interest groups**, **pressure groups**, or **social movements**, and they constitute an important part of Canadian political activity. The Canadian Chamber of Commerce, the Canadian Labour Congress, and the Canadian Federation of Students are prominent examples. Corporations and other institutions also make demands, either individually or in groups.

A special kind of group that is even more overtly political is the **political party**, and it can also be used to transmit demands to the government. People join

Figure 1.1   **A Model of the Political System**

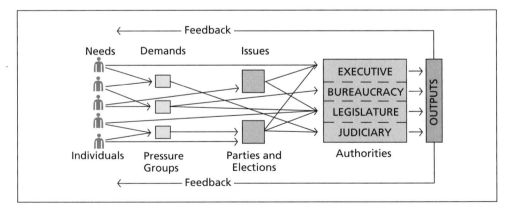

a political party or support it financially and try to get it to recognize their concerns in its platform or policies. If the party comes to power, it can incorporate the demand into government policy; if the party is in opposition, it may be able to use the mass media to bring the problem to national attention. Parties are particularly responsive to people's demands during an election campaign, as they appeal for the support of large numbers of individuals and groups by promising them to take the action they seek. Those dissatisfied with the manner in which existing parties are responding to their demands can create new parties. Examples are the creation of the Reform Party (which later became the Canadian Alliance and then absorbed the Progressive Conservative Party) and the Bloc Québécois.

Another means of transmitting the demand to the government is, as suggested earlier, via the **mass media** of communication. The media are usually eager to publicize controversial issues and often delight in pointing out problems that the government has failed to resolve. Although the media may be biased in their coverage, they give attention to individual and interest group concerns on a regular basis, cover political party activities, and are especially active in election campaigns, all of which helps to bring demands to the attention of the government. More than that, the media also provide the electorate with most of its information about politics, and in so doing serve to shape the whole nature of political discourse in Canada. All of these aspects of linking people to government are discussed in Chapters 6 to 10.

Despite the various avenues that can be used to transmit demands to the government, relatively few demands have any impact. The authorities are likely to ignore demands that do not concern very many people or that are contrary to their own values. Since the number of demands under serious consideration at any given time constitutes such a small proportion of the total number being made, it is sometimes useful to distinguish between demands and "issues," the latter including only those demands that the government has taken under serious consideration. It should be added that the authorities can make their own demands, which sometimes carry more weight than those arising from the wider society.

Government authorities are thus bombarded by demands from all directions, but even more striking than the vast quantity of demands is that there is usually intense conflict among them. The essence of politics and government, therefore, is choosing among competing demands, trying to resolve conflict, or making social choices in the midst of social conflict. **Politics** can be defined as that activity in which conflicting interests struggle for advantage or dominance in the making and execution of public policies. Politics is closely linked to the concept of **power**, which is often defined as the ability of one actor to impose its will on another, to get its own way, or to do or get what it wants.

Government

Having repeatedly mentioned **government**, we may now define it as the set of institutions that make and enforce collective, public decisions for a society. Backed up by armed forces, police, and punishments, if necessary, government possesses a particular kind of power called **coercion**. That is, the government has the ability to impose its will upon us by means of sanctions or penalties. Indeed, as a general rule, only the government, as an agent of the state, is allowed to use force or coercive power in society. But if we (or our ancestors) had a hand in the creation of such a government apparatus, as well as in the selection of the current governors, then we have in a sense agreed to be bound by its decisions. We have cloaked the government's power with legitimacy, that term being defined as "being accepted as morally binding." Such legitimate power is often called "authority," and a synonym for government is "the authorities." To some extent, we obey the government because of the threat or expectation of penalties if we do not, but we also obey because we accept government decisions to be binding upon us and necessary for the general good. Think of stopping at a red light or paying income taxes, for example.

Individuals and groups raise conflicting demands, but because there is a widespread consensus on the legitimacy of the government, people generally abide by its authoritative decisions, even when they disagree with them. (A current exception includes dissenters on gun registration). It is sometimes said, therefore, that politics and government are characterized by both conflict and consensus. The daily conflict normally operates within an underlying consensus about the decisionmaking apparatus and about remaining together as part of a united political community. Moreover, the authorities usually seek to develop some kind of consensus out of the conflicting demands.

Who are these government authorities? As can be seen in the diagram in Figure 1.1 (page 4), we usually divide them into four branches: the **legislature**, the **executive**, the **bureaucracy**, and the **judiciary**. The authoritative decision that a demand seeks can sometimes be made by a single branch of government. The legislature or Parliament passes laws, so if the demand requires the passage of a law, then action by the legislative branch will be necessary. The executive, consisting of the prime minister and cabinet, has a wide variety of powers. These include deciding where the government will spend money and appointing people to public positions. Thus, if the demand can be satisfied by an appointment or large monetary grant, it should be addressed to the executive. The bureaucracy is made up of public servants who work for the government, providing services and advising the politicians. If the demand is for the provision of routine government services or for changes in regulations, then bureaucratic action will probably suffice. Finally, the judiciary comprises the courts, which interpret the laws and make other decisions in case of dispute, and if the demand can be settled only by a judicial decision, it should be transmitted in that direction.

In many instances, however, the demand will require the combined actions of any two of the executive, legislative, and bureaucratic branches, or even all three working together, such as in the formulation, passage, and implementation of a new law. The courts normally stand somewhat apart from the other three organs of government. Judicial decisions usually follow authoritative actions in other branches of government, such as when the Supreme Court threw out the abortion provisions of the Criminal Code as being a violation of the Charter of Rights and Freedoms. But judicial decisions may also lead to subsequent legislative action. For example, after the Supreme Court ruled that a total ban on tobacco advertising was unconstitutional, the government introduced a revised law with fewer restrictions on tobacco advertising.

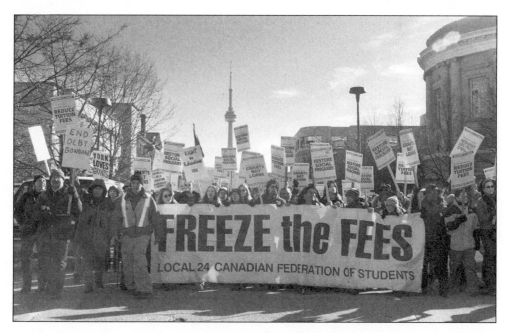

The Canadian Federation of Students demonstrates against rising tuition fees. (CP Photo/*Toronto Star*/Steve Russell)

Government decisions take many forms—laws, regulations, appointments, grants, contracts, services, and judgments—and can be collectively referred to as the "outputs" of the political system. Authoritative decisions are also made in the provinces and in an assortment of regional and local councils and boards, and they often require the agreement of two or more levels of government.

Completing the Picture

Whatever the type of output, it usually sparks a reaction in the rest of the system. This leads us to the concept of "feedback"—that is, a communication of the outputs back into the system. If an output satisfies a particular demand, that demand will no longer have to be articulated. For example, many French-speaking Canadians demanded that their language be designated as equal to English in government operations. The Pearson and Trudeau governments, which grasped at the opportunity to counter nationalism in Quebec, enacted the Official Languages Act as a result. But that was not the end of it: there was feedback or reaction to this decision. On the one hand, some francophones then demanded French-language services at the provincial as well as the federal level. On the other, many anglophones protested that the act (as well as Quebec language legislation favouring French) went too far. Thus, the reaction to one demand created a new pattern of demands; the language issue is still very much alive, especially in Quebec. The political system is thus characterized as a dynamic, circular process in which the authorities react to demands, convert some of them into outputs, and then respond in turn to whatever changes in the pattern of demands have resulted from the feedback from such outputs.

The modern world is composed of some 200 states such as Canada, and each has a government that makes its public decisions. Each state claims its own **sovereignty**, that is, its right to be self-governing; it has the final say over its own territory and people. But today's world is characterized by a tremendous amount of interplay among such states, as well as cross-border interaction and movement in terms of individuals, corporations, other organizations, and information. States often join international organizations and sign international agreements, and transnational corporations operate around the world. These developments constitute the phenomenon of **globalization**. Beyond the internal demands discussed above, such external actions increasingly serve as the source of demands on national political systems and as constraints upon domestic policymaking. As noted in Chapter 5, external pressures often lead a government into actions that it otherwise would not take, and no state is as sovereign as it would like to be.

Especially since the terrorist attacks on the United States in September 2001, governments have had to give additional attention to the adequacy of their security measures.

Foundations of Canadian Government Institutions

The Parliamentary System

Before going any farther, let us outline more specifically the basic institutions of government in Canada, which are dealt with in detail in Chapters 11 to 16. Within the central or national government in Ottawa (often called the "federal government"), the British parliamentary system provides the foundations of these governmental institutions. This system is based on the popular election of the members of the House of Commons. Parliament also has a second or "upper" chamber, the Senate, whose members are appointed by the prime minister. Such a two-chamber legislature is labelled "bicameral." The third part of Parliament is the monarch or the Crown. Because it was a British colony at the time the Constitution was adopted in 1867, Canada automatically shared the British monarch. The current monarch, Queen Elizabeth II, still resides in Britain, so on a practical basis, her representative, the governor general, exercises the functions of the Crown.

The British system is sometimes called the **Westminster model** or **parliamentary government**, but the latter label is somewhat misleading. The core of the parliamentary system, even in 1867, was the executive branch—the prime minister and the cabinet ministers. Although they must be members of Parliament, they are such an important part of Parliament that they often relegate both the monarch and other members of the House of Commons and Senate to a position of insignificance. Like the executive of any organization, the prime minister and cabinet are given the powers to lead and make the most important decisions. But the principle of **responsible government** holds that they retain their position and powers only as long as they are supported by a majority in the House of Commons. If the House of Commons declares a lack of confidence in the prime minister and cabinet, they must either resign, making way for another group to take their place, or call an election. Because the prime minister and cabinet ministers have seats in the legislative branch, mostly the House of Commons, the system is often described as involving a "fusion of powers"—that is, a combination of legislative and executive powers.

Evidence that the parliamentary system is executive-dominated can be seen in that the prime minister and cabinet ministers are given the power to introduce most laws and the right to control most of the agenda of the legislature. They have the exclusive power to introduce legislation of a financial nature—laws either to raise or to spend money. They have other wide powers as well: to make appointments, to draft subordinate legislation under the authority of laws, and to make decisions relating to international affairs—essentially all powers necessary to provide effective political leadership for the country. Other members of Parliament may criticize, delay, and propose amendments, but the prime minister and cabinet almost always get their way. This is so because a majority of the members of Parliament normally belong to the same political party as the prime minister and cabinet, and together they constitute a **majority government**. In this situation, prime ministers usually impose rigid party discipline on their MPs to support their every move. A **minority government** is somewhat less dominant.

The significance of the Senate has declined since Confederation because arriving there by appointment rather than election diminishes its members' legitimacy in a democratic age. The powers of the Senate have remained virtually equal to those of the House of Commons, but senators have rarely felt it proper to exercise them. Moreover, independent behaviour has been discouraged by the fact that the same party has usually held a majority both in the Senate and in the Commons. If for any reason the Senate should ultimately defeat a government bill, such an action does not affect the constitutional standing of the prime minister and cabinet. The model outlined here is also operational in each of the provinces, except that they all possess one-chamber (unicameral) legislatures.

Government was small and simple at the time of Confederation, but it has gradually developed another important branch, the bureaucracy or public service. The bureaucracy essentially advises the prime minister and cabinet on their decisions and then carries out whatever government programs have been authorized. The current Canadian bureaucracy consists of over 375 000 public servants who make a vast array of government decisions.

The British parliamentary system also incorporates the principle of **judicial independence**. Although courts are established by acts of Parliament, and judges are appointed by the prime minister and cabinet, the whole judicial system is expected to operate independently of the executive and legislative branches of government, as can be seen in Figure 1.2. In the case of Britain itself, judges have considerable discretion in interpreting laws but lack the power of **judicial review**,

Figure 1.2 An Outline of Canadian Political Institutions

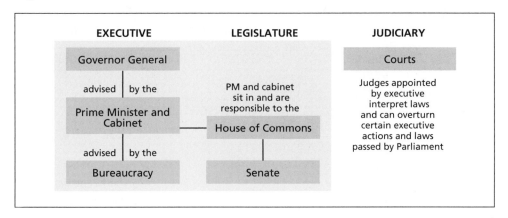

that is, the power to declare them invalid. The Canadian judiciary soon appropriated to itself the power to invalidate laws that violated the federal–provincial division of powers but was otherwise quite restrained.

Since the Canadian institutional structure was established in 1867, the only major change has been the adoption of the **Charter of Rights and Freedoms** in 1982. That action had the effect of expanding the scope of judicial review to include the new task of protecting individual rights and freedoms. Henceforth, the courts could disallow federal or provincial legislation or other government actions that violated the Constitution in terms of either the division of powers or the Charter of Rights and Freedoms.

The British parliamentary system is distinct in many ways from the presidential-congressional system of the United States. There, the president and the two houses of the legislature are independently elected, and no one is permitted to sit in more than one branch of government. The "separation of powers" means that executive, legislative, and judicial powers are distributed to three separate branches of government: president, Congress, and the courts respectively. Moreover, as indicated in Figure 1.3 (page 12), the U.S. system is also characterized by a maze of "checks and balances" designed to ensure that the actions of any one branch of government are subject to veto by another. Members of the House of Representatives and the Senate have much more legislative power than their counterparts in the parliamentary system, in terms of both initiating bills themselves and amending or vetoing those emanating from the executive. Party discipline is also much looser, so that even if a majority of the members of Congress belong to the same party as the president, there is no guarantee that the legislature

Figure 1.3   U.S. System of Separation of Powers and Checks and Balances

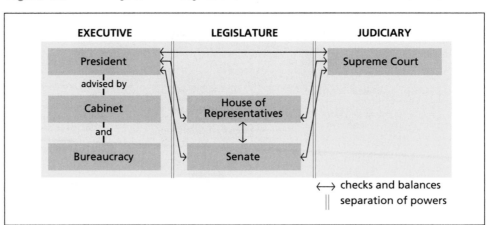

will pass the president's initiatives. The Supreme Court also has the power of judicial review and can overturn any legislation that it feels is in violation of the Constitution. Thus, even though it often appears that the U.S. president has enormous power, largely because of the manner in which that country tries to enforce its will across the globe, the fact is that, at least in domestic policy areas, the president actually has less control than the prime minister does in Canada.

Federalism

The Fathers of Confederation were dealing with a large piece of territory and were contending with colonies that had separate identities and a previous semi-autonomous existence. In this respect, the new country would have to be a **federation** of some kind, with two levels of government—central and provincial—and a division of powers between them.

Confederation was to a large extent the work of Sir John A. Macdonald, who went on to become the first Canadian prime minister. Macdonald preferred a unitary state or legislative union, in which the new central government would have almost all the powers and the provinces would be little more than municipalities. But Quebec and the Maritimes were not prepared to join such a system. Quebec demanded an autonomous provincial government so that its cultural concerns, such as education and civil law, would be placed in the hands of a French-speaking majority. Hence, the logical compromise was a system that contained a central government to deal with purposes common to the whole country and provincial governments to look after local concerns.

Macdonald accepted a federal form of government, allowing the former colonies to retain some of their political and economic independence, but he intended the new country to be a highly centralized federation. He felt that its economic and defensive objectives required a strong central government, a conviction reinforced by the conclusion among most of the other Fathers of Confederation that the American Civil War (which was ending just as they began their deliberations) had been the result of too much power at the state level. Thus, at their creation, the Canadian and American federations were quite different. The United States deliberately established a weak central government and strong states, while Canada preferred a strong central government and weak provinces.

Besides dividing powers between the two levels of government, constitutional architects in both the United States and Canada had to decide how the provinces or states would be represented at the national level. In both cases, the lower house of the legislature would be based on the principle of representation by population, so that the most populous provinces or states would have the largest number of members in that chamber. To protect the interests of the smaller states, however, the United States decided that each state, regardless of population, would have two senators at the national level. Some Fathers of Confederation also preferred this idea, but others wanted representation by population in both houses of Parliament. The Canadian compromise was to base the Senate on the principle of equal regional representation rather than equal provincial representation.

Fusing the Parliamentary System with Federalism

The basic governmental institutions established in 1867 thus combined the parliamentary system from Britain with a more centralized form of federalism than that found in the United States. But the whole ethos underlying the Canadian and U.S. systems was different. In the parliamentary system, everything is designed to *facilitate* government action by concentrating power in the hands of the executive, in terms of its relationship both with other institutions of government, such as Parliament and the courts, and with territorial units, such as provincial and local governments. In the American system, everything is designed to *inhibit* government action by preventing the concentration of power in the hands of any government. In the U.S., the individual institutions of the national government are able to veto each other and are collectively kept in line by a division of powers that gives most authority to the states. It is largely because the British system is designed to facilitate government action whereas the American system is designed to inhibit it that the fusion of the two systems in Canadian Confederation was such a distinctive creation. Macdonald saw the contradiction and therefore tried to establish a federal system that was much more centralized than that next door. He would turn over in his grave if he saw how powerful Canadian provinces have become and how much of a constraint they are on the actions of the national government!

As well, all provinces in Canada have found it convenient to delegate certain powers to local municipal governments. These are often headed by a mayor and council, usually include an autonomous school board, and sometimes incorporate other local elected or appointed authorities. Their responsibilities vary from province to province, and sometimes within a province, but municipal governments are often very significant. Unlike the federal and provincial governments, which are not subordinate to each other and whose specific powers are laid out in the Constitution, municipal governments are subordinate to provincial governments, and their responsibilities and taxing powers can be expanded or contracted at the province's whim. Municipalities typically have more responsibilities than their taxation powers can support, leading them to plead for increased provincial (or federal) funding.

This book concentrates on the federal or national system of government in Canada but does not deny the significance of the provinces and municipalities. Indeed, Chapter 12 deals with the relationship between the provinces and the national government. Especially since Paul Martin took over as prime minister, the federal government has been giving increasing attention to local governments.

SUMMARY

This chapter illustrated the many ways in which government action affects our everyday lives. It provided a model of the Canadian political system, showing how demands are transmitted from individuals and groups to the main institutions of government and sometimes transformed into public decisions. It outlined the main function of each organ of the Canadian government, emphasizing the concentration of power in the executive branch. The chapter contrasted this concentration with the separation of powers in the U.S. system of government, and it also showed the differences between Canada and the United States as federations.

DISCUSSION QUESTIONS

1. Which actions of the federal government or your own provincial or municipal governments do you disagree with? Should a different approach be used, or should these actions not be done at all? Which additional actions should one or more of these governments undertake?
2. What are the relative advantages and disadvantages of the structures of the Canadian and U.S. systems of government?
3. Do you feel that you are part of the political process? What would prompt you to be more involved?

KEY TERMS

Advocacy group/interest group/pressure group Any group seeking to influence government policy without contesting elections; an organization whose members promote their common interest by acting together to influence public policy.

Bureaucracy The permanent officials employed by the government, also known as the public service.

Charter of Rights and Freedoms Part of the Constitution Act, 1982, that guaranteed fundamental freedoms and legal, democratic, linguistic, mobility, and equality rights.

Coercion Power based on authorized physical force, including police, armed forces, and jails, on which government has a near monopoly.

Executive That branch of government that provides leadership and makes the major decisions.

Federalism (federation) A system of government characterized by two levels of authority (federal and provincial) and a division of powers between them, such that neither is subordinate to the other.

Globalization The modern phenomenon of nation-states declining in stature and power by giving way to the demands of transnational corporations via comprehensive free trade agreements, by massive diffusion of technological change, and by worldwide corporate competition or megamergers.

Government The set of institutions that make and enforce collective, public decisions for a society.

Judicial independence The constitutional principle that the courts should function independently of the rest of the government apparatus, especially the politicians, with implications for security of tenure and remuneration of judges.

Judicial review The power of the courts to overturn legislation or actions of the executive branch of government.

Judiciary The court system.

Legislature That branch of government whose function is to represent the people and make laws.

Majority government A situation in which the party in power has over 50 percent of the seats in the House of Commons.

Mass media Sources of information for the mass public—principally radio, television, and newspapers.

Minority government A situation in which the government party has fewer than 50 percent of the seats in the House of Commons.

Parliamentary government A form of government, distinct from the U.S. congressional system, characterized by parliamentary supremacy.

Political party An organized group that makes nominations and contests elections in the hope of influencing the policy and personnel of government.

Politics The activity in which conflicting interests struggle for advantage or dominance in the making and execution of public policies.

Power The ability of one actor to impose its will on another, usually considered to be the essence of politics and government.

Private sector That part of the economy operated by individuals, corporations, and other nongovernmental groups.

Public sector That part of the economy operated or financed by government.

Responsible government A form of government in which the political executive must retain the confidence of the elected legislature and resign or call an election if and when it is defeated on a vote of nonconfidence.

Social movement An informal network of organizations and individuals who on the basis of a collective identity and shared values engage in political struggle intended to expand the boundaries of the existing system, such as the women's and environmental movements.

Sovereignty Ultimate control or independence, such as Canadian national sovereignty vis-à-vis that of other countries.

Westminster model The model of government developed in Britain in which the political executive is given extensive power to provide effective leadership.

PART 1

The Societal Context

The next four chapters deal with the main elements of the societal or socioeconomic context of the Canadian political system. The aspects of Canadian society most relevant to politics are its regional, ethnic, and class features, primarily because they represent deep, persistent divisions called cleavages. In modern times, gender issues have also become a prominent feature of Canadian politics, while age will probably be of increasing significance in the future. Many of the demands with which the authorities have to contend originate from such cleavages.

Beyond the factors mentioned are the external forces that also affect the Canadian political system. The world has become a "global village," and international, multinational, transnational, and supranational—that is, "global"—factors are important elements of any national political system. This is especially true of Canada, which has always been open to such external influences, but all states are increasingly concerned with both international trade agreements and international terrorism.

Chapter 2

Economic Cleavages: Region and Class

Canada's deep-seated geographic and economic divisions are some of its most obvious characteristics. Such regional economic cleavages are a daily fact of Canadian political life, and many government decisions are direct responses to them. These cleavages can be most usefully discussed in terms of distance and division, regional economic differences, regional economic conflicts, and regional economic disparities. But economic divisions also exist in nongeographic terms, usually referred to as class—that is, disparities and conflicts among individuals with different levels of income and wealth and varied degrees of economic power. Governments must also deal with such class conflicts on a regular basis.

Chapter Objectives

After you have completed this chapter, you should be able to:

Discuss how distance, division, and the distribution of population affect the operation of the Canadian political system

Identify the principal regions in Canada and the relationship between regions and provinces

Identify the key economic factors that distinguish one region from another

Enumerate the principal regional economic conflicts in Canada, especially those that give rise to a feeling of Western alienation

Discuss different means of measuring regional economic disparities and programs that have been adopted to reduce them

Define the concept of class

Identify the traditional demands made by the upper class, middle class, and working class

Discuss the causes, extent, and implications of poverty in Canada

Regional Economic Cleavages
Distance and Division

Canada's tremendous distances have always had a crucial influence on its political system, especially in generating regional economic demands. The difficulties of dealing with such distances are immensely complicated by divisions caused by natural physical barriers running essentially in a north–south direction. Canada is usually divided into seven geographic regions, as shown in Figure 2.1.

The Great Lakes–St. Lawrence water route is an important means of linking several such regions to each other, rather than to neighbouring states to the south. Otherwise, however, transportation and communications linkages in Canada have had to be constructed across natural barriers. Demands to overcome distances and divisions have featured prominently in Canadian politics, and the establishment of some of these great transportation and communications projects has dominated whole eras of Canadian history. Governments have responded primarily by giving

Figure 2.1   Canada's Geographic Regions

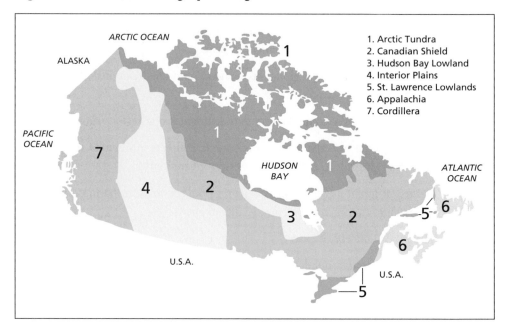

assistance to private corporations, establishing their own Crown corporations, and creating regulatory agencies in these fields.[1]

The major transportation and communications links and agencies with which the federal government has been associated are as follows:

- Canadian Pacific Railway
- Canadian National Railway
- VIA Rail
- Trans-Canada Highway
- Trans-Canada Airlines/Air Canada
- TransCanada Pipeline
- Canadian Broadcasting Corporation (CBC)
- Canadian Radio-television and Telecommunications Commission (CRTC)

In short, in order to create and hold together a nation, Canadians built east–west institutions that ran counter to the natural north–south geographic features of the continent and the perpetual pull of the United States. These ultimately included satellite services linking Canadians domestically (Telesat) and to the rest of the world (Teleglobe). In recent years, however, successive federal governments have deregulated, privatized, or reduced financial support for a number of these government operations.

Since people are not spread uniformly throughout Canada's gigantic territory, the distribution of population also complicates the distances involved. The overall density of the Canadian population is one of the lowest in the world, but what is really more significant is that there is no permanent settlement in nearly 90 percent of the country and that 75 percent of the population is huddled together within 150 kilometres of the U.S. border. The population of the various provinces in the 2001 census and in 2004 can be seen in Table 2.1 (page 22). Provincial population disparities affect the allocation of seats in the House of Commons—indeed, the whole power structure in Ottawa—and the calculation of federal transfer payments. Quebec is sensitive to the fact that in recent years its proportion of the total Canadian population has fallen below a symbolic 25 percent.

Ontario and Quebec combined contain about 62 percent of the population, and the Toronto–Ottawa–Montreal triangle obviously constitutes the "core" or "heartland" of Canada. While central Canada forms the political core of the country, it is also the economic heartland, with more large corporate head offices, especially in the Toronto area, than anywhere else. Moreover, it is the communications and cultural core, containing the headquarters of English and French

TABLE 2.1 POPULATION OF PROVINCES AND TERRITORIES

	2001 Census		April 1, 2004	
	Number	Percentage	Number	Percentage
Ontario	11 410 046	38.0	12 332 593	38.8
Quebec	7 237 479	24.1	7 520 938	23.6
British Columbia	3 907 738	13.0	4 177 443	13.1
Alberta	2 974 807	9.9	3 183 312	10.0
Manitoba	1 119 583	3.7	1 168 349	3.7
Saskatchewan	978 933	3.3	995 058	3.1
Nova Scotia	908 007	3.0	936 510	2.9
New Brunswick	729 498	2.4	750 540	2.4
Newfoundland and Labrador	512 930	1.7	518 955	1.6
Prince Edward Island	135 294	0.5	138 365	0.4
Northwest Territories	37 360	0.1	42 274	0.1
Yukon	28 674	0.1	31 512	0.1
Nunavut	26 745	0.1	29 567	0.1
Canada	30 007 094		31 825 416	

Source: Adapted from the Statistics Canada website, "Population and Dwelling Counts for Canada, Provinces and Territories, 2001 and 1996 Census," http://www12.statcan.ca/english/census01/products/standard/popdwell/Table-PR.cfm, and *The Daily*, Cat. 11-001, 23 June 2004, http://www.statcan.ca/Daily/p4p623/d040623b.htm (Retrieved 15 Aug. 2004).

CBC, CTV, CanWest Global, and private French-language television, the national newspapers, many other Canadian cultural institutions, and much of the Canadian high-tech industry. The rest of the country, the "periphery" or "hinterland," regularly complains that it is overlooked by both public and private decisionmakers, given such a concentration of population at the centre.

Regions, Provinces, and Territories

In speaking of **regionalism** in Canada, then, we begin with great distances complicated by geographic barriers and concentrations of population that cause variations in political and economic power. In addition, it is partly because of such distances and divisions that the provinces and territories were created. The constitutional basis of such units is somewhat different from the natural, geographic basis of regions, however, and the fit between regionalism and provincialism is not perfect. Feelings of regionalism can exist within a province, such as in the northern parts of many provinces; regional sentiment can cut across provinces, as in the case of people in northwestern Ontario feeling psychologically closer to Manitoba than to southern Ontario; and provinces can be lumped together into regions, such as the Maritimes or the Prairies. Nevertheless, as the 1979 Task Force on Canadian Unity pointed out, "the provinces ... are the basic building blocks of Canadian society and the logical units on which to focus a discussion of Canadian regionalism, even though they may not be the most 'natural' regions from an economic point of view."[2] It could be added that the creation of such provinces has served to enhance regional sentiment, as provincial politicians became exponents of regional problems and protectors of provincial interests.

In the 1990s, Quebec came closer than ever before to separating from the rest of Canada. If it were to leave with its existing borders intact (a somewhat debatable issue), Quebec would take with it almost one-quarter of the Canadian population, about 16 percent of the territory, and 21 percent of Canada's gross domestic product. From a strictly geographic point of view, the separation of Quebec would raise the question of continuing transportation links between Atlantic Canada and Ontario, border-crossing impediments, and jurisdiction over the St. Lawrence Seaway.

Regional Economic Differences

A discussion of the economies of the Canadian regions and provinces reveals striking regional economic differences that serve to reinforce their geographic distinctiveness and create another pattern of demands facing the Canadian political system.

Regional economic differences begin with primary industries or the natural resource base of the various provinces. The importance of natural resources to the national economy has been a central tenet of Canadian politics and economics for generations, usually termed the **staples theory** and identified with economic historian Harold Innis.[3] It postulates that Canadian economic development has relied on a succession of resource exports—furs, fish, timber, wheat, minerals, and energy—rather than manufacturing; Canadians are mere "hewers of wood and drawers of water."

Secondary industry consists of manufacturing, construction, and utilities. Manufacturing includes the initial processing and refining of primary products as well as the making of finished goods. Generally speaking, the secondary sector produces more revenue and more jobs than primary industry, is less seasonal, and commands higher wages. Primary and secondary industries are often combined as "goods-producing" industries.

Economists put transportation and communications, trade, finance, insurance and real estate, private services, and public administration into the "tertiary" or "services-producing" category. Manufacturing was never an important factor in the Canadian economy, and much political attention in this postindustrial era is focused on the services sector. The tertiary sector now furnishes about three-quarters of the employment in the country. With this background, let us highlight the economic differences among the various regions.

THE ATLANTIC PROVINCES

The Atlantic provinces have a distinctive and heavy reliance on fishing. This industry fell into deep trouble in the 1990s, primarily due to a dramatic reduction in cod stocks, but the abundance of shellfish has led to a partial recovery. The three Maritime provinces (New Brunswick, Nova Scotia, and Prince Edward Island) have a substantial agricultural base, while New Brunswick, Nova Scotia, and Newfoundland and Labrador also engage in forestry and mining, and there are great quantities of hydroelectric power in Labrador. Some processing and refining of natural resources takes place in the region, but the small local market and the distance from major population centres have left the region in a state of underdevelopment. Led by New Brunswick, however, a new emphasis on communications technology has revitalized the Atlantic provinces' economies to some extent, for in the modern technological world, physical distance is not the hindrance it was in the past. The Hibernia offshore oil project has already had an economic impact on Newfoundland, as has the Sable Island Offshore Energy Project (natural gas) on Nova Scotia. When the nickel mine is developed at Voisey's Bay in Labrador, it will also provide badly needed income and employment.

QUEBEC

The Quebec economy is more diversified than that of the Atlantic region and somewhat more prosperous. Quebec's outstanding primary industries include farming in the St. Lawrence Lowlands and mining and forestry in the Canadian Shield. The Shield is also traversed by numerous powerful rivers, making hydroelectricity Quebec's most valuable resource. Huge dams have been built on many of its rivers, including the controversial James Bay hydroelectric project. Hydro is the basis of Quebec's aluminum industry, as well as many other secondary industries. Quebec also stands out in the production of pulp and paper, especially newsprint, and is much stronger than the Atlantic region in the more sophisticated aspects of manufacturing, including aeronautics and pharmaceuticals. It also houses a large financial sector. The fact that economic power in Quebec used to rest largely in Anglo-Canadian and foreign hands fuelled the nationalist debate in that province. But since 1960 a major transformation has occurred, and both the public and francophone private sectors in Quebec have repatriated a great deal of industrial ownership.

ONTARIO

Ontario has always had the most diversified and strongest economy of any region. The province has an abundance of natural resources, including a great expanse of prime agricultural land in the south, as well as vast stretches of trees and almost every conceivable mineral in the Canadian Shield. Ontario's early development of hydroelectricity and of a steel industry gave it a head start over other regions. A skilled labour force, a large domestic market, proximity to the United States, and the advantage of federal tariff and banking policies also helped to make it the manufacturing heartland of the country. Sparked by the auto industry, it now produces over half of the Canadian manufacturing total. In addition, Ontario leads the country in the tertiary sector, including in areas such as finance, trade, and other services.

THE PRAIRIE PROVINCES

The Prairie provinces are historically associated with agriculture, especially wheat, other grain, and livestock. Alberta doubles as Canada's petroleum province and has become the richest part of the country by almost any measure. Petroleum is also of increasing significance in Saskatchewan, in concert with that province's other mineral resources, potash and uranium. Forestry is of some importance in Manitoba and Alberta, while Manitoba's hydroelectricity complements the petroleum of the other two Prairie provinces. The Prairies are also engaged in an increasing amount of manufacturing, and especially since 1960, the finance, trade, and service industries have expanded rapidly.

BRITISH COLUMBIA

Mountainous British Columbia is the leading forestry province and also specializes in mining, especially of natural gas, copper, and coal. Several fertile river and lake valleys provide for farming, and B.C. also possesses a significant fishing industry. The mountains are the source of several large rivers that have been dammed for the production of hydroelectricity. Manufacturing is primarily related to the forestry, mining, and agricultural bases of the B.C. economy, while recent Asian immigration has expanded the services sector, especially finance. British Columbia used to rank among the most prosperous provinces, but has recently fallen into the "have-not" category.

THE NORTH

In the North, the inhospitable climate, isolation, small and transient labour force, and poor transportation facilities conspire to retard economic development. It is primarily mining that has inspired many southerners to venture north over the years. Northern Aboriginal peoples used to be self-sufficient in hunting, fishing, and trapping, activities that continue to occupy them to some extent, but their lives have been disrupted by the arrival of newcomers. Settlement of many Aboriginal land claims and increased autonomy from Ottawa should better allow the Northern territories to respond to local needs in the future. Tourism is on the increase, a Mackenzie Valley natural gas pipeline may be in operation by 2009, and four producing or proposed diamond mines are already making a difference.

Regional Economic Conflicts

As a result of such regional economic differences, the national government regularly faces demands to assist the economy of a single province, region, or industry. Such demands do not necessarily involve conflict between one region and another, and sometimes they benefit them all. More often than not, however, demands from one region do conflict with those from another. Leaving aside Quebec, which will be examined in Chapter 3, the most common expression of such regional economic conflict has undoubtedly been the conflict between the Prairie and central regions. Since central Canada's regional interests have historically been persuasive with the federal government, the analysis is usually put in terms of the economic complaints of the West against the central core of the country.[4]

TRADITIONAL WESTERN COMPLAINTS

The traditional complaints of Western Canada relate to the following issues:

- Natural resources
- Tariffs
- Transportation
- Banking

While the Eastern provinces and British Columbia have always had jurisdiction over their own natural resources, Ottawa decided to retain such control when Manitoba was created in 1870, as well as with Saskatchewan and Alberta in 1905. The logic of this discrimination was that the federal government (i.e., central Canada) should control such resources in the national interest, allowing Ottawa to guide the development of the West. The Prairie provinces fought vehemently against this discrimination and were finally successful in gaining control of their natural resources in 1930.

The West complained for generations that Canadian tariff policy was designed in the interest of Ontario at the expense of the Prairies. In the 1879 **National Policy**, John A. Macdonald saw the tariff as a means of promoting and protecting the industrial heartland of central Canada. Adding a tariff (an import tax) to the price of imported manufactured goods would raise their price above that of goods manufactured in Canada, allowing domestic goods to be sold more cheaply than imports. Ontario thus gained employment in producing tractors, for example, but Western Canadians felt that this was contrary to their interests. In the absence of such a tariff, they would have been able to buy cheaper tractors from abroad. The West demanded lower tariffs at every opportunity, and in the 1920s sent its own farmer representatives—the Progressive Party—to the House of Commons to fight on this front.

Another aspect of Macdonald's National Policy that displeased the West was railway freight rates. Living so far from the central core of the country, Westerners expected to pay additional transportation costs, although they demanded that freight rates be subsidized by Ottawa. Indeed, the Crow's Nest Pass Act (or Crow Rate) of 1897 was an attempt to do just that, and it provided a low rate for transporting Prairie grain to eastern ports. Westerners successfully fought to retain the Crow Rate in the 1920s but were later greatly upset by the Trudeau government's decision to increase these rates, as well as by the Chrétien government's decision to abolish the subsidy entirely in 1995. A related complaint centres on peculiar inequities within the freight rate structure, including higher rates for finished goods than for raw materials, which discouraged the development of manufacturing in the West.

Canada deliberately developed a centralized branch banking system in an attempt to construct a sound, stable banking community that would avoid frequent local collapses. The result was a handful of large national banks, with headquarters in Toronto or Montreal and with local branches spread across the country. From a hinterland perspective, money deposited in the local branch of a national bank did not remain in the community to be lent out for local purposes but was sent to headquarters in central Canada to be used in the economic development of Ontario or Quebec. This was another reason for the farmers' revolt of the 1920s, and displeasure with the Canadian banking system had much to do with the rise of the Social Credit party in Alberta in the 1930s.

These four policy areas—natural resources, tariffs, transportation, and banking—can be put in a broader context. The metropolitan–hinterland thesis suggests that the West was created as a colony of central Canada and was intended to be held in a subordinate and dependent relationship.[5] The flavour of this relationship is captured in the cartoon below.

"The Milch Cow," by Arch. Dale (1882–1962), from the *Grain Growers Guide*, 15 December 1915. (Glenbow Archives NA-3055-24)

MODERN WESTERN ALIENATION

Some of these traditional issues continue to rankle the West, and additional concerns have emerged in recent times. The conflict over natural resources re-emerged in the 1970s and 1980s, especially with respect to petroleum pricing. After the OPEC (Organization of Petroleum Exporting Countries) cartel agreed on an artificial rise in the international price of oil in 1973, federal policy began to favour the consumer/manufacturing interest of central Canada at the expense of the producer interest of the West. The height of the regional economic conflict occurred in 1980 with the Trudeau government's **National Energy Program** (NEP), which imposed new federal taxes, kept the national price below the world level, encouraged frontier development, and promoted Canadianization of the industry, all objectives opposed by most Westerners. Eventually, a partial compromise between central and Western interests was reached in 1981, and the Mulroney government later scrapped the NEP entirely. Nevertheless, the NEP had a profound effect on the Western Canadian psyche, especially when combined with the West's simultaneous opposition to Ottawa's constitutional initiatives and official bilingualism policy.

Tariffs among all countries have gradually come down since 1945, but the issue took on a new life in the 1980s with the Western demand for a free trade agreement between Canada and the United States. By this time, business interests in central Canada also supported such a measure, and it was adopted to their mutual satisfaction.

In the 1970s, when the West became stronger in spite of the traditional banking policy, the federal government finally allowed regional banks to be established. Several of these new Western financial institutions faltered in the 1980s, however, largely because of a downturn in the Western economy that Westerners blamed on Trudeau's National Energy Program.

Dissatisfaction with the Liberal Party's focus on Quebec issues in the 1970s and 1980s and again in the early 1990s—constitutional initiatives and official bilingualism policy—led to a new outburst of **Western alienation**, defined as follows:

> *A regionally distinct political culture through and within which are expressed economic discontent, the rejection of a semi-colonial status within the Canadian state, antipathy towards Quebec and French-Canadian influence within the national government, the irritation of the West's partisan weakness within a succession of Liberal national governments, and the demand from provincial political elites for greater jurisdictional autonomy.*[6]

The fact that after 1984 the Mulroney Conservative government continued to put priority on Quebec led to the formation of the Reform Party, whose initial slogan was "The West Wants In." The Reform Party won the majority of seats west of Ontario in the 1993 and 1997 elections, including almost all of the seats in British Columbia and Alberta. In 2000, the party changed its leader and name (to the Canadian Alliance) in an effort to become more appealing to the rest of the country. In 2003, it reabsorbed the Progressive Conservative Party and adopted another new name, although it retained its Alberta-based leader, Stephen Harper. Table 2.2 illustrates the regional support of the various political parties in the 2004 federal election and shows that the new Conservative Party of Canada still had a predominant Western base.

TABLE 2.2 REGIONAL DISTRIBUTION OF POPULAR VOTE BY PARTY, 2004 ELECTION (PERCENTAGES)

	Liberal	Conservative	NDP	Bloc
Atlantic	43.8	30.0	22.6	—
Quebec	33.9	8.8	4.6	48.9
Ontario	44.7	31.5	18.1	—
West	26.8	45.5	20.3	—

Source: Data compiled and used to create the above chart was taken from the website of Elections Canada: http://www.elections.ca (Retrieved 15 Aug. 2004). It is used with the permission of the Chief Elector Officer but extrapolation and analysis rests with the author.

The majority of Westerners remain extremely sensitive to any federal government interest in the petroleum industry; they share with Quebec an inclination for decentralization of the federal system; they remain suspicious of Ottawa's apparent preference toward Quebec and the Atlantic provinces in its policies and finances; and, given their relative prosperity, they tend to prefer individual self-reliance over collective, public solutions to demands being made. They also propose to give the Senate more power to protect regional interests against the voting power of central Canada in the House of Commons.

Albertans generally take the most extreme positions on such issues. Despite its prosperity, that province continues to exhibit feelings of alienation, including opposition to the Kyoto Accord, to liberal interpretations of the Charter of Rights and Freedoms, and to the requirement in the Canada Health Act that publicly funded health services be provided in the public sector. The Alberta government wants an elected Senate, a scaled-down gun registry, and a role for provinces in international agreements that affect provincial jurisdiction.

OTHER ASPECTS OF REGIONAL CONFLICTS

Many of the Western economic conflicts with central Canada have been echoed by the Atlantic provinces. Nova Scotia and New Brunswick entered Confederation in 1867 as proud and prosperous colonies, but their economies quickly declined. While changes in marine technology (from wooden sailing ships to steel steamships) were probably the principal factor responsible, Maritimers blamed federal economic policy for much of their difficulty. Post-Confederation tariff policy appeared to do the Maritimes more harm than good; the Atlantic provinces shared the West's concerns about freight rates, although they received subsidization in this area, too; and they fought for provincial ownership of offshore petroleum in the 1990s. They also complained that the federal government was not sufficiently aggressive when it came to protecting Atlantic fish stocks from foreign overfishing.

Smaller-scale regional economic disputes are also a routine occurrence in Canadian politics. Awarding the CF-18 maintenance contract to Canadair of Montreal infuriated supporters of Bristol Aerospace of Winnipeg; extending drug patent protection for multinational pharmaceutical firms in Quebec offended Canadian generic drug producers in Ontario; and promoting frontier petroleum exploration (including federal assistance to Newfoundland's Hibernia project)

Case Study
The CF-18 Maintenance Contract

In 1986, the Mulroney government had to choose between two bids for the contract to maintain Canada's then new, sophisticated CF-18 fighter aircraft. The bid from Winnipeg's Bristol Aerospace was cheaper and technically superior to that of Montreal's Canadair. Yet the government gave the contract to Quebec for political reasons: Quebec had more seats in the House of Commons than Manitoba; the PC party was already strong in the West and needed to deepen its newfound roots in Quebec; Quebec felt that it was owed this contract because it considered itself the aerospace centre of Canada and because of previous preferential treatment of Ontario; and, of course, Quebec separatism was always an option. The move outraged Manitoba and all of Western Canada and inflamed feelings of Western alienation.

upset conventional oil and gas producers in Alberta. Former Ontario premier Mike Harris complained that employment insurance premiums were too high, especially when Ontarians paid a large part of the premiums and residents of the five Eastern provinces collected a disproportionate amount of the payments.

Regional Economic Disparities

Conflicts between regions are exacerbated in Canada because of regional economic inequalities or disparities. Whatever the fault of federal policies, Canada's primary resources are not evenly distributed, the regions have different sizes and populations, and they are located at variable distances from key export markets.

Among the available ways to measure regional economic disparity is provincial gross domestic product (GDP), that is, the total value of all goods and services produced in a province. Because of great differences in the size of provincial populations, it is more useful to divide each province's GDP by its population, giving the GDP per capita. A third measure of provincial disparities is per capita income, and a fourth is provincial unemployment rates. These measures are provided in Table 2.3, which generally indicates three categories of provinces: two rich ones, Ontario and Alberta; four poor ones, the Atlantic provinces; and four intermediate ones, British Columbia, Quebec, Manitoba, and Saskatchewan (although Saskatchewan moved into the "have" category in 2005).

In addition to developing national social programs and assisting various industries in a general way, successive governments have focused on two principal means to deal with the specific question of regional economic disparities. One is to give federal funding to have-not provincial governments, and the other is to provide grants to individual firms in designated have-not regions of the country.

EQUALIZATION PAYMENTS

In 1957, Ottawa finally responded to repeated demands and began to make **equalization payments**, payments that are funded by various federal taxes levied in all provinces. These annual cash grants to the have-not provinces are designed to allow them to raise their services to an acceptable national level but can be spent for any purpose. In other words, they are unconditional grants, with no strings attached. The sums involved are quite impressive, as Table 2.4 (page 34) reveals. Atlantic provinces in particular complain, however, that when they take in additional natural resource revenues, they experience a proportional decrease in their equalization payments. This issue, along with the question of whether offshore

TABLE 2.3 REAL PROVINCIAL GROSS DOMESTIC PRODUCT, GDP PER CAPITA, ESTIMATED PER CAPITA INCOME, AND UNEMPLOYMENT RATE, 2003

	Real GDP ($ Millions)	GDP per Capita ($)	Estimated per Capita Income ($)	Unemployment Rate (Percent)
Newfoundland and Labrador	15 364	29 569	23 536	16.7
Prince Edward Island	3 397	24 652	23 885	11.1
Nova Scotia	25 057	26 770	25 939	9.3
New Brunswick	20 627	27 481	25 520	10.6
Quebec	232 611	31 068	27 454	9.1
Ontario	456 822	37 327	31 651	7.0
Manitoba	34 522	29 689	27 182	5.0
Saskatchewan	32 148	32 316	25 587	5.6
Alberta	128 490	40 743	32 243	5.1
British Columbia	130 914	31 571	28 032	8.1
Canada	1 092 891	34 553		7.6

Source: Adapted from the Statistics Canada website, "Real Gross Domestic Product, Expenditure-Based, by Provinces and Territories," http://www.statcan.ca/english/Pgdb/econ50.htm (Retrieved 15 Aug. 2004) [column 1]; Column 1 divided by 2003 provincial population [column 2]; Conference Board of Canada, *Provincial Outlook* (Spring 2002) [column 3]; and the Statistics Canada website, "Labour Force, Employed and Unemployed, Numbers and Rates, by Provinces," http://www.statcan.ca/english/Pgdb/labor07a.htm (Retrieved 15 Aug. 2004) [column 4].

petroleum–producing provinces should be able to keep all the revenues from that industry, caused a major conflict with the federal government in 2004.

REGIONAL ECONOMIC DEVELOPMENT PROGRAMS

The second means of trying to reduce regional economic disparities is to establish federal regional economic development programs. The basic thrust of these programs is to designate those parts of the country that are in need of economic assistance, and then to provide grants to firms that would locate or expand existing operations in such areas. Some grants also go to provinces or municipalities in order to provide the basic infrastructure that might attract industry, such as highways, water and sewage systems, and industrial parks. Several separate regional economic development agencies now exist, principally the Atlantic Canada Opportunities Agency (ACOA), Federal Economic Development Initiative for Northern Ontario (FedNor), Western Economic Diversification Canada (WD), and Canada Economic Development for Quebec Regions (CED).

TABLE 2.4 EQUALIZATION PAYMENTS ($), 2004–05

Quebec	3 761 000 000
Manitoba	1 341 000 000
New Brunswick	1 155 000 000
Nova Scotia	1 146 000 000
British Columbia	824 000 000
Newfoundland and Labrador	726 000 000
Saskatchewan	462 000 000
Prince Edward Island	246 000 000
Total	9 661 000 000

Source: Adapted from Department of Finance Canada, "Federal Transfers to Provinces and Territories" (March 2004), http://www.fin.gc.ca/fedprov/mtpe.html (Retrieved 15 Aug. 2004). Reproduced with the permission of the Minister of Public Works and Government Services Canada, 2004.

Class Cleavages

Turning from economic disparities based on geography to inequalities in individual incomes, wealth, and power, we come to class cleavages. The concept of class is not as clear-cut as that of region, and Canadians are generally more aware of their regional and ethnic identities. In fact, because of such other divisions, class may not be as important a generator of political activity in Canada as it is in most countries. We do have significant class cleavages but lack a strong consciousness of class and class conflict. This part of the chapter will begin by discussing various definitions and measurements of class and then examine the political role of the different classes.

Defining and Measuring Class

When dealing with the concept of class, it is customary to start with Karl Marx, who predicted that every capitalist economy would produce a class system consisting primarily of the bourgeoisie, the owners of the means of production, and the proletariat, the workers. The proletariat would sell their labour for a price; the bourgeoisie would pay them as little as possible (and less than they were worth), thereby accumulating profit or surplus value. While religion and the prospect of a pleasant afterlife might keep them content for a while, the workers would come to resent their low wages and state of exploitation and eventually engage in a violent revolt.

Some social scientists continue to provide a neo-Marxist analysis of class cleavages in society, but others divide individuals and families into the upper, middle, and working classes, based on such interrelated factors as income, occupation, and education. When such measures are used, the divisions between the classes are less clear-cut than in Marxist analysis. Income is the simplest measure to employ in discussing this subject.

One means of measuring income inequality is to divide the population into five equal groups, or quintiles, from highest to lowest income, and to indicate the share of total income received by each group. Figure 2.2 presents such proportions for the year 2002. It also shows that the income shares before social program transfers (such as employment insurance and social assistance) were dramatically inequitable, and that the tax system takes only a little away from the rich to redistribute to the poor. Thus, even after taxes and transfers, the highest-earning 20 percent of the population still receive nearly 40 percent of the total income, while the lowest 20 percent receive just 7.5 percent.

Figure 2.2   Income Shares of Quintiles: Market Income, Total Income (Income after Transfers and before Tax), and Income after Tax, 2002

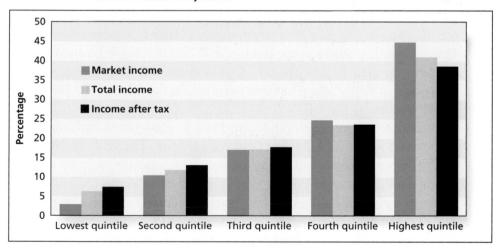

Source: Adapted from the Statistics Canada publication, "Income in Canada, 2002," cat. no. 75-202 (May 2004), 86.

One of the problems in using the concept of class is the distinction between "objective" and "subjective" class. Objective class refers to the class into which analysts place a person, according to criteria such as type of work or level of income, while subjective class means the class to which people think or feel they belong, even if it contradicts objective standards. Many people who consider themselves to be middle class would be categorized as working class by social scientists. Behaving as if they belonged to a different class than they really do, such people could be said to be lacking in **class consciousness**, something that Marx also foresaw and called "false consciousness." This factor reduces the significance of class in motivating political activity.

The Upper Class

Canada is home to many fabulously rich entrepreneurs and some of the wealthiest families on earth. At the top of the 2004 edition of *Canadian Business's* "The Rich 100" list were Ken Thomson, at $22 billion; Galen Weston, at $9 billion; Jeff Skoll, at $7 billion; the Irving family, at $5 billion; and Jimmy Pattison and Paul Desmarais, at $4 billion each.[7] Thomson owns a large number of firms in the information and publishing fields, especially online databases; Galen Weston is the proprietor of Loblaws, Holt Renfrew, and Weston Bakeries; and Jeff Skoll made his money from eBay Inc. The Irving family owns most of New Brunswick, including large tracts of woodlands, pulp mills, all the English-language daily newspapers in the province, oil refineries, gas stations, shipbuilding companies, trucking firms, bus lines, railways, and potato operations. Jimmy Pattison owes his wealth to a wide variety of enterprises, while Paul Desmarais's holdings include Power Corp, Investors Group, and Great-West Life. Among other Canadian billionaires are Ted Rogers (Rogers Communications), Barry Sherman (Apotex Pharmaceuticals), Wallace McCain (Maple Leaf Foods), and the Bombardier and Asper families.

Another category of wealthy Canadians comprises the corporate chief executive officers who do not necessarily own their firms. The *Globe and Mail* survey of CEO compensation in 2003 reported that 29 Canadians received remuneration packages in excess of $5 million that year, and 81 in excess of $1 million. These packages include the value of salary, bonus, incentives, shares, stock options, and other benefits.[8]

The general lines of the public policy demands of the economic elite are easily drawn. Essentially, they want to be left alone; they prefer to minimize the role of government and have society rely more extensively on private market forces.

They want to cut government spending on social programs so that their taxes can be minimized, balance the annual government budget, and reduce the accumulated national debt. If taxes are necessary, they want governments to avoid corporate and progressive individual taxes as much as possible and to provide generous loopholes, write-offs, and tax shelters. Their goal is to minimize government regulation, labour and environmental protection, and anti-combines laws and other restrictions on corporate takeovers.

What Do You Think?

Do the economic elite—corporate owners and CEOs—owe their wealth and power to their own efforts? Or have they largely inherited their wealth or gained it through exploiting their workers and manipulating the political system—the tax laws, the labour laws, the environmental laws, etc.? Why don't more people see the political system in class terms?

Governments have normally responded to such demands with alacrity. The Canadian state gives priority to big business demands in the first place because it depends on the private sector to create jobs. Politicians are especially sensitive to a corporate threat to move to a country with more favourable policies. Second, corporate executives and politicians often come from the same ranks, including prime ministers and ministers of finance. Brian Mulroney and Paul Martin provide ideal examples. Third, companies have many avenues of influence available: making a direct, personal pitch for favourable decisions, using professional lobby firms to help them make contact with public decisionmakers for a fee, and taking advantage of their membership in pressure groups. Among the hundreds of business pressure groups in existence, the **Canadian Council of Chief Executives**, formerly known as the Business Council on National Issues, is probably most powerful, representing the chief executive officers of the 150 largest firms in the country. Fourth, the corporate elite also control the mass media to a large extent. Finally, throughout their history, both the Conservative and Liberal parties have been financed primarily by large corporate contributions. Such donations guaranteed access to decisionmakers, if not specific favours, and it was not difficult to establish a link between corporate contributions and general public policy. In its last days in office, however, the scandal-plagued Chrétien government significantly reduced the opportunity for corporations to donate money to political parties and candidates.

The progressive nature of the personal income tax was reduced when the Mulroney government reduced 10 tax brackets to 3, and capital gains continue to be taxed at a lower rate than other forms of income. In her book *Behind Closed Doors*, Linda McQuaig shows how the rich use their political influence to obtain tax breaks that are paid for by those with lesser incomes.[9] Personal and corporate income taxes are riddled with loopholes, and Canada is one of the few countries in the world without a tax on wealth or inheritance. Beyond the recent moves toward deregulation, the various free trade agreements represent a commitment on the part of governments not to restrict the operations of corporations. Moreover, for a fee of $500 000, a corporation could send its CEO to address the national leaders at the Summit of the Americas in Quebec City in April 2001, while anti-globalization protesters were kept outside by a high fence and tear gas.

Three principal exceptions to this corporate pressure to minimize the role of government must be noted. First, while the economic elite demands that government minimize spending on others, it often expects sizable chunks of public funds for itself, such as in government contracts and grants. Even after 20 years of primary reliance on free market forces, the Canadian government continues to give generous financial assistance to some of the largest companies in the country. A second exception is the rare occasion on which the economic elite has actually favoured new social programs. Such programs tend to increase the purchasing power of lower-income people, reduce the amounts that companies themselves have to pay in employee benefits, and ensure the basic stability of society so that upper classes do not have to worry about violent protests from the poor or unemployed. Third, business leaders expect government to provide such basics as roads, railways, and electricity that decrease their costs or increase their profits. Despite the overwhelming tendency of governments to respond to demands from the corporate elite, however, it should not be forgotten that politicians ultimately get elected by voters, the great majority of whom belong to other classes. Thus, other classes can influence events to some extent, but only if they act as a class.[10]

The Middle Class

On a subjective basis, probably a majority of Canadians think that they belong to the middle class. Academic analysts challenge this view, although they do agree that there is a large middle class in a modern society. They often divide their smaller version of the middle class between the upper middle class and the new middle class, the former being made up of small-business people, self-employed professionals (e.g., lawyers and doctors), and affluent farmers. The **new middle class** incorporates middle managers (who take orders from the corporate elite and give them to the working class), civil servants, teachers, nurses, and other salaried professionals. While the middle class is far from being a unified force, its members are normally well educated and receive above-average levels of income. Their main assets are their homes, their cars, and assorted other material possessions. While members enjoy such tax shelters as RRSPs, the middle class often claims that it pays a disproportionate amount of the taxes to finance government programs of all kinds. With the many tax changes of recent years, however, this claim is difficult to document. On the other hand, such groups as teachers and nurses increasingly feel that they are being treated by governments as if they belonged to the working class.

The Working Class

The working class is generally identified as doing manual or routine work. Members of the working class are typically engaged in resource exploitation, assembly line production, secretarial and clerical work, sales, and a variety of crafts and trades. Less affluent farmers could also be included. Academic analysts put the bulk of the population into this category, even though many who are so labelled identify subjectively with the middle class. Normally lacking post-secondary education, members of the working class usually receive less income than those in the middle class.

Karl Marx's predictions of a violent proletarian revolt were dealt a blow when governments unexpectedly legalized trade unions and extended the franchise to the working class. Nevertheless, most governments and companies have been hostile toward the formation of labour unions, and Canada has experienced a large number of violent strikes, either over the formation of a union or over its subsequent demands. Among the key labour struggles in Canadian history were the 1919 Winnipeg General Strike, the 1937 General Motors Strike in Oshawa, the 1945 Ford Strike in Windsor, the 1949 Asbestos Strike in Quebec, and the woodworkers' strike in Newfoundland in 1959.[11] While legislation dealing with conciliation, mediation, arbitration, picketing, labour standards, occupational health and safety, and compensation for injury on the job is ostensibly passed to protect the working class, governments usually avoid offending their own corporate supporters in the design or implementation of labour laws. Some, like the former Mike Harris government in Ontario, systematically undermine existing labour standards.

Others things being equal, it is in the interests of members of the working class to belong to a trade union. Unionized employees usually have higher wages, more adequate benefits, better working conditions, and more protection against arbitrary dismissal than those who do not engage in collective bargaining. For example, unionized workers are twice as likely to have private medical, dental, life, and disability insurance, as well as pension coverage, as those who are not unionized. In spite of these advantages, the rate of unionization among "paid workers" in Canada is very low (except in comparison to the United States!) and is in decline. Total union membership in 2002 was 3.9 million, or 30 percent of the 12.8 million paid workers in the country.[12]

Moreover, the number of blue-collar jobs is declining in such areas as resource industries, construction, and manufacturing, where unionization used to be most common. New jobs in the postindustrial society are found largely in sales and services, especially in the private sector, where workers are traditionally part-time, poorly paid, and hard to organize. Lacking a union, and given the nature of their job, those in sales and service occupations are not as likely to be class-conscious or to develop social democratic values as those who produce goods.

An employee stands outside the Wal-Mart store in Chicoutimi, Quebec, after it became the first Wal-Mart in Canada to become unionized. The company promptly closed the store.
(CP Photo/Chicoutimi Le Quotidien/Jeannot Levesque)

The composition of the unionized workforce is also changing in other ways. Once comprising primarily private sector, male, manual workers, it is increasingly composed of public sector unions, and women constitute about 47 percent of union members. Public sector unions now make up three of the seven largest unions in the country: the Canadian Union of Public Employees, with 505 000 members; National Union of Public and General Employees, with 325 000; Canadian Auto Workers, with 220 000; United Food and Commercial Workers, with 220 000; United Steelworkers, with 190 000; Communications, Energy and Paperworkers Union, with 149 000; and Public Service Alliance, with 148 700.[13]

Given that most labour legislation is passed at the provincial level, the principal federal measure is the Employment Insurance act (EI). This program, originally called Unemployment Insurance, was introduced in 1941 to tide workers over between jobs, but given the high national unemployment rates in many years since, and the even higher rates in certain regions in every year, it is relied upon much more heavily than was originally anticipated. With such large numbers of workers drawing on the fund, it became a vital source of both individual and regional income, although governments repeatedly restricted its coverage in the 1980s and 1990s. The Chrétien and Martin governments siphoned off the significant surplus in the EI account to pay down the national debt and then loosened up the program, especially for Atlantic Canada, just prior to the 2000 and 2004 elections.

The **Canadian Labour Congress** (CLC) is the main lobbying body for over 2.5 million workers. The CLC is thus one of the largest pressure groups in the country and represents a significant number of voters. Its influence is diminished, however, by its outsider status in Ottawa, as well as by the fact that not all unions belong to it. The historic factionalism within the Canadian union movement is another factor that has not helped the cause of the working class.[14] Governments are often justified in assuming that a gap exists between labour leaders and rank-and-file members with respect to policy positions and party support. Union leaders often support the NDP, while large numbers of rank-and-file members vote for each of the other major parties.

The Poor

The poor can be defined as those living below the **poverty line**. The most widely accepted definition of poverty in Canada is the low-income cutoff provided annually by Statistics Canada. According to this measure, any individual or family that spends more than 55 percent of its income on food, clothing, and shelter is living in poverty (given that the average family spends 35 percent of its income on these three necessities). By this definition, Canada has about 5 million residents living in poverty, or about 16 percent of the population. That includes over 55 percent of female lone-parent families. Even more disturbing, a large proportion of these people live far below the poverty line, and these figures do not include the large group of near-poor that exists just above it.[15]

Probably the most heartbreaking and most intractable aspect of poverty is that it includes over one million children. The high-school dropout rate among children from poor families is much higher than that of others, and the tie between low income and low education is self-perpetuating. *The Canadian Fact Book on Poverty* documents how children from low-income families stand out from their better-off peers:

> *They are less healthy, have less access to skill-building activities, have more destructive habits and behaviours, live more stressful lives, and are subject to more humiliation. In short, they have less stable and less secure existences and as a result they are likely to be less secure as adults.*[16]

Many poor people work full-time, and others part-time; in fact, the poor can be about equally divided between those who work and those who are unemployed or unemployable. The working poor try to scrape by on the minimum wage or on more than one low-paying job, and they are sometimes better off if they go on social assistance. Rather than raising the minimum wage, some provincial governments actually reduced welfare benefits in the last half of the 1990s, and only Quebec provided an adequate daycare program. From about 1995 to 2004, the most common government action was to cut taxes, even at the expense of social programs. The Centre for Social Justice points out that people living in poverty have no taxable income, so that tax cuts are of no benefit to them; tax cuts create only larger income disparities.[17]

Campaign 2000 is a national public education movement working to end child poverty in Canada. In its 2004 report, *Pathways to Progress: Structural Solutions to Address Child Poverty*, it called for a comprehensive anti-poverty plan involving government action to:

- Raise the minimum wage
- Provide better protection through Employment Insurance

- Create an effective child benefit system that provided enough income support to keep parents out of poverty
- Build a universally accessible system of early child education and child care
- Expand affordable housing to end homelessness
- Renew the national social safety net through the new Canada Social Transfer, with increased federal funding[18]

One of the great weaknesses of the poor in the political system is that they are generally unorganized and collectively inarticulate. They lack the skills to organize effectively as pressure groups, primarily because they are without the education, money, and time to develop such skills. Because of their low voter turnout rate, they tend to be ignored by both federal and provincial governments. Nevertheless, several pressure groups and think tanks exist to research the poverty problem and to speak for the poor in the cacophony of the political process: the Canadian Council on Social Development, the National Council of Welfare, the National Anti-Poverty Organization, the Centre for Social Justice, the Caledon Institute of Social Policy, the Canadian Centre for Policy Alternatives, and Campaign 2000. But no one should expect any degree of equality in the struggle among interest groups representing different classes.

SUMMARY

The first part of the chapter dealt with regional economic cleavages. It began by showing how distance, division, and the distribution of population have given rise to demands on the political system and influenced the nature of its responses. It noted the imperfect relationship between regions and provinces and provided an overview of the economic differences among the various regions. It explained why many Western Canadians have felt a sense of alienation from the federal government, both historically and in contemporary times, presented statistics on measures of regional economic disparities, and identified policies adopted to reduce them. The second part of the chapter discussed class cleavages, beginning with various definitions of class and the general lack of class consciousness in Canada. It then listed the typical demands made by each of the main classes, along with the typical government responses. The chapter concluded with a discussion of poverty in Canada—who and how many are poor and what policies have been or could be adopted to improve the lot of poor Canadians.

DISCUSSION QUESTIONS

1. What should be the role of the federal government in overcoming Canada's great distances and divisions? To what extent can the private sector fulfill this function?
2. Are you conscious of living in a particular region, and if so, what regional and provincial complaints do you have about federal policies?
3. What, if anything, can be done to lessen the problem of regional economic disparities?
4. Why is union membership among the working class not higher? Why is class consciousness in Canada relatively low?
5. Should Canada make a more concerted effort to reduce poverty? If so, how?

KEY TERMS

Canadian Council of Chief Executives The most powerful peak business pressure group in Canada, representing the 150 largest firms in the country.

Canadian Labour Congress The largest labour pressure group in Canada; the political voice of over 2.5 million members.

Class consciousness An awareness of the social class to which one belongs.

Equalization payments Large annual cash payments made by the federal government to have-not provinces to help them provide a satisfactory level of public services.

National Energy Program The 1980 policy associated with Pierre Trudeau designed to skim off petroleum tax revenue for Ottawa, keep the price of petroleum below world levels, encourage conservation, and Canadianize the industry, which met with great opposition in Western Canada.

National Policy A broad nation-building 1879 policy of John A. Macdonald that included tariff protection for central Canadian manufacturing, massive immigration, and the construction of a national transportation system.

New middle class A term from class analysis describing salaried professionals such as teachers, public servants, and nurses.

Poverty line An amount of income such that anyone who received less would be living in poverty.

Regionalism Strong feelings of attachment to the region or province where one lives that often generate political activity.

Staples theory The notion that Canadian economic development has gone through a series of stages based on the exploitation of one natural resource or another and the export of such resources, without the development of a secondary or manufacturing sector.

Western alienation The feeling shared by many Western Canadians that their interests are not taken seriously in the national policymaking process.

FURTHER READING

Abella, Irving, ed. *On Strike*. Toronto: James Lewis & Samuel, 1974.

Braid, Don, and Sydney Sharpe. *Breakup: Why the West Feels Left Out of Canada*. Toronto: Key Porter Books, 1990.

Clement, Wallace, ed. *Understanding Canada: Building on the New Canadian Political Economy*. Montreal: McGill-Queen's University Press, 1996.

Gagnon, Alain-G. *Québec: State and Society*. 3rd ed. Peterborough: Broadview Press, 2004.

Gibbins, Roger, and Loleen Berdahl. *Western Visions, Western Futures*. Peterborough: Broadview Press, 2003.

Kilgour, David. *Inside Outer Canada*. Edmonton: Lone Pine Publishers, 1990.

McQuaig, Linda. *Behind Closed Doors*. Toronto: Penguin, 1987.

Palmer, Bryan. *Working-Class Experience: The Rise and Reconstitution of Canadian Labour, 1800–1980*. Toronto: Butterworths, 1983.

Ross, David P., Katherine J. Scott, and Peter J. Smith. *The Canadian Fact Book on Poverty—2000*. Ottawa: Canadian Council on Social Development, 2000.

Chapter 3

French Canada and the Quebec Question

Among all the ethnic/cultural/linguistic issues in Canadian politics, it is the English–French cleavage that has always been of greatest significance. The prominence given to concerns of French Canadians primarily reflects the large number of people involved, their historical rights, and the territorial base of Canada's francophones in Quebec. The French–English cleavage is at least as problematic as the regional economic cleavages in Canadian politics, and the two reinforce each other in the question of Quebec's place in Confederation.

Chapter Objectives

After you have completed this chapter, you should be able to:

Outline the historical evolution of French–English interaction in Canada

Enumerate the French–English crisis points in our history

Explain and appreciate the concept of Quebec nationalism

Contrast the values, attitudes, and demands of the Québécois before and after the Quiet Revolution

Distinguish between contrasting approaches to protect and promote the French language and culture in Canada

Comment on the responses of federal, Quebec, and other provincial governments to francophone demands

Outline the attempts at constitutional change since 1980

Discuss optional mechanisms for dealing with the Quebec question in the future

Historical Overview of French–English Relations

Pre-Confederation Developments

Almost every Canadian political decision for over 200 years has reflected the French–English division to some extent, and the tensions that threaten the continued existence of the country are best understood in historical context. The French first colonized what is now the province of Quebec, and populated it with farmers, clergy, and seigneurs. But when the British defeated the French on the Plains of Abraham in 1759, the conquerors took control of the nonagricultural economy and the government.

Time Line

Constitutional Developments, 1759–1867

1759	British conquest of Quebec
1774	Quebec Act
1791	Constitutional Act
1840	Act of Union
1867	British North America Act (Constitution Act, 1867)

The people, however, continued to speak French and attend the Roman Catholic Church, which became a highly influential and autonomous organization. It would probably have been impossible to make Quebec into an Anglo-Protestant colony; in any case, after a brief attempt at assimilation, the British exhibited a policy of tolerance and accommodation, and in the 1774 **Quebec Act**, they guaranteed the French their religious rights and their own system of civil law.

A large component of "English" immigrants—especially the United Empire Loyalists from the new United States—moved into what is now Ontario in the 1780s. The colony was divided into two by the **Constitutional Act** of 1791: Lower Canada (Quebec) would be essentially French-Catholic, and Upper Canada (Ontario) would be Anglo-Protestant. In the 1830s, conflict erupted in both colonies between the elected assembly and the appointed executive, which in the case of Lower Canada translated into discord between the French (assembly) and the English (executive).

The colonies were reunited by the 1840 **Act of Union** on the recommendation of Lord Durham, who believed that the ethnic problem in Canada could be solved only by another attempt to assimilate the French. This objective was quickly abandoned, and the French language came to be used alongside English in the government of the pre-Confederation period. The governments of the day were usually alliances between English and French leaders, and the legislature operated on the informal principle of the double majority—legislation had to have the approval of a majority of members from both sections of the colony.

Given this historical evolution, the federal union incorporated in the British North America Act (BNA Act), now called the **Constitution Act, 1867**, is perfectly understandable. As a separate province, Quebec would have considerable autonomy, as provided by the division of powers between the federal and provincial governments. Not all Quebec participants, however, were satisfied that the degree of autonomy was sufficient. Most adhered to the "compact theory of Confederation," according to which Confederation was a compact between two equal founding nations, and any change in the Constitution would require unanimous provincial consent, or at least the consent of Quebec.

As for cultural guarantees, both French and English were given official status in all operations of the federal Parliament, and laws were to be passed in both languages. Both languages could also be used in whatever federal courts were later established, as well as in the legislature and courts of Quebec.

Post-Confederation Conflicts

Although the two language groups have been regularly accommodated in government circles since 1867, a number of serious linguistic/ethnic conflicts erupted from the time of Confederation to the Second World War. The first of two Riel Rebellions, led by French Catholic Métis Louis Riel, precipitated the creation of the province of Manitoba in 1870. In 1884–85, Riel re-emerged in what is now Saskatchewan to lead the second Riel Rebellion on behalf of Western Natives and Métis, who had been treated shamefully by the government. After quelling the rebellion, the federal government charged Riel with treason. This raised ethnic and religious tensions across the country to a fever pitch, for while Anglo-Protestants regarded Riel as a murderer, traitor, and madman, French Catholics believed he was a patriot and a saint. Riel's hanging heightened the level of French-Catholic outrage, especially in Quebec, and permanently damaged the close attachment of the people of that province to the Conservative Party.

The second linguistic conflict occurred in Manitoba. The small settlement was about equally divided between French and English, and (at Riel's insistence) the 1870 Manitoba Act followed the Quebec precedent of giving the two languages official status in the new province's legislature and courts. After its creation, however, Manitoba attracted thousands of English-speaking immigrants and others who chose to identify with the anglophone community. Hence, in 1890, the anglophone majority passed the Official Language Act, removing the official status of French.

Time Line

Post-Confederation French–English Conflicts to 1945

1870	First Riel Rebellion
1885	Second Riel Rebellion
1890	Manitoba's Official Language Act
1913	Ontario's Regulation 17
1917	First conscription crisis
1944	Second conscription crisis

The third linguistic conflict concerned minority French-language education rights in Ontario. In 1913, the government's Regulation 17 virtually abolished the use of French in the Ontario school system; English was to become the sole language of instruction after the third year, and the study of French as a subject was limited to one hour a day.

The **conscription crisis** of the First World War was the fourth major French–English confrontation. Having little in the way of standing armed forces, the Canadian military effort rested on appeals for volunteers. These appeals initially had promising results, but as reinforcements were needed later in the war, few recruits came forward. The government therefore decided to resort to conscription—compulsory military service—in 1917. Isolated for centuries from Europe, French Canadians felt that the war was of no concern to them and certainly did not justify the risk of their lives. Prime Minister Robert Borden knew that French Canada generally felt indifferent to the conflict and that conscription would divide the country along ethnic lines. He therefore appealed to Liberal leader Wilfrid Laurier to join him in a coalition government. Laurier refused the offer, although most English-speaking Liberal MPs did join in the Union government. The subsequent enforcement of conscription entailed considerable violence, including a riot in

Quebec City in the spring of 1918 that left four people dead and many others injured. This confrontation destroyed what little French-Canadian support for the Conservative Party was left after the execution of Louis Riel.

Ontario repealed Regulation 17 in 1927, and French–English tensions returned to their normal, controllable level until they were inflamed by the fifth conflict, another conscription crisis during the Second World War. But in 1939 Canada was led by Liberal Prime Minister Mackenzie King, with a strong contingent of ministers and MPs from Quebec. King knew that French Canada would resist conscription, so on the basis of the slogan "conscription if necessary, but not necessarily conscription," he held a national referendum in 1942 to release his government from an earlier pledge not to conscript. Happily, King then managed to postpone the adoption of compulsory military service until almost the end of the war.

Quebec Nationalism

Central to the question of French–English relations and the position of Quebec in Canada is the phenomenon of Quebec nationalism. This feeling of primary loyalty to Quebec emanates from the widely held notion that it is home to a distinctive French-Canadian nation, centred on language, ethnicity, culture, and territory, and—prior to 1960—religion. Over the centuries, Quebec nationalism has taken many twists and turns, but it remains a driving force in both provincial and federal politics, where it always stood for a substantial degree of political autonomy or self-determination. Quebeckers valued autonomy because Quebec was different and because they felt such autonomy had been guaranteed in 1867. Quebec sometimes also considered itself to be morally superior to the rest of the country and often believed that it was fighting for its life. Before 1960, Quebec nationalism was largely inward-looking and defensive, primarily concerned with ensuring that the federal government kept out of that province's affairs. After 1960, it was activist and self-confident, as the province wanted to take over many federal responsibilities. Quebec nationalism also sought to reverse the dominance of Anglo and external economic power in the province.

Moderate nationalists now advocate the protection and promotion of the French language and culture, increased powers for the province, and more French-Canadian control of the economy. More extreme nationalists fight for provincial sovereignty with a loose connection to Canada or outright separation.

Somewhat complicating the picture, however, is the declining French-Canadian birthrate in Quebec and the presence in the province of about one million residents (including Aboriginal peoples, anglophones, and those of other origins) who do not embrace the same ethnic/linguistic/cultural objectives. As noted in Chapter 2, Quebec's population has recently fallen below a symbolic 25 percent of the total Canadian population.

The French–English Cleavage, 1960–82

The Quiet Revolution: Quebec in the 1960s

Until 1960, Quebec was a traditional, conservative, rural, poorly educated, patronage-oriented society, heavily influenced by the Roman Catholic Church. Dominated by the authoritarian Premier Maurice Duplessis from 1935 onward, the inward-looking population was taught that only he could protect them from evil external influences, such as Ottawa. The Quebec of the past 45 years, however, is quite a different province and society. In the 1960s, Quebec francophones experienced a **Quiet Revolution**, consisting of a dramatic change of values and attitudes, especially toward the state, a new collective self-confidence, and a new brand of nationalism. These features of the new Quebec had many implications for French–English relations in both the Quebec and Canadian political systems.

QUEBEC'S CHANGES AND DEMANDS

The government of Jean Lesage (1960–66) took over many functions previously administered by the Church.[1] The most important of these, education, was radically modernized, and health and welfare programs were also made public rather than charitable responsibilities. With the nationalization of private power companies, Hydro-Québec became a huge Crown corporation supplying most of the electricity in the province and serving as an engine of economic development. Lesage also reformed almost every piece of legislation on the books, especially labour and electoral laws, added reams of new ones, and created many government agencies. All these new and expanded public responsibilities required substantial additional revenues, and Lesage put immense pressure on Ottawa to increase federal–provincial grants, to allow Quebec to opt out of the conditions attached to them, and to give the province a greater share of joint taxation. In areas of provincial jurisdiction, Quebec began to move toward distinctive pro-

Time Line

French–English Relations, 1945–70

1945–59	Opposition to Maurice Duplessis grows
1960–66	Quiet Revolution
1963–68	B&B Commission
1968	Pierre Trudeau becomes PM
1968–69	Official Languages Act
1970	FLQ crisis

grams, designing its own pension plan, which was then used as a model for the Canada Pension Plan. As time went on, the province began to demand ever larger jurisdiction, leading to perpetual federal–provincial discord.

Federally oriented Quebec francophones such as future prime minister Pierre Trudeau had a different vision of French Canada that did not focus on Quebec. This group of Québécois began to demand that French be used as a language equal to English in the corridors of power in Ottawa. They were also concerned about the fate of francophone minorities in the other provinces, helped by the fact that the new self-confidence of the Québécois inspired these dwindling minorities to greater self-assertiveness.

FEDERAL RESPONSES

During the 1960s, the federal government grappled somewhat haphazardly with these demands. The Diefenbaker government (1957–63) introduced simultaneous interpretation into Parliament, began printing federal government cheques in a bilingual format, and appointed a French-Canadian governor general. Immediately upon taking office, the Pearson government (1963–68) established the Royal Commission on Bilingualism and Biculturalism (the B&B Commission). Pearson also gave Quebec and the other provinces more federal funds and taxation powers, removed conditions from many shared-cost programs, and permitted Quebec to make international arrangements with France and other francophone countries.

Since the federal Parliament and courts were already theoretically bilingual, the main gap in official bilingualism at the national level was in the executive branch, where English was essentially the working language of the public service, at least at policymaking levels. Pearson therefore introduced the **Official Languages Act** to make the Canadian public service bilingual. Since its passage under Trudeau in 1969, Canada has become officially and effectively bilingual in its federal institutions. Ottawa also began to assist francophone minorities in other provinces in order to try to stem their increasing assimilation into the anglophone majorities as well as to support French immersion educational programs.

The question of French–English relations, or "national unity," was the principal political issue throughout the Trudeau era (1968–79, 1980–84). Around that time, it became clear that two basic models existed to deal with the problem. The first was to recognize Quebec as the homeland of French Canada and to give that province powers and resources to protect and promote its linguistic and cultural distinctiveness. Quebec would be essentially "French" and the rest of Canada primarily "English." The second option was to treat Quebec as *une province comme les autres* and to promote bilingualism at the federal level and in the other provinces so that any Canadian could use either language anywhere in the country.

English Canadians had difficulty accepting these demands, which seemed excessive and contradictory: making Quebec more French and more autonomous at the same time as promoting French in Ottawa and the other provinces. Most people did not understand that the two demands came largely from two different groups of francophones, the vast majority concentrating on Quebec and a minority that wanted to expand French Canada beyond that province. Trudeau was not representative of mainstream thought in Quebec in his fight against the recognition of Quebec as the homeland of French Canada and in his opposition to giving that province any special status or power, which he thought would be the first step toward separation. Part of Trudeau's popularity in English Canada stemmed from the perception that he was "anti-Quebec," but he was passionately "pro-French" in promoting French power and bilingualism in Ottawa and across the country.[2]

THE SEPARATIST OPTION

During the 1960s, advocates of a third option—Quebec separatism—began to emerge. Most people supporting this option were committed to democratic processes, but one wing of the separatist movement, the **Front de libération du Québec (FLQ)**, resorted to violence. It believed that the normal political process was not responding quickly enough to the demands of the Quiet Revolution, and its periodic bombings killed two people and injured many others. In October 1970, two small cells of the FLQ kidnapped a British diplomat, James Cross, and abducted and murdered a Quebec cabinet minister, Pierre Laporte. Trudeau invoked the **War Measures Act**, giving the police and armed forces special powers to quell the violence. In the process, over 400 innocent, peaceful supporters of separatism were arrested. By crushing the FLQ, by giving French Canadians more clout in Ottawa, and by guaranteeing pan-Canadian bilingualism in the Constitution in 1982, Trudeau hoped to undercut any Quebec demand for special status or separatism in the defence of French Canada.

Quebec–Canada Relations, 1970–82

The first Robert Bourassa government in Quebec (1970–76) passed Bill 22 to give primacy to the French language in many spheres in the province, such as in the operations and documents of public authorities. As far as education was concerned, immigrant children were generally forced to attend French-language schools. This was an attempt to have such children join the majority French linguistic group in the province rather than become "English," as so many previous immigrants had done. In fact, relying on immigration to bolster the francophone segment of the population became a vital point after the French-Canadian birthrate plummeted in the 1960s. Bill 22 also aimed at the francization of the private sector by pressuring companies to use French as the language of internal corporate operations. The more Quebec moved in the direction of French unilingualism, of course, the greater became English Canada's resistance to Trudeau's policy of national bilingualism, and the greater grew the number of anglophones who left Quebec.

Time Line
Quebec–Canada Relations, 1970–82

1976	Election of Parti Québécois
1977	Quebec Bill 101
1980	First Quebec referendum
1982	Constitution Act, 1982

The Parti Québécois (PQ) was elected to office in 1976 under René Lévesque with an even more nationalistic program.[3] Faced with a hostile Trudeau government in Ottawa, the PQ made few gains in provincial autonomy. But in 1977 it passed **Bill 101**, the Charter of the French Language, which considerably extended Bill 22 in making French the predominant language in the province. The bill generally turned the persuasive and optional aspects of Bill 22 into coercive and mandatory ones. It made French the only official language of the legislature (although laws continued to be translated unofficially into English); only individuals (not corporations) could use English in Quebec courts; essentially the only children who could go to English-language schools in the province were those who had at least one parent who had done so; and all commercial signs had to be in French only. Over the next decade or so, all four of these clauses were ruled unconstitutional by the courts, but they were subsequently modified to comply with the court decisions. Thus, most of Bill 101 still stands, and French continues to be the official language of the province.

In 1980, the PQ government held a **referendum** on the question of pursuing a more independent relationship with Canada called **sovereignty-association**. Many prominent politicians, including Trudeau, Justice Minister Jean Chrétien, and several provincial premiers, encouraged Quebeckers to defeat the PQ proposal, promising them "constitutional renewal" if they did so. When sovereignty-association was turned down by a vote of 60 percent to 40 percent, new federal–provincial constitutional negotiations began, culminating in the **Constitution Act, 1982**.[4] Ironically, even though the whole effort was supposed to appeal to the residents of Quebec, that province alone objected to the act as reflecting the Trudeau vision of a bilingual Canada rather than recognizing the distinctive francophone character of Quebec. Nevertheless, it became law in all parts of the country. As far as language was concerned, the act reinforced official bilingualism at the federal level and in New Brunswick, and it guaranteed **minority language education rights** in all provinces wherever numbers warranted. Many Quebeckers never forgave Trudeau and Chrétien for adopting such a significant constitutional document without Quebec's consent.

French–English Relations in the Other Provinces

The distribution of French- and English-language communities in the various provinces is shown in Table 3.1. Defined by mother tongue, the largest francophone minorities are located in Ontario (509 000) and New Brunswick (239 400), where they respectively constitute 4.5 and 33.2 percent of the provincial population.

TABLE 3.1 MOTHER TONGUE AND HOME LANGUAGE BY PROVINCE, 2001 (PERCENTAGES)

| | Mother Tongue | | Home Language | |
	English	French	English	French
Newfoundland and Labrador	98.4	0.5	99.2	0.2
Prince Edward Island	94.0	4.4	97.4	2.1
Nova Scotia	93.0	3.9	96.2	2.2
New Brunswick	65.0	33.2	69.0	30.3
Quebec	8.3	81.4	10.5	83.1
Ontario	71.3	4.5	82.7	2.7
Manitoba	75.4	4.2	89.1	1.9
Saskatchewan	85.4	1.9	95.2	0.5
Alberta	81.5	2.1	91.2	0.7
British Columbia	73.6	1.5	84.8	0.4
Nunavut	26.9	1.5	41.5	0.8
Northwest Territories	77.8	2.7	89.9	1.1
Yukon	86.8	3.3	95.8	1.5
Total	59.1	22.9	67.5	22.0

Source: Adapted from the Statistics Canada websites, "2001 Census, Population and Growth Rate of Language Groups, Canada, Provinces, Territories and Canada less Quebec, 1991, 1996 and 2001," http://www12.statcan.ca/English/census01/products/analytic/companion/lang/tables/growthrate.cfm, and "Population by Language Spoken Most Often at Home, Canada, Provinces, Territories and Canada less Quebec, 1991, 1996 and 2001," http://www12.statcan.ca/English/census01/products/analytic/companion/lang/tables/langhome.cfm (Retrieved 15 Aug. 2004).

The Quebec government and most Quebeckers have been more concerned about internal linguistic matters than about what happened to French-language minorities in other provinces. Nevertheless, the Quiet Revolution led francophones outside Quebec to make a last-ditch attempt to preserve their language and culture. Often under pressure from Prime Minister Trudeau, some provincial premiers hoped that by extending rights or services to their francophone minority, they would help to forestall separatism in Quebec. Thus, many provinces have made considerable improvement in minority francophone rights since 1965. As mentioned, all were bound by the Constitution Act, 1982, to provide education in the minority official language where numbers warrant. Under an amendment to the Official Languages Act in 1988, all provinces were also committed to provide for criminal trials in French if demanded by the accused.

New Brunswick went farthest with its own Official Languages Act of 1969, which was constitutionalized at provincial request in 1982. New Brunswick also improved the Acadian educational system at all levels and provided provincial government services in both languages. The province strengthened the act further in 2002, and it can now be said to be effectively bilingual.

Even before Trudeau, Ontario began to provide for French-language secondary schools, and it later established the right of every Franco-Ontarian to go to a French-language school. Ontario then guaranteed French trials in the provincial courts and gradually extended French-language provincial services. Bill 8, coming into effect in 1989, provided for provincial government services in French in designated regions of the province as well as for the translation of laws. Meanwhile, simultaneous interpretation in the legislature began in 1987, and Franco-Ontarians were granted the right to have their French-language schools run by trustees elected by the francophone population.

Manitoba moved very slowly in this direction on its own but was pushed by a series of Supreme Court of Canada decisions beginning in 1979. The result was that the 1890 Official Language Act was declared unconstitutional, all laws had to be passed in both languages, trials had to be available in French, and most government documents had to be bilingual.

Quebec–Canada Relations since 1982

Three years after the controversial adoption of the Constitution Act, 1982, Quebeckers defeated the Parti Québécois and put Robert Bourassa's Liberals back in power. The second Bourassa government was first able to persuade the more receptive Mulroney government to allow Quebec to play a fuller part in the international French-speaking community, the Francophonie. Then, in 1988, the Supreme Court of Canada declared the sign provision of Bill 101 to be unconstitutional as a violation of freedom of expression, even "commercial expression." Bourassa responded by using the "notwithstanding clause" in the federal and Quebec charters of rights to pass Bill 178, providing for French-only outdoor signs but allowing some bilingual signs indoors. Such violation of a constitutional right of anglophones produced a vehement reaction among Anglo-Quebeckers and an anti-Quebec and anti-French response in the rest of the country. On the other hand, some aspects of Bill 101 had been voluntarily relaxed in 1983, and in 1986 Quebec had ensured the provision of social and health services in English to its anglophone minority. Moreover, when the five-year limit on Bill 178 ran out in 1993, Bourassa replaced it with Bill 86, which allowed bilingual signs outside as well as inside stores.

Time Line

Quebec–Canada Relations since 1982

1987–90	Meech Lake Accord
1992	Charlottetown Accord and national referendum
1995	Second Quebec referendum
1998	Supreme Court decision on Quebec independence
2000	Clarity Act

The Meech Lake Accord

The Constitution Act, 1982, including the Charter of Rights and Freedoms, was operative in Quebec even though the government of that province refused to endorse it. When Brian Mulroney became prime minister, however, he was determined that Quebec should symbolically rejoin the Canadian constitutional family "with honour and enthusiasm." He included several Quebec nationalists in his cabinet and, in 1985, asked Bourassa to outline his conditions for such a reunion. The Quebec government proceeded to make five demands:

1. Constitutional recognition of Quebec as a "distinct society" within Canada
2. Increased jurisdiction over immigration
3. Participation in Supreme Court appointments
4. Power to veto constitutional amendments
5. Right to opt out, with compensation, of national programs within provincial jurisdiction

Mulroney called the premiers together at Meech Lake in April 1987, where they agreed to a document that addressed Quebec's demands and became known as the **Meech Lake Accord**.[5] The prime minister secured unanimous provincial consent by extending to the other provinces the same rights as were demanded by Quebec, except for the distinct society clause. The document also would have constitutionalized the Supreme Court of Canada, guaranteed annual first ministers' conferences on the Constitution and the economy, and—at the behest of the Alberta delegation—provided for provincial participation in Senate appointments.

Despite the relative ease with which it was drafted, the Meech Lake Accord generated much controversy. Led by ex-prime minister Trudeau, its critics did not approve of Quebec's designation as a distinct society within Canada, and they objected to the phrase that it was the role of the government and legislature of Quebec to "preserve and promote" that distinctiveness. No one was sure of the implications of the **distinct society clause** for the federal–provincial division of powers, leaving the interpretation of it to the courts on an issue-by-issue basis. Some argued that, armed with that constitutional support, Quebec would immediately begin to challenge federal powers in a variety of fields; others worried about the status of the English and Aboriginal minorities within Quebec, as well as of the francophone minorities in other provinces.

A second objection to the accord was that it enlarged the list of subjects that required unanimous provincial consent in the constitutional amending formula. Many critics felt that Senate reform and the transformation of the Northern territories into provinces would be virtually impossible if such changes required agreement of all 10 provinces instead of only 7.

Much concern was expressed about the provision allowing provinces to opt out of national programs within provincial jurisdiction and be compensated by Ottawa. Fears were expressed that satisfactory new national social programs (such as daycare) would never materialize because provinces would be compensated for programs that met merely national objectives, not national standards.

Others condemned the process through which the accord had emerged—a behind-the-scenes gathering of (male) first ministers. In the post-Charter era, individual Canadians in all parts of the country insisted on being part of the constitutional amendment process; moreover, the primacy of Quebec's concerns was rejected by those given constitutional standing by the Charter—women, Aboriginal peoples, and multicultural and other minorities.[6]

Supporters of Meech Lake argued that it would symbolically bring Quebec back into the constitutional fold and overcome the isolation and betrayal that many residents of that province felt after 1982. Indeed, it was the most modest list of demands ever to come out of Quebec. Defenders called this the "Quebec round" and argued that Aboriginal, Northern, Western, and other concerns would be the next items on the constitutional agenda. They felt that rather than promote incremental separatism, the accord would give Quebec the flexibility to remain satisfied within Confederation. Its proponents contended that in demo-

André-Philippe Côté/Reproduced with permission of *Le Soleil*.

graphic, linguistic, and cultural terms, the distinctiveness of the Quebec society
could not be denied.

Many political scientists and others had long argued that the provinces should
have a say in the appointment of senators and Supreme Court judges. In the
former case, this was because the Senate was intended to represent the provinces
within Ottawa's decisionmaking structure; in the latter, because the Supreme
Court rules on federal–provincial disputes and hence its judges should not be unilaterally appointed by one side. Many true federalists also contended that Ottawa
should not be able to invade provincial jurisdiction with its spending power and
set up national programs without provincial consent, as had often happened in
the past.

According to the constitutional amending formula adopted in 1982, the
Meech Lake Accord then had to be approved by the federal and all provincial legislatures within three years, that is, before June 1990. In most cases, such legislative approval came rather easily, but new governments in Newfoundland and
Manitoba had reservations about the accord. In the end, it was not approved by
the legislatures in either of those provinces, the latter because Aboriginal MLA
Elijah Harper delayed passage beyond the deadline in the absence of any advance
for Native peoples.

The Charlottetown Accord

With the death of the Meech Lake Accord, many Quebeckers felt betrayed again, and nationalist and separatist sentiment in Quebec mushroomed. Both the Quebec Liberals and Parti Québécois issued more nationalistic constitutional positions, and demands arose for a referendum on sovereignty to be held in 1992. Meanwhile, several Quebec members of Parliament quit the Conservative and Liberal parties to sit as Quebec *indépendantistes* in the Bloc Québécois (BQ) led by Lucien Bouchard, a former minister in the Mulroney cabinet.

Prime Minister Mulroney appointed Joe Clark as the minister responsible for constitutional affairs, and Clark tried to develop a collective federal–provincial –territorial–Aboriginal response to offer to Quebec before its constitutional referendum. After several rounds of negotiations, Clark, the nine premiers, and territorial and Aboriginal leaders all agreed on a comprehensive constitutional proposal in July 1992. Quebec then entered the bargaining, and the participants unanimously signed a new constitutional accord in Charlottetown in August.[7] The **Charlottetown Accord** had four main parts, two of primary concern to Quebec: the "Canada clause" and changes to the division of powers. The other two major components of the accord, Aboriginal self-government and the Triple-E Senate, are dealt with in Chapters 4 and 15 respectively.

The Canada clause that began the accord would recognize Quebec as a distinct society within Canada as well as enumerate the other fundamental values and characteristics of the country. These included democracy, the rule of law, parliamentary and federal systems, the Aboriginal peoples of Canada and their enhanced rights, official language minorities, cultural and racial diversity, individual and collective rights, gender equality, and the equality and diversity of the provinces.

The second main issue of interest to Quebec was the federal–provincial division of powers. As in the Meech Lake Accord, provinces could have a larger role in immigration matters. They could also opt out of new national shared-cost programs set up within provincial jurisdiction and receive federal financial compensation if the programs met national objectives. In addition, if they wished, the provinces could have full or partial power over 10 additional fields of public policy: forestry, mining, tourism, recreation, housing, municipal and urban affairs, culture, labour-market training, telecommunications, and regional development.

The accord would be of no effect until ratified by Parliament and the 10 provincial legislatures. Before ratification, however, the federal government announced that a national referendum would be held on the new constitutional deal on October 26, 1992. The decision to hold such a nationwide referendum was based on two main points. First, Quebec was already committed to a referendum on constitutional change on that date, while Alberta and B.C. laws required a referendum on constitutional amendments. If these three provinces would be voting on the accord in any case, the opportunity had to be extended to the others. Second, a referendum would avoid the criticism that Meech Lake encountered—lack of public input—and public approval would lend legitimacy to the agreement and spur the 11 legislatures into speedy affirmative action.

On a national basis, 55 percent of the people who cast their ballots voted no and 45 percent voted yes. Majorities voted no in Quebec, Nova Scotia, the four Western provinces, and the Yukon. Even though the referendum was not legally binding, there was no point in bringing the constitutional package before legislatures for ratification: the Charlottetown Accord was dead.

Public opinion polls showed that rather than basing their decision on the contents of the accord as such, many of the people who voted no did so to vent their anger and frustration against Prime Minister Mulroney, the premiers, and politicians and governments in general. Voters were not in a generous frame of mind, and rather than seeing the accord as a multisided compromise, they generally felt that it gave too much to others and not enough to themselves. Indeed, while the accord was primarily designed to address the constitutional insecurity of Quebec, Aboriginal Canadians, and Western and smaller provinces, a majority in all three groups believed that their elites had not bargained hard enough on their behalf.[8]

What Do You Think?

What is the harm in recognizing Quebec's distinctiveness in the Constitution? Is such a designation unfair in any way to other provinces? Is it the first step toward separation?

The Chrétien Government Record and the 1995 Referendum

After this disheartening if not traumatic experience, all federal parties decided that it would be wise to leave the constitutional issue alone. For example, the Chrétien Liberals were elected a year later on the promise that they would concentrate on improving the economy. In 1994, however, the Parti Québécois was returned to power in Quebec. With Ottawa largely ignoring the issue, the new

Quebec premier, Jacques Parizeau, wanted a quick vote on a clear-cut separatist position. Others, however, including Bloc Québécois leader Lucien Bouchard, preferred a scheme that retained significant ties to Canada. When the polls showed that Parizeau could not achieve the support of a majority of Quebec voters on the question of his choice, he succumbed to the pressure of public opinion (and of Bouchard) and promised an extensive list of continuing links to Canada.

Parizeau's referendum was held in October 1995. The proposal involved a convoluted and unclear question incorporating a kind of sovereignty that retained significant ties to the rest of Canada. In the final week of the campaign, Prime Minister Chrétien finally woke up to the possibility of a PQ victory and made a vague promise of reform if the "no" vote prevailed. The result of the referendum could not have been closer: 50.6 percent voted no, while 49.4 percent voted yes. This narrow defeat precipitated Parizeau's abrupt resignation, and Lucien Bouchard moved from leading the BQ in Ottawa to the PQ in Quebec.

Fulfilling his last-minute promises, but not being able to persuade all provinces to make an actual amendment to the Constitution, Chrétien had Parliament pass a resolution recognizing Quebec as a distinct society within Canada. He also promised that regardless of the official constitutional amending formula, no such amendments would be passed without the approval of each region of the country (including Quebec). Labour-market training was then transferred from federal to provincial jurisdiction.

In 1997, the prime minister referred a hypothetical question to the Supreme Court of Canada, asking it to rule on the legality of a unilateral declaration of independence by Quebec. In August 1998, the Supreme Court issued its decision in the reference case: under the Canadian Constitution, secession of a province could not be achieved unilaterally. To separate, Quebec would have to use the constitutional amending formula and seek the approval of the other participants in Confederation. Neither did Quebec gain such a right under international law because its residents did not constitute an oppressed people. On the other hand, if Quebec obtained a clear majority vote in a provincial referendum on a clear question in favour of secession, it would be hard for the rest of the country to ignore.[9]

With Bouchard threatening another referendum as soon as "winning conditions" prevailed, Chrétien introduced his controversial **Clarity Act**, which essentially translated the Supreme Court decision into legislation. Chrétien believed that such legislation was required because the questions asked in the Quebec referendums of 1980 and 1995 were deliberately vague. Although the act stopped

In the Words of the Court
The Legality of Quebec's Secession

"Quebec does not meet the threshold of a colonial people or an oppressed people, nor can it be suggested that Quebecers have been denied meaningful access to government to pursue their political, economic, cultural and social development ... [But] a clear majority vote in Quebec on a clear question in favour of secession would confer democratic legitimacy on the secession initiative which all of the other participants in Confederation would have to recognize."

Source: Reference re Secession of Quebec, [1998] 2 S.C.R. 222.

short of articulating what a "clear majority" would be in numerical terms, it specified that the federal government would not recognize a Quebec referendum result that did not involve a clear expression of the will of the population that the province should cease to be part of Canada. The federal government would not tolerate a question that involved continuing economic or political arrangements with Canada. Neither would it support a constitutional amendment unless the amendment addressed the division of assets and liabilities; border changes; the rights, interests, and territorial claims of Aboriginal peoples; and the protection of minority rights. While the Quebec government obviously opposed the new rules, the act did not incite the inflammatory backlash in that province that some opponents had expected.

Bouchard resigned as premier of Quebec without having called another referendum, and his successor, Bernard Landry, was defeated by Jean Charest's provincial Liberal Party in 2003. With a federalist party in power in Quebec, the rest of the country relaxed to some extent, but a strong core of sovereignty supporters remained. In the 2004 federal election, the Bloc Québécois gained nearly 50 percent of the vote in Quebec, although much of that was from people upset by the Chrétien sponsorship scandal rather than from genuine sovereigntists.

Prime Minister Paul Martin shakes hands with Quebec Premier Jean Charest after reaching a deal at the First Ministers' Conference on Health in September 2004. (CP Photo/Tom Hanson)

The Future of French–English Relations

Given that francophones constitute nearly 25 percent of the Canadian electorate, and given their historic constitutional rights, geographic concentration in Quebec, majority control of such a large province, and modern-day self-consciousness and self-confidence, French Canadians cannot be ignored. If English Canada wants Quebec to remain part of the country, it cannot go back to the easy days of pre-1960 unilingualism and federal government domination.

Despite much confusion on the question, five alternatives with regard to the future of French–English relations in Canada can be identified:

- Complete independence of Quebec (Jacques Parizeau)
- Sovereignty of Quebec with links to Canada (René Lévesque, Lucien Bouchard)
- Quebec as a distinct society within Canada (Robert Bourassa, Brian Mulroney)

- All provinces equal; strong central government; national bilingualism (Pierre Trudeau)
- All provinces equal; strong provinces; bilingualism confined to Quebec (Preston Manning as leader of the Reform Party)

It appears to many observers that the only way to accommodate the French presence within Canada is the "middle way."[10] Given that 85 percent of French Canadians are located in Quebec and that 82 percent of Quebeckers are French-speaking, it is logical to recognize that Quebec is the heartland of French Canada. In the words of Brian Mulroney and Robert Bourassa, Quebec constitutes a "distinct society within Canada." This approach would give that province special recognition and responsibility to protect itself in the North American English linguistic environment. Justified or not, Quebec retains something of a siege mentality with respect to its language and culture, and language has replaced the Church as the focus of the French identity. The Quebec corporate elite is now a francophone group, and they, along with the new middle class in the Quebec public sector, see themselves benefiting from increased provincial autonomy.[11] Unfortunately, the oratory of Pierre Trudeau and Preston Manning probably hardened English-Canadian opinion toward the idea of recognizing Quebec as a distinct society, despite the passage of the parliamentary resolution to this effect.

It seems unlikely that Jean Charest and Paul Martin will need to raise the constitutional issue again during their concurrent regimes, as they easily agreed to give Quebec slightly different treatment from the other provinces at the health care summit in September 2004.

SUMMARY

This chapter demonstrated that the French–English problem has always been with us. It discussed the main developments in this relationship before and since Confederation. Then it turned to the evolution of Quebec society and Quebec nationalism, concentrating on the changes resulting from the Quiet Revolution of the 1960s. The chapter showed that two main strategies emerged for dealing with Quebec and French-Canadian demands for the protection of the French language and culture, one focused on Quebec and the other on the country as a whole. It then examined the government responses to these demands in Ottawa and in the various provinces, including Quebec. The chapter concluded with an outline of the successful and unsuccessful attempts at constitutional change since 1980 and proposed five options for dealing with the Quebec question in the future.

DISCUSSION QUESTIONS

1. Which of the options listed previously is closest to your vision of Canada?
2. To what extent should individual provinces operate on a bilingual basis?
3. If a future referendum were won by the Quebec separatists, what sort of scenario do you see unfolding?

KEY TERMS

Act of Union The 1840 act that united the colonies of Upper and Lower Canada into the colony of Canada and that was partly designed to assimilate the French.

Bill 101 The 1977 Quebec language law that made French the official language of Quebec and put restrictions on the use of English in the public and private sectors, including French-only signs.

Charlottetown Accord The 1992 constitutional agreement that responded to Quebec's demands for distinct society status, Aboriginal demands for self-government, and the West's demand for a Triple-E Senate, but was defeated in a national referendum.

Clarity Act The 2000 act that specified the conditions under which the federal government would recognize a referendum result in Quebec on the issue of independence.

Conscription crises Two political crises during the two world wars, in 1917 and in 1944, in which the population and government were divided, largely along ethnic lines, over the necessity of compulsory military service.

Constitution Act, 1867 The new name for the British North America Act, 1867, which united the four original provinces.

Constitution Act, 1982 The act sponsored by Prime Minister Trudeau that contained a made-in-Canada constitutional amending formula and a Charter of Rights and Freedoms.

Constitutional Act The 1791 British law that divided Canada into two separate colonies—Upper and Lower Canada—each with a governor, executive and legislative councils, and assembly.

Distinct society clause A controversial clause in the Meech Lake Accord, and slightly modified in the Charlottetown Accord, claiming that Quebec constituted, within Canada, a distinct society.

Front de libération du Québec (FLQ) The terrorist wing of the Quebec separatist movement in the 1960s and 1970s.

Meech Lake Accord The 1987 package of constitutional reforms intended to bring Quebec back into the constitutional fold that was turned down in 1990.

Minority language education rights Rights established in section 23 of the Charter of Rights and Freedoms whereby French-speaking Canadians can send their children to French-language schools wherever their numbers warrant, a principle also extended to English-speaking Canadians where they are a minority.

Official Languages Act The 1969 federal act that established official bilingualism in Canada and gave citizens the right to deal with certain offices of the federal government in either English or French.

Quebec Act The 1774 British law that provided for a system of government for the colony of Quebec that included certain privileges for the French-language, Roman Catholic majority.

Quiet Revolution The dramatic change of values and attitudes, especially toward the state, the new collective self-confidence, and the new brand of nationalism in Quebec in the 1960s.

Referendum A populist device in which a public policy proposal is submitted directly to the electorate.

Sovereignty-association The Parti Québécois proposal in which Quebec would be sovereign while maintaining an economic association with the rest of Canada.

War Measures Act The law invoked in both world wars and during the 1970 FLQ crisis under which the federal cabinet was given emergency powers to deal with the crisis.

FURTHER READING

Cairns, Alan C. *Disruptions: Constitutional Struggles, from the Charter to Meech Lake*. Toronto: McClelland and Stewart, 1991.

Clarke, Harold D., Allan Kornberg, and Peter Wearing. *A Polity on the Edge: Canada and the Politics of Fragmentation*. Peterborough: Broadview Press, 2000.

Fraser, Graham. *René Lévesque and the Parti Québécois in Power*. Toronto: Macmillan, 1984.

Johnston, Richard, et al. *The Challenge of Direct Democracy: The 1992 Canadian Referendum*. Kingston: McGill-Queen's University Press, 1996.

McRoberts, Kenneth. *Misconceiving Canada: The Struggle for National Unity*. Toronto: Oxford University Press, 1997.

———. *Quebec: Social Change and Political Crisis*. 3rd ed. Toronto: McClelland and Stewart, 1993.

———, and Patrick Monahan, eds. *The Charlottetown Accord, the Referendum and the Future of Canada*. Toronto: University of Toronto Press, 1993.

McWhinney, Edward. *Canada and the Constitution, 1979–82: Patriation and the Charter of Rights*. Toronto: University of Toronto Press, 1982.

Romanow, Roy, J. Whyte, and H. Leeson. *Canada … Notwithstanding: The Making of the Constitution, 1976–1982*. Toronto: Methuen, 1984.

Russell, Peter. *Constitutional Odyssey: Can Canadians Become a Sovereign People?* 2nd ed. Toronto: University of Toronto Press, 1993, 3rd ed., 2004.

Chapter 4

Aboriginal Peoples, Other Ethnic Groups, and Gender Issues

The French–English question has been a constant of Canadian politics since before Confederation, but until recently Aboriginal and other ethnic issues were largely ignored. Similarly, once women achieved the vote around 1920, the system paid little attention to them. About 1970, however, Aboriginal, other ethnic, and gender issues suddenly became prominent items on the political agenda. This chapter explores these three relatively new concerns: the first section examines Canada's Aboriginal peoples; the second discusses other ethnic groups; and the last deals with the women's movement and other gender issues.

Chapter Objectives

After you have completed this chapter, you should be able to:

Discuss the historical evolution of Aboriginal–European interaction and the factors that have contributed to the deplorable state of life of many Aboriginal people in Canada

Understand different kinds of Aboriginal land claims, the concept of Aboriginal self-government, and the current negotiating process involved in both

Distinguish between pre-1970 and post-1970 Canadian immigration patterns

Trace the evolution of multiculturalism policy

Discuss the implications of Canada's active immigration policy

Enumerate the milestones of women's political participation in Canada, as well as the factors that have inhibited such participation

Discuss the issues that have concerned the women's movement since 1970

Understand the public policy concerns of the gay and lesbian communities

Canada's Aboriginal Peoples
History and Numbers

The Native or Aboriginal peoples who have inhabited Canada for as long as 40 000 years are an extremely varied group. They are officially categorized as North American Indians, Inuit, and Métis, but none of these groups is homogeneous. Because the early explorers mistakenly thought they were in India and named the local inhabitants accordingly, Canadian Indians now prefer to be known by the term **First Nations**. Before Europeans came to the continent, the Aboriginal peoples were self-sufficient and self-governing. They made decisions on the basis of consensus rather than by voting, and in many cases women (sometimes called clan mothers) played a significant role. In their close attachment to the land, they did not think in terms of private ownership; instead, they believed in the shared use of land and saw themselves as trustees of it for future generations. The fur trade, which led to the invasion by Europeans, was devastating for the Aboriginal peoples, totally disrupting their way of life and introducing new diseases that severely reduced their population.

Terminology

What does "First Nations" mean? This term came into common usage in the 1970s and can be applied in different contexts. It can refer to the Indian peoples of Canada, both status and non-status, but does not include the Métis or the Inuit. It can also replace the word "band." It can be used as a noun (for example, "the Whitefish Lake First Nation") or as an adjective (for example, "life in a First Nations community").

In the **Royal Proclamation of 1763**, which divided up the territory acquired by Britain, an attempt was made to define Indian lands. In a large area called Indian Territory, the purchase or settlement of land was forbidden without Crown approval, that is, without a treaty between the Crown and the Aboriginal peoples concerned. This policy was not always followed, and Europeans often occupied Indian land without a treaty. Even when treaties were signed, there was much question about the fairness of the negotiations. Later on, the Crown set aside reserves in exchange for the cession of Indian land, in addition to providing benefits such as the right to hunt and fish on unoccupied Crown land.

The 1867 Constitution Act gave jurisdiction over Indians and lands reserved for the Indians to the federal government. In 1876, Parliament passed the **Indian Act**, providing for federal government control of almost every aspect of Aboriginal life. The Indian Act aimed to assimilate Aboriginal people into the new white majority and represented a colonialist mentality—the exploitation, domination, and subjugation of a people by an imperial power. One of its provisions allowed for "enfranchisement," which encouraged Indians to give up their Indian status. Thus began the distinction between "status Indians," those registered with the federal government according to the terms of the Indian Act, and "non-status Indians," those not so registered.

Meanwhile, the treaty-making process continued apace, covering most of northern Ontario and the Prairie provinces. These treaties were designed primarily to clear Aboriginal title so that the transcontinental railway could be built and Western immigrant settlement could begin. In return for surrendering title to the lands involved, Indians received tracts of land for reserves as well as other benefits such as small annuities, schools, hunting and fishing rights, agricultural implements, cattle, and ammunition. In retrospect, almost everyone agrees that the Aboriginal peoples were taken advantage of in these negotiations; the land given them for reserves was usually small, remote, and lacking in resources. Even worse off, however, were those Indians in much of Eastern Canada, British Columbia, and the Arctic, with whom no treaties were signed at all.

The Métis were the descendants of European fur traders and Indian women. Found largely on the Prairies, Métis combined nomadic hunting with farming. Not covered by the Indian Act or by treaties, they were left to the mercy of new white settlers and provincial and territorial governments. It is not surprising that Louis Riel, leader of the rebellion that led to the creation of Manitoba in 1870, took up their cause in 1884–85 in the second Riel Rebellion in Saskatchewan. After the rebellion was crushed, the Métis found themselves in an even weaker position.

In the 2001 census, some 1.3 million people, or 4.4 percent of the total Canadian population, reported Aboriginal ancestry, but only 976 000 (3.3 percent of the total population) identified with an Aboriginal group. The Department of Indian and Northern Affairs reports a slightly higher number of Aboriginal people: approximately 1.6 million, or 4.5 percent of the population. These numbers are distributed as follows: status Indians on reserve, 400 000; status Indians off-reserve, 260 000; non-status Indians, 425 000; Métis, 212 100; and Inuit, 60 000.[1] There are 2370 reserves in Canada, with an average size of about 1160 hectares.

They are divided among some 600 bands or First Nations, with an average population of about 650 persons.

The Living Conditions of Aboriginal Peoples

The above statistics present only part of the picture. Of equal significance are the distressing statistics on Aboriginal poverty. Many reserve families have incomes far below the poverty line, and apart from a few urban professionals, the same is true for most of those who live off-reserve. Related to this level of poverty are alarming rates of Aboriginal alcoholism, low educational attainment, and unemployment. The overall life expectancy of Aboriginal Canadians is seven years shorter than that of non-Aboriginal Canadians, largely a result of poor health services and on-reserve housing that is overcrowded and lacking in running water, indoor toilets, and central heating. The infant mortality rate among registered Indians is almost twice the rate among Canadians as a whole, and Aboriginal people suffer far more than non-Aboriginal people from tuberculosis and many other diseases. The suicide rate among Aboriginal youth is at least five times the national average, and Aboriginal people are much more likely to be murdered or die from accidents, poisoning, or violence.

Much of the current predicament of Aboriginal peoples in Canada can be traced to the Indian Act and government attitudes behind it. Having lost their land, original livelihood, and culture, and being placed on unproductive reserves, many Aboriginal people find themselves with little to do. The resulting unemployment, idleness, and reliance on welfare often lead them to seek solace in substance abuse. In this intoxicated state, they may resort to family and other violence, which in turn brings them into trouble with the law. Not being able to pay their fines, and being subject to discrimination at the hands of the police, the courts, and other aspects of the justice system, they then go to jail, where they become even more alienated, depressed, and abused.

Aboriginal peoples have suffered from untold discrimination and indignity at every turn. In the past, the Indian Act required non-Aboriginal bureaucratic approval for almost any band decision. Aboriginal babies were frequently removed from the reserves to be adopted by non-Aboriginal parents, and until the 1970s, many Aboriginal children were forced to go to residential schools, where they were punished, sometimes to the point of assault, for speaking their Aboriginal language or engaging in Aboriginal customs. Aboriginal languages and cultures have been systematically discouraged, and traditional forms of government and medicine have been outlawed. Registered Indians did not even have the right to

vote in federal elections until 1960, and between 1927 and 1951, the Indian Act
made it an offence for them to hire a lawyer to bring a claim against Canada
without government consent. Another factor contributing to the disruption of
Aboriginal people's lives is the exploitation of Indian lands by mining, petroleum,
lumber, and hydroelectricity companies.

Aboriginal Political Issues since 1970

Although Aboriginal people struggled against public policies from the time of the
Riel rebellions, it was not until 1970 or so that governments in Canada began to
pay much attention to them or their problems. Aboriginal people were particularly vocal in their opposition to the Trudeau–Chrétien **White Paper on Indians**
of 1969 that called for their complete integration into the wider Canadian society.
With the proposed repeal of the Indian Act and treaties, they would become
equal, ordinary Canadian citizens. On the other hand, Aboriginal peoples finally
sensed support in the sympathetic Berger Inquiry into the proposed Mackenzie
Valley gas pipeline in 1977. By this time, their problems had become so serious
that they simply could no longer be ignored, and the incidence of sit-ins, road-
blocks, rallies, court cases, hunger strikes, and international protests increased.
Several Aboriginal organizations came into existence, including the **Assembly of
First Nations**, to spearhead the demand for change. Post-1970 Aboriginal issues
are related primarily to land and to governance.

LAND ISSUES

As noted earlier, in much of the country, North American Indians signed treaties
with the Crown under which they ceded the land to the government in return for
protected reserves (see Figure 4.1, page 76). But, especially in Eastern Canada,
British Columbia, and the North, few such treaties were signed, leaving Indians
and Inuit in these regions without a land base, similar to the Métis, who have
never legally possessed any land. This situation gives rise to the issue of
Aboriginal title, that is, a claim to land on the basis of traditional occupancy and
use rather than treaty. The existence of such Aboriginal title was first recognized
in the *Calder* case in 1973 in connection with the Nisga'a band in British
Columbia. In response, the government of Canada announced its intention to
negotiate Aboriginal title. A great many Aboriginal land claims have been
launched in the past 30 years. They fall into two categories: comprehensive claims
based on Aboriginal title (that is, traditional occupancy and use of land) that

Figure 4.1   Map of Historic Indian Treaties

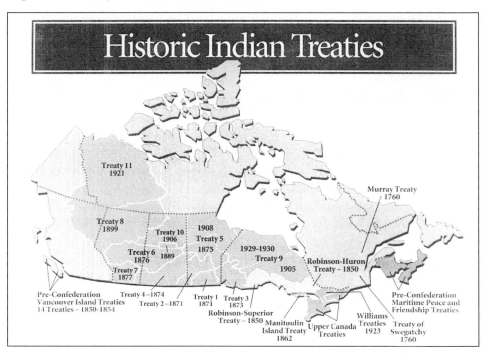

Source: Treaties: Agreements for Building the Future. Ottawa: Indian and Northern Affairs Canada, 2000. Reproduced with the permission of the Minister of Public Works and Government Services Canada, 2004.

have not been dealt with by treaty or other legal means, and specific claims arising from misinterpretation or nonfulfillment of the terms of Indian treaties and other lawful obligations.

Such claims have moved relatively faster in the North than in the south, since north of the 60th parallel the federal government has jurisdiction over the land as well over the Aboriginal peoples. In fact, agreement has been achieved in several comprehensive land claims in the North. Besides providing land and money, such comprehensive claims clarify Aboriginal hunting, fishing, and trapping rights and clear obstacles to future economic development.

In the south, because Ottawa has responsibility for Aboriginal peoples and lands reserved for the Indians but the provinces have jurisdiction over public lands, such claims have moved more slowly. Aboriginal peoples have generally found provincial governments even less sympathetic to their issues than Ottawa, and conflict has often developed between Indian bands and large natural resource companies as well as non-Aboriginal people who now live on the land in question. Ottawa insists that the provinces be party to such settlements and contribute to their costs. Thus far, relatively few comprehensive land claim successes can be reported below the 60th parallel.

The first major provincial comprehensive land claim settlement was the 1975 **James Bay Agreement** between the Cree and Inuit and the government of Quebec. In return for allowing Quebec to construct a giant hydro development project in the area, the James Bay Agreement gave the Aboriginal peoples exclusive use of 13 700 km^2 of land and additional territory of exclusive hunting, fishing, and trapping rights, along with $225 million in cash. One terrible side effect of the development, due to an unanticipated chemical reaction between water and rock in the flooded land, was the mercury poisoning of the fish and of the Aboriginal people who ate them. This problem and the growing perception that the deal may otherwise have been less generous to the Aboriginal community than originally thought led the Cree of Quebec to reject the second, "Great Whale" phase of the James Bay project in the 1990s.

Since the province of British Columbia contains a large proportion of North American Indians who have not signed treaties, the comprehensive land claims issue has been particularly significant there. Progress was slow until the 1997 *Delgamuukw* case established a definition of Aboriginal title and approved the admissibility of oral history evidence in making such a claim. The Nisga'a tribe in northwest B.C., which had been seeking recognition of their Aboriginal title for over 100 years, finally arrived at an agreement-in-principle in 1996. The treaty ratified by the federal and provincial governments in 2000 provided the Nisga'a with 1930 km^2 of land and $190 million in cash, along with several powers of self-government.

Specific land claims are those resulting from dissatisfaction with treaties—especially when bands did not receive the full amount of land that the treaties promised. Between 1973 and 2002, Canada settled over 230 specific land entitlement claims, although not always to First Nations' satisfaction, leaving several hundred others under negotiation or assessment. Everyone involved hoped that the new claims commission established in 2002 would produce faster results.

Another dimension of land issues concerns the activities that treaties allow Aboriginal peoples to pursue on public or Crown lands. Aboriginal **treaty rights**, especially hunting and fishing rights, frequently conflict with provincial law. After many court cases, some progress has been made on this front, including on the issue of logging. However, the issue of Aboriginal peoples' fishing out of season erupted in 2001–02 in Burnt Church, New Brunswick. In the *Marshall* cases, the Supreme Court of Canada recognized a treaty right for local Aboriginal peoples to make a moderate livelihood from the sea, but it also acknowledged that the Department of Fisheries and Oceans could regulate the fishery in the interests of conservation. A recent Supreme Court of Canada decision held that the Métis have a constitutional right to hunt for food, just as other Aboriginal peoples do.

Yet another aspect of the land question arose in the most violent Aboriginal–government conflict of modern times—the crisis at Oka, Quebec, in the summer of 1990.[2] The municipal council's decision to expand a golf course on land claimed by resident Mohawks as sacred ground led to an armed standoff between Mohawk warriors and the Quebec Provincial Police, during which one police officer was killed. The Canadian Armed Forces were later brought in, and Aboriginal demonstrations took place across the country. Then, in 1995, an unarmed Aboriginal demonstrator, Dudley George, was killed by a police officer in a peaceful land claims demonstration at Ipperwash, Ontario. The controversy over the involvement of the Mike Harris government in this affair continues.

GOVERNANCE ISSUES

Aboriginal Canadians have long demanded improvements in government health, social, and educational services, and some minor improvements have been made over the years. Aboriginal peoples began to feel, however, that they were too constrained by the Indian Act and that their problems required Aboriginal solutions. They were tired of living at the mercy of non-Aboriginal politicians and bureaucrats. Yet most Aboriginal peoples did not want to gut the Indian Act and existing government programs until they had something better to put in their place.

Shortly after their rejection of the 1969 White Paper, Aboriginal peoples began to argue that they should be able to choose their own decisionmaking processes, for they could hardly be expected to support the apparatus that created their current problems. Before the passage of the Indian Act, they had sophisticated and distinctive forms of government; many wanted to return to such traditional ways, feeling that the system of elected band councils was an alien imposition.

But going well beyond such decisionmaking machinery was the demand for **Aboriginal self-government**. The specific structures of such proposed self-government are not clear-cut. Some advocates would accept a kind of super-municipality, and some progress has been made toward greater community-based control at the local level. While an array of self-government arrangements and institutional models has been developed within the existing constitutional setup, other Aboriginal peoples have more ambitious plans that would be harder to fit into the Canadian constitutional framework.

The first improvement in the constitutional recognition of Aboriginal rights occurred in the Constitution Act, 1982. Section 25 guaranteed that Charter rights would not be construed so as to abrogate or derogate from any Aboriginal, treaty, or other rights or freedoms that pertained to the Aboriginal peoples of Canada, including any rights recognized by the Royal Proclamation of 1763 and any rights or freedoms "that now exist by way of land claims agreements or may be so acquired." Section 35 recognized and affirmed the existing Aboriginal and treaty rights of the Aboriginal peoples of Canada. Inspired by the equality rights clause in the Charter, the Indian Act was amended to rescind the clause that had previously removed Indian status from Aboriginal women who married white men but granted such status to white women who married Indian men. Bill C-31 led to the reinstatement of nearly 100 000 Aboriginal women and their children, but since bands were allowed to control who could actually live on the reserve, many

National Chief of Assembly of First Nations Phil Fontaine meets with provincial premiers in Niagara-on-the-Lake in July 2004. (CP Photo/Fred Chartrand)

of those reinstated in status had difficulty in returning. In general, the Charter of Rights and its interpretation by the courts have been of some help to Aboriginal peoples, given their inclination to take their claims to court when dealing with uncooperative politicians and bureaucrats.[3]

Although mid-1980s constitutional talks on Aboriginal self-government broke down, two pieces of legislation were passed to provide for self-government in specific localities. The 1984 Cree-Naskapi (of Quebec) Act set in place self-government arrangements for the Aboriginal peoples of Quebec who were parties to the James Bay land claim agreement, and the 1986 Sechelt Indian Band Self-Government Act allowed the Sechelt band in British Columbia to assume control over its lands, resources, health and social services, education, and local taxation in what is usually called the "municipal model."

THE MEECH LAKE AND CHARLOTTETOWN ACCORDS AND BEYOND

Canadian Aboriginal peoples were understandably opposed to the 1987 Meech Lake Accord, which addressed Quebec's constitutional demands but completely overlooked their own. Even supporters of the accord empathized with Elijah Harper when he blocked it in the Manitoba legislature in 1990. This action, together with the Oka affair, precipitated a dramatic breakthrough in constitutional concern with Aboriginal issues and in the participation of Aboriginal leaders in constitutional negotiations. Aboriginal leaders were given the same status as premiers in the talks leading up to the 1992 Charlottetown Accord, and that document addressed Aboriginal concerns in a more extensive and satisfactory way than it did the demands of Quebec.

The Charlottetown Accord would have recognized the inherent right of Aboriginal peoples to self-government within Canada and regarded such Aboriginal governments as a third order of government in Canada, analogous to provinces. The document also provided for self-government agreements to be negotiated among the three levels of government. Federal and provincial laws would remain in place until superseded by Aboriginal laws, but the latter would have to be consistent with the preservation of peace, order, and good government in Canada. As mentioned in Chapter 3, the Charlottetown Accord was turned down in a national referendum, but the Aboriginal section of the accord was not primarily to blame.

Since 1992, activity in the area of Aboriginal governance has been limited to legislative and administrative changes, such as delegating federal or provincial government powers to First Nations communities. In 1995, the Chrétien government declared that in its view the inherent right to Aboriginal self-government was already incorporated in section 35 of the Constitution Act, 1982. In consequence, a ministerial statement formally launched a negotiating process to implement that right, with arrangements varying from one group to another. A large number of Aboriginal groups are involved in these negotiations. Aboriginal peoples have increased their control over how federal funding is spent and have assumed responsibility for delivering many of their own educational, social, and health care services.

Much hope for the solution of Aboriginal problems was placed in the Royal Commission on Aboriginal Peoples, appointed in 1991 and reporting in 1996. The commission endorsed Aboriginal self-government in its widest sense and the basic separation of Aboriginal and non-Aboriginal societies. Among other things, it proposed an Aboriginal Parliament, dual Canadian–Aboriginal citizenship, an independent lands and treaties tribunal, an Aboriginal development bank, an action plan on health and social conditions, and an Aboriginal-controlled education system. Whether because of the magnitude or the direction of the recommendations, the Chrétien government seemed reluctant to rush into their implementation. It did, however, issue a Statement of Reconciliation, apologizing for past wrongs, especially the horrors of the residential school system.

Comprehensive land claims and self-government agreements are now often negotiated simultaneously, and two prominent examples should be mentioned. A plebiscite in 1992 ratified the division of the Northwest Territories, and a land claim in the eastern Arctic was finalized in 1993. As a result, in 1999, the territory of **Nunavut** was created and separated from the Northwest Territories. It has all the governmental institutions associated with a province or territory but represents a kind of Aboriginal self-government, in the sense that the population is almost completely composed of Inuit. The 2000 **Nisga'a Treaty** incorporated self-government powers somewhat beyond those of municipalities and was secured by federal–provincial–Aboriginal agreement. It includes sections on forestry, mining, wildlife and the environment, the administration of justice, finance, and taxation (including Aboriginal peoples' surrender of their tax-exempt status).[4]

In 2002, the Chrétien government introduced a new First Nations Governance Act, which it claimed advanced Aboriginal self-government. Most Aboriginal peoples saw it differently, however, and the act was abandoned when Paul Martin took over as prime minister. Martin declared Aboriginal issues to be a higher priority for his government, but it remains to be seen if greater progress will occur. While Statistics Canada reported in 2003 that off-reserve Aboriginal youth are achieving higher levels of education than in the past, the off-reserve population in general continues to suffer from a long list of health problems. Meanwhile, the Auditor General found that on-reserve housing is in a crisis situation.[5]

ABORIGINAL JUSTICE

Aboriginal peoples constitute only about 4 percent of the Canadian population but comprise between 15 and 20 percent of the inmates in Canadian correctional institutions. Two horrendous cases in 1971 attracted much public attention to this problem. Donald Marshall was a Nova Scotia Micmac who was imprisoned for over 10 years for a murder he did not commit. At the same time, in Manitoba, Helen Betty Osborne, an Aboriginal girl in The Pas, was raped and murdered by four white men who were protected from prosecution. Then, in 1988, J.J. Harper, an Aboriginal leader, was shot and killed by a Winnipeg police officer. More recent cases in Saskatoon and Toronto involving police mistreatment of Aboriginal people have even attracted the ire of Amnesty International. These cases and others, and the inquiries they precipitated, illustrate the misunderstanding, prejudice, harassment, abuse, and brutality inflicted on Aboriginal people by police, courts, and jails. They have also led to calls for a parallel Aboriginal justice system in which Aboriginal convictions and sentences would be based on Aboriginal values and community traditions.

While governments have generally ruled out a wholesale parallel Aboriginal justice system, several provinces have allowed experimental judicial processes involving Aboriginal input. More Aboriginal peoples have been hired as police officers. In addition, some reserves have their own Aboriginal police force, and a few even maintain their own correctional facilities. Increasingly, judges dealing with Aboriginal defendants are following Aboriginal traditions such as sentencing circles or consulting with elders in imposing sentences; these sentences can involve restitution or banishment. Perhaps with the high rate of Aboriginal incarceration in mind, Parliament amended the Criminal Code in 1995 to read: "All available sanctions other than imprisonment ... should be considered for all offenders, with particular attention to the circumstances of Aboriginal offenders."

Other Ethnic Groups and Multiculturalism

A third aspect of ethnic cleavage, involving other ethnic groups and multiculturalism, increasingly vies with the French–English and Aboriginal questions on the political agenda. The 2001 census showed the presence of over 200 different ethnic origins in Canada. The three principal issues in this area are amending immigration policy, preserving and promoting the identity of ethnic groups (or multiculturalism), and ensuring that individuals belonging to such groups are treated equitably under the law and in society.

Canadian Immigration Patterns

Beyond the French and the British, the first dramatic surge of immigrants arrived in Ontario and the Prairies during the 1880s. It included Danes, Dutch, Icelanders, Poles, Ukrainians, Finns, Norwegians, and Swedes. In British Columbia, on the other hand, Asians were a leading group: between 1881 and 1884, nearly 16 000 Chinese were brought in as contract labourers to work on the Canadian Pacific Railway. Nova Scotia and Ontario also became home to a substantial number of Blacks who were escaping from slavery in the United States.

An even larger number and variety of immigrants arrived between 1903 and 1914, and the prosperous 1920s were another active decade on the immigration front. After the Second World War, a further huge wave of immigrants came to Canada, largely from southern Europe, supplemented by postwar refugees from around the world. The numbers have swelled further in the past 15 years.

Overall, Britain was the leading source of immigrants between 1900 and 1965. During that period, immigration policy favoured British, American, and European newcomers, since they were considered well educated and skilled and, being predominantly Caucasian, better able to assimilate. After the Immigration Act was significantly amended in 1967, however, Canadian immigration patterns changed radically, as Table 4.1 shows. In 1957, over 90 percent

TABLE 4.1 COMPARISON OF BRITISH, EUROPEAN, AND ASIAN IMMIGRANTS TO CANADA IN SELECTED YEARS (PERCENTAGE)

	Britain	**Continental Europe**	**Asia**
1957	38.6	52.6	1.3
1967	28.0	43.8	9.3
1977	15.7	19.8	21.0
1987	5.6	19.1	44.3
1997	2.1	15.8	54.3

Source: Citizenship and Immigration Canada, *Immigration Statistics* (annual) and "Facts and Figures, 1998: Immigration Overview," http://www.cic.gc.ca/english/pdf/pub/facts1998.pdf (Retrieved 15 Aug. 2000). Adapted with permission of the Minister of Public Works and Government Services, 2004.

of immigrants were from Britain or continental Europe, a figure that fell to 17.9 percent by 1997. In contrast, Asian immigrants constituted less than 2 percent of the total in 1957, increasing to 54 percent in 1997. The top 10 source countries over the 2000–02 period are listed in Table 4.2.

TABLE 4.2 TOP 10 SOURCE COUNTRIES OF IMMIGRANTS TO CANADA, 2000–02

Country	Number of Immigrants
China	110 262
India	82 751
Pakistan	43 689
Philippines	34 002
Korea	24 559
Iran	19 087
U.S.A.	17 005
Sri Lanka	16 316
Romania	15 702
United Kingdom	14 717

Source: "Facts and Figures 2002: Immigration Overview," http://www.cic.gc.ca/english/pub/facts2002/immigration/immigration_5.html (Retrieved 24 May 2004). Calculations by author. Adapted with permission of the Minister of Public Works and Government Services, 2004.

As a result of this immigration pattern, the term **visible minorities** came into usage. Members of visible minorities are defined in the Employment Equity Act as "persons, other than Aboriginal peoples, who are non-Caucasian in race or non-white in colour." They now constitute 13.4 percent of the Canadian population—that is, approximately four million people. Well over three-quarters of the members of visible minorities in Canada reside in the six largest cities, especially Toronto, Vancouver, and Montreal. Indeed, over 37 percent of the residents of Toronto and Vancouver belong to visible minorities. Immigrant groups can thus be subdivided between the more recent visible minorities—essentially those from Asia, Africa, the Caribbean, South America, and the Middle East—and those less visible immigrants who came earlier from Britain and continental Europe. Some public policies, such as multiculturalism, include both groups, while others, such as employment equity, apply only to visible minorities.

Multiculturalism, Equity, and Inclusiveness

After the revision of the Immigration Act in 1967, the composition of the Canadian population changed significantly. Moreover, the increase in the numbers of people of "other" ethnic origin naturally gave them more leverage to push for policy changes in areas where they encountered indifference or discrimination.

Due largely to pressure from Ukrainian Canadians, the 1963 Royal Commission on Bilingualism and Biculturalism was ultimately asked to examine the contribution made by other ethnic groups to the cultural enrichment of Canada and the measures that should be taken to safeguard that contribution. While focusing primarily on the English and the French, the commission recommended that increased government attention be given to other ethnic groups, including public funding in certain areas. With this encouragement, such groups began to demand public financial assistance in addition to verbal or moral support, and the term "multiculturalism" came into use.

In 1971, the Trudeau government announced a new policy of multiculturalism within a bilingual framework. **Multiculturalism** is the official recognition of the diverse cultures in a plural society; it involves encouraging immigrants to retain and foster their linguistic heritages and ethnic cultures instead of abandoning them. The government argued that the Canadian identity would not be undermined by multiculturalism; on the contrary, cultural pluralism was the very essence of the Canadian identity. Multiculturalism is based on the idea that having a population of diverse origins makes Canada a more interesting place to live. By providing links to virtually every other country in the world, such a population also enhances Canada's international image and influence.

Basic Objectives of Multiculturalism Policy
- To assist cultural groups in retaining and fostering their identity.
- To assist cultural groups in overcoming barriers to their full participation in Canadian society.
- To promote creative exchanges among all Canadian cultural groups.
- To assist immigrants in acquiring at least one official language.

The policy of multiculturalism legitimized demands for many other changes both in terms of promoting ethnic identities and removing barriers to equity. A federal multiculturalism ministry took form in the 1970s, and the Canadian

Human Rights Commission was created in 1978 to complement equivalent bodies at the provincial level. Another advance for multiculturalism was the 1982 Charter of Rights and Freedoms, which provided constitutional protection against discrimination by federal and provincial governments in the **equality rights** clause, section 15. Moreover, the Charter endorsed affirmative action programs in order to overcome past discrimination. Under pressure from various ethnic groups, another section was added, stipulating that the Charter would be interpreted "in a manner consistent with the preservation and enhancement of the multicultural heritage of Canadians" (section 27). In 1988, the Mulroney government extended the 1982 provision by passing a new Canadian Multiculturalism Act.

On a different front, the 1986 federal Employment Equity Act designated visible minorities—along with women, people with disabilities, and Aboriginal peoples—as groups that could benefit from affirmative action programs with respect to hiring in the public service. While some ethnic leaders criticized the lack of specific goals and timetables in the legislation, those not included complained about reverse discrimination. The act was strengthened in 1995, but

New Canadians take the oath of citizenship. (CP Photo/Aaron Harris)

removing legal barriers to equity and/or giving visible minorities an occasional boost does not ensure that those belonging to visible minorities will be free from discrimination in the daily interactions of life. Besides instances of personal abuse, they still encounter situations where their skills are underutilized and not fairly remunerated, and many live in state of poverty.

In 1988, the Mulroney government also took action to compensate Japanese Canadians for their mistreatment during the Second World War. Unjustly suspected of being loyal to Japan, Canadian citizens of Japanese background were uprooted from the West Coast, interned in "relocation centres," and had their property confiscated. The 1988 Japanese Redress Agreement provided $21 000 for each of the surviving internees. This led to demands from other ethnic groups that they be similarly compensated for wartime discrimination in Canada.

Recent Developments in Multiculturalism and Immigration

If the responses to demands from the multicultural community were largely positive in the 1970s and 1980s, such was not entirely the case in the 1990s. Opposition surfaced toward immigration in general and visible minority immigration in particular, as well as to multiculturalism, employment equity, and other policies and practices.[6]

Such opposition was partly in response to the recession of the early 1990s and the continuing high unemployment rate afterward. Whatever the real merits of immigration in economic terms, ordinary voters saw recent immigrants in jobs that they felt would otherwise have gone to Canadian residents of longer duration. As for the source of immigrants, while the level of Canadian acceptance and tolerance of nontraditional immigrants is high, it is not unlimited. From the point of view of established citizens, the integration of new immigrants costs money (not that either level of government provides adequate services in this area), and it is difficult to teach classes made up largely of immigrant children who have yet to learn English or French. The Reform Party (later the Canadian Alliance) was the first to break rank with an all-party consensus on this issue and called for a sizable cut in annual immigration levels, with a greater emphasis on skills. For a time, even the pro-immigration Chrétien government responded to these pressures.

The policy of official multiculturalism has been criticized even by members of the multicultural community, such as writer Neil Bissoondath, who maintains that official multiculturalism is divisive, ghettoizes visible minorities, fosters racial animosity, and detracts from national unity.[7] Critics also argue that it is not appropriate for the government to be fostering the maintenance of foreign traditions

Immigration Report Card, 2002

Immigrants	203 947
Family	65 277
Economic	136 525
Other	2 145
Refugees	25 111
Total	229 058

Source: "Facts and Figures 2002: Immigration Overview," http://www.cic.gc.ca/english/pub/facts2002/immigration/immigration_2.html (Retrieved 24 May 2004). Adapted with permission of the Minister of Public Works and Government Services, 2004.

while starving national cultural institutions; they say that the money might be better spent teaching immigrants about basic Canadian values.

Less opposition to visible minorities was evident at the beginning of the new century, even as the number of visible minorities increased. This could have been the result of a more prosperous economy and/or the growing recognition that immigration was essential to economic growth.

In 2002, the Chrétien government enacted new immigration and refugee legislation. It aimed to increase the number of immigrants, place more emphasis on education and experience, and streamline the refugee system. Because of the heightened concern about terrorism after the events of September 11, 2001, however, the government increased security measures at Canada's borders. Indeed, after 9/11, many Canadian Muslims and Arabs were victims of a backlash, and some suffered grievously at the hands of U.S. authorities.

The Women's Movement and Other Gender Issues
Evolution of Women's Rights to 1970

Men and male-oriented issues virtually monopolized Canadian politics before 1900. In those early years, when all women were expected to marry and then become chattels of their husbands, they first had to fight for educational and occupational rights, such as admission to universities and to the medical and legal professions. Women demanded the right to make contracts and to own property, and they increasingly began to work in factories and offices and to become teachers and nurses; others continued to make major contributions on the farm. About 1900, farm women in particular became active in reform organizations of many kinds, including those that pressed for the prohibition of alcohol and the establishment of new public health facilities, better housing, and improved working conditions for women and children.

As influential as women were in promoting these causes, many began to feel that their impact would always be limited until they could vote. Thus, in what is sometimes called the "first wave" of the women's movement, women demanded the franchise. After the outbreak of the First World War, proponents of female suffrage had an additional argument: women should be rewarded for their contribution to the war effort. Thus, Manitoba, Alberta, and Saskatchewan, containing some of the most articulate women of the day, pioneered the female franchise in 1916; Ontario and British Columbia joined them in 1917; and all the other provinces except Quebec followed shortly afterward.

At the federal level, the Borden government deliberately manipulated the franchise for the 1917 election, in part by giving the vote to women in the armed services (mostly nurses) and by allowing soldiers fighting abroad to appoint their nearest female relative at home—women who would likely support the war effort—to cast their vote by proxy. A year later, the vote was extended to all women (except those excluded for ethnic reasons, such as Aboriginals and Asians), and they had their first chance to exercise this new right in the 1921 election.

Two women were elected to the Alberta legislature in 1917, while Agnes Macphail became the first woman elected to the House of Commons in 1921. She served alone until 1935, however, when a second woman was elected. Macphail stayed on until 1940 and then, in 1943, became the first woman elected to the Ontario legislature. Vigorous and articulate, she promoted radical and progressive causes of many kinds but could do only so much by herself to advance women's issues in such an entrenched male bastion.

It was not until 1940 that Quebec women were enfranchised in provincial elections. Moreover, the legal status of a married woman under the Quebec Civil Code was such that until 1955 she could not seek a separation on grounds of adultery by her husband, and until 1964 she had no right to carry on a trade without her husband's consent.

The number of women who won seats in the House of Commons was minuscule right up to 1970, and many of those elected were the widows or daughters of

Time Line
Milestones in Women's Rights

1916	Women obtain vote in three provinces
1917/18	Women obtain vote in federal elections and in most other provinces
1921	First woman MP
1929	*Persons* case
1940	Women obtain vote in Quebec provincial elections
1957	First woman federal cabinet minister
1967/70	Royal Commission on Status of Women
1982	First woman on the Supreme Court
1989	First woman federal party leader
1993	First woman prime minister

male members of Parliament. Female political participation was inhibited by many factors. First, people were traditionally socialized into the view that politics was a masculine pursuit and that women should remain in the home. Second, most women were constrained by the responsibilities of homemaking and child-rearing. The long hours and unpredictable schedules of politicians conflicted with most women's family commitments, which prevented them from being away from home for any length of time. Homemaking roles had little prestige and prevented women from accumulating the money, contacts, and experience that political careers usually require. Third, political parties discouraged female candidacies, and when consciousness of the lack of female candidates increased, parties frequently nominated them as sacrificial lambs against a strong male incumbent.

Until the late 1920s, no women had been appointed to the other house of Parliament, the Senate. When an enterprising group of Western women took this issue to court, the Supreme Court of Canada ruled that women were not "qualified persons" within the meaning of section 24 of the 1867 Constitution Act and were therefore ineligible to sit in the Senate. This decision was appealed to the Judicial Committee of the Privy Council, which in the 1929 *Persons* case overruled the Supreme Court. The women's movement continues to celebrate this decision to this day in the form of the "Persons Day Breakfast." As well, the Governor General's Awards in Commemoration of the Persons Case are given out every year. After the case was decided, Prime Minister Mackenzie King immediately appointed Cairine Wilson to the Senate, but the second woman was not appointed until 1935, and 18 years would pass before three more received the call.

In the Words of the Court
The Judicial Committee of the Privy Council on the *Persons* Case

"The exclusion of women from all public offices is a relic of days more barbarous than ours ... [T]heir Lordships have come to the conclusion that the word 'persons' in s. 24 includes members both of the male and female sex."

Source: Henrietta Muir Edwards v. Attorney-General for Canada, [1929] (better known as the *Persons* case), Richard A. Olmsted, *Decisions of the Judicial Committee of the Privy Council*, vol. 2 (Ottawa: Queen's Printer, 1954).

It was not until 1957 that the first woman, Ellen Fairclough, was appointed to the federal cabinet; she was followed by Judy LaMarsh in 1963. The advance of women to the cabinet at the provincial level was generally even slower. Nevertheless, gradual improvements continued to be made in federal and provincial legislation and programs of benefit to women. The federal Family Allowances Act of 1944, for example, provided a small monthly payment to each Canadian mother to help care for her children, often representing the only independent income the woman possessed. In 1952, Ontario passed the first equal pay legislation, to be followed by federal legislation two years later. The birth control pill became available about 1960, amendments to the Criminal Code in 1969 made it legal to advertise birth control devices, and a new Divorce Act made it easier to get out of an unfulfilling marriage.

The Women's Movement since 1970

By 1970, attitudes had changed sufficiently that it was possible to speak of a **women's movement**, and the word "feminist" became common. In their most general sense, such terms are used to apply to those who seek to establish complete gender equality, to free men and women from restrictive gender roles, and to end any semblance of the subordination of women.

This "second wave" of the women's movement coincided with the Royal Commission on the Status of Women, appointed in 1967 and reporting in 1970. That report "provided a solid statistical base and a framework for most of the feminist action that followed during the 1970s"[8] and made 167 recommendations. Since that time, gender issues have become an important, daily factor in Canadian politics, and most governments now designate a minister to be responsible for women's issues. Ottawa also issued a Federal Plan for Gender Equality in 1995.

The number of women's groups has increased remarkably in recent years, the foremost pressure group being the National Action Committee on the Status of Women (NAC). NAC was established in 1972, largely because of government inaction on the Status of Women report, and functions as an umbrella lobbying group for over 700 local and national member groups representing over three million women. Although its membership is large, its chronic shortage of funds has hampered its effectiveness, a problem exacerbated by the withdrawal of much federal government funding in recent years.

POLITICAL REPRESENTATION

In the post-1970 era, women's participation in politics and government increased substantially. Table 4.3 charts this progress. Many of the factors mentioned above that inhibited women from becoming politicians before 1970 are still present, although in recent years most parties have created special funds to support female candidates.

TABLE 4.3 REPRESENTATION OF WOMEN IN THE HOUSE OF COMMONS, 1921–2004

Election	Number Elected	Election	Number Elected	Election	Number Elected
1921	1	1957	2	1979	10
1925	1	1958	2	1980	14
1926	1	1962	5	1984	27
1930	1	1963	4	1988	39
1935	2	1965	4	1993	53
1940	1	1968	1	1997	62
1945	1	1972	5	2000	62
1949	0	1974	9	2004	65
1953	4				

Source: Compiled from "Women Candidates in General Elections, 1921 to Date," http://www.parl.gc.ca/information/about/process/house/asp/WomenElect.asp?lang=E&Hist=N&Source=hoc (Retrieved 5 Aug. 2004). Reproduced with permission of the Library of Parliament/Bibliothèque du Parlement, 2004.

At the cabinet level, the token one or two female ministers were clearly considered to be insufficient by the 1980s, and Brian Mulroney appointed six women to his 1984 cabinet. In the provinces, the number of women ministers gradually increased, too, with Bob Rae coming close to gender equality in his Ontario NDP cabinet in 1990.

It was also in the post-1970 period that Canada finally saw women elected as political party leaders. Alexa McDonough (NDP, Nova Scotia) led the way in 1980, to be followed by a host of others. After Rosemary Brown made a serious stab at the NDP national leadership in 1975 and Flora Macdonald sought the PC's in 1976, it remained for Audrey McLaughlin to make history when she was elected leader of the federal New Democratic Party in 1989, the first woman to lead a major national party. Alexa McDonough moved from Nova Scotia to succeed her as federal NDP leader in 1995.

Two women have become provincial premiers, and Kim Campbell served briefly as prime minister. Jeanne Sauvé was the first female Speaker of the House of Commons and first female governor general, while Bertha Wilson became the first woman to sit on the Supreme Court of Canada in 1982. Women judges have been appointed at an ever-increasing rate in other courts, and about 25 percent of federally appointed judges are now women. In 2000, Beverley McLachlin became the first female chief justice of Canada.

Within the federal bureaucracy, the first women joined the RCMP in 1974, and the first female deputy minister was appointed in 1975. Women gradually became eligible for full combat roles in the armed forces, and the first female general was named in 1988. In 1993, Jocelyne Bourgon became the first woman to hold the top public service position in Ottawa, Clerk of the Privy Council and Secretary to the Cabinet.

EMPLOYMENT ISSUES

Since the majority of women of working age are now in the labour force—of which women constitute about 46 percent—one major feminist concern is employment. Women have traditionally been discriminated against in pay, underrepresented in managerial positions, and discouraged from undertaking nontraditional occupations. In 1985, full-time female workers earned on average 65.5 percent of what men earned, leading women to demand "equal pay for work of equal value" or **pay equity**. Most Canadian governments now have pay equity laws, and there has been considerable improvement in the situation, although a recent federal task force on the subject called for more vigorous legislation.[9]

Beyond pay equity is the broader subject of **employment equity**, that is, the elimination of discrimination in hiring and promoting women. Employment equity is sometimes combined with **affirmative action** programs to give women preference in order to make up for past inequities. In 1983, affirmative action with respect to the hiring of women was made mandatory in all federal government departments, and the report of the 1984 Commission of Inquiry on Equity in Employment became the foundation of the 1986 Employment Equity Act. The act extended employment equity requirements to all Crown corporations, all federally regulated companies with over 100 employees, and other large companies in receipt of major government contracts. Nevertheless, while women now constitute about 50 percent of the federal government workforce, they occupy only 30 percent of executive-level jobs. Ontario passed an even more extensive Employment Equity Act in 1993, which was quickly repealed by the Conservative government of Mike Harris, but Ottawa strengthened its legislation in 1995.

The area in which women are most severely underrepresented is at the top of private corporations. A 1999 survey of the top 500 industrial companies in Canada found only 13 women who held the position of chief executive officer. One notable example is Heather Reisman at Indigo Books and Chapters.

What Do You Think?

How do you feel about employment equity and affirmative action laws in support of women, Aboriginal peoples, visible minorities, and people with disabilities? Are they necessary to combat systemic discrimination, or do they constitute reverse discrimination? Have they ever benefited or disadvantaged you?

For those women who choose to have children as well as seek employment outside the home, the issue of child care is often a serious problem. Daycare for children of such parents, especially children of single mothers, remains one of the major unresolved "women's issues" of the day. Some single mothers or two-parent families are happy to rely on relatives, friends, or unlicensed facilities, but in 2001 there were fewer than 360 000 licensed full-time daycare spaces available across the country. These provided care for only 12 percent of the three million children under the age of 13 who had mothers in the paid labour force. Both PC and Liberal governments reneged on promises of a national daycare program, leaving the provinces to fund such programs on their own, at least until the Martin government took the commitment more seriously.

LEGAL, REPRODUCTIVE, SEXUAL, AND VIOLENCE ISSUES

As the 1982 Charter of Rights and Freedoms emerged from federal–provincial negotiation, gender equality was to be lumped into equality rights along with such other factors as race, religion, and age, which governments would be allowed to override with the notwithstanding clause. Such treatment at the hands of 11 male first ministers galvanized the women's movement as never before; as a result of its tremendous pressure, section 28 was added to the final document to give gender equality a place of its own, protected from the notwithstanding clause.[10]

There followed a series of feminist challenges to laws that women believed discriminated against them. The government itself encouraged such legal activity with the Court Challenges Program, under which it subsidized the Legal Education and Action Fund (LEAF) in making such challenges. Women have not won every such case, but among their victories was the right to maternity leave under the Unemployment Insurance Act.

One of the main feminist rallying cries of the post-1970 period is that women must be able to control what happens to their own bodies. Many women's organizations supported Dr. Henry Morgentaler in his long fight to reform the Criminal Code's provisions on abortion.[11] Although amendments had been made in 1968, feminists did not regard these as sufficient, and the Supreme Court of Canada threw out the abortion law in the famous 1988 *Morgentaler* case. Two years later, the Mulroney government introduced a compromise abortion law, but it was defeated in the Senate, leaving Canada with no federal law restricting abortion. Even so, access to abortion varies widely across the country. Prostitution and pornography have also been subject to judicial decision, while sexual stereotyping, sexual harassment, and physical and sexual assault are other major issues of concern to women. Women gained a partial victory in "rape-shield" sexual assault cases, when questions to defendants about past sexual history were somewhat restricted and when the Supreme Court ruled that "no means no."

THE FEMINIZATION OF POVERTY

Chapter 2 revealed that there is a relatively high incidence of poverty among women. About 55 percent of sole-support mothers raise their children below the poverty line. With or without a male partner, large numbers of women with preschool children find it necessary to work outside the home to support themselves and their families.[12] This has continued to be the case even after the Canada Child Tax Credit was added to the income tax system to replace the Family Allowance for lower-income families. To decrease the incidence of women

Hemant Morparia/artizans.com

living in poverty, measures such as pay equity, employment equity, higher minimum wages, increased unionization, and improved job training and literacy programs will be required.

Gay and Lesbian Issues

A variety of issues related to homosexuality have arisen in recent years, and these
also figure prominently on today's political agenda. In most cases, politicians are
reluctant to deal with demands coming from the gay, lesbian, and bisexual communities, leaving such groups to take their concerns directly to the courts.

One of these groups' first demands was for protection in human rights codes
from individual discrimination. Somewhat surprisingly, the breakthrough came in
Quebec. When the Charter of Rights and Freedoms was adopted in 1982, section
15 prohibited discrimination by government or in law on the basis of sex, but
sexual orientation was not explicitly included. In the 1995 *Egan* case, however,
the Supreme Court of Canada unanimously added sexual orientation to the
equality rights clause, although it was subject to reasonable limits. By the late
1990s, whether by legislation or court action (as in the *Vriend* case in Alberta),

sexual orientation had been added to all the human rights codes in Canada. Such federal and provincial legislation primarily protects homosexuals from discrimination in the private sector. The Criminal Code was also amended in 2004 to ban the incitement of hatred against gays and lesbians.

The next phase of the battle for equality in this area centred on gay and lesbian couples. In two cases from Ontario, *Rosenberg* and *M. v. H.*, the courts recognized same-sex equality rights in pension benefits after death and in financial support after separation. In the latter case, the Supreme Court advised Ontario to amend other laws that continued to treat same-sex couples differently from others. Afterward, both federal and provincial governments passed omnibus legislation to make such amendments across the board. In some cases, however, they continued to define "marriage" as a union between a man and a woman and made a distinction between a "same-sex partner" and a "spouse." A number of homosexual couples challenged such distinctions, as well as restrictions on adoption. Through a series of judicial decisions, both same-sex adoption and same-sex marriage have been authorized, on the ground that anything less would violate equality rights.

The Chrétien government chose not to appeal controversial provincial court of appeal decisions approving same-sex marriage. Instead, it sent a reference case to the Supreme Court of Canada on this issue, which was approved in 2004. In the meantime, the 2001 census included a question on same-sex partners for the first time. Regardless of the Constitution and the law, many employers in both the public and private sectors have extended employee benefits (such as health, dental, and retirement plans) to same-sex couples.

SUMMARY

This chapter discussed the political significance of issues relating to Aboriginal peoples and other ethnic groups, as well as gender issues, all of which have become much more prominent in Canada since about 1970. It established that the quality of Aboriginal life was generally much better before the arrival of Europeans on the continent, partly as a result of self-government. The discussion then turned to current Aboriginal demands, primarily involving land claims and demands for more autonomy in daily affairs, and the responses thereto since 1970. The second part of the chapter dealt with ethnic groups in Canada other than British, French, or Aboriginal. It tracked their arrival and their changing composition and mentioned that a majority of recent immigrants are of Asian origin.

The chapter then discussed the adoption of a policy of multiculturalism and of related policies designed to remove discrimination and to enhance equality and inclusiveness. It also noted divergent views on the subjects of multiculturalism and immigration. The third part of the chapter traced the evolution of women's political participation in Canada. It also noted the factors that have contributed to the lower level of female, as compared to male, involvement, but it also showed that issues of primary interest to women are now firmly on the political agenda. The chapter concluded with the relatively new political issues relating to the gay and lesbian communities, including removal of discrimination in such areas as employment, adoption, and marriage.

DISCUSSION QUESTIONS

1. To what extent should Aboriginal peoples in Canada be able to govern themselves?
2. To what extent should Canada pursue the policy of multiculturalism?
3. What are the most significant current public policy issues of interest to women?
4. How far should we go in public or private policies recognizing same-sex relationships?

KEY TERMS

Aboriginal self-government A demand made by Aboriginal groups that they be able to govern themselves.

Aboriginal title The Aboriginal claim to land based on traditional occupancy and use rather than treaty.

Affirmative action A law or program that provides preference in the hiring or promotion process to individuals with certain characteristics.

Assembly of First Nations The largest interest group representing status and non-status Indians (who now prefer to be called First Nations peoples).

Employment equity A policy that seeks to guarantee complete fairness in hiring, promotion, or remuneration, regardless of gender, ethnicity, or disability.

Equality rights A category of rights in the Charter of Rights and Freedoms that prohibit governments from discriminating against certain categories of people.

First Nations A term that came into common usage in the 1970s that can refer to the Indian peoples of Canada, both status and non-status, or that can replace the word "band."

Indian Act The act that governed almost all aspects of Aboriginal life in Canada after the 1870s, giving extensive authority to government bureaucrats and minimal discretion to Native people themselves.

James Bay Agreement The 1975 deal signed by the government of Quebec and its northern Aboriginal residents that gave the latter land, cash, and hunting rights in return for surrendering land for the James Bay hydroelectric project.

Multiculturalism A policy of encouraging ethnic and cultural groups to maintain their customs and traditions, often with public financial assistance.

Nisga'a Treaty The 2000 treaty signed by the Nisga'a First Nation and the governments of Canada and British Columbia that incorporated a land claim settlement and powers of self-government, considered the first modern-day Aboriginal treaty.

Nunavut The eastern half of the Northwest Territories that was established as a separate, Inuit territory in 1999.

Pay equity An element of employment equity programs designed to ensure that all employees are paid equally for work of equal value and are not discriminated against on the basis of gender or other factors.

Royal Proclamation of 1763 The British policy enunciated after conquering Quebec that in a large area called Indian Territory forbade the purchase or settlement of land without a treaty between the Crown and the Indian peoples concerned.

Sexual orientation One's sexual preference, usually either heterosexual or homosexual; it now constitutes a ground on which discrimination is prohibited.

Treaty rights Aboriginal rights based on treaties signed with the Crown.

Visible minorities Members of ethnic groups, other than Aboriginal peoples, whose skin colour is not white.

White Paper on Indians The 1969 Trudeau–Chrétien policy proposal to do away with the Indian Act and treaties and to fully integrate Aboriginal peoples into Canadian society.

Women's movement The collection of women's groups that mushroomed across the country, starting around 1970, demanding complete equality for women.

FURTHER READING
Aboriginal Peoples

Alfred, Taiaiake. *Peace, Power, Righteousness: An Indigenous Manifesto*. Toronto: Oxford University Press, 1999.

Berger, Thomas. *A Long and Terrible Shadow: White Values, Native Rights in the Americas*. Vancouver: Douglas and McIntyre, 1991.

Boldt, Menno. *Surviving as Indians: The Challenge of Self-Government*. Toronto: University of Toronto Press, 1993.

Frideres, James S. *Aboriginal Peoples in Canada: Contemporary Conflicts*. 5th ed. Scarborough: Prentice-Hall Canada, 1998.

Long, David, and Olive Dickason. *Visions of the Heart: Canadian Aboriginal Issues*. Toronto: Harcourt Brace, 1996.

Mercredi, Ovid. *In the Rapids: Navigating the Future of First Nations*. Toronto: Viking, 1993.

Morrison, Andrea. *Justice for Natives: Searching for Common Ground*. Montreal: McGill-Queen's University Press, 1997.

Other Ethnic Groups

Abu-Laban, Yasmeen, and Christina Gabriel. *Selling Diversity: Immigration, Multiculturalism, Employment Equity, and Globalization*. Peterborough: Broadview Press, 2002.

Bissoondath, Neil. *Selling Illusions: The Cult of Multiculturalism in Canada*. Toronto: Penguin, 1994.

Kymlicka, Will. *Finding Our Way: Rethinking Ethnocultural Relations in Canada*. Toronto: Oxford University Press, 1998.

Troper, Harold, and Morton Weinfeld. *Ethnicity, Politics and Public Policy*. Toronto: University of Toronto Press, 1999.

Gender

Andrew, Caroline, and Sanda Rodgers, eds. *Women and the Canadian State*. Montreal: McGill-Queen's University Press, 1997.

Bashevkin, Sylvia. *Women on the Defensive*. Toronto: University of Toronto Press, 1998.

Dobrowolsky, Alexandra. *The Politics of Pragmatism: Women, Representation, and Constitutionalism in Canada*. Toronto: Oxford University Press, 1999.

Herman, Didi. *Rights of Passage: Struggles for Lesbian and Gay Legal Equality.* Toronto: University of Toronto Press, 1994.

Johnson, Holly. *Dangerous Domains: Violence against Women in Canada.* Scarborough: Nelson Canada, 1996.

MacIvor, H. *Women and Politics in Canada.* Peterborough: Broadview Press, 1996.

Smith, Miriam. *Lesbian and Gay Rights in Canada: Social Movements and Equality-Seeking, 1971–1995.* Toronto: University of Toronto Press, 1999.

Trimble, Linda, and Jane Arscott. *Still Counting: Women in Politics Across Canada.* Peterborough: Broadview Press, 2003.

Chapter 5

The Global Context of Canadian Politics

Canada does not exist in a vacuum; instead, it is linked to the rest of the world by all sorts of political, economic, defensive, cultural, demographic, individual, and technological ties. In colonial times, all basic governmental decisions for the country were made in Britain. As Canada emerged into a sovereign state, however, the world was becoming increasingly interdependent. Thus, even though Canada gained the legal powers to make decisions for itself, it became particularly susceptible to influence from the United States. The U.S. remains the most constant external pressure, especially as it pursues its own interests as the sole superpower in the world, in what is sometimes called the "new world order." But nowadays the outside forces are much more numerous and could be said to constitute the "global" environment of the Canadian political system. A multitude of states, international organizations, international agreements, and transnational corporations have an ever-increasing impact upon Canada, complicating the efforts of the government to pursue its own policy preferences. Moreover, since September 11, 2001, the forces of globalization have been complicated by those of international terrorism.

Chapter Objectives

After you have completed this chapter, you should be able to:

Trace the evolution of Canadian autonomy from Britain

Discuss the American influences on Canadian defence and foreign policies

Comment on American influences on Canadian economic policies

Identify policies adopted to promote and protect Canadian culture

Discuss the concept of globalization and its effects on Canadian policymaking

Comment on the effects of international terrorism on the Canadian political system

The Road to Canadian Sovereignty from Britain

The British North American colonies were largely self-governing in internal affairs even before 1867. Contrary to popular belief, the **British North America Act (BNA Act)** of 1867 (later renamed the Constitution Act, 1867) did not directly advance the cause of Canadian independence. Although the act of confederation made Canada a more respectable and viable entity and ultimately strengthened its case for greater autonomy, it did not alter the British–Canadian relationship. In theory, the British government could still overturn any statute passed by the Canadian Parliament, although in practice, it rarely did so.

In external relations, Canada had succeeded in claiming the right to control its own tariffs even before Confederation, and between 1867 and 1914 it became increasingly autonomous in making treaties with other countries. At the turn of the century, Canada sent an official contingent to the South African (Boer) War more in response to Canadian public opinion than to British pressure. In the Alaska boundary dispute of 1903, however, the British representative on the Anglo-Canadian half of the judicial tribunal voted with the three American representatives to award the United States a long strip of the northern British Columbia coastline.

The ultimate independence of Canada and several other British colonies is usually attributed to developments connected to the First World War. Although Canada was automatically at war in 1914 as a result of British action, a series of conferences of Dominion prime ministers began in 1917, as Canada and the other Dominions demanded a say in return for their wartime contributions. Prime Minister Robert Borden participated in the Paris Peace Conference and signed the peace treaties, and the Dominions became individual members of the League of Nations. Thus, by 1919, Canada had gained new international status as a result of accomplishments on the battlefield and subsequent demands for recognition at the conference table.

The Imperial Conference of 1926 ended with a proclamation of the complete equality of the United Kingdom and the Dominions in internal, international, and imperial affairs. They were proclaimed

> *autonomous Communities within the British Empire, equal in status, in no way subordinate one to another in any aspect of their domestic or external affairs, though united by a common allegiance to the Crown, and freely associated as members of the British Commonwealth of Nations.*[1]

Besides giving Canada complete autonomy in all policy fields, the development of 1926 had implications for the position of governor general. This official would no longer be an agent of the British government, but rather only a personal representative of the Crown. These arrangements were constitutionalized in the **Statute of Westminster** of 1931.

After 1931, therefore, Canada was completely independent of Britain, but a number of anomalies helped to disguise this fact. First, Canada continued to share a head of state with Britain, although from the Canadian perspective, that person was the king or queen of Canada. Of more importance, since Canada had not been able to decide how to amend the BNA Act within Canada, such amendments still had to be passed by the British Parliament, albeit only at Canadian request. Also of great significance, but due to Canadian inaction, the Judicial Committee of the Privy Council remained Canada's final court of appeal until 1949.

Canada made an autonomous decision to take part in the Second World War, after which British–Canadian ties declined. As time went on, Canada's population became more diversified in its ethnic origins, Britain occupied a diminished role in world affairs, and Canada drew closer to the United States.[2] The 1982 Constitution Act removed the Constitution from any kind of British custody, with a new formula for amending it in Canada. After that, Canada shared only the Queen with Britain (and several other states), but in her capacity as the Canadian head of state she provides no official link between the two countries.

Time Line
Canadian Independence

1919	Member of the League of Nations
1926	Imperial Conference confers autonomy on Dominions
1931	Statute of Westminster
1949	Supreme Court of Canada becomes final court of appeal
1982	Made-in-Canada constitutional amending formula

The American Sphere of Influence

Even before becoming fully autonomous from Britain, Canada began its slow but steady absorption into the U.S. sphere of influence. The United States serves as a model for many Canadians, but it also pressures Canada on a daily basis to do things its way. Its influence can thus be seen in such areas as defence and foreign policy, economic policy, and culture.

Defence and Foreign Policy

After the Second World War, the United States became increasingly obsessed with containing Soviet communism, and in 1949 it persuaded Canada and most Western European countries to form a new military alliance, the North Atlantic Treaty Organization (NATO). Commitments to NATO required a considerable increase in the size of the Canadian armed forces. U.S. attention was then drawn to the confrontation between North and South Korea, and the United Nations military intervention in the Korean War was effectively a U.S. effort to which Canada made a significant military contribution, losing 1550 lives.

The next phase of the North Americanization of Canadian defence was a series of radar screens built across the United States and Canada during the 1950s to intercept anticipated Soviet bombers. These arrangements logically led in 1958 to what is now called the North American Aerospace Defence Command (NORAD). The agreement provided for a joint Canada–U.S. air defence system with headquarters in Colorado. A Defence Production Sharing Program was added to these collaborative schemes in 1959.

Prime Minister John Diefenbaker encountered two serious missile crises with the United States in the 1957–63 period. When U.S. President John F. Kennedy used the establishment of Soviet missile bases in Cuba as an excuse to announce a naval blockade of that country, the Canadian cabinet waited three days before putting its armed forces in a state of highest alert. Kennedy's anger at this delay was compounded by American annoyance at Canada's stand with respect to Bomarc missiles. These had been established by the United States at two bases in Canada as part of the NORAD Agreement and were intended to be armed with nuclear warheads. Some cabinet ministers argued that placing the warheads on Canadian soil would proliferate the nuclear arms race, and the Canadian–American defence relationship thus became a prominent issue in the 1962 and 1963 election campaigns. The Diefenbaker government fell apart over the issue in 1963 and was defeated on a nonconfidence motion. The Liberals won the resulting election under Lester Pearson, and the new prime minister had the warheads installed as part of Canada's international commitments.

Pearson's successor, Pierre Trudeau, removed the warheads, cut military spending, and—in a new emphasis on protecting domestic sovereignty—halved Canada's NATO contingent. Nevertheless, the NORAD Agreement was repeatedly renewed. Trudeau then allowed the United States to test yet another new weapon, the cruise missile, over Canadian territory because of the resemblance of its terrain to that of the Soviet Union.

The Mulroney government promised to make defence a much higher priority and published a hawkish white paper on the subject in 1987. Public opposition and budgetary considerations prevented the paper's implementation, however, a decision that appeared to have been farsighted when the Cold War effectively ended about 1990.

Canada participated in the U.S.–led Gulf War coalition when Iraq invaded Kuwait, and then in the various phases of the Balkan war. Canada also responded quickly to the call to join the American-led "war on terrorism." While the Chrétien government declined to take part in the second Iraq war in 2003, it did preside over an increasing "interoperability" between the armed forces of the two countries. Canada also found itself under pressure to agree to the new U.S. missile defence system, Ballistic Missile Defence (BMD). Despite much expert advice that the system is unproven and unnecessary, Canada agreed in August 2004 to house it within NORAD, moving one step closer to joining it.

What Do You Think?

How close should Canada–U.S. cooperation be in the realm of defence? Should we have joined (or still join) the U.S. ballistic missile defence program? Are we already too integrated militarily with the U.S., or can we still pursue our own priorities in this field?

Thus it is clear that for over 50 years the United States has exerted significant pressure on Canadian defence policy. Even though Canada did not always respond as energetically as the U.S. wished, such external demands influenced many Canadian political outcomes. Some Canadians were satisfied with the arrangement because the country was essentially protected by the U.S. military arsenal and had to pay relatively little for its own defence. Others did not like the U.S. pressure and the loss of control of a vital aspect of public policy.

To the extent that foreign policy can be distinguished from defence policy, the degree of U.S. influence in this field has also been a controversial question. Canada sees itself as a "middle power" that staked out an independent position on recognizing and/or trading with countries such as Cuba and—during the Cold War—China and the Soviet Union. On the other hand, the United States expects Canadian support of its initiatives to be automatic. The Canadian government was quick to respond to U.S. demands to contribute to its military efforts in Kuwait and its peacekeeping mission in Somalia, both ostensibly in the name of the United Nations.

More independently, Canada responded to international pressure and made a major humanitarian contribution in the Bosnian civil war, as well as in Rwanda. Canada was also a leader in the campaign to ban anti-personnel land-mines and to establish an International Criminal Court. Prime Minister Chrétien made aid to Africa one of Canada's top foreign policy priorities and then, as noted, stayed out of the second Iraq war because it lacked legitimacy in the eyes of the United Nations.

Economic Policy

The economic influence of the United States on Canada is even more pervasive than the U.S.'s impact on defence and foreign policy. This influence is felt in almost every aspect of Canadian life, including investment, trade, the environment, and energy. In many ways, Canada constitutes a zone within the American economy rather than a distinctive national economy.

FOREIGN INVESTMENT

A new country is not likely to produce enough domestic capital to finance all the development projects desired. Therefore, in the early years, a great deal of investment in Canada came from Britain. Some of this foreign capital consisted of British companies operating in Canada, such as the Hudson's Bay Company, but to a large extent it took the form of Canadian borrowing in the London bond market. Interest had to be paid on such loans, but ownership remained largely in Canadian hands.

Later, the main source of foreign investment shifted from Britain to the United States. Moreover, the form of investment switched from loans to "direct" or "equity" investment, that is, control through the ownership of shares. Table 5.1 indicates the shift from British to U.S. investment in Canada between 1900 and 1999. To a large extent, the Canadian economy has come to consist of branch plants of U.S. parent corporations; since these companies typically operate in many other countries, too, they gain the label of "multinational" or "transnational" corporations.

TABLE 5.1 PERCENTAGE OF BRITISH, U.S., AND OTHER FOREIGN INVESTMENT IN CANADA, 1900–99

	1900	1914	1930	1939	1946	1950	1960	1967	1985	1999
U.S.	13.6	23.0	61.2	60.0	71.8	75.5	75.2	80.7	75.6	72.2
U.K.	85.2	72.4	36.3	35.8	23.2	20.1	15.1	10.3	9.5	5.9
Other	1.1	4.6	2.4	4.1	4.9	4.2	9.6	8.9	14.9	21.8

Source: *Foreign Direct Investment in Canada*, Table titled: Percentage of British, U.S., and Other Foreign Investment in Canada, 1900–1967, The Commission, (c. 1972) p. 15. Reproduced with permission of the Minister of Public Works and Government Services, 2004, and courtesy of the Privy Council Office, and Statistics Canada, *Canada's International Investment Position* (March 2000), cat. no. 67-202, 40.

This pattern of economic development was fostered in the first instance by the **National Policy** of 1879, which put a tariff on imported manufactured goods. Rather than export to Canada from the United States and pay the tariff, U.S. companies set up branch plants within Canada behind the tariff wall. This was advantageous for the creation of employment in Canada and contributed to the general prosperity of the country, especially Ontario. As time went on, however, considerable capital was generated within Canada, but the degree of foreign ownership continued to increase.

It was not only manufacturers that moved into Canada but also foreign companies that sought to exploit Canadian natural resources. "A large proportion of the investment in resource exploitation reflected the needs of the United States investors for raw materials for their processing and manufacturing plants in the United States." This integration often had the practical impact of "reducing the likelihood of further processing activity of Canadian natural resources in Canada."[3] In fact, Canada has more foreign ownership than any other advanced industrial country, although, as Table 5.1 shows, the sources of recent international investment in Canada are more diversified than in the past. Some of the largest multinationals operating in Canada are identified in Table 5.2 (page 110).

Most advocates of the free market system are enthusiastic boosters of unlimited foreign investment. They claim that maximum efficiency results from capital being able to flow to wherever it will yield the greatest returns. In this case, defenders of foreign investment argue that Canada still needs foreign capital and that such investment creates jobs, which in turn raise the Canadian standard of living. They also claim that efficiency is enhanced when multinationals transfer state-of-the-art technology as well as well-trained managers and management techniques to their branch plants.

TABLE 5.2 LARGE MULTINATIONAL COMPANIES IN CANADA

• General Motors of Canada (U.S.)	• Sears Canada Inc. (U.S.)
• Ford Motor Co. of Canada (U.S.)	• Honda Canada Inc. (Japan)
• DaimlerChrysler Canada (U.S.)	• Shell Canada Ltd. (Netherlands)
• Imperial Oil Ltd. (U.S.)	• Canada Safeway (U.S.)
• Imperial Tobacco Canada (U.K.)	• Toyota Canada (Japan)
• Cargill Ltd. (U.S.)	• General Electric Canada (U.S.)
• Costco Wholesale Canada (U.S.)	

Source: Report on Business Magazine, "The Top 1000" (July/August 2004), 59. Reproduced with the permission of *The Globe and Mail.* Wal-Mart does not figure in such tables because it is a private, family-owned company.

Others take the view that these advantages are short-term or short-sighted.[4] First, multinationals are likely to purchase supplies and component parts from the parent company or parent country, rather than buying them and creating employment in Canada. Second, their plants usually remain small and inefficient because they are designed to serve only the Canadian market, rather than being encouraged to compete in export markets with the parent plant or with branches set up in other countries. Critics also claim that a branch-plant economy suffers because most of its research and development (R & D) is done in the parent plant in the parent country. This limits the number of challenging jobs in science, engineering, and technology located in Canada. As convenient as it is to import such technology, this process hinders Canadian innovative efforts to develop distinctive export products, for most studies indicate that R & D is the secret of future economic success. Critics of the situation also worry that if layoffs or shutdowns are necessary, these are usually slated for branch plants first.

The ultimate symbolic disadvantage of foreign-owned companies is that they may occasionally choose or be required to conform to the laws of the country in which their parent is located rather than those of Canada. The extension of U.S. laws to branch plants located in Canada is called "extraterritoriality," and it has regularly occurred, especially in the case of the Trading with the Enemy Act and the Helms-Burton Act. When branch plants in Canada have tried to do business with countries on the U.S. "enemy list" (Cuba, in terms of Helms-Burton), they have been told that they must follow U.S. law, thus reducing production and job opportunities in Canada.

The policies that Canadian governments have adopted to counter this threat of U.S. or other foreign ownership of the Canadian economy can be divided into four main categories. First, **Crown corporations**—government-owned enterprises—have been established to ensure that the company involved remains in Canadian hands. Atomic Energy of Canada Ltd. and Petro-Canada, for example, were created by the federal government in response to demands that a Canadian presence in strategic industries be retained.

Second, while leaving other corporations to function privately, the federal government often created **regulatory tribunals**. The main such agency was the Foreign Investment Review Agency (FIRA), established in the early 1970s. FIRA screened foreign takeovers of large Canadian companies and new ventures by foreign firms, approving the deal if it involved "significant benefit to Canada." In fact, FIRA rarely disallowed any such initiatives and imposed minimal conditions; even so, it became a major irritant to the United States, and the Mulroney government replaced it with Investment Canada. In this new form, the agency's goal was to attract increased foreign investment to Canada. Other regulatory agencies include the National Energy Board and the Canadian Nuclear Safety Commission, which were designed to protect the Canadian national interest in certain important respects.

Third, ownership restrictions and tax incentives have been introduced. Maximum foreign-ownership limits exist in fields such as broadcasting, financial institutions, and newspapers and publishing; banking was also among these before the Free Trade Agreement took effect. Incentives to Canadian ownership were exemplified by the **National Energy Program** (NEP) of 1980, under which, largely via tax write-offs, several oil companies in Canada were purchased from their American owners. Finally, the government has established funding agencies such as the Business Development Bank of Canada, whose mandate is to encourage Canadian entrepreneurs when the commercial banks are not interested in lending them money.

Many of these policies were half-hearted and others were diluted under U.S. pressure. Many were weakened or withdrawn by the Mulroney government, both to increase foreign investment and to remove irritants in the Canada–U.S. relationship. The proportion of foreign control has increased after 1984, and for much of that period, the low value of the Canadian dollar made Canadian firms ripe for sale to foreigners. Thus, economic nationalists regard the situation as more critical than ever, while others remain indifferent or take the opposite side of this issue, seeing foreign investment as the source of badly needed jobs and a natural aspect of globalization.

TRADE

Because of geographic proximity, it is only logical that Canada and the United States are closely linked by trade. It is even more likely because of their complementary resources and industries—the abundance of primary resources in Canada and the extent of manufacturing in the United States. Thus, Canadian dependence on the United States as a market for its exports and as a source of its imports has gradually increased over time. Indeed, most provinces now trade more with neighbouring states than with each other, although much of this trade is of an intrafirm character rather than truly international.

Canadian exports to the United States exceeded those to the United Kingdom after 1921 and edged up to over 80 percent of all exports since 1990. Imports from the United States constituted nearly 50 percent of the Canadian total from the start and rose to over 70 percent in each of the past 15 years. The 2003 proportions can be seen in Figure 5.1. Canada's free trade agreements with the United States are discussed later in the chapter.

Given the degree to which Canadian prosperity depends on export trade, it is advantageous to have ready access to the U.S. market; it is also convenient to

Figure 5.1   **Canada's Exports from and Imports to Its Trading Partners, 2003**

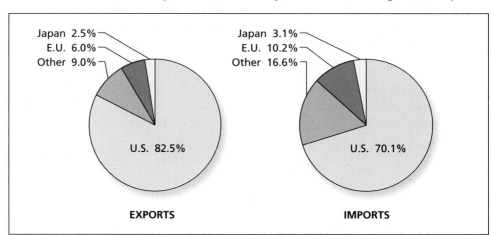

Source: Adapted from the Statistics Canada website, "Imports and Exports of Goods on a Balance-of-Payments Basis," CANSIM, tables 228-0001, 228-0002, and 228-0003, http://www.statcan.ca/english/Pgdb/gblec02a.htm (Retrieved 15 Aug. 2004).

have such a close supply of goods that are not produced in Canada. On the other hand, to have so many eggs in one basket means that in times of U.S. recession, demand for Canadian goods falls off and the Canadian economy declines, whereas in prosperous periods, U.S. inflation also tends to increase prices in Canada. Furthermore, protectionist pressure in the United States for new or increased tariffs or quotas against Canadian exports can have a devastating effect on certain industries, such as softwood lumber. The relative value of the Canadian and U.S. dollars can also be an important factor, and at least from a strictly import-export point of view, it is good for Canada if our dollar has a lower value. There is also the potential that U.S. security concerns might delay "just-in-time" cross-border shipments, as well as the threat that the U.S. might retaliate economically if Canada does not support it on foreign policy and security issues.

THE ENVIRONMENT

Canadians have seriously damaged their own environment over the years, but the situation has been aggravated by proximity to the United States and by some of its even less restrictive anti-pollution laws. The largest transboundary environmental issue is that of acid rain. Canadian research generally shows that about 50 percent of the acid rain falling north of the border comes from U.S. sources, primarily coal-fired power plants in the Midwest. These emissions fall into Canadian lakes and rivers, killing plant and animal life and damaging trees, cars, and buildings.

The pollution of the Great Lakes is the other serious bilateral environmental problem. Here again, each side is to blame, but most of the chemicals are discharged from the larger number of factories and waste dumps situated on the U.S. shores of the lakes. Phosphorous levels were reduced in the 1970s, but the Great Lakes are still in a critical state because of toxic pollution. Indeed, recent government cutbacks in environmental protection on both sides of the border have made the problem worse.

An external influence of a different kind is the Kyoto Protocol, which Canada signed in 1997. It is a multilateral agreement in which countries commit to reduce the emissions of greenhouse gases, which are widely believed to cause global warming and climate change. While many Canadians welcomed Kyoto, those industries most affected demonstrated considerable concern. Opposition was heightened when the United States decided not to ratify the treaty, leaving Canadian corporations at a comparative disadvantage.[5]

Graham Harrop/artizans.com

ENERGY

In the energy sector, the voracious U.S. industrial complex usually wants to import Canadian electric power, oil, and natural gas. Governments in Quebec, Manitoba, and B.C. have been eager to export electricity, and those of Alberta, Saskatchewan, B.C., Nova Scotia, and Newfoundland want to supply oil and/or natural gas. The federal government has normally approved these sales with little hesitation, although the National Energy Board is charged with ensuring that long-term Canadian needs will not be compromised in the process. Native and environmental groups in some provinces have not been so favourably disposed toward the hydro necessary to produce the electricity, however, and Canadian nationalists worry about the future supply of petroleum for domestic purposes, as well as rising prices because of such exports. George W. Bush's obsession with energy pleased Alberta petroleum exporters and put back on the political agenda the issue of pipelines to transport northern petroleum to the United States.

The degree of U.S. ownership of the Canadian petroleum industry has also caused considerable conflict between the two countries. The National Energy

Program of 1980 set a target of 50 percent Canadian ownership of the oil and gas industry by 1990 and gave certain preferences to Petro-Canada and private Canadian firms. U.S. petroleum companies in Canada protested, and their government pressured Canada to remove these incentives to Canadianization. The Mulroney cabinet dismantled the NEP completely and began the privatization of Petro-Canada; more recently, there have been many American takeovers of Canadian oil companies.

TRADE UNIONS

Historically, Canadian trade unions have been just as closely allied with those in the United States as the corporations for which their members worked. Many unions in Canada, such as the United Steelworkers and the United Food and Commercial Workers, are part of "international unions" with their headquarters in the United States. The Canadian union movement justified the relationship by arguing that as long as it had to bargain with multinational corporations, it needed the support of international unions, especially their larger strike funds. Membership in international unions peaked in 1965 at 67 percent of all union members in Canada. Since then, however, a nationalist trend has been apparent in the Canadian labour movement, of which the creation of an autonomous Canadian Auto Workers union is the most striking example. Thus, by 2001, only 1 212 000, or 29.5 percent of Canadian union members, belonged to international unions,[6] and the current president of the United Steelworkers of America is a Canadian.

American Influence on Canadian Culture

People around the world enjoy U.S. popular culture. Canadians are a particularly captive market, given their geographical proximity, their linguistic similarity, their small domestic market, their chronic feeling of dependence and inferiority, and the degree of economic integration between the two countries. The general public has little consciousness of the origin of most pop culture fare, and even less concern that so much of it comes from the United States. But many nationalists among the intellectual elite are disturbed by the high proportion of television programs, magazines, movies, books, and music in Canada that emanates from the United States. They claim that this cultural invasion stifles the development of a distinctive Canadian national identity, worry about its influence on Canadian attitudes and values, and wonder how long a separate political system can be maintained in these circumstances.

Television was the most significant cultural institution of the second half of the 20th century. Today, the average Canadian watches about 22 hours of television per week, and 60 percent of that is foreign (mostly American) programming.[7] Broken down by language group, anglophones watch about twice as much foreign programming as do francophones. Some Canadians live close enough to the U.S. border to receive U.S. channels directly; failing that, most Canadian stations, except for the CBC, broadcast a large proportion of U.S. programming. In addition, over 85 percent of Canadian households have cable television or direct-to-home satellite dishes that offer them all the U.S. networks, as well as pay and specialty channels of various origins.

Canadian television networks broadcast so much U.S. programming for two reasons. First, it is much cheaper to buy a U.S. show or series than to produce a Canadian one—about one-tenth the cost. Second, although Canadians generally prefer their own news, public affairs, and sports programs, U.S. programs shown in Canada otherwise attract a larger audience. They therefore command higher advertising rates than the Canadian programs. In fact, Canadian television has a higher reputation abroad than it does at home, and those few Canadian series that are produced are readily sold to foreign networks.

Magazines are perhaps the second most important vehicle of popular culture, and this Canadian industry is also permeated by U.S. content. While Canadian magazines lead foreign magazines in subscriptions in Canada, foreign magazines account for the bulk of English-language newsstand sales. Overall, Canadian magazines constitute about 50 percent of the total circulation, but as with television, the picture is much more positive in French-speaking Canada than in English-speaking areas.

The Canadian motion picture industry is even weaker than television or magazines, and the average Canadian moviegoer has rarely, if ever, seen a Canadian feature film. Less than 5 percent of screen time in Canadian movie theatres is devoted to Canadian films, and most of that is in the large Toronto and Montreal markets or at film festivals. U.S. movie producers make many feature films in Canada every year, taking advantage of its low prices, scenic locations, and technical expertise, but these are almost always disguised as U.S. movies. The problem has many causes, including the fact that the film distribution system is U.S.–controlled, the undeniable Canadian fascination with Hollywood, the small Canadian market, and a shortage of funds. Canadian productions do slightly better in the home video market.

When it comes to books, the Canadian market is also amply supplied with U.S. content, and it is estimated that a majority of the books bought in Canada are imported.[8] Both Canadian-owned companies and foreign-owned publishers operating in Canada sell foreign as well as Canadian titles, for books are like television shows: they are cheaper to import than to make domestically. Moreover, most Canadian bookstores make no special effort to sell Canadian books.

Sound recording is another cultural industry dominated by external firms and content. Although the Canadian music industry is stronger than most other areas of culture, it depends for support on CRTC regulations (see the next section) and financial assistance from government sources.

In short, in the five cultural industries of television, magazines, movies, books, and sound recordings, Canadian-owned companies produce virtually all of the Canadian output. But these companies are marginal players in a market dominated by subsidiaries of large, mainly U.S., multinationals. That there is a Canadian presence at all in such industries is primarily the result of demands made by the nationalist minority for protection from U.S. domination and for promotion of Canadian content.

COUNTERING THE U.S. INFLUENCE

The Crown corporation is a nationalistic instrument in the cultural field, as it is in economic matters. The **Canadian Broadcasting Corporation (CBC)**, in its radio and television networks, and Radio-Canada, its French-language equivalent, is perhaps the most crucial agent of Canadian cultural expression. Today, CBC radio has virtually 100 percent Canadian content and can be heard in almost every part of the country. Its programs are widely regarded as crucial links in keeping the country together. CBC television is less successful, mainly because the television medium is so expensive. The Mulroney and Chrétien governments slashed millions of dollars from the CBC budget, making the corporation's task even harder.

Another Crown corporation, the National Film Board, has also had an illustrious existence, making impressive Canadian films and winning many international awards. It has two serious disadvantages, however: insufficient funding to make feature films, so that it has specialized instead in documentaries and shorts, and no effective mechanism for giving the general public access to its films.

A second policy instrument to protect and promote Canadian culture is a regulatory tribunal called the **Canadian Radio-television and Telecommunications**

Commission (CRTC). This agency issues broadcasting licences and Canadian-content regulations, the latter being more stringent for the CBC than for private stations and networks. CBC television now airs a virtually all-Canadian lineup in prime time, whereas news, public affairs, and sports take up most of the required Canadian time on the private television networks, which produce very little Canadian drama. The CRTC also requires that radio stations play 35 percent Canadian music, a regulation that is generally seen as the catalyst for the explosion of the Canadian music industry over the past 35 years.

Because the CRTC has been under strong industry and popular pressure to allow more U.S. outlets in Canada, it permitted cable and pay television that diluted the audiences of Canadian channels. In 1995, the CRTC also authorized direct-to-home satellite services. Many nationalists fear for the fate of Canadian content in the not-too-distant future when the largely American 500-channel universe is beamed directly into Canadian homes.

A third policy instrument consists of Canadian ownership restrictions and financial incentives. Ownership restrictions in the cultural field apply to radio, television, and newspaper companies in Canada. In addition, Canadian magazine policy from 1965 allowed firms to deduct magazine advertising expenses from their income tax only if those advertisements were placed in Canadian magazines. The same policy also prohibited the entry into Canada of split-run editions of foreign magazines containing advertisements directed at Canadians. In the 1990s, however, *Sports Illustrated* started to produce a Canadian split-run edition that challenged the law because such editions could now be physically printed in Canada via satellite. Capitulating to U.S. pressure and a WTO ruling, the Chrétien government allowed foreign magazines sold in Canada to carry up to 18 percent of Canadian ads without any Canadian editorial content and raised the limit on foreign ownership of a Canadian magazine from 25 to 49 percent.

A fourth device to promote Canadian culture is the funding agency. The Canada Council for the Arts, set up in 1957, gives life-saving grants to hundreds of individual writers, artists, musicians, and playwrights, as well as to almost every orchestra, theatre centre, art gallery, and ballet and opera company in the country. Telefilm Canada subsidizes the production of feature films, and the Department of Canadian Heritage offers special funding to most cultural industries.

Globalization

In the new millennium, Canada has to contend with many external influences beyond those of the United States. These can be lumped together under the label of **globalization**. Globalization is usually understood to be based on the following new developments:

- Comprehensive free trade agreements, involving removal of state controls on corporate behaviour
- Massive diffusion of computerization and other technological change, permitting instantaneous communication around the globe
- Megamergers of large transnational corporations, cross-border capital and investment flows, and worldwide corporate competition

Such globalization can be discussed under four headings—foreign governments, international organizations, international agreements, and transnational corporations—with an addendum regarding international terrorism.

Foreign Governments

Foreign governments make decisions every day, in both foreign and domestic policy, that can have some effect on Canada. Sometimes this impact is deliberate, but often it is unintentional. It is the responsibility of our foreign affairs department to put pressure on such governments so that their decisions are not harmful to Canada. The case of the United States has already been discussed, but such influences now come from all directions. For example, the European Union, Canada's second-largest trading partner, frequently raises objections to Canadian policies. It banned the import of furs from animals caught using leg-hold traps, rejected Canadian lumber exports because of concerns about Canadian forestry practices, and contested the use of words such as "champagne" on Canadian labels. The pressure that the United States, the European Union, and many other foreign governments apply to Canada to change its policies are often made on behalf of their own multinational corporations. On the other hand, Canada has complaints of its own, especially with regard to the overfishing by a number of European countries in Canadian territorial waters and the unmatchable subsidies that European and American governments pay their wheat farmers.

International Organizations

As Table 5.3 shows, Canada has joined a multitude of international organizations with the aim of taking advantage of opportunities to influence other countries' policies, to expand its external trade, and to promote joint objectives with other states. Nevertheless, such membership often entails obligations that influence Canadian domestic or foreign policies. The United Nations is probably the most important of such organizations. It gives a middle-ranking country such as Canada a platform to promote its altruistic as well as its self-interested objectives. But the UN also makes claims on Canada, such as to answer the call whenever it decides to set up a peacekeeping force in trouble spots around the world. Moreover, the UN has criticized several domestic Canadian policies, including Quebec language legislation; federal and provincial laws on labour, Aboriginal peoples, and women; and the deterioration of social programs. Of course, many Canadians welcomed these criticisms as contributing to the effort to change such laws.

TABLE 5.3 LEADING INTERNATIONAL ORGANIZATIONS TO WHICH CANADA BELONGS

• United Nations	• The Commonwealth
• World Trade Organization	• La Francophonie
• NATO	• Organization of American States
• International Monetary Fund	• The G8
• World Bank	• Asia-Pacific Economic Cooperation Council

In 1947, Canada was among the signatories of the General Agreement on Tariffs and Trade (GATT), under which countries pledged to remove trade restrictions on a multinational basis. The successor to GATT, the **World Trade Organization (WTO)**, can actually order its members to change their trading practices. The WTO has disallowed a large number of Canadian laws and policies in recent years in connection with agricultural marketing boards, magazines, dairy products, drug patents, aircraft company subsidies, and even the Canada–U.S. Auto Pact. The WTO has thus become a huge impediment to the pursuit of Canadian government policies, that is, to Canadian **sovereignty**, in a wide range of sensitive fields. The WTO has attracted opposition around the world from those who feel that its decisions prevent countries from making reasonable policies in their own national public interest and that, instead, it acts in the interests of transnational corporations.

Other international organizations also have an effect on Canadian policy. They include the International Monetary Fund, the Asia-Pacific Economic Cooperation Council (APEC), the Summit of the Americas, and even those to which Canada does not belong, such as the Organization of the Petroleum Exporting Countries (OPEC). The leaders of the G8 (the group of eight leading industrialized countries) meet annually to try to come to a consensus on economic and other matters.

International Agreements

Canadian policymakers had been concerned for some time that the country was being left out of the regional trading blocks being formed, especially the European Union. Then, in the early 1980s, a protectionist mood descended upon the U.S. Congress, and new barriers to many Canadian exports were imposed: on shakes and shingles, softwood lumber, potash, potatoes, fish, and specialty steel. Such protectionist measures were among the factors that converted Brian Mulroney to the concept of free trade. Mulroney found an ally in the White House, so he and Ronald Reagan set the negotiations in motion. The **Canada–U.S. Free Trade Agreement** (FTA) was finalized in October 1987 and took effect on January 1, 1989. It was a wide-ranging pact covering almost every aspect of the relationship between the two countries—far more than "trade."[9] It was clearly designed to enshrine neoconservative and neoliberal values, give corporations more leeway from government regulation, and prevent the recurrence of such nationalistic measures as FIRA and NEP.

The agreement removed almost all barriers to the flow of goods and services between the two countries over a 10-year period. Firms in each country could henceforth send their products to the other without tariffs, quotas, or other impediments. Each country had to treat the other's firms the same as its own (the "national treatment" principle), but each continued to apply its own tariffs to imports from other states.

In the area of financial services, U.S. investors were exempted from the 25 percent ceiling on foreign ownership of Canadian banks. As for other investment, U.S. businesses would now be able to start new operations in Canada without restriction (and vice versa), and Investment Canada could screen only acquisitions of firms with a value over $150 million and could not impose any performance requirements.

Energy, agriculture, the Auto Pact, and cultural industries were four of the other most controversial sections of the agreement. A North American energy pool was created in which Canada had to sell oil, gas, or electricity to the United States at the Canadian domestic price; if cutbacks were ever necessary, domestic sales had to be reduced by the same proportion as exports. In agriculture, Canada had to remove import restrictions on chickens, turkeys, and eggs, as well as tariffs on processed food. The Auto Pact was also changed to some extent in order to incorporate U.S. concerns. In theory, the agreement did not affect existing cultural programs; however, any new support of cultural industries could be met by retaliation of equivalent value by the other country.

For any future conflicts in trade between the two countries, a complex dispute-settlement mechanism was set up that involved binational panels and binding arbitration. If either country refused to abide by the final decision of the arbitrators, however, the other could retaliate ("countervail"), as before.

The free trade debate went on for many years, with proponents regarding the agreement as the solution to all Canadian economic problems and the source of perpetual prosperity and opponents seeing it as leading to the complete integration of Canada and the United States.[10] Some 15 years later, the results seem to be mixed. Ontario did lose 200 000 manufacturing jobs in the early 1990s, but how much of this was due to the free trade agreement as such and how much to the recession and other globalizing factors is hard to determine. More significantly, the number of conflicts under the agreement has been large. Some of the same issues that precipitated the Free Trade Agreement have continued to be problems, especially Canadian exports of softwood lumber. Other areas of dispute include uranium, beer, government procurement, magnesium, steel, swine, wheat, sugar, potatoes, peanut butter, tobacco, milk, meat, paper, salmon and herring, poultry products, magazine publishing, and country-music television. On the other hand, trade between the two countries has expanded enormously in both directions, and few of the most dire predictions have come to pass.

The ink was hardly dry on the Canada–U.S. Free Trade Agreement when the Mulroney government entered talks with the United States and Mexico that produced the 1994 **North American Free Trade Agreement (NAFTA)**. It essentially extended FTA to Mexico; most provisions in the two agreements were identical. This initiative was not so much Canada's choice; Canada entered it mainly to preclude the other partners from endangering its position, although some corporations saw the agreement as a means of enhancing the efficiency of their operations. Opponents feared that companies would move from Canada to

A semi-trailer loaded with lumber sits idle in a Vancouver sawmill as a result of the United States' imposition of duties on Canadian softwood lumber. (CP Photo/Richard Lam)

Mexico because of the low wages and environmental standards in that country, and they complained that Mexico was able to negotiate a stronger energy clause with the United States than Canada had under the FTA.[11]

Under Chapter 11 of NAFTA, a foreign company can sue a country on the grounds that a government policy reduced its profits. Canada has lost at least two multimillion-dollar lawsuits in this connection, the most infamous involving the gasoline additive MMT. Ethyl Corporation of Virginia used such NAFTA rules to force Canada to roll back its ban on this ingredient, which is widely regarded as a hazard to health.

In the wake of these agreements, Canada signed the "Open Skies" agreement with the United States in 1995, which deregulated the cross-border airline industry, giving U.S. and Canadian companies equal access to routes between the two countries. The Chrétien government also signed a separate free trade deal with Chile and participated in talks aimed at establishing a Free Trade Area of the Americas, encompassing all the countries of the hemisphere except Cuba. To this end, the Summit of the Americas was held in Quebec City in April 2001, and amid considerable anti-globalization violence in the streets, the assembled governments set a target date of 2005 for the completion of the treaty.

Stephen Clarkson has advanced the interesting notion that the two North American trade agreements plus the WTO constitute an external or "supraconstitution" for Canada, which is just as constraining on the operation of government as the internal Constitution. At the same time, Clarkson adds that it is hard to know whether government decisions since 1990 are the result of globalization as such or of its companion ideologies, neoliberalism and neoconservatism.[12]

Transnational Corporations

As noted, the pressures exerted by a foreign government are often made on behalf of corporations with head offices in that country, and comprehensive trade agreements are basically about removing government controls on corporate behaviour. Indeed, at the heart of globalization is the changed role of **transnational corporations**. More and more companies are outgrowing their domestic state; they are introducing new forms of technology at an incredible rate; they are merging and taking each other over; and they are opening or closing operations strictly on the basis of economic efficiency and without regard to traditional location. The world is increasingly becoming one integrated global economic unit in which national boundaries are much less significant than in the past. Corporate money, banking, finance, and investment flow between countries almost at will. In these circumstances, it is becoming more difficult for national or provincial governments to maintain distinctive labour, tax, or environmental laws because such companies (and their senior employees) regularly threaten to move to other jurisdictions that they find more congenial.[13]

On the other hand, many observers feel that governments do not have to cave in completely to such corporate blackmail.[14] The forces of globalization suffered at least a temporary setback in 1998 with the abandonment of the Multilateral Agreement on Investment (MAI). To its supporters, the MAI was merely an international investment agreement that would set rules for the operation of the global economy. But its critics argued that governments would be hobbled in their objectives of taxing, regulating, and setting standards, and that Canada would no longer be able to give preference to its own people via tax breaks, subsidies, grants, or other support to promote employment, research and development, or Canadian content. These critics around the world engaged in a remarkable effort of multinational grassroots organization largely via the Internet (perhaps an example of the more positive side of globalization), such that the sponsors of MAI abandoned the project, although it may resurface again in another form.[15]

Other Canadians who accept the inevitability of globalization have suggested refinements: The process of globalization should be more open or transparent than it has been to date; it should involve a commitment to democracy and human rights; and it should ensure a fairer distribution of the increased wealth that globalization generates.

International Terrorism

Terrorism, an act or threat of violence perpetrated by an ideological group that is intended to produce fear or change, can be committed by domestic or external groups. Canada has been happily free of much domestic terrorism, but after the bombing of the World Trade Center and Pentagon on September 11, 2001, concern with international terrorism greatly increased even in this country. These actions represented a significant addition to the global context within which individual states operate. While they had the greatest impact on the United States, most other governments took actions in response, some of their own volition and some at U.S. insistence. Canada passed a comprehensive piece of anti-terrorism legislation that gave sweeping powers to the government and was persuaded to become part of the military operations in Afghanistan. The Paul Martin government appointed a minister of Public Safety and Emergency Preparedness, a sign that international terrorism has become a new constant in the Canadian policy-making process.[16]

SUMMARY

This chapter concerned the external forces that impinge upon the Canadian political system. It began with a discussion of the period during which Canada was a British colony, which officially ended in 1931. It then examined how Canada fell into the American sphere of influence and discussed U.S. influences on Canadian defence and foreign policies, on economic policies such as investment, trade, the environment, energy, and trade unions, and on Canadian culture. It outlined the four main devices that Canadian governments have utilized to counter such influences: Crown corporations, regulatory tribunals, ownership restrictions, and funding agencies. The third part of the chapter dealt with globalization and discussed in turn the impact of foreign governments, international organizations, international agreements, transnational corporations, and international terrorism.

DISCUSSION QUESTIONS

1. What are the advantages and disadvantages of the close defensive, economic, and cultural relationship between Canada and the United States?
2. On balance, have the free trade agreements been good or bad for Canada?
3. How much scope does globalization leave to nation-states to make distinctive domestic policies?
4. What are the implications of international terrorism for Canada?

KEY TERMS

British North America Act (BNA Act) The 1867 act of the British Parliament that created Canada by uniting the four original provinces, that provided some of the essential elements of the new country's Constitution, and that in 1982 was renamed the Constitution Act, 1867.

Canada–U.S. Free Trade Agreement The agreement signed by Canada and the United States in 1987 and taking effect in 1989 that gradually eliminated tariffs between the two countries and otherwise prohibited governments from interfering in the private marketplace.

Canadian Broadcasting Corporation (CBC) The large national Crown corporation with radio and television divisions whose mandate is to promote meaningful communication among all parts of the country.

Canadian Radio-television and Telecommunications Commission (CRTC) The regulatory agency established to police the communications industry, including radio, television, telephones, and telecommunications.

Crown corporation A corporation owned by the government that assumes a structure similar to that of a private company and that operates semi-independently of the cabinet.

Globalization The modern phenomenon of nation-states declining in stature and power by giving way to the demands of transnational corporations via comprehensive free trade agreements, by massive diffusion of technological change, and by worldwide corporate competition or megamergers.

National Energy Program The 1980 policy associated with Pierre Trudeau designed to skim off petroleum tax revenue for Ottawa, keep the price of petroleum below world levels, encourage conservation, and Canadianize the industry, which met with great opposition in Western Canada.

National Policy A broad nation-building 1879 policy of John A. Macdonald that included tariff protection for central Canadian manufacturing, massive immigration, and the construction of a national transportation system.

North American Free Trade Agreement (NAFTA) The 1994 extension of the Canada–U.S. Free Trade Agreement to Mexico.

Regulatory tribunal A government agency established to regulate an area of public policy, such as transportation or communications, that operates at arm's length from the cabinet.

Sovereignty Ultimate control or independence, such as Canadian national sovereignty vis-à-vis that of other countries.

Statute of Westminster The 1931 British law that declared Canada and the other Dominions to be fully independent.

Terrorism An act or threat of violence perpetrated by an ideological group that is intended to produce fear or change.

Transnational corporations Corporations operating simultaneously in many countries throughout the world that often take orders from company headquarters and that individual states find difficult to control.

World Trade Organization (WTO) An international organization to which Canada and most other countries belong that has the power to disallow national policies and practices that it deems discriminatory against companies from other states.

FURTHER READING

Barlow, Maude, and Tony Clarke. *Global Showdown: How the New Activists Are Fighting Global Corporate Rule*. Toronto: Stoddart Publishing, 2000.

Cameron, Duncan, and Mel Watkins, eds. *Canada under Free Trade*. Toronto: Lorimer, 1993.

Clarkson, Stephen. *Uncle Sam and Us: Globalization, Neoconservatism, and the Canadian State*. Toronto: University of Toronto Press, 2002.

Cohen, Andrew. *While Canada Slept: How We Lost Our Place in the World*. Toronto: McClelland and Stewart, 2003.

Doern, G. Bruce, et al., eds. *Border Crossings: The Internationalization of Canadian Public Policy*. Toronto: Oxford University Press, 1996.

Doern, G. Bruce, and Brian Tomlin. *Faith and Fear: The Free Trade Story*. Toronto: Stoddart, 1991.

Dorland, Michael, ed. *The Cultural Industries in Canada: Problems, Policies and Prospects*. Halifax: Lorimer, 1996.

Helliwell, John F. *Globalization and Well-Being*. Vancouver: UBC Press, 2002.

McQuaig, Linda. *The Cult of Impotence: Selling the Myth of Powerlessness in the Global Economy*. Toronto: Viking, 1998.

Watson, William. *Globalization and the Meaning of Canadian Life*. Toronto: University of Toronto Press, 1998.

PART 2

Linking People to Government

Having outlined the societal and global contexts in which Canadian politics operates, we are now ready to examine how people are linked to the government. The three traditional elements of Canadian politics are the electoral system, political parties, and pressure groups. At a minimum, each citizen can have a modest impact on the government by voting in an election. If people wish to have more influence on government policy, they can join or support the political party whose platform is closest to their way of thinking or choose the vehicle of social movements and pressure groups. Each of these three links between people and government is discussed in its own chapter in the following section.

But the context of values, attitudes, opinions (and how they are acquired), and patterns of political participation must also be examined. Moreover, no one can deny the importance of the mass media and public opinion polls in linking people to government. Thus we begin with a chapter on the Canadian political culture, socialization, and participation, followed by a chapter on the mass media and public opinion polls.

Chapter 6

Political Culture, Socialization, and Participation

Understanding how Canadians feel about politics and government, how they develop such feelings, and how they participate politically provides a useful context in which to study elections, political parties, and pressure groups. This chapter therefore examines Canadian political values and attitudes—the Canadian political culture; how these values and attitudes are acquired—political socialization; and the related subject of patterns of Canadian political participation.

Chapter Objectives

After you have completed this chapter, you should be able to:

Define democracy and discuss the extent to which Canadians are committed to it

Enumerate the principal differences that have been identified between basic Canadian and American political values

Evaluate the extent to which the traditional political culture remains intact, and comment on the forces that threaten it

Identify the main agents of political socialization

Comment on variations in the voter turnout rate and reasons for voting or not voting

Enumerate forms of nonelectoral participation

Political Culture

Political culture can be defined as the sum total of the political values, beliefs, attitudes, and orientations in a society. Vague and elusive as these values and attitudes may be, most political scientists think they are worthy of analysis because they influence what is done within a political system.

Political culture includes feelings people have toward the overall political community of Canada, such as their reaction to national symbols—flag, anthem, Constitution—and feelings of patriotism, nationalism, and pride. It also includes people's feelings toward their province as opposed to the whole country. A second aspect of political culture involves beliefs regarding the role of the state—how large a part Canadians want it to play in their lives. Another variable consists of orientations to the decisionmaking apparatus. Are people aware of it, and to what extent do they want to control it? How do Canadians feel, in general, about the police, the bureaucracy, the courts, and the politicians? Do citizens trust them? Do

International hockey prowess always ignites strong feelings of Canadian nationalism. (CP Photo/Frank Gunn)

people feel that their participation in the political system can make any difference? When such values and attitudes are widely shared, they can be said to constitute the collective political culture. While political culture in Canada is usually considered to be fairly stable, this chapter will also examine how it seems to be changing.

Democracy

The first conclusion that emerges from a quest for Canadian political values is that almost all Canadians believe in **democracy**. The preamble to the Charter of Rights and Freedoms acknowledges democracy to be a foremost value in the country when it speaks of Canada as a "free and democratic society," but the Charter is not very specific about what this means. Democracy is derived from the Greek words "demos" (meaning people) and "kratia" (meaning power), and in the modern Western world usually includes the following elements:[1]

- Popular sovereignty
- Political equality
- Political freedom
- Majority rule

POPULAR SOVEREIGNTY

Popular sovereignty means that the people have the final say, which in large, modern political systems usually takes the form of elections at specified intervals. For most Canadians, this is a sufficient opportunity for the exercise of popular sovereignty, although few would be content with anything less. Some states use plebiscites or referendums on a regular basis, but these devices have largely been foreign to the Canadian mentality. Only three national **referendums** have occurred since 1867 (prohibition in 1898, conscription in 1942, and the Charlottetown Accord in 1992), although the incidence is slightly higher at the provincial and municipal levels. Popular sovereignty is thus normally exercised in periodic elections that are essentially opportunities to select those who will make the big political decisions over the next four years or so, although any effective democracy also involves popular participation between elections. At least in the past, Canadians cherished **representative democracy** in which such elected and appointed authorities made decisions on their behalf.

POLITICAL EQUALITY

Given the significance of elections as the means of implementing the principle of popular sovereignty, a second aspect of Canadian democracy is **political equality**—that is, the idea that everyone is equal on election day. In essence, this means that each person has one vote and each vote has equal weight. It is only in relatively recent times, however, that Canada has met this ideal; at one time or another in the past, several groups were excluded.

POLITICAL FREEDOM

The 1982 Charter of Rights and Freedoms provided an explicit constitutional statement of **political freedom** in Canada. It says: "Everyone has the following fundamental freedoms: freedom of conscience and religion; freedom of thought, belief, opinion and expression, including freedom of the press and other media of communication; freedom of peaceful assembly; and freedom of association." The Charter did not create these political freedoms, however; it put into writing the freedoms that Canadians had always enjoyed, and it provided a new means of protecting them—using the courts to invalidate legislation that infringed them rather than having to persuade politicians to do so.

MAJORITY RULE

Canadian democracy also incorporates the notion of **majority rule**—that is, in case of dispute, the larger number takes precedence over the smaller number. This principle is generally accepted in elections and in the legislatures that result from elections. Of course, if the number of options is greater than two, as in the case of Canadian elections, the winning candidate or party may not actually have a majority (over 50 percent), but just a plurality.

On the other hand, it is sometimes felt necessary to protect minorities from the actions of the majority, so that specific minority rights are given constitutional protection. The Constitution Act, 1867, recognized certain religious and linguistic minority rights, while the Charter of Rights and Freedoms extended constitutional minority rights to a considerable degree.

Distinguishing between Canadian and American Values

Once we get beyond the consensus on democracy, it is difficult to find widespread agreement on other Canadian political values. One approach that bears promise, however, is to contrast widely held Canadian values with those of the United States. Of course, Canadian and American values are very much alike. But some analysts have found at least subtle differences that have their foundation in the revolutionary origins of the United States and in the Canadian reaction against that revolution.

Many make the point that the American Declaration of Independence lists the objectives of "life, liberty and the pursuit of happiness," while Canada's Constitution Act, 1867, talks about "peace, order and good government." Seymour Martin Lipset goes on to outline a basic distinction: "Canada has been and is a more class-aware, elitist, law-abiding, statist, collectivity-oriented, and particularistic [group-oriented] society than the United States."[2] Pierre Berton has similarly noted that Canadians are law-abiding, peaceful, orderly, deferential toward authority, cautious, elitist, moralistic, tolerant, diffident, and unemotional.[3] The results of a 1995 Allan Gregg survey of what ordinary Canadians thought was distinctive about Canada included nonviolence, tolerance of minorities, humane treatment of the poor and disadvantaged, official bilingualism, and reluctance to boast.[4] This approach leads us to identify five basic Canadian values that can be distinguished from those in the United States:

- Canadians prefer a closer balance between individualism and collectivism.
- Canadians value diversity more than homogeneity and are more tolerant of minorities.
- Canadians are more deferential toward authority.
- Canadians have a stronger belief in egalitarianism.
- Canadians are more cautious, more diffident, and less violent.

BALANCE BETWEEN INDIVIDUALISM AND COLLECTIVISM

If there is one value other than democracy to which most Canadians adhere, it is probably that of **individualism**, often expressed as the sanctity of private enterprise or individual economic freedom. Canadians generally believe that those with the greatest talent or those who work hardest should reap the benefits of their abilities and/or labour. The extent of such commitment can be best gauged, however, in comparison to attitudes in the United States.

While both countries have "mixed economies" today—that is, a combination of private enterprise and government involvement—the United States remains the world's last stronghold of individualism, with a relatively smaller public sector than other modern states. Canada, on the other hand, has been less hostile toward public intervention and more inclined to rely on government. This is partly because of the distinctive geographic environment of the Canadian political system and the desire to protect Canada from various U.S. influences. But it also stems from the basic Canadian value of **collectivism**, or community, originally derived from the United Empire Loyalists who opposed the American Revolution. They saw society not as a mass of grasping, ambitious, "free" individuals, but as an organic community in which all people had their place and did their respective part to contribute to the welfare of the whole. It is not part of the Canadian psyche to be instinctively suspicious of the state; indeed, Canadians have not seen the government in terms of an alien imposition but as the authorized agent to respond to their individual and collective demands.

Canada is generally less collectivist than Western Europe, and the difference between the two North American countries should not be overstated, but much concrete evidence of a significant variation exists. The Canadian public health insurance system stands out in great contrast to that of the United States; the Canadian social safety net is also considered more adequate; and the extent of federal and provincial Crown corporations is unheard of south of the border. Taxes in Canada are generally higher in order to finance such collective activity. In just about every policy field, in fact, the extent of government intervention is greater in Canada than in the United States.

DIVERSITY AND TOLERANCE

A second difference between the basic values of the two countries is commonly expressed in terms of the melting pot and the mosaic: immigrants to the United States are urged to become "unhyphenated" Americans, whereas Canada encourages the retention of cultural diversities. Canada celebrates heterogeneity in society and tolerance of minorities, and it expects its public institutions to accommodate immigrants' practices and beliefs. The distinctiveness of the French-Canadian Roman Catholic community based in Quebec was the original basis of this value, but it has now spread to policies of multiculturalism and recognition of other group rights, including those of Aboriginal peoples. Multiculturalism is seen as a means of enriching and enlivening the country, encouraging new Canadians to feel at home, promoting tolerance and minimizing discrimination, and perhaps enhancing Canada's contribution to world harmony. Will Kymlicka makes the point that Canada was a world leader in constitutionalizing multiculturalism and Aboriginal rights and in accommodating national minorities through territorial autonomy.[5]

Diversity also has a territorial dimension—the fact that Canadian provinces are much stronger than the American states relative to the central government. Decentralization in Canada is accompanied by stronger regional or provincial loyalties and identities, due again to the example set by Quebec. Most studies have indicated that Ontarians feel closer to Canada than to their province, while the residents of Quebec, Newfoundland, and Alberta identify more with their province. Even so, the provincial orientations of Albertans or Quebeckers should not be overstated. In a recent survey, 67 percent of Albertans disagreed with the suggestion that the province should replace national programs with its own, and 87 percent of Albertans had a strong sense of belonging to Canada.[6] Table 6.1 reveals how francophone Quebeckers typically balance loyalties to Quebec and Canada.

TABLE 6.1 FRANCOPHONE QUEBECKERS' ATTITUDES TO QUEBEC AND CANADA, 2001

Question: Which of the following do you consider yourself?	Percentage of Respondents
Solely a Quebecker	29
A Quebecker first, then a Canadian	29
Equally a Quebecker and a Canadian	24
A Canadian first, then a Quebecker	12
Solely a Canadian	5

Source: Léger marketing poll, *The Globe and Mail* (9 Feb. 2001), 4. Reprinted with permission of Léger Marketing.

DEFERENCE TO AUTHORITY

Another fundamental difference between Canadian and American values is the greater **deference to authority** in Canadian society. Canadians demonstrate more respect toward the law, judges, police, religious leaders, and many others with "legitimate power." Peace, order, and good government rather than individual liberty constitute the Canadian ideal, and many observers have noted that Canada is probably the only country where a police officer is a national symbol. Less obsessed with material success than Americans, Canadians are more likely to obey a law even if they do not like it. Crime rates are considerably lower in Canada (the homicide rate typically being one-quarter that of the United States on a per capita basis), gun control laws are stronger, and the drug problem is less severe.

EGALITARIANISM

Canada values **egalitarianism** more than the United States. That is, Canada is more concerned with removing barriers that prevent individuals or groups from achieving their full potential. One striking example is in the constitutional equality of women. Canada adopted a strong guarantee of gender equality (including affirmative action) in the 1982 Charter of Rights and Freedoms at the very time that a similar proposal failed in the United States. The health and welfare programs that flow from Canadian collectivism similarly ensure a greater degree of socioeconomic equality for the poor and working classes. Studies of income distribution in the two countries consistently reveal smaller disparities between rich and poor in Canada. For example, a 2000 Statistics Canada study showed that the poorest 25 percent of Canadian families have more purchasing power than their U.S. counterparts, while the opposite is the case at the top of the income scale.[7] Even in the realm of higher education, Canada now appears to be more egalitarian than the United States: in contrast to earlier times, a larger proportion of young adults in Canada have access to postsecondary education.[8] Canada also extends this redistributive egalitarianism to have-not provinces through equalization payments.

CAUTION, DIFFIDENCE, AND NONVIOLENCE

A final difference in values to emerge from this analysis relates to Canadian caution and diffidence, sometimes called a national inferiority complex. It includes a historical dependence on other countries and the absence of a spirit of innovation and risk-taking. Canadians delight in the security of savings and understatement. Of course, there have been many Canadian "winners" in all walks of life, in whose accomplishments Canadians vicariously share: Margaret Atwood, Céline Dion, Glenn Gould, Wayne Gretzky, Karen Kain, Bryan Adams, Frederick Banting, Lester Pearson, John Polanyi, and others. But Canadians are obsessed with "survival" rather than success; they are especially good at deprecating themselves and almost always think that things American are superior. Canadians are prudent and cautious, sober and solemn, introverted, uncertain, and always questioning themselves. Most Canadians take quiet satisfaction in their achievements—the 1995 survey showed that 89 percent of Canadians felt proud when they saw the Canadian flag or heard the national anthem—but they rarely proclaim it aloud.

Along similar lines, although Canada made major contributions to two world wars, Canadians are not a warlike people and abhor violence at home and abroad. We have tried to be peacemakers and peacekeepers in international relations,

Reprinted with permission from *The Globe and Mail*.

putting special emphasis on the United Nations, trying to reduce the militancy of the foreign policy of the United States in quiet, backroom diplomacy (though perhaps not as hard as we should have), and helping to remove the causes of war through assistance to developing countries.

The Changing Canadian Political Culture

As Canada approached the 21st century, many aspects of this traditional value structure seemed to be changing. Different concepts of democracy emerged, and the distinction between Canadian and American values appeared to be in decline. Much of this transformation can be attributed to the presence of the United States, directly or indirectly, although some of it is part of a worldwide change in political values.

As far as democracy is concerned, the 1990s saw an upsurge in interest in the means of more direct popular participation in government. The most common prescription in this regard is the referendum, in which legislators would be guided or bound by the frequent referral of policy questions to the electorate as a whole. Quebec has used this device repeatedly on the question of sovereignty; certain other provinces now require it for approval of constitutional amendments, and some have prescribed its use for other issues such as significant tax increases. With the widespread access to computers in the modern world, many have raised the possibility of "e-democracy," in which people could regularly vote on issues on-line. Somewhat similarly, British Columbia has established a mechanism for the **recall** of MLAs between provincial elections.

What Do You Think?

Do you think e-democracy—which involves regular consultation with voters by means of the Internet—is a valid or viable idea? On what kind of issues should we hold referendums? On what grounds should it be possible to recall a member of Parliament? (In answering these questions, do not forget that you are probably more computer-literate than the majority of the population and are the bearer of superior political knowledge.)

As for the distinctions between Canadian and American values, these are threatened in at least three ways. First, given the widespread U.S. influence over Canada and the Canadian exposure to the United States, values implicit in that country's popular culture, as transmitted by television, movies, books, magazines, and music, are likely to have considerable impact on those north of the border. It is debatable whether distinctive Canadian values can withstand the homogenizing force of modern technology, especially that emanating from the south. Second, Canadian nationalists see all these influences increasing under free trade agreements with the United States, which restrict government intervention to protect Canadian culture. Third, some observers feel that the adoption of a U.S.–style Charter of Rights and Freedoms will further diminish distinctive Canadian values by challenging rather than deferring to government authority.

In a country that articulates its basic values so diffidently to start with, these powerful threats are not to be taken lightly. There are several indications that support for collectivism and feelings of deference in Canada are on the decline.[9] Although it cannot be blamed entirely on Americans, the obsession with government debts, deficits, and tax cuts at both federal and provincial levels has seriously eroded social programs and shifted the basis of pensions and child benefits from universality to selectivity. Privatization of Crown corporations and deregulation have also become rampant. Moreover, Canadians seem increasingly concerned with the legal equality of all citizens, rather than with their socioeconomic equality or well-being. Nevertheless, the most authoritative recent study of com-

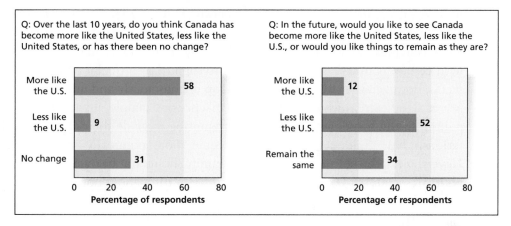

Figure 6.1   Canada–U.S. Differences

Q: Over the last 10 years, do you think Canada has become more like the United States, less like the United States, or has there been no change?

- More like the U.S.: 58
- Less like the U.S.: 9
- No change: 31

Percentage of respondents

Q: In the future, would you like to see Canada become more like the United States, less like the U.S., or would you like things to remain as they are?

- More like the U.S.: 12
- Less like the U.S.: 52
- Remain the same: 34

Percentage of respondents

Source: EKOS Research Associates Inc., "Canadian Values and Identities in North America" (July 2002). © 2002. Reproduced with permission of EKOS Research Associates Inc.

parative values finds that Canadian distinctiveness remains clear,[10] and Figure 6.1 indicates that the desire to remain distinct is still strong.

Political Socialization

Political socialization is the process through which individuals acquire their political values, attitudes, information, and opinions. The process consists in part of direct, individual exposure to political phenomena but is mostly performed by intermediaries or agents of socialization. It is relatively easy to identify the main agents of political socialization in Canada, but evaluating their relative impact is much more difficult. We begin with the four traditional agents—family, school, peers, and the media—and then examine other such influences.

The Family

Despite many modern pressures that have transformed the role of the family, including the increasing incidence of mothers working outside the home and the high divorce rate, the family remains the basic cell of Canadian society. Parents, stepparents, or sometimes grandparents are the first major influence on a child's attitudes and values. Most children absorb attitudes and values, some of which are of political significance, in a kind of osmosis from their family's talk and behaviour. Parents' casual comments about politics, politicians, parties, and police are good examples. Some parents also deliberately try to indoctrinate their children with certain political values or get them to support a particular political party. It seems, however, that what children pick up unconsciously and unintentionally is just as significant as what parents try to teach. For example, if parents talk about politics in the home, with or without attempting to guide their children's orientations, their children will usually become more politically interested later. Nevertheless, the political impact of the family should not be overemphasized, for political socialization is a process that continues throughout one's life.

The School

The school is the second main agent of political socialization. All school systems in Canada and elsewhere deliberately attempt to inculcate certain basic values and attitudes, including some of a political nature, such as a feeling of affection or support for the country, the governmental apparatus, the head of state, the police, the flag, and the national anthem. Like the family, the school is an early enough influence that it may shape basic lifelong values.

The fact that students are now entering some form of institutionalized educational setting earlier than in previous generations has probably increased the school's importance relative to that of the family, a phenomenon that may be of particular significance in immigrant households.

Given the diversity of Canadian society, many questions arise about the role of the school in the political socialization process. Since the provinces have jurisdiction over education, for example, do they deliberately contribute to the development of distinctive provincial political cultures at the expense of the overall country? The radically different accounts of certain historical events found in French- and English-language textbooks are often cited as an example of the biased role of formal education in this process.[11] One point is clear: the forces of dualism, regionalism, and continentalism in Canadian society make it difficult for the school system to develop any pan-Canadian sense of national identity.[12]

Just as happens in the family setting, however, the school also contributes informally and unintentionally to the development of attitudes and values. Such unconscious transmissions occur in teachers' remarks beyond the formal curriculum, in class discussions and excursions, and in extracurricular activities.

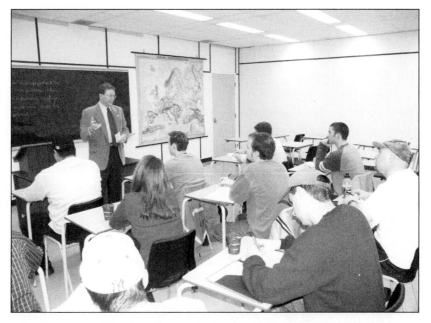

Political socialization in the classroom setting. (Rand Dyck)

Moreover, exposure to an authoritarian teacher or principal is likely to produce different attitudes toward participation and dissent than those resulting from a more democratic setting. Corporations are also becoming increasingly involved in the educational system, promoting their own goods, services, and values.

Students are not only starting school at a younger age but also staying in school longer. The 2001 census showed that only 23 percent of the population over the age of 24 had not completed high school, down from 48 percent in 1981. University graduates represented another 23 percent of the population, while 31 percent had postsecondary college or trade certificates or diplomas.

Peers

Peers are the third main agent of political socialization. Peers are simply friends, colleagues, acquaintances, and associates. The concept of "peer pressure" is probably most familiar at the adolescent level and is not usually concerned with political values, attitudes, and opinions. But we are all susceptible to peer influence at any stage of our lives. In any group setting, including peer-group discussions that turn to politics, one person often becomes dominant, whether because of knowledge, position, or strength of character. At this stage, given the likelihood that basic values have already been established, attitudes and opinions are most likely to be influenced.

The Mass Media

The mass media are the fourth main agent of socialization. They are more often instruments of entertainment than enlightenment, however, and personal inter-action with family members, teachers, or peers normally carries greater impact than passive, impersonal exposure to the media. When it comes to politics, the media transmit opinions primarily on topical issues and personalities and are less likely to influence lifelong values and attitudes. Nevertheless, there is evidence that Canadians do learn from this coverage,[13] and such short-term stimuli are becoming more important in determining how people vote.

Once again, media influence can be divided between the unconscious and the deliberate. In their editorials, newspapers explicitly attempt to influence opinions, while on the other pages of the paper, Canadians expect news coverage to be as unbiased and factual as possible. Whether newspapers can keep such a fine line between subjective editorials and objective reporting is an interesting question, and some observers have detected bias in the headlines, positioning, pictures, and selection of items to be included or excluded. Even though television does not usually have editorials as such, it has much greater scope for presenting biased news coverage than do newspapers, as noted in the fuller account of the mass media in Chapter 7. Moreover, some observers argue that the images portrayed on television, even in its provision of entertainment, convey powerful messages with political implications.

Other Agents of Political Socialization

The family, school, peers, and media are probably the main agents of political socialization in Canada, but they are certainly not the only ones. Political parties, churches, interest groups of various kinds, corporations, and the government itself are secondary influences on political values, attitudes, information, and opinions.

Political parties practise the art of persuasion and seek to influence opinions and party preferences on a daily basis. Those people who already identify with a particular party find that the simplest means of forming an opinion on any issue is by taking their cue from the party leader.

Churches often take stands on political issues. First and foremost, the Roman Catholic Church strongly influenced political values, attitudes, and opinions in Quebec prior to 1960. It had a close relationship with political authorities and did not hesitate to tell its members how to behave politically. The influence of religion in Canadian society may be on the decline, but its political role remains significant. When the Canadian Alliance party was led by Stockwell Day, for example, it was highly attractive to those with fundamentalist Christian values.

Over half the population belongs to an organized group of some kind, and although the orientation of such groups is primarily nonpolitical, all have the potential to influence their members' political views. Some, such as the Canadian Medical Association and the Canadian Labour Congress, are quite determined to do so. As with parties and churches, taking one's opinions from the urging of a group leader obviates the need to make further individual effort to understand the issue. Other groups—such as the Boy Scouts or Girl Guides—try to instill in children an informed affection for the country.

Like political parties, individual corporations are in the business of persuasion, trying to sell their own goods and services. Sometimes, however, companies also try to influence political attitudes and opinions, an effort that is called **advocacy advertising**. Many corporations were involved in the free trade debate, especially during the 1988 election campaign, expressing their support through "speeches, debates, letters, advertisements, information sessions with employees, and inserts in newspapers."[14] Before and since 1988, employers often tried to influence the voting preferences of their own employees with internal memos about how different parties or policies would affect the firm.

Finally, the government itself is often engaged in efforts to influence public views and behaviour. Sometimes these efforts are widely recognized as legitimate, such as in the cases of encouraging physical fitness and discouraging smoking, impaired driving, racial discrimination, domestic violence, and the use of drugs. Sometimes attempts to influence people are made for broadly acceptable political purposes, such as promoting vacations in Canada and the purchase of Canadian-made goods. Governments are also expected to inform the public about new laws, regulations, and programs, but there is a fine line between providing simple information and extolling the virtues of such initiatives for partisan purposes. The Mulroney government, for example, spent large sums of public funds promoting the merits of the Free Trade Agreement and the Goods and Services Tax in advertising campaigns that most observers felt were excessive and self-serving. The sponsorship of various events in Quebec by the Chrétien government to try to engender greater support for the federal government was not only counterproductive but also resulted in scandal.

> ## Should Government Try to Influence People's Values?
>
> After almost losing the 1995 Quebec referendum, the government of Jean Chrétien spent hundreds of millions of dollars on a pro-Canada advertising campaign in that province. The money was spent to boost the federal government's profile by flying the Canadian flag as widely as possible in Quebec and by sponsoring sporting and cultural events. Quebeckers were generally insulted that they were considered so easily bought; even worse, the Auditor General revealed that the money was mismanaged. In fact, much of it was wasted by advertising companies with close ties to the Liberal Party.

How Canadians individually and collectively acquire their political values, attitudes, information, and opinions is a complicated question. Because the process is so haphazard and complex and the stimuli in each person's environment so diverse, no deliberate effort is guaranteed to be successful. Instead, Canadians acquire many of their political values, attitudes, and opinions in a completely unconscious way. Moreover, many Canadians are only semi-socialized: they simply do not have many political values, attitudes, and opinions or much political information. The general level of political awareness is not high, which in turn is reflected in patterns of political participation.

Political Participation

Political participation consists of "those voluntary activities by citizens that are intended to influence the selection of government leaders or the decisions they make."[15] Numerous avenues of political participation exist, but actual participation takes initiative and effort, which many people are not willing to exert. Participation is also related to the possession of **political efficacy**—a sense of political competence and a feeling that one can have some impact on the system. Table 6.2 reveals that about two-thirds of Canadians think that MPs soon lose touch with the people and that people like themselves have no say in what the government does. Participation also depends on the possession of such resources as time, money, and information, although perhaps not as much as many people think. Regrettably, the opportunities for participation in Canada far exceed actual levels of involvement.

TABLE 6.2 CANADIANS' FEELINGS ON GOVERNMENT RESPONSIVENESS, 2000

	Agree (Percentage)	Disagree (Percentage)	Don't Know (Percentage)
Those elected to Parliament soon lose touch with the people	69	26	5
People like me do not have any say over what the government does.	63	35	2

Source: Adapted from Paul Howe and David Northrup, "Strengthening Canadian Democracy: The Views of Canadians," *Policy Matters* 1, no. 5 (July 2000). Reprinted by permission of the Institute for Research on Public Policy, Montreal. www.irpp.org

Electoral Participation

Voting on election day is a crucial aspect of democracy and is the most common form of political participation in Canada. The voter turnout rate is also one of the few forms of participation that can be regularly and reliably measured. The overall average national turnout rate between 1900 and 1988 was about 73 percent, or nearly three-quarters of those eligible to vote. These figures disguise the fact that the turnout rate varied considerably from one province to another. Prince Edward Island stands out with the highest average turnout, while the rate in Alberta, the North, and Newfoundland was much lower. The rate for each federal election between 1974 and 2004 is provided in Table 6.3.

Those who do not vote have consistently been shown to be alienated from or uninformed about the political system, and they include primarily the young, the poor, and the working classes. Other traditional reasons for not voting include

TABLE 6.3 PERCENTAGE VOTER TURNOUT IN FEDERAL ELECTIONS, 1974–2004

Year	Turnout	Year	Turnout
1974	71	1993	70
1979	76	1997	67
1980	69	2000	64
1984	75	2004	61
1988	75		

Source: Data compiled and used to create the above chart was taken from the website of Elections Canada: www.elections.ca (Retrieved 15 Aug. 2004). It is used with the permission of the Chief Electoral Officer but extrapolation and analysis rest with author. "Voter Turnout at Federal Elections and Referendums, 1867–2000," http://www.elections.ca/content.asp? section+pas&dir=&document=turnout&lang=e&textonly=false.

lack of interest, unappealing alternatives, weak party identification, passivity engendered by watching television, feelings that government is irrelevant to one's life or is not listening, or thinking that the result is predetermined. The voter turnout rate dramatically decreased over the 1990s and after, to an all-time low of about 61 percent in 2004. In general, the largest group that abstained were poorly educated young people, those who were less interested in politics, and those who were less informed.[16] Another probable factor for the decline in voter turnout rates is the "dismantling of the state," including globalization; since government performs fewer functions than previously, people have less confidence in it and fewer expectations. Canada's turnout falls between the extremes found in other countries, being well above the rate in the United States but behind that in most comparable states, including Britain.

Why Don't Young People Vote?

It is estimated that only 25 percent of people under the age of 30 voted in the Canadian federal election of 2000. The three most common reasons for not voting given by those in this group were as follows: lack of interest (28 percent); lack of time (23 percent); and lack of appeal on the part of, or lack of faith in, parties, leaders, and candidates (20 percent). Most such young people lack a sense of civic duty and do not feel that voting is important for its own sake and an essential obligation of living in a democracy.

Source: Jon H. Pammett and Lawrence LeDuc, "Explaining the Turnout Decline in Canadian Federal Elections: A New Survey of Non-Voters" (March 2003), http://www.elections.ca/loi/tur/tud/TurnoutDecline.pdf (Retrieved 22 Nov. 2004).

Within the group of those who do vote, other degrees of electoral involvement can be distinguished. For one thing, the level of information of the typical voter should not be overestimated. Even if around 80 percent claim to have exposed themselves to television or newspaper coverage of the election campaign, only about 20 percent follow politics closely on a daily basis between elections.[17] A 2000 study revealed that only 26 percent could name the current prime minister, the minister of finance, and the Leader of the Opposition.[18] The level of factual and conceptual knowledge increased with the level of education and reading about politics in newspapers and magazines, but viewing political programs on television had negligible impact.[19]

Beyond those who cast an "informed vote," a smaller proportion of the electorate actually becomes actively involved in the election campaign: attending an all-candidates meeting; joining a political party; voting at the party's local nomination meeting; contributing money to a political party; or helping a local candidate to do mailing, telephoning, door-to-door canvassing, and election-day work. A small number in each constituency become totally preoccupied with the local campaign; these people, including candidates themselves, are sometimes called "gladiators," as distinct from the great bulk of the population, who are primarily "spectators."

Nonelectoral Participation

The political participation of most Canadians peaks at election time, but many avenues are open between elections in which to make demands or otherwise become involved in the political process. One option is to join a political party. Most Canadian political parties do not maintain reliable lists of their members, but Ken Carty estimates that only about 2.7 percent of the population belongs to a party.[20] It is known, however, that many people sign up before or during the election campaign (often to participate in the nomination of candidates) or before a leadership contest and then let their membership lapse.

Another means of political participation is to join an organized interest group, an action that some 60 percent of Canadians claim to do. As seen in Chapter 10, any group, whatever its primary orientation, can become a pressure group, so that membership in any group is potentially political. Even if the group itself takes a political turn, however, passive members rarely do more than send the occasional preprinted postcard to their MP or the prime minister.

On the other hand, the purpose of some groups is primarily political, and political activists increasingly prefer involvement in social movements and interest groups over joining a political party. Active executive and staff members of such groups may become highly involved in political campaigns and the pressure-group politics that goes on in Canada every day. Even more initiative is required to form such a group, usually to protest against some political decision or lack of action at the municipal, provincial, federal, or even global level.

Such group participation usually involves communicating with the authorities in routine ways, but occasionally it takes the form of peaceful demonstrations (locally or on Parliament Hill), sit-ins and other types of civil disobedience, and the rare case of violent protest. As noted above, Canadians are generally a peaceful lot, and political violence is uncommon. The main historical incidents of such violence in Canada were the Riel Rebellions of 1870 and 1885, the conscription riots in Quebec City in 1918, the Winnipeg General Strike of 1919, the

Regina Riot of 1935, the various FLQ incidents of the 1960s culminating in the FLQ crisis of 1970, and the Mohawks' armed standoff at Oka in 1990.[21]

Canadians can also participate politically between elections as individuals— writing, faxing, or e-mailing letters to MPs or the prime minister, writing letters to the editors of newspapers, calling radio or television phone-in shows, signing petitions, or telephoning or meeting an MP. Statistics Canada provides some data on the degree of individual involvement in these activities, as shown in Figure 6.2. Hardly more than 25 percent signed a petition, an action that does not require much effort, and the degree of engagement declined from there. Moreover, there is probably a large element of overlap among the people who participated in any of these activities.

Figure 6.2   Percentage of Canadians Who Engaged in Selected Political Activities over the Previous Year, 2003

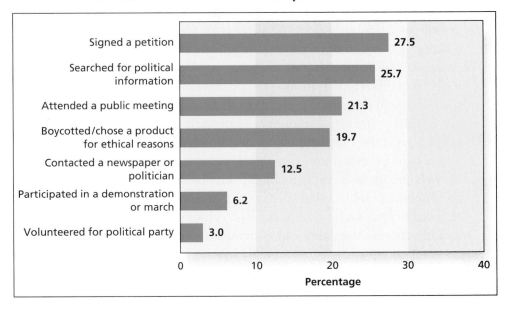

Source: Adapted from the Statistics Canada publication, "2003 General Social Survey on Social Engagement, Cycle 17: An Overview of Findings," 2003, cat. no. 89-598 (July 6, 2004), http://www.statcan.ca/english/freepub/89-598-XIE/2003001/Figures/chart19.htm (Retrieved 15 Aug. 2004).

SUMMARY

This chapter examined political culture, political socialization, and political participation in Canada. After defining political culture, it focused on the adherence to democracy, as well as five other basic political values that distinguish Canadians from Americans. It suggested that while Canadians' political values are undergoing a certain amount of change, they remain quite distinct. The chapter then discussed the concept of political socialization and the principal agents thereof, including family, school, peers, mass media, and government itself. The third part of the chapter dealt with political participation. It showed that the voter turnout rate in Canada has seriously declined in recent years, especially among young people. It also indicated that while various forms of nonelectoral political participation are available, the extent to which Canadians avail themselves of these opportunities is not particularly impressive.

DISCUSSION QUESTIONS

1. Are periodic elections a sufficient means of exercising the principle of popular sovereignty? In what situations are referendums appropriate?
2. To what extent are basic Canadian political values still distinct from those in the United States?
3. Thinking about the relative importance of the agents of political socialization in your own life, can you decipher your own socialization process?
4. How high a level of political information and political participation does a democracy require?

KEY TERMS

Advocacy advertising Advertising that advocates a political point of view rather than trying to sell a good or service.

Collectivism As opposed to individualism, an ideology that holds that the public interest is enhanced by substantial collective action, normally via government.

Deference to authority A value considered to be part of the Canadian political culture in which citizens are respectful of government authority and accept its word and orders with little question.

Democracy A political system characterized by popular sovereignty, political equality, political freedom, and majority rule.

Egalitarianism As opposed to elitism, the philosophy or practice of providing everyone with an equal amount of power and/or treating everyone more or less equally.

Individualism An ideology that holds that individuals should have maximum freedom or liberty to do as they please, especially in economic terms, and that governments should not get involved in taxation, regulation, redistribution, or ownership.

Majority rule An element in the definition of democracy that in any decision-making setting involving a difference of opinion, the larger number should carry the day.

Political culture The sum total of the politically relevant values, beliefs, attitudes, and orientations in any political system.

Political efficacy The feeling that one has political influence and that one's political participation can make an impact.

Political equality An element in the definition of democracy that entails the principle of "one person–one vote," that is, every citizen has a vote and each counts equally.

Political freedom An element in the definition of democracy that entails freedom of speech, press, assembly, association, etc., such that people can organize and advocate in order to influence election results and public policy.

Political socialization The process whereby individuals acquire their political values, attitudes, beliefs, information, and opinions.

Popular sovereignty An element in the definition of democracy that entails periodically allowing the public at large to exert its will—to have the final say—normally through general elections.

Recall A populist device in which the signing of a petition by a certain proportion of the local electorate to recall their legislative representative means that the representative must resign.

Referendum A populist device in which a public policy proposal is submitted directly to the electorate.

Representative democracy A system of government based on periodic election of representatives to Parliament, as opposed to more direct participation by voters in making public decisions.

FURTHER READING

Adams, Michael. *Fire and Ice: The United States, Canada and the Myth of Converging Values*. Toronto: Penguin Canada, 2003.

Bell, David. *The Roots of Disunity: A Look at Canadian Political Culture*. Rev. ed. Toronto: Oxford University Press, 1992.

Berton, Pierre. *Why We Act Like Canadians*. Toronto: McClelland and Stewart, 1982.

Friedenberg, Edgar J. *Deference to Authority*. White Plains, N.Y.: M.E. Sharpe, 1980.

Gidengil, Elisabeth, et al. *Citizens*. Vancouver: UBC Press, 2004.

Lipset, Seymour Martin. *Continental Divide*. New York: Routledge, 1990.

Nevitte, Neil. *The Decline of Deference*. Peterborough: Broadview Press, 1996.

Ostry, Sylvia. "Government Intervention: Canada and the United States Compared." *Policy Options* (March 1980), 26–31.

Pammett, Jon H., and Lawrence LeDuc. "Explaining the Turnout Decline in Canadian Federal Elections: A New Survey of Non-Voters." March 2003. http://www.elections.ca/loi/tur/tud/TurnoutDecline.pdf.

Thomas, David, ed. *Canada and the United States: Differences That Count*. 2nd ed. Peterborough: Broadview Press, 2000.

Chapter 7

The Mass Media and Public Opinion Polls

The **mass media**, principally television, newspapers, and radio, are the primary source of most Canadians' knowledge and opinions about topical political issues and current political personalities. Public policymakers also depend on the media to provide much of the information they need for their own work as well as to transmit the messages that they want the public to hear. The media thus provide an important two-way communications link between the governors and the governed. A second crucial link is the public opinion poll. Political parties rely heavily on polls to guide their actions immediately before and during election campaigns, but governments and the media also seek to discover Canadians' opinions on a daily basis. This chapter examines both of these important and interconnected features of the political system.

Chapter Objectives

After you have completed this chapter, you should be able to:

Outline the ownership of different media and evaluate the significance of public, private, and concentrated ownership

Discuss the agenda-setting function of the media

Distinguish between the virtues of newspapers and television as sources of political information

Understand the mutually dependent relationship between politicians and the media

Appreciate the extent to which public opinion is not well informed

Enumerate the practitioners and discuss the techniques of public opinion polling

Evaluate the extent to which public opinion polls influence voting behaviour and the policies adopted by governments

The Mass Media

In surveying the newspaper, radio, and television industries today, it should first be noted that the privately owned media exist primarily to make a profit and that whatever political functions they serve are incidental to that purpose. In addition, since the media—even television—usually rely on words and language, and since a majority of Canadians are unilingual, the country is characterized by a "media apartheid," in which English and French are virtually two solitudes.

Newspapers

The Canadian daily newspaper industry has been characterized by chain owner-ship for several decades, but owners have frequently exchanged newspapers in recent years. An earlier era was dominated by the Ken Thomson and Southam newspaper chains. Then, in the 1990s, Conrad Black, proprietor of the Hollinger chain, added the Southam and most of the Thomson papers to his holdings and established *National Post*. After 2000, the Asper family, proprietors of CanWest Global Television, became active in the newspaper industry and purchased most of Black's Canadian dailies. Meanwhile, Thomson sold *The Globe and Mail* to BCE (Bell Canada Enterprises), also owners of the CTV television network, although he retained a minority interest.

At the time of writing, the largest chain in terms of the number of papers is Michael Sifton's new Osprey Media Group, which publishes 22 small dailies in Ontario. The second largest chain is Quebecor, which consists of 17 dailies owned by the Péladeau family and includes the English-language Sun Media chain. The Asper family owns 13 papers, including the *National Post*; a new chain named GTC Transcontinental owns 11; and Hollinger still has 10. Smaller chains include Desmarais's seven Quebec papers, led by *La Presse* of Montreal; Horizon, with five; TorStar, with four, including the *Toronto Star*, the largest single daily in the country; and the three-paper Irving chain. In addition, there are approxi-mately nine independents or members of smaller chains.[1]

Thus, some of the wealthiest families in Canada—Asper, Irving, Desmarais, and Péladeau—control most of the country's newspaper industry. Moreover, one chain or another often has an overwhelming dominance in a single province. Such concentrated ownership of Canadian newspapers has always caused consid-erable concern. Many fear that the owner of several papers will gain an unhealthy degree of influence over public opinion by establishing a common point of view for all papers in the chain. The Trudeau government appointed the Kent Royal

Commission on Newspapers to investigate this question, but responding to strong pressure from the industry, that government abandoned a bill aimed to restrict concentrated media ownership. All conglomerate-owned newspapers are likely to betray a pro-business bias,[2] and most of the newspaper-owning families have substantial holdings beyond newspapers. This leads to the question of whether such media outlets provide fair coverage of the operations of other firms under the same ownership. Especially in the small confines of New Brunswick, for example, it has been suggested that Irving newspapers refrain from critical comment on all the Irving family's other holdings. Moreover, many media analysts find the new trend toward companies owning both television networks and daily newspapers to be somewhat troubling.

Dangers of Chain Ownership of the Media

The Asper family's ownership of many daily newspapers across Canada illustrates the dangers of chain ownership when a single owner is determined to mould Canadians' thinking on public issues. CanWest Global headquarters prepares national editorials that have to be carried by every newspaper in the chain and with which local editorials cannot disagree. Headquarters has often spiked—denied publication—of items, including editorial cartoons, to which it objected. Furthermore, the owners have fired columnists, editors, and publishers who did not share their point of view, and they insisted on positive coverage of politicians or issues close to their heart.

Radio and Television

The radio and television industries are distinct from newspapers in two respects: the degree of public ownership involved and the presence of government regulation. As for public ownership, the **Canadian Broadcasting Corporation (CBC)** operates radio stations in both official languages nationwide. CBC radio has a relatively large and sophisticated audience, and it plays a major role in transmitting information and opinion among its listeners. The CBC/Radio-Canada television network also has stations across the country, with English-language production centred in Toronto and French-language production in Montreal. These are supplemented by agreements with a number of privately owned affiliated stations, which agree to telecast a certain amount of CBC programming.

Apart from CBC/Radio-Canada, the Canadian radio industry consists of nearly 650 local AM and FM stations. These stations used to be independently owned but are increasingly characterized by chain ownership, just as in the newspaper industry. Ownership changes quite frequently, but by 2000, some 60 percent of the radio market in Canada was controlled by the 10 leading firms. Like newspapers, radio stations must be Canadian-owned. When the limited Canadian content on private radio stations became a problem, the CRTC issued Canadian-content rules, as noted in Chapter 5.

The privately owned CTV network, centred on CFTO in Toronto, consists of 30 television stations and, as noted, is now owned by BCE. The Toronto-based CanWest Global system is owned by the Asper family of Winnipeg, who succeeded in cobbling together a third national English-language network. Several major cities also have an unaffiliated, independent private English-language station. On the French side, TVA, whose focal point is Télé-Métropole in Montreal, is a 10-station network now owned by the Péladeau family, and a second private French network, Quatre Saisons, is owned by BCE.

The **Canadian Radio-television and Telecommunications Commission (CRTC)** is the federal regulatory agency in this field. The commission requires Canadian television stations to be domestically owned and to telecast 50 percent or more Canadian content. But such regulations are virtually meaningless when almost all residents are within reach, either directly or via cable or satellite, of a large assortment of U.S. television channels. On this point, Fred Fletcher talks of "American images crowding out Canadian ones,"[3] and Ed Black writes of the problem of trying to serve a small population in two language groups "who live in tempting, embarrassing, and almost smothering proximity to [10 times as many] Americans who speak the language of Canada's majority ... They also have the world's most penetrating and effective system for transmitting ideas en masse."[4] Peter Trueman adds, "Think of the overwhelming preponderance of American programming, which in an unobtrusive way pumps us full of American values, American hopes, American history, even American patterns of speech."[5]

CBC television has a strong commitment to Canadian programming but suffers from a chronic shortage of funds. After severe bloodletting under the Mulroney government, the CBC hoped for better treatment under the Chrétien regime. Instead, that government slashed the CBC budget even further, precipitating the resignation of the corporation's president.

Private stations and networks realize that profits can be maximized by telecasting as much U.S. programming as the CRTC will allow. Nevertheless, the importance and popularity of CBC, CTV, and Global national newscasts, *The*

Morning News, The Fifth Estate, Marketplace, Royal Canadian Air Farce, This Hour Has 22 Minutes, Téléjournal, Le Point, Canada AM, and *W5* should not be underestimated. As mentioned in Chapter 5, the overall percentage of time spent watching Canadian-content programs on Canadian conventional, pay-TV, and specialty channels in 2002 was 40 percent, but this rate is twice as high among francophones as anglophones. English-speaking Canadians watch more Canadian than foreign coverage only in the categories of news and public affairs and sports.

The establishment of CBC Newsworld in 1989 (and a French-language equivalent in 1995) was another effort to strengthen Canadian television content. These all-news channels cover many political events live and more extensively than regular CBC, with which they work closely, and provide regional coverage, documentaries, and in-depth interview programming. While their audience is small, most members of the political elite tune in regularly. CTV also has a national all-news channel, while several provinces have an educational television channel and/or another that carries provincial legislative proceedings. The national parliamentary channel on cable is called CPAC.

About 85 percent of Canadian homes are hooked up to (and hooked on) cable television or satellite services, more than in any other country. The CRTC regulates which channels cable systems carry, but cable television brings the major U.S. networks into most Canadian homes and permits subscribers to watch U.S. news, public affairs, and sports programs. The Canadian cable industry is essentially dominated by three regional giants: Rogers Communications, Shaw Cablesystems, and Vidéotron. The variety of other channels on cable television is constantly increasing, and some of them are of Canadian origin; CBC, CTV, Global, and others have established their own specialty channels. CRTC approval of new specialty channels, including pay-per-view channels and direct-to-home (DTH) satellite services, has further served to dilute the audience of conventional Canadian television stations.

The Changing Media World: Convergence in Canadian Media Ownership

Probably few aspects of the political system are in such a state of rapid change as the mass media. This change is usually referred to as a **convergence** of technologies and corporations, as television, telephone, satellite, cable, computer, and Internet companies merge.[6] Spectacular media conglomerations have taken place in the United States in recent years (which in themselves have a considerable impact on Canada), but in this respect Canada is not far behind. The merging of

BCE with CTV, Sympatico, and *The Globe and Mail*; the purchase of many newspapers by CanWest Global Television; and the multilayered Quebecor and Rogers Communications empires represent similar cross-media conglomerates, as shown in Table 7.1.

The increased concentration of ownership of such sources of public information is not a healthy development in any democracy that values the maximum diversity of opinions. Moreover, it tends to reduce the resources devoted to news and investigative reporting at the expense of profit-oriented entertainment. On the other hand, the opposite trend toward a fragmentation of audiences allows individuals to ignore broader public questions as they expose themselves to media coverage of only a few personal interests through specialized television channels.

Finally, the Internet is starting to rival newspapers, radio, and television as a medium of mass communications. Like them, it can be used as a source of information and entertainment; indeed, as one of its features, the Internet actually provides access to the other three mass media. Nearly 70 percent of Canadians now have access to the Internet at home, work, or school. Nevertheless, the potential of the Internet in this realm has not yet been fully realized. As well, while the Internet can be a liberating force that permits people to gain information from around the world, connect with others having similar concerns, and provide direct feedback to government, it can also be used for antisocial purposes.

TABLE 7.1 FOUR LARGEST MEDIA CONGLOMERATES IN CANADA, 2005

CanWest Global	Bell Globemedia	Quebecor	Rogers Communications
11 conventional TV stations	CTV television network	17 daily newspapers	Cable television
Independent, affiliated, and specialty channels	Specialty channels	TVA television network	Specialty channels
13 daily newspapers	*The Globe and Mail*	Internet services	Internet services
Southam magazines	Teleglobe TV satellite	Publishing houses	Magazines
Internet services	Bell ExpressVu satellite service	Cable television	Radio stations
	Internet services	Magazines	Video rentals
	Quatre Saisons television network	Video rentals	
	Bell telephone		

The Media and the Public

The influence of the mass media on the political system is profound and appears to be constantly increasing.[7] Most of the information Canadians receive about the political process comes from television, newspapers, or radio, and perhaps *Maclean's*, rather than from direct observation or other sources such as books or magazines. Some recipients may be able to separate this information from whatever commentary or biases accompany it, but many are swayed by the particular perspective that the media give to the data they present.

The current consensus on the role of the media is that they set the political agenda for the country.[8] In other words, the media tell people what to think about, what the important issues are, and which political personalities are significant. They help to define what is political.[9] This is a function that the media share with political parties, and while parties may be more important as initiators of issues, these are not likely to remain on the agenda without media attention. The **parliamentary press gallery** seems to have a "herd instinct" or to engage in "pack journalism" in developing a consensus about what these significant issues are.[10] In part, this reflects the influence of the daily oral Question Period in the House of Commons, which provides the media with short, superficial, and controversial issues that are well suited to television coverage.

When asked to choose among the various media, a majority of people say they prefer to get their political information from television rather than newspapers. Those who prefer television feel it is more fair and believable for all kinds of information, as well as more complete, except perhaps for business and economic news.[11] These results are somewhat distressing to those who know the real advantages and disadvantages of the two main media in question. Because of cost and time constraints, television newscasts must present a shorter and more superficial account of political events than newspapers. Coverage of any item rarely exceeds a 60- to 90-second "news clip" with a 10-second "sound bite" of the voice of political leaders, in which *how* something is said is usually more important than *what* is said. The transcript of a 30-minute newscast would make up about one-third of a single newspaper page.[12] Moreover, because it is a visual medium, television must seek out colourful, dramatic, emotional, conflictual, or entertaining pictures. Riots, demonstrations, and political conventions usually make for good television, but the daily routine of politics does not lend itself so well to compelling visual coverage. Witness the efforts taken by politicians, protesters, and the media to find contrived and engaging settings in which to stage political happenings, make announcements, or tape interviews.

Peter Mansbridge holds up his Gemini Award for Best News Anchor at the awards ceremony in Toronto in October 2003. Most Canadians get their political information from television. (CP Photo/Frank Gunn)

Television portrays images and impressions, and it is therefore much better at dealing with political leaders and personalities than with issues. When Liberal leader John Turner issued a 40-point policy manifesto just before the 1988 election, for example, "the electronic media, which have trouble transmitting more than a single idea in a 30-second clip, could not cope with such a cornucopia of ideas that had not been pre-digested into a simple theme wrapped around a few easily grasped issues."[13] These characteristics make television the most open of the three media to distortion and exploitation, so that it is actually the *least* believable and—however unintention-ally—the *most* biased.[14] Television meets the needs of the average citizen with a short attention span who is looking for visual stimulation and does not wish to invest much effort in understanding the political system.

This situation is exacerbated by the increasing tendency of political parties and politicians to gear their activities to the demands of television rather than those of the other media or the public. Press conferences are now dominated by television lights and cameras; leaders' tours during election campaigns are "photo opportunities" designed to generate a sound bite on the evening news; and party conventions and leaders' debates are scheduled at the television networks' convenience. In preparing for elections, parties put greater effort into designing television commercials and trying them out before focus groups than into devising solutions to the country's problems. The leaders' debate has become the single most important event in an election campaign because elections usually turn more on leader images than issues, policies, local candidates, or other leading figures in the party. The appearance, style, and general image of the party leader, including the ability to perform on television, has become of crucial importance. This emphasis on appearance is often said to trivialize politics.

It would be too soon, however, to write off the political importance of newspapers. Daily newspapers generally offer more comprehensive coverage of political

What Do You Think?

Even if the mass public prefers to get its day-to-day political information from television, is this medium good enough for students of politics such as yourself? Do you try to read a respectable daily newspaper on a regular basis? If you could not afford to buy a newspaper regularly, would you go to your university or college library to read one? Do you read newspapers on the Internet?

events, and they excel at covering issues, which they can do at length, in depth, and in detail, presenting both greater factual information and a wider range of interpretation. While the "average" Canadian relies on television for political information, those with political influence, whether in government, parties, pressure groups, or peer-group situations, depend on newspapers. Those who prefer newspapers over television have higher levels of education and higher incomes, and they are better informed. Furthermore, even though print journalists must often defer to the paraphernalia of their television colleagues, the broadcast media and opposition parties tend to take their cues from newspapers.

It should be added that the degree of a person's political participation increases sharply with his or her level of newspaper consumption. In other words, those who make the effort to increase their political information by reading a newspaper (as opposed to sitting passively in front of a TV set) are not only better informed but also most likely to go on to engage in some form of political participation.[15]

The Globe and Mail calls itself "Canada's national newspaper" and publishes a national edition transmitted by satellite to several printing locations, so that it is available every morning in all major centres across the country. It is read by most of the top-level decisionmakers and media executives and thus tends to set the agenda for other news organizations. Over the past few years, however, it has had competition from the *National Post*. The independent but financially troubled *Le Devoir* occupies a similarly influential position in French Canada, and it has always been an advocate of Quebec nationalism. In fact, all French-language media in Quebec have played a part in communicating a sense of the French-Canadian nation, from the famous Plouffe family television series in the 1960s to the federally owned Radio-Canada.

The Media and the Politicians

Politicians and their bureaucratic advisers need publicity and therefore have a great interest in how the media cover their behaviour. Even though they have their own direct sources, they also depend on the media to provide information they need about what is happening at home and abroad. The media in turn often rely on government sources for most of their information, and much media reporting of politics is of the "government handout" variety.

OWNERS, EDITORS, AND JOURNALISTS

The Canadian daily newspapers are expected to present news coverage in an objective manner and reserve the opinions of the owner or editor for the editorial page. Even so, one can often detect biases in the tone or selection of news items, such as a rightward slant in *The Globe and Mail* and a centre-left, Liberal inclination in the *Toronto Star*. Conrad Black made such biases more overt when he assumed ownership of the Southam chain, especially in his creation of the *National Post*: a clear-cut preference for the Reform/Alliance party and its right-wing policies pervaded the whole paper. The newspaper maintained this tradition even after it was purchased by the Asper family and after the Alliance and PC parties merged.

In principle, reporters should remain distant from politicians to cover them objectively; on the other hand, it is often necessary to cultivate close relations in order to get the kind of information that those in the media seek. Allan Fotheringham writes that "the narrowest line in journalism is the line between exploiting your sources (without ever destroying them) and being captured by them."[16] Furthermore, since politicians often confidentially seek out the opinions of working reporters, the latter sometimes have to agonize over whether to reveal information that was given to them "off the record," that is, in the expectation that it would not be used.

The media also have to confront the issue of politicians' privacy. When do excessive drinking, sexual infidelity, or family and financial problems begin to interfere with a politician's public functions, and when should they be revealed? Beyond personal privacy is the question of whether the media should transmit information they are not supposed to have, such as when Global Television came into advance possession of a summary of the 1988 budget.

THE GOVERNMENT SIDE: NEWS MANAGEMENT

The increasingly common problem of **news management** and manipulation relates especially to the deliberate timing and selective distribution of government information. It includes exaggerating positive news while keeping secret or delaying release of that which is negative, giving preference to friendly reporters over others, making prime ministerial requests for network television time for less than important announcements, and outright lying. News management also involves putting the best face on a deficient government action or politician's performance by having a partisan official tell the media how successful it actually was, in the hope that the media will transmit this evaluation to their audience. Those involved in such efforts are often called media handlers or **spin doctors**, because they try to put the best face, or "spin," on any event.

News leaks are another issue in news management. When governments do not know what course to follow, they sometimes leak a proposal to the media as a "trial balloon," hoping for guidance from the public reaction received. Ed Black points out that this practice is helpful in the modern, instantaneous world, where politicians usually have little time to respond to problems or give them comprehensive consideration.[17]

The ultimate problem in media–government relations is political interference with the "freedom of the press," one of the sacred principles of democracy, as discussed in Chapter 6. The most blatant examples of such political interference have occurred at the provincial level. In Quebec between 1935 and 1960, Premier Maurice Duplessis kept the press under control by awarding advertising and printing contracts to newspaper owners and financial gifts to members of the press gallery. In Alberta in the 1930s, the Social Credit Party tried to force newspapers to retract any criticisms of the government. Occasional attempts have apparently been made by the Prime Minister's Office over the years to have the CBC take a certain perspective on a vital national issue. The most celebrated case in English Canada was the cancellation in 1966 of the highly popular but critical CBC public affairs program *This Hour Has Seven Days*.[18] The Trudeau government later accused the Radio-Canada network of being riddled with separatists who gave a biased interpretation of federal–provincial relations. Although there was probably some truth to the charge, it smacked of political interference. Short of actual government interference or censorship is the highly secretive tradition of Canadian governments. In 1982, the Access to Information

Act made it somewhat easier for the media as well as other interested parties to obtain access to government information, but the secrecy habit is difficult for politicians and bureaucrats to overcome.

Public Opinion Polls

The phrase **public opinion** sometimes implies that a unanimous, informed view on a particular issue is held by all members of the public. In actuality, many opinions are held on any issue, and each issue interests only a certain segment of the population—that is, each issue has its own public. Furthermore, most political opinions are not well informed. They are often based on little information, they are simplifications of complex issues, and they can even be internally contradictory. Indeed, people often form their opinions first and then look for information to confirm them; at the very least, they "seek out information that conforms to their predispositions ... and avoid or reinterpret any contrary and non-supportive messages."[19] Nevertheless, public opinions about topical issues frequently influence the actions of government.

Measuring Public Opinion

Given this great conglomeration of viewpoints, public opinion is very difficult to gauge. Haphazard methods such as reading editorials or letters to the editor or listening to open-line programs are obviously unreliable, but so are many amateur public opinion surveys. On the other hand, professional polling agencies claim to be able to select a small representative sample of people, ask carefully worded questions, and report with a high degree of accuracy the opinions of the whole population. Such polls have assumed an immense importance in contemporary Canadian politics: "no political party plans campaign strategy without them, no government is prepared to risk major policy initiatives without gauging public opinion, and for major news organizations they are an indispensable reporting tool, both between and during elections."[20]

Beyond the now common procedure for conducting a **public opinion poll**, two special techniques deserve mention. The first is "tracking," which entails telephoning samples of 100 to 500 people nightly during an election campaign in order to see how day-to-day developments are affecting them. The second is the "focus group," in which a small number of people are gathered together behind a one-way mirror with a group leader who encourages them to voice their "gut" reactions to various leaders, issues, and slogans. Their responses are recorded and then analyzed. The importance of polls and focus groups in constructing a party's campaign message and even picking the language to be used to convey that message can hardly be overemphasized.

Who are these professional pollsters? The leading pollsters all do much non-political polling as well, and a number of lobbying firms also do polling as part of their comprehensive consulting work. Professional pollsters include the following:

- Compas Inc.
- EKOS Research Associates
- Environics Research Group
- Ipsos Canada
- Léger Marketing
- POLLARA
- SES Research

Reprinted with permission of *The Globe and Mail*.

How accurate are the polls? The only way a survey's accuracy can really be tested is through a comparison of its results immediately prior to an election with the electoral outcome itself. The immediate pre-election findings of most professional agencies have usually been within the range of accuracy claimed—typically plus or minus 4 percent 19 times out of 20. This is impressive, considering that results can be influenced by the way a question is worded, the optional responses available, the sequence of the questions, the degree to which respondents are telling the truth, the willingness of respondents to participate, the timeframe, and many other variables. In the June 2004 election, however, almost all of the polls underestimated the Liberal vote. Pollsters explained this inaccuracy by claiming that a large shift in voter preference occurred in the last two days of the campaign. The most accurate prediction came from the SES Research poll, as revealed in Table 7.2.

The discrepancies that sometimes occur give rise to a concern that those with ulterior motives can deliberately manipulate polling results by tailoring the sample or the wording of the questions. Moreover, those with significant financial resources can resort to advocacy advertising and then continue polling until the correct "public opinion" is forthcoming.

TABLE 7.2 SES RESEARCH POLL ON FINAL FEDERAL VOTING PREFERENCE VS. ELECTION RESULTS, 2004

	SES Research Prediction (Percentage of Votes)	Election Results (Percentage of Votes)
Liberals	34.2	36.7
Conservatives	30.4	29.6
NDP	19.5	15.7
BQ	12.2	12.4
Green	3.7	4.3

Source: Poll June 24, 2004 and Election Results June 28, 2004. Reproduced with permission of SES Research. www.sesresearch.com.

Impact of Polls on the Public

One of the main issues that arises in the discussion of polls and pollsters is whether their pre-election predictions influence the election results. This question cannot be answered categorically, but it is unlikely that their direct effect is that great. First, most voters do not pay much attention to poll results; second, not everyone believes them; and third, it is not important to everyone to vote for the winning side even if this is clear in advance. While some voters may want to jump on the victorious bandwagon—the **bandwagon effect**—at least a few are likely to switch to the predicted loser—the "underdog effect"—either out of sympathy or to try to prevent an overwhelming victory for the prospective winner.[21]

On the other hand, the polls probably have a significant indirect effect on the election results. The media are just as obsessed with the polls as the politicians are, and survey results may well entice the media to concentrate on those parties and politicians who are in the lead and to ignore those who are trailing. Furthermore, polls have a considerable impact on party morale. A positive poll usually generates greater enthusiasm and effort, better candidates, and larger financial contributions, while a negative poll saps the spirit of leaders, candidates, and foot soldiers alike. In other words, such poll results affect the momentum of the campaign.

Another issue can be addressed more categorically: polls definitely detract from the discussion of real issues in the election campaign.[22] The media are fascinated by polls—primarily because they are good for business—and therefore they usually emphasize the **horse-race effect** of the contest. The media tend to spend more time on who is ahead than on comparative analysis of party platforms, asking leaders to comment on the latest poll results, for example, rather than on how the party would deal with a particular public problem. Now that the media actually hire or own polling firms, survey results are becoming major news items in themselves. Responding to this problem, the CBC announced at the start of the 2004 federal election campaign that it would not conduct any public opinion surveys. But the more remarkable aspect of that campaign was that the final results were considerably at odds with the pollsters' predictions, as already mentioned.

Many political losers have blamed their fate on negative public opinion polls, and some have called for the prohibition of polls during part or all of the campaign. Such bans do exist in many countries. Whatever their faults, however, polls enliven the campaign and increase the information available, and prohibiting their publication in the media would not prevent parties, candidates, and others from conducting their own surveys. The main effect of a publication ban would be to give certain crucial information to those who could afford a survey and to deny it to the general public, a rather undemocratic suggestion.

One of the amendments to the Canada Elections Act made in the wake of the Royal Commission on Electoral Reform was to prohibit, in the final three days of the campaign, the broadcast, publication, or dissemination of public opinion poll results. This restriction was soon challenged by the Thomson and Southam newspaper chains as a violation of freedom of the press, and their objection was upheld by the Supreme Court of Canada. The revised Canada Elections Act of 2000 prohibits the publication of new polling results only on election day itself and requires polling organizations to provide a full account of their methodology.

Impact of Polls on the Authorities

The other main question in the study of public opinion is the relationship between it and the response of the authorities. For nearly 100 years after Confederation, governments had to act in the absence of a reliable survey, but it now sometimes seems that they are reluctant to make any decision until it can be based on a poll. Given that opinion is likely to be considerably divided, however, clear-cut guidance from such polling cannot always be found.

Sometimes, even when public opinion is clearly in favour of a certain course of government action, the authorities will decide to act otherwise. This may be the consequence of the politicians' own convictions, the recommendations of the public service, the pressure from lobbyists and interest groups, or the rigidity of party discipline. Indeed, some hold the view that even in a democracy, politicians are not obliged to follow public opinion; they may also lead it. This is especially true now that we realize how uninformed, superficial, and changeable most public opinions really are. While politicians and bureaucrats may be accused of acting in their own self-interest if they do not follow a clear preference among the public, they may actually be relying on a deeper understanding of the issue, the greater information at their disposal, a more sophisticated analysis of its implications, or a concern for minority rights. For many years, for example, capital punishment was an issue on which public opinion clearly supported one side but on which the authorities repeatedly went their own way. Should Parliament have reinstated capital punishment in response to popular opinion based on a mistaken impression about rising crime rates, a desire for retribution, and a questionable assumption of deterrence? Most political issues are even more complicated than capital punishment, and on most public opinion is much more divided; thus the correlation between public opinion and public policy is not as strong as might be expected.

On the other hand, Claire Hoy reveals just how many public policies over the years were adopted, and how many election dates were set, on the basis of public opinion polls. He also shows how important polls were in the 1988 election campaign. First, the governing Conservatives used publicly funded polls to determine their election platform. Second, the Liberals surveyed public opinion in Quebec to see if a Senate veto of the Free Trade Agreement would detract from their support in that province. Third, the NDP avoided the free trade issue (and left the Liberals to capitalize on it) because party polling indicated that the NDP lacked public credibility on economic issues.[23] Indeed, the NDP used focus groups as early as 1984 to find that the phrase "ordinary Canadians" was preferable to "working Canadians" for use in its slogan.[24] When even the NDP starts to base its slogans and strategies on focus groups and public opinion polls, it is hard to overstate their significance.

It should be added that the incidence of and government reliance on public opinion polls severely undercuts the argument in favour of referendums. Public opinion polls already provide a quick, cheap, frequent, and accurate picture of the public's views, so there is little danger that the government will not know how the population feels about an issue.

SUMMARY

This chapter considered the political significance of the mass media and of public opinion polls. It began with a discussion of the ownership of the various media in Canada, especially newspapers and television, and an analysis of how much the owner of any medium influences its coverage. This question arises in particular because of the tradition of chain ownership in the Canadian newspaper industry and the more recent emergence of cross-media conglomerates or convergence. The chapter then went on to discuss the important agenda-setting function of the media and the relative merits of newspapers and television as sources of political information. In this regard, media analysts heavily favoured newspapers, while television was more popular among the general public. The section on the media ended with an account of the mutually dependent relationship between the media and politicians. The next section, on public opinion polls, emphasized that each political issue has its own public and that a large proportion of public opinions are not well informed. It identified the leading polling firms in Canada and noted the techniques they use in producing their reports. The chapter considered the extent to which public opinion polls influence voting behaviour as well as the policies adopted by governments, concluding that the impact is not as strong as might be expected in either case.

DISCUSSION QUESTIONS

1. Is there something distinctive about media companies that would provide justification for more restrictions on concentrated ownership than in other industries?
2. What are the advantages and disadvantages of obtaining political information from television and newspapers?
3. Should public opinion polls be prohibited at some stage of an election campaign?
4. Should the authorities always do what public opinion polls show a majority wants?

KEY TERMS

Bandwagon effect The notion that if and when they know which party or candidate is going to win the election, voters will move en masse in that direction.

Canadian Broadcasting Corporation (CBC) The large national Crown corporation with radio and television divisions whose mandate is to promote meaningful communication among all parts of the country.

Canadian Radio-television and Telecommunications Commission (CRTC) The regulatory agency established to police the communications industry, including radio, television, telephones, and telecommunications.

Convergence The recent phenomenon in the mass media of companies and technologies merging to create multimedia conglomerates, with ownership of newspaper, television, telephone, satellite, cable, Internet, and magazine businesses.

Horse-race effect The notion that election campaigns have degenerated into a "horse race" where everyone, especially the media, is concerned with which party is ahead, not with how parties would tackle serious public issues.

Mass media Sources of information for the mass public—principally radio, television, and newspapers.

News management A variety of techniques used by politicians and governments to ensure positive media coverage.

Parliamentary press gallery Those members of the media who are registered to sit in the press gallery in the House of Commons and who report on its proceedings or on government in general.

Public opinion The sum total of opinions held by members of the public on any subject.

Public opinion poll A survey conducted to ascertain the opinions of the public on assorted matters.

Spin doctors Party officials and ministerial aides who talk to the media and try to influence media coverage by putting the best face on an event from their party's point of view.

FURTHER READING

Centre for Research and Information on Canada. *CRIC Papers.* http://www.cric.ca/en_html/cric.html.

Frizzell, Alan, et al. *The Canadian General Election of 1997.* Toronto: Dundurn Press, 1997.

Levine, Allan. *Scrum Wars: The Prime Ministers and the Media.* Toronto: Dundurn Press, 1993.

Lorimer, Rowland, and Mike Gasher. *Mass Communications in Canada.* 4th ed. Don Mills: Oxford University Press, 2001.

Miller, John. *Yesterday's News: How Canada's Daily Newspapers Are Failing Us.* Halifax: Fernwood Publishing, 1998.

Nash, Knowlton. *Trivia Pursuit: How Showbiz Values Are Corrupting the News.* Toronto: McClelland and Stewart, 1998.

Nesbitt-Larking, Paul. *Politics, Society, and the Media: Canadian Perspectives.* Peterborough: Broadview Press, 2001.

Taras, David. *Power and Betrayal in the Canadian Media.* Peterborough: Broadview Press, 1999.

Winter, James. *Democracy's Oxygen: How Corporations Control the News.* Montreal: Black Rose, 1997.

Chapter 8

Elections and the Electoral System

Elections are one of the most important features of a democratic political system and usually one of the most exciting. This chapter examines the formal, legal aspects of the electoral system, as well as the party campaign organization at both the national and local levels. It also contains an evaluation of the electoral system and suggestions for reform; a discussion of party and election finance; and an assessment of electoral behaviour and party support.

Chapter Objectives

After you have completed this chapter, you should be able to:

Outline the redistribution process

Understand how the formal election machinery is organized at both national and local levels

Comment on how parties organize their election campaigns at both national and local levels

Understand the concern of political scientists about the relationship between a party's popular vote and the percentage of seats it wins

Enumerate and evaluate the main provisions of the laws on party and election finance, including the problem of third-party advertising

Assess various aspects of Canadian voting behaviour

The Election Organization
Drawing the Electoral Map

Canadian elections are based on single-member electoral districts. Hence, before Canadians go to vote, an electoral map must be established to divide the country into electoral districts or **constituencies**. The term **redistribution** is used to describe this process. It involves two stages: first, deciding how many seats in the House of Commons to allot to each province and territory, and second, drawing constituency boundaries within each province.

The Constitution Act, 1867, requires that the readjustment process be repeated after each decennial census, such as after 2001 and 2011. Given the federal character of Canada with its strong provincial loyalties, the search for a reasonably fair means of distributing seats in the House of Commons among the provinces has been a long and unsatisfactory one. The formula used following the 2001 census and the one that resulted in the current 308 seats in the House of Commons involved the following four steps:

1. Starting with 282 seats, 1 seat is allocated to each of the Northwest Territories, Nunavut, and the Yukon, leaving 279 seats.
2. The total population of the 10 provinces is divided by 279 to obtain the electoral quota or quotient.
3. This electoral quota is divided into the population of each province to obtain the number of seats each is entitled to.
4. Additional seats are then awarded so that each province has as many House of Commons seats as it has senators and as many seats as it had in 1985.

Thus, for the 2004 election, the House of Commons seats were distributed as follows: Ontario, 106; Quebec, 75; British Columbia, 36; Alberta, 28; Manitoba and Saskatchewan, 14 each; Nova Scotia, 11; New Brunswick, 10; Newfoundland and Labrador, 7; Prince Edward Island, 4; Northwest Territories, 1; Nunavut, 1; and Yukon, 1. Because the territories and smaller provinces are overrepresented as a result of points 1 and 4, the four largest provinces actually deserve more seats than they have been given.[1]

The second phase of the redistribution process, drawing constituency boundaries within each province, was historically the prerogative of the politicians. They regularly engaged in the process of "gerrymandering," that is, manipulating constituency boundaries so as to ensure as far as possible the re-election of the members of the government party. A new system was adopted in the Electoral

Boundaries Readjustment Act of 1964, however, so that this task is now performed by nonpartisan commissions. An electoral boundaries commission is appointed for each province, chaired by a judge, with the other two members of each commission appointed by the Speaker of the House of Commons. All commissions draw extensively on the support staff of Elections Canada.

The commissions swing into action as soon as the provincial population figures are available from the census. Theirs is a very delicate task of trying to arrive at a design that will provide constituencies of approximately equal population size throughout the province at the same time as accounting for geographic characteristics or identity and historical patterns (for example, trying not to divide a town into two separate electoral districts). The most difficult problem is in dealing with sparsely populated rural or northern regions at the same time as concentrated urban centres. In recognition of this problem, the commissions are allowed to deviate from the average population figure in any province to a maximum tolerance of plus or minus 25 percent and even to exceed this limit in extraordinary circumstances. Thus, rural and northern constituencies tend to be below the provincial quotient and southern, urban ones somewhat above it. In general, since it takes fewer votes in smaller provinces and in rural parts of all provinces to elect a member of Parliament, such votes are worth more than those in large provinces or in urban areas. Whether out of charity, ignorance, or recognition of the fact that the population is peculiarly distributed, Canadians seem generally unconcerned about this deviation from the principle of representation by population or political equality.

The Official Election Organization

SETTING THE DATE

The prime minister normally has the prerogative to call the election within five years of the previous one. Largely based on the government party's standings in the public opinion polls, the election is typically called about four years after the previous campaign. Going into the fifth year, especially to the five-year limit, is usually a sign that the government expects to be defeated. Public opinion polls can be wrong, of course, or public opinion can change between the calling of the election and the actual voting day, since Canadian party preferences are highly volatile. The apparent advantage for the party in power in choosing the date is therefore not absolute, as several prime ministers and premiers have discovered to their chagrin. Nevertheless, allowing the governing party the discretion to choose the election date gives it an advantage in terms of readiness, the ability to "bribe" the electorate at the last minute with new spending and other initiatives, and the opportunity to use government money for advertising. Several provinces have recently moved to fixed election dates.

The governor general must approve the prime minister's request to **dissolve Parliament** in order to call an election, but this is normally automatic. Only once in Canadian history (1926), in rather peculiar circumstances, did a governor general refuse such a request. The defeat of a government in a nonconfidence vote in the House of Commons is the alternative method of precipitating an election, in which case the prime minister's leeway is limited to choosing the exact date.

ELECTION OFFICIALS

The **chief electoral officer** is responsible for the overall administration of the election and must act with absolute impartiality. On the other hand, the **returning officers**, who organize the election in each of the 308 electoral districts (also called constituencies or ridings), are chosen by the cabinet on a partisan basis. Once appointed, however, they are expected to function in a nonpartisan fashion. The 2000 U.S. presidential election, whose results remain questionable to this day, reinforced the wisdom of having Canadian federal elections run on a uniform basis by Elections Canada.

THE VOTERS LIST

In Canadian federal elections, the voters list used to be compiled from scratch by means of a door-to-door enumeration after the election writ was issued. Reforms introduced in 1996 provided for a permanent National Register of Electors, the base of which was compiled in one last door-to-door enumeration in April 1997. Ever since, it has been automatically updated from such sources as income tax returns and files on citizenship and immigration, driver's licences, and vital statistics. Although such a permanent voters list is considered less reliable than a door-to-door enumeration, it made it possible to reduce the length of the election period to 36 days. Homeless people were allowed to vote in federal elections for the first time in 2000.

NOMINATION

Most candidates are nominated by a political party, but they must submit formal **nomination** papers endorsed by 100 people on the local voters list accompanied by a $1000 deposit. Candidates are now reimbursed for the full $1000 upon filing their financial statement after the campaign. Official candidates of registered parties must obtain the party leader's endorsement in order to use the party name on the ballot. This requirement was adopted mainly to make it easier for voters to identify candidates with their party, but it effectively gives the leader a veto over nominations. There is no longer a minimum number of candidates that a party must run in order to have the party label placed under the candidates' name.

ELECTION DAY

After nomination day, the returning officer arranges for the ballots to be printed and allows people to vote in advance polls or by special ballot. Recent reforms have made voting much more convenient for those not expecting to be at home on election day, including those living or travelling outside the country. The returning officer also hires and trains deputy returning officers and poll clerks to look after each polling station on election day and finds appropriate polling station locations.

Canadian federal elections are held on Mondays, and the polls used to be open from 9 a.m. to 8 p.m. local time. Because voters in the Western part of the country complained that the winner was often decided even before their votes had been counted, a system of staggered hours for different time zones was introduced in 1997. This means that the polls close at approximately the same time all across the country, and ballots can be counted and the results announced more or less simultaneously. Until the 2004 election, there was a media blackout on reporting official results from eastern parts of the country in provinces where the polls were still open, but a B.C. court decision ruled this invalid. Voters are entitled to three consecutive hours off work in which to cast their ballot, and the sale of liquor is no longer prohibited during polling hours.

Voters mark their X in private with a pencil on the ballots provided, and when the polls close, the deputy returning officer and poll clerk count them by hand, usually in the company of scrutineers from the various candidates who are allowed to challenge unorthodox markings on ballots and generally keep the whole process honest. Results are announced an hour or two after the polls close, and the candidate with the most votes—the first past the post—is declared elected. The winner usually does not actually have a majority of the votes cast, only a plurality. If the difference between the first and second candidate in any electoral district is less than 1/1000 of all votes cast, an automatic recount is held.

THE BALLOT

The secret ballot was introduced in federal elections in 1874. The candidates are listed in alphabetical order, and since 1970 the ballot has contained their party affiliation, if any. The chief electoral officer keeps a registry of political parties, and following a recent decision by the Supreme Court of Canada, a party that runs even a single candidate can place its label on the ballot. Such parties must also register their national and constituency official agents and auditors for the purposes of keeping track of the party's and

A sample ballot. (Canada Elections Act, 2000, c. 9, Schedule 1. Reproduced with the permission of Elections Canada)

candidates' finances. Twelve parties were registered for the 1988 election, 14 for 1993, 10 for 1997, 11 for 2000, and 12 for 2004.

THE FRANCHISE

The extension of the franchise (the right to vote) beyond males with substantial property was mentioned in earlier chapters. This process was complicated by the use of different provincial franchises in federal elections between 1867 and 1917. Moreover, the franchise was manipulated in 1917 so as to maximize support for the incumbent government. The vote was extended to women serving in the war as well as to female relatives of men overseas, but it was denied to Canadian citizens who had come from "enemy alien" countries. In 1918, all women were granted the federal vote, and since 1920 a uniform federal franchise has existed. Even so, until all such restrictions were removed by 1948, most Canadians of Asian ancestry (especially those from Japan, China, and India) were denied the right to vote in federal elections because the federal law disqualified anyone who for reasons of race was denied the vote under provincial electoral statutes. The vote was extended to Inuit people in 1953 and to status Indians in 1960. The voting age was reduced from 21 to 18 in 1970, and British subjects who were not Canadian citizens lost their vote in 1975.

　　By that time, the Canada Elections Act mainly disqualified returning officers (except in the case of a tie), federally appointed judges, prison inmates, those deprived of their liberty by reason of mental disease, and those convicted of corrupt or illegal electoral practices. In the course of the 1988 campaign, however, three of these disqualifications were challenged in the courts in terms of the Canadian Charter of Rights and Freedoms, which guarantees the vote to every Canadian citizen. In the case of judges and those in mental institutions, the provisions of the act were declared unconstitutional and the disqualifications were removed. The courts made a number of contradictory decisions on whether prison inmates should be able to vote, and another recent Supreme Court decision finally resolved the issue: at least in federal elections, all inmates have a right to vote. The Canada Elections Act of 2000 gave returning officers a vote, and in case of a tie, a **by-election** would be held in the constituency. By-elections are otherwise necessitated by the resignation or death of an MP between elections.

The National Party Campaign

At the national level, political parties usually set up a campaign committee about two years before they expect the election to be called. They start to think about strategy, policy, image, and budget, as party headquarters conduct public opinion polls to see how the voters perceive the various leaders, parties, and issues.[2] For the party in power, such polls are central to deciding when to call the election in the first place, and for all major parties, polls serve to guide general strategy, media advertising, and the selection of priority ridings once the campaign begins.

Another national activity that begins before the calling of the election is the search for good candidates. While party headquarters rarely impose a candidate on an unwilling constituency association, they may try to guide the local decision or even parachute a few "star" candidates into safe seats. Parties usually run a full slate of candidates, so where local organizations are weak, the national level of the party sometimes has to take the initiative to find a candidate for them. In order to ensure a minimum number of candidates of cabinet calibre, especially women, and to avoid nominations falling into the wrong hands, Jean Chrétien had the party give him the power to appoint candidates in certain cases. Paul Martin also used this power in 2004 but upset many local partisans in the process.

The NDP once hoped to achieve gender parity in its candidates, but it was later content with nearly 50 percent being either women or visible minorities. Meanwhile, because of the Reform Party's tendency to attract a certain number of extremists, that party made prospective candidates complete a form detailing their background, a practice continued by the Canadian Alliance. If an "undesirable" person still managed to get nominated, the party leadership could expel a candidate, as it did in one case of an alleged racist in 1993.

Party headquarters organize training sessions for campaign managers and candidates (right down to personal deportment) and produce mounds of election material for local candidates. One of the Liberals' great assets in the 1993 campaign was their election platform, commonly called the "Red Book." It provided a tremendous prop for a leader who was otherwise not overly policy oriented in his public appearances.[3] "Red Book II," used in 1997, was less effective, and "Red Book III," in 2000, even less so.

The Leader's Tour and Its Media Coverage

Once the campaign begins, party headquarters organize each leader's tour, prepare the party's national media campaign, and gear up for the televised leaders' debate. Each party leader crisscrosses the country over the campaign period in an effort both to give a boost to promising local candidates and to generate daily stories for

Jack Layton, federal NDP leader, arrives in Sudbury during the 2004 election campaign. (CP Photo/Andrew Vaughan)

the national media. Such "free" coverage is eagerly sought, and parties spare no trouble or expense to obtain it.

The leader is accompanied by a horde of strategists and support staff, as well as by reporters who pay to travel aboard the party-chartered plane or bus. In general, national television newscasts contain one item per leader per day and have usually provided almost equal time to the main parties.

National Media Advertising

Each party also buys media advertising during (and sometimes immediately before) the campaign, and most parties spend huge amounts of money on the production of television commercials alone. The purchase of broadcast time is regulated by the Elections Act, requiring each broadcaster to make available, for purchase by registered political parties, six and a half hours of prime time during the campaign. The broadcasting arbitrator allocates time among the parties based primarily on the number of seats held in the House of Commons and on the popular vote received in the previous election. As a result of a Reform Party court challenge, parties can now purchase more than these allotments, subject to their overall expense ceiling, so that the significance of the allocation of time has diminished. In addition to purchasable time, parties are awarded free radio and television time in the same proportions.

The Leaders' Debate

The other main aspect of the national campaign is the televised leaders' debate. The debates have become crucial aspects of the campaign because of the combined importance of leaders and television. Separate debates are held in English and French, putting a premium on a party leader's bilingual capacity.

The debates are not mentioned in the law, so the consortium of television stations that carry them essentially sets the rules. The debates have to fit into the television networks' schedule and are held when least advertising revenue would be lost. In 1993, with a large number of parties in the race, the consortium agreed that only five parties would take part—that is, those represented in Parliament and those that have had a consistent impact in public debates and public opinion. Mel Hurtig, leader of the new National Party of Canada, went to court to try to force his way into the debate but did not succeed. The leaders of the same five parties participated in 1997 and 2000; in 2004, the leader of the Green Party was excluded under protest.

The frontrunner in the campaign basically tries to avoid a knockout punch, while the other party leaders attempt to score one. After the debate, each party sends forth its **spin doctors** to persuade reporters that its leader won, but whether the public makes up its own mind on the winner or awaits the verdict of media commentators is not certain. About two-thirds of the electorate watched at least one debate in both 1984 and 1988, and nearly 60 percent did so in 1993.[4] Although 45 percent of respondents told a *Maclean's* poll that the 1988 debate had helped them decide how to vote,[5] mostly to the advantage of the Liberals, much of this advantage had worn off by election day. The Conservatives had strategically insisted on having the debate early in the campaign in case they needed time to recover from just such an inferior performance. The 1997 and 2000 debates were of little significance in the overall result; in 2004, the French debate was more important than the English debate, as Bloc leader Gilles Duceppe consolidated his hold on francophone Quebeckers.

Conservative leader Stephen Harper, Liberal leader Paul Martin, NDP leader Jack Layton, and Bloc Québécois leader Gilles Duceppe (left to right) pose for a photograph before the start of the English version of the leaders' debate in June 2004. (CP Photo/Tom Hanson)

The Local Candidate Campaign

Nomination

At the local level, each party's first priority is to nominate its candidate. Holding the nomination meeting even before the election is called allows many preparations to be made ahead of time, so the campaign can get off to a strong and early start.

The Local Campaign

Once the nomination has taken place, each party sets up a campaign committee under a campaign manager (see Figure 8.1). The official agent is responsible for ensuring that the candidate complies with the Canada Elections Act. In most campaigns, the other key official is the canvass organizer, who organizes the door-to-door "foot canvass" to distribute literature and/or a telephone canvass. Whether canvassers contact voters on the doorstep or on the phone, the object is both to spread the party's message and to seek out its own supporters. Armed with a voters list, canvassers put a positive, negative, or "undecided" mark beside the name of all voters contacted. To cover an entire constituency in this fashion requires a veritable army of volunteers and an elaborate organization. If money is more plentiful than volunteers, the local campaign may rely instead on media advertising. In recent elections, some parties in targeted constituencies engaged in local polling and computer-assisted mail and telephone campaigning directed

Figure 8.1   Structure of a Typical Local Campaign Committee

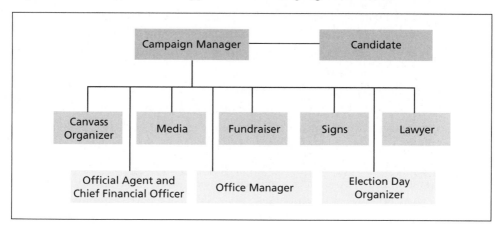

to members of key groups. In the past, much of this work was voluntary, but since the opportunity to use "volunteers" paid by a business or union has now been seriously reduced, parties increasingly engage paid staff. The local campaign is a complex operation requiring ever more sophistication, staffing, and funding.

All this activity culminates on election day, when the organization tries to have a party scrutineer placed in each of the polls. Ideally, an inside scrutineer keeps track of which people on the list have cast their ballot, while an outside scrutineer periodically collects this information and heads out to round up all those previously identified as party supporters.

Evaluating the Electoral System

In each constituency, the candidate with the most votes wins, even if this is less than 50 percent. Among the advantages of this **first-past-the-post system** are its simplicity, its quick calculation of results, and its provision for each constituency of a clear-cut representative. When all the local results are cumulated nationally, however, the proportion of seats a party wins does not necessarily bear much relationship to its overall share of the total **popular vote**. Take as an extreme, hypothetical example a two-person race in each constituency in which the Liberal candidate beat the Conservative candidate by one vote in every case. The Liberal Party would then win 100 percent of the seats from just over 50 percent of the vote, and the Conservative Party would have 0 percent of the seats from just under 50 percent of the vote. In fact, this example is not so hypothetical: in the New Brunswick election of 1987, the Liberals won 100 percent of the seats with about 60 percent of the popular vote. Many political scientists and other observers are therefore concerned that such overall disparities can occur between percentage of seats won and percentage of popular vote, advocating a more proportional system.

Overall, in 25 elections starting in 1921, the party with the largest popular vote won more seats than it deserved on 24 occasions. The system also favoured third parties with concentrated regional support (Social Credit, Reform/Alliance, and the BQ), but those with broad national support usually lost out—the CCF (Co-operative Commonwealth Federation) and the NDP, for example, regularly received only about half as many seats as their popular vote merited.

Some observers tolerate these disparities because the first-past-the-post electoral system usually produces a **majority government**—the leading party obtaining more than 50 percent of the seats—even though a party rarely wins over 50 percent of the popular vote. Table 8.1 indicates that on 3 occasions (1940, 1958, and

TABLE 8.1 COMPARISON OF PERCENTAGE OF POPULAR VOTE AND PERCENTAGE OF SEATS
WON BY PARTY IN FEDERAL ELECTIONS, 1921–2004

| | Liberal | | Conservative | | CCF/NDP | |
	% Vote	% Seats	% Vote	% Seats	% Vote	% Seats
1921	41	49	30	21	—	—
1925	40	40	46	47	—	—
1926	46	52	45	37	—	—
1930	45	37	49	56	—	—
1935	45	71	30	16	9	3
1940	52	74	31	16	9	3
1945	41	51	27	27	16	11
1949	49	74	30	16	13	5
1953	49	64	31	19	11	9
1957	41	40	39	42	11	9
1958	34	18	54	79	10	3
1962	37	38	37	44	14	7
1963	42	49	33	36	13	6
1965	40	49	33	36	18	8
1968	45	58	31	27	17	8
1972	38	41	35	40	18	12
1974	43	53	36	36	16	6
1979	40	40	36	48	18	9
1980	44	52	33	37	20	11
1984	28	14	50	75	19	11
1988	32	28	43	57	20	15

		Liberal	PC	NDP	Ref/All	BQ
1993	% Vote	41.3	16.0	6.9	18.7	13.5
	% Seats	60.0	0.7	3.1	17.6	18.3
1997	% Vote	38.4	18.9	11.1	19.4	10.7
	% Seats	51.4	6.6	7.0	19.9	14.6
2000	% Vote	40.8	12.2	8.5	25.5	10.7
	% Seats	57.1	4.0	4.3	21.9	12.6

		Liberal	Conservative	NDP	BQ
2004	% Vote	36.7	29.6	15.7	12.4
	% Seats	43.8	32.1	6.2	17.5

Source: Data compiled and used to create the above chart was taken from the website of Elections Canada: http://www.
elections.ca (Retrieved 15 Aug. 2004). It is used with the permission of the Chief Electoral Officer but extrapolation and analysis
rest with the author.

1984) the winning party obtained at least 50 percent of the vote, and this auto-matically produced a majority government. On 13 other occasions out of 25, this electoral system manufactured a majority government in terms of seats, even though the leading party did not win a majority of the vote. This left 9 occasions when a **minority government** resulted, including the 2004 election. While applauding the system for its tendency to produce majority governments, how-ever, we should note that it weakens the opposition. Moreover, on three occasions (1957, 1962, and 1979) the party with the second-largest popular vote ended up with more seats than the party that came first and therefore went on to form the government.

It is worth noting that if parties had received as many seats as their popular vote justified in 1993, the PCs and NDP would have been recognized as official parties in the House of Commons, and the Reform Party, instead of the Bloc Québécois, would have been the official opposition. The 1997 and 2000 elections rectified the situation but continued to underrepresent the PCs and NDP. In 1997, for example, the PCs and Reform were virtually tied in votes, but they were awarded 20 and 60 seats respectively. In 2000, if seats were awarded in proportion to votes, the Liberals would have won about 50 fewer seats; the Bloc, about 5 less; the Alliance, at least 10 more; the NDP, twice as many; and the PCs, three times as many. In 2004, the Liberals, Conservatives, and Bloc were all overrepresented, while the NDP and Greens did not get the representation they deserved.

Another set of disparities between popular vote and seat figures exists on a province-by-province basis. What is particularly striking is the disparity between the Conservative vote and seats in Quebec (1896–1984) and that between the Liberal vote and seats in Western Canada (since 1957). Table 8.2 provides the fig-ures for the 2004 election, and Figure 8.2 (page 190) shows the 2004 election results in graphic form.

Alan Cairns observed that such disparities affect parties in three principal ways: image, strategy, and policy.[6] When the Conservatives had virtually no mem-bers from Quebec prior to 1984, they gained an anti-French image, even though they usually obtained at least 13 percent of the popular vote in that province. Similarly, after 1957, the Liberals acquired the image of an anti-Western party because they rarely elected members west of Ontario, even though they normally received over 20 percent of the Western vote.

As far as strategy is concerned, when Conservatives despaired of electing members from Quebec and felt they could form a government without much rep-resentation from that province, they ignored it. The Liberals often similarly felt

TABLE 8.2 COMPARISON OF SEATS, PERCENTAGE OF SEATS, AND VOTES WON BY PARTY BY PROVINCE, 2004 FEDERAL ELECTION

	Liberals			Conservatives			NDP			BQ		
	Seats	%S	%V	Seats	%S	%V	Seats	%S	%V	Seats	%S	%V
Nfld.	5	71.4	48.0	2	28.6	32.3	–	–	17.5	–	–	–
P.E.I.	4	100.0	52.5	–	–	30.7	–	–	12.5	–	–	–
N.S.	6	54.6	39.7	3	27.3	28.0	2	18.2	28.4	–	–	–
N.B.	7	70.0	44.6	2	20.0	31.1	1	10.0	20.6	–	–	–
Quebec	21	28.0	33.9	–	–	8.8	–	–	4.6	54	72.0	48.9
Ontario	75	70.8	44.7	24	22.6	31.5	7	6.6	18.1	–	–	–
Man.	3	21.4	33.2	7	50.0	39.1	4	28.6	23.5	–	–	–
Sask.	1	7.1	27.2	13	92.9	41.8	–	–	23.4	–	–	–
Alta.	2	7.1	22.0	26	92.9	61.7	–	–	9.5	–	–	–
B.C.	8	22.2	28.6	22	61.1	36.3	5	13.9	26.6	–	–	–
Nunavut	1	100.0	51.3	–	–	14.4	–	–	15.2	–	–	–
N.W.T.	1	100.0	39.4	–	–	17.2	–	–	39.1	–	–	–
Yukon	1	100.0	45.7	–	–	20.9	–	–	25.7	–	–	–
Total	135	43.8	36.7	99	32.1	29.6	19	6.2	15.7	54	17.5	12.4

Source: Data compiled and used to create the above chart was taken from the website of Elections Canada: http://www.elections.ca (Retrieved 15 Aug. 2004). It is used with the permission of the Chief Electoral Officer but extrapolation and analysis rest with the author.

that campaigning in the West was a waste of time and money and concentrated their effort elsewhere. In the 2000 election campaign, for example, Jean Chrétien did not bother to make a single campaign stop in Calgary. These strategies are not good for keeping the country together, one of the functions that political parties and elections are supposed to perform.

Finally, since the elected members of the party have a major role to play in the development of party policy, Conservative policy did not reflect the concerns of French Canada when the party lacked francophone and Quebec MPs, just as Liberal policy tended to ignore Western concerns. This is especially serious for the party that forms the government, for it has few or no MPs from a province or region to put into the cabinet. Because of such regionalized party standings between 1962 and 1984, either Quebec or the West was effectively left out of national decisionmaking at the cabinet level. Residents of those neglected regions understandably felt that national policy did not reflect their interests and turned

Figure 8.2   **Seats Won by Party by Province, 2004**

to provincial governments to defend these interests or started to think in separatist terms.

In 2000, the Liberals succeeded in electing at least two MPs from each province—enough to ensure minimal cabinet representation. Even so, they received more votes but fewer seats than the Bloc in Quebec; the Alliance had only two seats to show for its 24 percent of the vote in Ontario; and the Liberals gained 25 percent of the vote in the West but were rewarded with only 14 of 88 seats.

Since Cairns first brought these problems to scholarly attention, reform of the electoral system has been frequently discussed. Many observers would like to overcome the lack of representation of important segments of opinion in party caucuses and the cabinet, as well as to avoid the sense of regional–ethnic alienation that stems from this situation. A full-scale system of proportional representation is probably too extreme a reform in the circumstances, but a hybrid scheme combining constituency MPs with "supplementary MPs" based on popular vote has much merit.

Several authorities have suggested the addition of 50 or 60 supplementary MPs, who would overcome the worst problems of the existing system but still make majority government possible. This system would start with the regularly elected constituency MPs who are necessary to ensure the representation of all parts of Canada. But the supplementary MPs would be added, to be distributed on the basis of popular vote by party by province. They would correct the greatest discrepancies between the proportion of seats and votes. For the party in power, such supplementary MPs could provide provincial representation in the cabinet.[7] They might also be used to correct gender or minority imbalances. The results of the 2004 election encouraged further consideration of some form of proportionality.

Financing Elections

Parties and Candidates

Prior to 1974, Canada had virtually no laws with respect to party and election finance. The Liberal and Conservative parties relied almost completely on contributions from big business at the national level, which usually produced a surplus to be distributed to candidates' campaigns as well. Candidates were otherwise dependent on donations from local small firms. Both parties had fundraisers or "bagmen"—often senators who could exploit their corporate connections and make use of their abundant spare time—assisted by corporate volunteers. Business also made contributions in kind, such as skilled personnel. The CCF/NDP depended primarily on individual membership fees supplemented by union contributions, but in this case the flow of funds was reversed: the local candidates had to help finance the central campaign. Overall, the Liberals and Conservatives raised and spent far more than the CCF/NDP, both at the national and local levels.

The secrecy surrounding party and election finance before 1974 makes it difficult to know exactly how many irregularities and scandals actually took place, but they were probably numerous. Small-scale scandals in the 1960s, together with increasing public expectations of political morality, caused the Pearson government to appoint a commission on the subject of party and election finance in 1964. Opposition pressure in the minority government period of 1972–74 finally forced the reforms that commission recommended. Amendments to the Canada Elections Act were passed in 1974 but did not take effect until the election of 1979. The legislation had six basic provisions, some of which have been adjusted since:

- Ceiling on candidate spending
- Ceiling on party spending
- Disclosure of the identity of contributors
- Tax credit for contributions
- Public subsidy for serious candidates
- Public subsidy for major parties

While no limit was placed on the size of contributions, a ceiling was imposed on how much a national party could spend; a ceiling was also placed on each candidate's expenditures. A disclosure provision required that the names of those contributing over a certain amount be filed with the chief electoral officer and that such records be open to public inspection. A tax credit provision gave contributors an income tax credit for contributions, and candidates who received at least 15 percent of the vote had roughly 50 percent of their expenses subsidized by the public purse. Finally, parties that won at least 2 percent of the popular vote were subsidized for 22.5 percent of their total national expenditures.

The objectives of the legislation were thus to increase the fairness, openness, and participatory nature of the electoral system. Fairness was enhanced by limiting national party and candidate spending, as well as by the public subsidy provision; the disclosure clause made it difficult for large secret contributions to be made in return for some favourable government decision, policy, or grant; and the tax credit encouraged individual contributions, reducing Liberal and Conservative dependence on corporations. For all the difficulties and loopholes remaining in the act, it produced a more honest, equitable, and participatory system of election finance. Table 8.3 shows the total amount spent by the local and national campaigns of the major parties in the 2000 election.

The results were fairer than they would have been in the absence of such legislation, but the disparities continued to concern many observers. Data from the 2000 election showed that the Liberals received $12 million from corporations of their total intake of $20 million, and the Canadian Alliance had $7 million from corporations of a $19 million total. Those two parties vastly outspent the others, and this heavy reliance on the corporate sector gave rise to many suspicions about what those corporations expected from government in return. In fact, the Gomery Inquiry into the sponsorship scandal revealed a significant amount of corruption

TABLE 8.3 TOTAL ELECTION EXPENSES OF FIVE MAIN PARTIES, 2000 ELECTION (DOLLARS)

	Candidates	National	Total
Liberal	14 633 510	12 525 174	27 158 684
Alliance	9 514 889	9 669 648	19 184 537
NDP	3 954 481	6 334 585	10 289 066
PC	4 572 457	3 983 301	8 555 758
Bloc	4 254 434	1 968 693	6 223 127

Source: Data compiled and used to create the above chart was taken from the website of Elections Canada: http://www. elections.ca (Retrieved 15 Sept. 2004). It is used with the permission of the Chief Electoral Officer but extrapolation and analysis rest with the author. "Election Expenses and Reimbursements," http://www.elections.ca/content.asp?section=fin& document=table&dir=rem&lang=e&textonly=false.

in Liberal party finance in Quebec. Since taxpayers ultimately pay for much of these party expenditures via tax credits and tax rebates, an argument could be made that government financing of the whole campaign would not cost the public purse much more than it already did and would eliminate the suspicions of sleaze. Alternatively, contributions could be limited to individuals, as is the case in provincial elections in Quebec and Manitoba.

The Chrétien government ran into an abundance of ethical problems in its third term, and as part of a package to clean up the way political parties and government operate, a new regime for election finance came into effect in January 2004. The following are its main features, divided into three areas: elections, leadership contests, and nomination meetings.

ELECTIONS

- Individuals are limited to an annual contribution of $5000 to a party or its candidates.
- Corporations and trade unions are limited to an annual contribution of $1000 to a constituency association or a party's candidates but are prohibited from donating to national political parties.
- Individual contributions are eligible for a 75 percent tax credit for contributions up to $400, with the percentage declining thereafter.
- A candidate who receives at least 10 percent of the votes (down from 15 percent) is eligible to be reimbursed for 60 percent (up from 50 percent) of his or her election expenses.

- National parties that receive at least 2 percent of the national vote (or 5 percent in the constituencies they contest) are eligible for an annual public subsidy of $1.75 per vote received in the previous election.
- National parties also were eligible to be reimbursed for 60 percent of their election expenses in 2004 and 50 percent thereafter (up from 22.5 percent).

LEADERSHIP CONTESTS

- Individual contributions are limited to $5000.
- Corporate and trade union contributions are prohibited.
- Contributions and expenditures must be disclosed.

NOMINATION MEETINGS

- Contributions and expenditures must be disclosed.
- Expenditures are limited.

Third-Party Advertising

Another major problem in the realm of election finance is **third-party advertising**. Legislation in 1983 prohibited all advocacy-group spending during an election campaign that was not channelled through a party or candidate campaign. It was argued by sponsors of the legislation that the only way party and candidate spending ceilings could be effective was if any spending on their behalf was included in the parties' budgets. But more and more groups began to advertise on their own, for or against various parties or candidates. While such advertising was clearly a violation of the spirit of the law as well as its specific terms, the National Citizens Coalition (NCC) challenged these sections of the legislation in the Alberta courts. The courts ruled the clauses unconstitutional as a violation of the freedom-of-expression provisions of the Charter of Rights and Freedoms.

Third-party advertising increased enormously in the 1988 election campaign, especially in the case of the pro–free trade group, the Canadian Alliance for Trade and Job Opportunities. With only the Conservative Party in favour of free trade, any advertising that promoted the Free Trade Agreement also promoted the Conservative Party. Thus the Conservatives benefited from some $5 million in advertising by advocacy groups on top of its own national budget of nearly $8 million. Such third-party advertising made a mockery of party spending ceilings and is widely thought to have helped the Conservatives achieve re-election by turning the momentum of the campaign back in their favour.

In response to widespread public criticism of this problem and to address other electoral issues, the Mulroney government appointed a Royal Commission on Electoral Reform and Party Financing shortly after the 1988 election. On this issue, the commission recommended that spending by individuals or organizations other than candidates and political parties be restricted to $1000 during the election period. The commission argued that given the significance of the issue, to limit paid advertising of such advocacy groups during 36 days every four years was a "reasonable limit" on freedom of expression and would stand up to judicial scrutiny.

The law was so amended just prior to the 1993 election, but it was successfully challenged by the NCC again. The amendments of 2000, however, allowed third parties to spend up to $150 000, of which no more than $3000 could be spent in each electoral district on advertising for or against candidates. The Supreme Court of Canada finally upheld this version of the law in 2004.[8]

Electoral Behaviour and Party Support

Given the fact that the Liberals were so regularly victorious in Canadian federal elections between 1935 and 1984 and again after 1993, it is tempting to believe that a large proportion of voters have a strong identification with that party and that any result other than a Liberal triumph is unlikely. Research in psephology—the study of voting behaviour—shows, however, that a great many voters—roughly 50 percent—have no enduring **party identification**. In most other Western democracies, the degree of voter identification with a specific party is much higher, and the flexibility of the Canadian electorate demands explanation. Jon Pammett accounts for this phenomenon as follows:

> *The most basic [factor] is that Canadian political culture is relatively apolitical. While Canadians are moderately interested in politics, this interest does not translate for most into substantial political involvement. The amount of detailed political information possessed by the average Canadian is low. Studies of children's political learning, or socialization, show a relatively weak transference of preference for a political party from parent to child ... because these feelings may not be strongly or persistently held in the adult "socializer."[9]*

Underlying such party identification as does exist are certain sociodemographic characteristics and basic ideological orientations. The former include such factors as region, religion, ethnic background, gender, and class, which relate to the cleavages discussed in Chapters 2, 3, and 4. First, there are wide variations in regional support for different parties. In Quebec, only the Bloc Québécois and the Liberals are serious factors; the new Conservative Party is heavily concentrated in Western Canada; the Liberals are strong in the Atlantic region; and the NDP has pockets of strength throughout English-language Canada. There is also an urban–rural divide in terms of party preference.

Somewhat surprisingly, a second marked pattern in Canadian voting behaviour has been religion. Roman Catholics have been strongly inclined to vote Liberal, whether they were French, English, or of other ethnic background, and regardless of where they lived in the country. Ethnicity has been a third significant factor in Canadian electoral behaviour. The French-Canadian preference for the Liberal Party is well known and exists outside as well as within Quebec. Among those of non-British and non-French origins, the Liberals also did best, especially among post–Second World War immigrants (largely of Mediterranean and Indian subcontinental origins), who apparently reacted with gratitude to the fact that the Liberal Party was in office when they arrived. Gender now seems to be more important than in the past, with women generally being more left-leaning than men.

In terms of class, the expectation would be that upper-class citizens would vote Conservative, the middle class would support the Liberals, and the working and poorer classes would vote NDP. In most Western democracies, such a pattern is quite significant, but it is not borne out well in Canada.[10] The Liberal Party has usually attracted nearly the same degree of support from all classes except farmers. Only a small proportion of the working class actually votes for working-class parties. The NDP, for example, normally gets relatively more support from skilled and unskilled labour than from other groups, but not as much as does each of the other parties. The low level of **class consciousness** and class-based voting in Canada is quite striking, and many explanations have been offered.[11]

Although there is a low level of class voting, ideology is quite important in Canadian electoral behaviour. At least outside Quebec, there is something of a traditional ideological division between left and right that relates to faith in the free market system as opposed to the desirability of government intervention. Those adhering to market forces tend to vote for the Conservatives, while those more inclined to government intervention choose the Liberals or the NDP.[12]

The voting decision is an extremely complex and subtle one and is not easily explained. Beyond sociodemographic characteristics, ideology, and party identification come such short-term considerations as perception of economic prosperity, opinions on issues, and evaluations of the government's performance and of the respective leaders. For those without a strong party identification, it is usually the leaders and issues that are most important; the local candidate is not normally a crucial factor. Voters often say that they were moved by the issues in their voting decision, but many have trouble identifying the issues that supposedly influenced them. The relative importance of issues and leaders also varies from one election to another. Such flexibility means that over half of the electorate makes up its mind during the course of the campaign and that elections remain highly unpredictable.

These revelations also cast doubt on the question of whether elections provide a policy **mandate** for the successful party.[13] First, Canadian parties rarely present a comprehensive election platform in the campaign. Next, victorious

Reprinted with permission from *The Globe and Mail*.

parties do not seem to feel bound by the specific policies that they proposed. In the third place, the limited extent to which issues play a part in the campaign seriously detracts from the claim of any government that it has a mandate to pursue a particular policy. Finally, even on the rare occasion that a single issue figures prominently, the winning party almost never obtains a majority of the total votes cast, and certainly not a majority in all regions of the country. The free trade issue in 1988 provided the closest thing to a policy mandate for any Canadian government in recent times, yet the Conservatives received only 43 percent of the overall popular vote and less than 40 percent in six provinces and territories. The Liberals made much of their "Red Book" during the 1993 campaign, but even though a large part of it was unfulfilled, the electorate returned them to office in 1997.

As for the 2004 election, the Liberals would probably have won a majority had it not been for the sponsorship scandal, which angered people both inside and outside Quebec.[14] Even though it happened on Jean Chrétien's watch, many voters thought Paul Martin knew or should have known about it and, in any case, did not handle it well.

Early analysis of the campaign indicated that despite efforts to be more moderate than the Canadian Alliance, Stephen Harper and his new Conservative Party were still seen by many voters as too extreme. The Liberals ran television commercials to exactly this effect (often called "attack ads"), which helped to reinforce this perception. Jack Layton's NDP achieved levels twice as high as in 2000, but he was abandoned by many of his new supporters at the end of the campaign. Some of them were seduced by the Liberal call to vote strategically—for Liberals instead of the NDP—in order to keep the Conservatives out.

The last-minute upsurge in Liberal support appears to have come from those who were undecided until the last 48 hours, as well as those who left both the Conservatives and NDP as decision time arrived. Many were traditional Liberals who overcame their anger at the sponsorship scandal at the last minute.

There were essentially two parallel campaigns. In Quebec, it was Liberals and the Bloc. Voters in that province were upset at the Liberal sponsorship scandal and certain provincial Liberal government policies, but nationalists and separatists were also very impressed with the performance of Bloc leader, Gilles Duceppe. In the rest of Canada, it was a two- or three-party contest. None of the leaders stood out, so most voters were guided by values and issues, such as same-sex marriage, gun control, and social programs. The Liberals tried to differentiate themselves on health care, but in fact the Conservatives and NDP also stressed this issue. Some people in Ontario probably voted against the federal Liberals because of recent actions taken by the provincial Liberal government in that province.

SUMMARY

This chapter discussed elections and the Canadian electoral system. It began by outlining how the electoral map is redrawn every 10 years in what is called the redistribution process. It then set out the operation of the formal election machinery, including the voters list, the ballot, and the franchise, and recent changes thereto. The next two sections dealt with the national party campaign—including the leader's tour, media advertising, and the leaders' debate—and the local candidate campaign—including the nomination process and the effort to get the candidate elected. The chapter then switched focus to analyze the advantages and disadvantages of the first-past-the-post electoral system, noting in particular the unfairness of the system in awarding seats to political parties in relation to their share of the popular vote. It also proposed that an element of proportionality be added to the system. The next part examined how elections are financed and outlined the many recent changes to electoral financing legislation. Changes regarding third-party advertising were also noted. Finally, the chapter discussed what we know about Canadians' voting behaviour, including the concept of party identification and the effects of sociodemographic characteristics and ideological factors. The limited extent to which issues figure in the campaign cast doubts on the concept of a mandate for the victorious party.

DISCUSSION QUESTIONS

1. Should Canada adopt fixed election dates? Are there any other aspects of the formal electoral organization that should be changed?
2. Is the current Canadian first-past-the-post electoral system fair to parties and conducive to national unity? If not, what changes could be made to improve it?
3. Are the recent changes to laws governing party and election finance completely satisfactory? If not, what should be changed?
4. What could be done to give more emphasis to the substance of each party's campaign (i.e., its platform) and less to its presentation (personality, image, and advertising)?

KEY TERMS

By-election An election held between general elections in a specific electoral district due to the death or resignation of the MP or a tie on election night.

Chief electoral officer The independent and impartial official who is in charge of the operation of the whole electoral system.

Class consciousness An awareness of the social class to which one belongs.

Constituency An electoral district that sends one member to the House of Commons.

Dissolution of Parliament The ending of a Parliament, usually after four or more years, by calling an election, an act normally in the hands of the prime minister but one that formally requires the approval of the governor general.

First-past-the-post system The kind of single-member electoral system used in Canada in which the candidate with the most votes wins the constituency, regardless of whether it is over 50 percent.

Majority government A situation in which the party in power has over 50 percent of the seats in the House of Commons.

Mandate The concept that the winning party has an obligation to enact policies it promised during the election campaign.

Minority government A situation in which the government party has fewer than 50 percent of the seats in the House of Commons.

Nomination The act of becoming a candidate in an election, normally entailing being selected to represent a party at a nomination meeting and then completing official nomination papers.

Party identification The tendency of a voter to feel attached to a particular political party over an extended period of time.

Popular vote The percentage of all votes cast for a candidate or party, regardless of who was elected.

Redistribution The process of reallocating seats in the House of Commons among the provinces after each decennial census and then redrawing constituency boundaries within each province.

Returning officer The official in charge of running the election in each electoral district.

Spin doctors Party officials and ministerial aides who talk to the media and try to influence media coverage by putting the best face on an event from their party's point of view.

Third-party advertising Advertising by advocacy groups, as opposed to political parties, during an election campaign.

FURTHER READING

Blais, André, et al. *Anatomy of a Liberal Victory: Making Sense of the Vote in the 2000 Canadian Election*. Peterborough: Broadview Press, 2002.

Cairns, Alan C. "The Electoral System and the Party System in Canada." *Canadian Journal of Political Science* (March 1968), 55–80.

Canada Election Study. Assorted publications. http://www.ces-eec.umontreal.ca.

Clarke, Harold D., et al. *Absent Mandate: Canadian Electoral Politics in an Era of Restructuring*. 3rd ed. Toronto: Gage, 1996.

Courtney, John C. *Elections*. Vancouver: UBC Press, 2004.

Elections Canada. Assorted publications. http://www.elections.ca.

Frizzell, Alan, and Jon H. Pammett, eds. *The Canadian General Election of 1997*. Toronto: Dundurn Press, 1997.

Frizzell, Alan, Jon H. Pammett, and Anthony Westell, eds. *The Canadian General Election of 1993*. Ottawa: Carleton University Press, 1994.

Law Commission of Canada. *Voting Counts: Electoral Reform for Canada*. Ottawa, 2004.

Milner, Henry, ed. *Making Every Vote Count: Reassessing Canada's Electoral System*. Peterborough: Broadview Press, 1999.

Nevitte, Neil, et al. *Unsteady State: The 1997 Canadian Federal Election*. Toronto: Oxford University Press, 2000.

Pammett, Jon. "Class Voting and Class Consciousness in Canada." *Canadian Review of Sociology and Anthropology* 24, no. 2 (1987), 269–90.

Pammett, Jon H., and Christopher Dornan, eds. *The Canadian General Election of 2000*. Toronto: Dundurn Press, 2001.

———. *The Canadian General Election of 2004*. Toronto: Dundurn Press, 2004.

Chapter 9

Political Parties

Political parties are integral to the operation of almost every aspect of a modern political system, and they are mentioned in almost every chapter of this book. This chapter discusses them in five main sections: the functions of political parties; the historical evolution of Canadian political parties; the number and kinds of parties in Canada; party organization; and party ideology. Party and electoral finance and the role of parties in the electoral campaign, including electoral behaviour and party support, were discussed in Chapter 8.

Chapter Objectives

After you have completed this chapter, you should be able to:

Understand the functions and roles of political parties

Trace the evolution of the Canadian party system

Differentiate between one-party dominant, two-party, two-plus, and multi-party eras

Discuss the pros and cons of broker and class-based parties

Discuss the various theories accounting for the numerous minor parties in Canada

Enumerate the factors that are contributing to the decline in the importance of parties

Contrast parties in terms of membership, leadership selection and review, policymaking, and general structures and operations

Define the concepts of left, right, liberalism, conservatism, social democracy, collectivism, individualism, equality, and inequality, and apply them to Canadian parties

The Functions of Political Parties

A **political party** can be defined as an organized group that nominates candidates and contests elections in order to influence the policy and personnel of government. Its truly distinctive feature is that it runs candidates in an election campaign. When one sees political parties at their worst (for example, in the televised daily Question Period in the House of Commons), it is sometimes tempting to ask why we have them at all or to ask why we cannot make up a government consisting of the best people from each party. Why do we have political parties, and what do they do?

First, parties recruit and train politicians. While many ambitious or public-spirited persons would likely seek public office without them, parties ensure that we have candidates for federal (and provincial) elections. In the best-case scenario, parties provide qualified, representative candidates, nominating the best person they can find and (time permitting) educating that candidate in the issues of the day. In so doing, parties avoid some of the problems of municipal elections: they eliminate acclamations, filter out kooky candidates, and give voters a notion about what the candidate stands for.

Second, political parties provide experienced political leadership. The most able and successful MPs eventually become potential party leaders. Again, in an ideal case, those who seek the leadership of the party and the country will have served in the House of Commons for an extended period of time, so that they are experienced in the operation of the complex government machine. Parties usually serve to preclude the situation where a person will become prime minister out of the blue.

The third function of political parties flows from the earlier points and from the definition above: each provides a united team of people attached to a coherent policy platform. Parties simplify the electoral process as each one aggregates a number of interests together in its platform, thus providing a limited number of alternative packages from which voters can choose. In the process of combining, consolidating, or appealing to many different interests, parties also help to integrate the country and reduce the number of demands to a manageable quantity sometimes called "issues." In the exchange of election rhetoric, as well as in the partisan crossfire in Parliament, parties educate the public about the issues and help to ensure that the electorate is exposed to a variety of viewpoints.

Besides these electoral functions of parties, they are crucial to the operation of government once the election is over. It is hard to imagine that a cabinet could make efficient, coherent decisions without the shared bond of party loyalty or that the House of Commons could organize its business without a strong element of party discipline. A Parliament of 308 independents would be a recipe for chaos, and although coalition governments work well in some countries, a cabinet made up of the best MPs from each party is likely to be unstable.

Finally, political parties keep government accountable. One or more opposition parties in Parliament criticize government decisions on a daily basis, providing fodder for media coverage so that the public can remain well informed. Such opposition parties ultimately provide an organized alternative for the voters to support in the next election if they are dissatisfied with the incumbent government's performance.

Of course, political parties rarely live up to the theoretical ideals listed above. But given the fact that they are engaged in a serious struggle for power, some inadequacies or excesses are to be expected. That political parties develop in virtually all national political systems in the world, even where not provided for in the Constitution or the law, surely attests to the utility or necessity of such organizations.

Historical Evolution of Canadian Political Parties

When attempting to understand the current Canadian party system, it is helpful to be familiar with the evolution of political parties since the time of the Confederation. This evolution can be divided into three periods.

1867–1921

The first 30 years of Confederation were dominated by Sir John A. Macdonald's Conservative party. Hence, the period from 1867 to 1896 is often labeled as a **one-party dominant** system. After Macdonald was disgraced in the Pacific scandal over fundraising practices, the Liberals were in office between 1873 and 1878 under Alexander Mackenzie, but his government reflected a lack of party cohesion. Although Macdonald returned to power in 1878, his decision to execute Louis Riel caused French-Canadian support to fall away from the Conservative Party, helped by the fact that an appealing French Canadian, Wilfrid Laurier, became leader of the Liberal Party shortly afterward. Macdonald died in 1891, and his party experienced a period of great instability in the subsequent five years.

Thus, with the Liberals finally showing the marks of a well-organized national party, it is not surprising that Laurier won the watershed election of 1896. At that time, Canada moved to a classic **two-party system**, in which Liberals and Conservatives competed on equal terms.

Time Line
Prime Ministers, 1867–1921

John A. Macdonald	Conservative	1867–73
Alexander Mackenzie	Liberal	1873–78
John A. Macdonald	Conservative	1878–91
John Abbott	Conservative	1891–92
John Thompson	Conservative	1892–94
Mackenzie Bowell	Conservative	1894–96
Charles Tupper	Conservative	1896
Wilfrid Laurier	Liberal	1896–1911
Robert Borden	Conservative	1911–20
Arthur Meighen	Conservative	1920–21

Laurier governed quite successfully until he was beaten in 1911 by Robert Borden's Conservatives. The new government was soon confronted with the monumental task of managing Canada's war effort. After three years of war, Borden concluded that conscription—compulsory military service—would have to be adopted. Most English-speaking Liberal MPs agreed to join the Conservatives in a Union government in 1917, but Laurier and the French-Canadian Liberals remained aloof. With conscription, the Conservative Party almost totally alienated French Canada, at the same time as the policies of both parties upset the farming community in English Canada, notably the West. On the other hand, when Mackenzie King succeeded Laurier as Liberal leader, he skillfully pursued party reconciliation.

1921–93

Mackenzie King led the Liberals back to victory in 1921. That election marked the end of the two-party system in Canada, however, as farmers entered the contest with their own Progressive Party candidates. Because various minor parties made their presence felt but did not seriously challenge the dominance of the Liberals and Conservatives between 1921 and 1993, the Canadian party system during that period can be called a **two-plus party system**.

By the late 1920s, most of the Progressive MPs had either become Liberals or been defeated. The Liberals themselves were defeated in 1930, primarily because of the onset of the Depression. The unlucky victors, the Conservatives led by R.B. Bennett, could not cope with the unemployment, poverty, and general devastation wrought by the Depression. Along with almost every other government in office during this period, they were defeated in the next election.

The Depression was also the catalyst for the creation of a number of new political parties. The Co-operative Commonwealth Federation (CCF) was formed in 1932, an amalgam of farmer and Labour MPs, Eastern intellectuals, and various farmer, labour, and socialist groups and parties, primarily from the West. The party elected several MPs in 1935 and took office in Saskatchewan in 1944 under T.C. Douglas.

The Social Credit Party was born in Alberta in 1935 around charismatic evangelist William Aberhart. The party was originally concerned with the reform of the banking system as a means of dealing with the Depression, but all attempts to do so were disallowed by the courts or the federal government. Alberta soon became prosperous with the discovery of oil, and Social Credit transformed itself into an orthodox conservative party under E.C. Manning. The party remained in power in Alberta for 36 years, came to power in British Columbia in 1952, and repeatedly elected several Western MPs.

None of these developments impeded the Liberal Party at the federal level, as Mackenzie King led his party back to power in 1935. King's conciliatory skills were severely tested during the Second World War (1939–45), and the second conscription crisis was much less severe than the first. After also presiding over the initiation of the Canadian welfare state, King retired in favour of Louis St. Laurent in 1948.

The Conservative Party floundered for 20 years after 1935, having previously alienated French Canada and having been blamed, however unfairly, for the Depression. It changed leaders repeatedly, changed party policy to some extent, and changed the party name to Progressive Conservative in 1942, all to no avail. The political climate was suddenly transformed in 1956, however, with the choice of John Diefenbaker as party leader. Benefiting from the public's increasing resentment of Liberal arrogance and complacency, especially over the pipeline scandal, Diefenbaker led the Conservatives to victory in 1957. But his government fell apart over defence policy in the early 1960s and was defeated in 1963.

Meanwhile, the CCF had seen its fortunes decline throughout the 1950s and decided to combine its efforts with those of the new Canadian Labour Congress. The result was the creation of the New Democratic Party (NDP) in 1961. T.C. Douglas was persuaded to leave the premiership of Saskatchewan to become the first national NDP leader.

Lester Pearson's Liberals were elected in 1963 and re-elected in 1965, but they were always denied a majority of seats. Nonetheless, Pearson tackled many controversial issues, particularly the new nationalism in Quebec, the Canada Pension Plan, medicare, and a new Canadian flag. One opposition party or another supported each of Pearson's measures, so that he was able to continue in office until he retired in 1968.

Time Line
Prime Ministers, 1921–93

Mackenzie King	Liberal	1921–26
Arthur Meighen	Conservative	1926
Mackenzie King	Liberal	1926–30
R.B. Bennett	Conservative	1930–35
Mackenzie King	Liberal	1935–48
Louis St. Laurent	Liberal	1948–57
John Diefenbaker	Progressive Conservative	1957–63
Lester Pearson	Liberal	1963–68
Pierre Elliott Trudeau	Liberal	1968–79
Joe Clark	Progressive Conservative	1979–80
Pierre Elliott Trudeau	Liberal	1980–84
John Turner	Liberal	1984
Brian Mulroney	Progressive Conservative	1984–93
Kim Campbell	Progressive Conservative	1993

The Liberals then gained a majority government under their new leader, Pierre Elliott Trudeau. After 11 years in office, however, the Liberals were defeated in 1979 by the Conservatives, now led by Joe Clark. Nine months later, the Clark government fell with parliamentary rejection of its budget, and Trudeau led his party back to power in early 1980.

After helping to defeat the 1980 referendum proposal of the Parti Québécois, Trudeau patriated the Constitution, together with a Charter of Rights and

Freedoms, but without the consent of Quebec. He also alienated the West with his controversial National Energy Program. Upon his retirement in 1984, the Conservatives won a landslide victory under their new leader, Brian Mulroney, which included a startling majority of the seats in Quebec. After the negotiation of the Canada–U.S. Free Trade Agreement and the Meech Lake Accord, Mulroney led his party to a second successive majority in 1988, in which the free trade issue played a pivotal role. But by 1990, Meech Lake failed to acquire the unanimous approval of new provincial governments, and in 1992 the successor Charlottetown Accord failed to gain the support of a majority of Canadians.

1993–Present

The Liberal Party's obsession with Quebec was the main reason that the West preferred the Conservatives after 1957. But when the Mulroney Conservatives proved to be primarily concerned with holding on to their unprecedented Quebec support after 1984, many Westerners turned to the new Reform Party, headed by Preston Manning, son of the former Social Credit premier of Alberta. Besides being an expression of Western alienation, Reform was a manifestation of right-wing populism in its opposition to big government, its desire for lower taxes, and its concern with law and order.

With the collapse of the Meech Lake Accord in 1990, sovereignist sentiment increased in Quebec, giving rise to a second new federal party, the separatist Bloc Québécois. Thus, five parties of considerable strength contested the 1993, 1997, and 2000 federal elections, and produced unusual results: under Jean Chrétien, the Liberals did especially well in Ontario; the Bloc Québécois displaced the Conservatives in Quebec; and the Reform Party/Canadian Alliance usurped the Conservatives in the West. It seemed that a new highly regionalized Canadian-style **multiparty system** had developed.[1] In the 2000 election, the Liberals won seats in every province and territory but lacked depth west of Ontario; the Bloc weakened its grip on Quebec; and the Alliance made modest gains east of Manitoba, winning two seats and 24 percent of the vote in Ontario.

The post-2000 election period was characterized by four weak opposition parties—the NDP on the left, the BQ in Quebec, and the competition between the PCs and Alliance on the right. Moreover, the Alliance lost much of its popular support because of decreasing confidence in its leader, Stockwell Day. As noted in the following box, Day was replaced by Stephen Harper, and soon afterward Peter MacKay succeeded Joe Clark as leader of the Progressive Conservatives. Harper and MacKay then engineered a merger of the two parties, forming the Conservative Party of Canada. Paul Martin finally took over the leadership of the Liberals from Jean Chrétien in 2003, and Canada suddenly seemed to possess a four-party system. In 2004, this four-party system translated into a minority Liberal government.

Profile
Division and Reunification on the Right

A group of Western Canadians, upset with various decisions of both Liberal and PC parties, met in Vancouver and Winnipeg in 1987 and founded the Reform Party of Canada, with Preston Manning as its leader. After disappointing results east of Manitoba in the 1993 and 1997 elections, Manning unveiled a plan to broaden the party, especially seeking to attract the support of Progressive Conservative sympathizers in a "United Alternative." Party members supported this initiative, as well as the change of name to the Canadian Alliance. In a vote among party members in mid-2000, Stockwell Day defeated Manning for the leadership of the new party. Day was not an impressive leader, however, and in 2002 he was replaced by Stephen Harper. After Peter MacKay succeeded Joe Clark as leader of the PCs, he collaborated with Harper to form the new Conservative Party of Canada.

The Number and Kinds of Parties

Political scientists have proposed several perspectives on the number and kinds of political parties in Canada. They have also theorized about the future of such parties.

Broker Parties

One kind of political party that has been identified is the **broker party**.[2] Those who advocate such a type of party focus on the multiple cleavages in Canadian society and the function of parties to aggregate interests. These advocates argue that political parties in Canada should be conciliators, mediators, or brokers among such cleavages as regions, ethnic and linguistic groups, classes, and genders. They suggest that maximizing their appeal to all such groups is not only the best way for parties to gain power but also necessary in order to keep the country together. Thus, in their search for power, parties should act as agents of national integration and attempt to reconcile as many divergent interests as possible.

Throughout most of Canadian history, the two overriding cleavages that have concerned people as well as parties have been region and culture. Thus, broker parties make appeals to the different regions and try to bridge the English–French divide in their election platforms, government policies, and party leadership. Now that other interests have also claimed a place on the political agenda—Aboriginal peoples, other ethnic groups, and women, for example—they must also be accommodated. The one cleavage that tends to get overlooked by broker parties is that of class, but defenders of the broker system argue that parties should not foment artificial class conflicts and ideological differences in a country that is already seriously divided; they should bring people together rather than drive them apart.

However appealing the broker system may seem, its negative implications should not be overlooked. By concentrating on regional and ethnic cleavages, parties minimize the role of ideology in Canadian politics. Such parties are opportunistic and pragmatic rather than offering the electorate a choice of principles and genuinely distinctive programs. They are unlikely to generate innovative policy approaches, resting content to respond to public opinion polls and interest group demands. What such parties offer to the electorate in the place of alternative solutions to national problems are alternative leaders and slogans. Especially in a television age, leader images, unfortunately, have often become the focus of election campaigns.

Mackenzie King, the longest-serving prime minister, thwarted class politics with his successful pursuit of brokerage politics. (Library and Archives Canada/C-027645)

Class-Based and Ideological Parties

A second kind of political party is one that is based on a set of principles (an ideology) or that seeks the support of a particular socioeconomic class. There is usually a direct or indirect connection between class and ideology, such that these can be called **class-based parties**.[3]

Class analysts expect that in the pre-democratic period of any country all parties will defend the capitalist system, but when the vote is extended to the working class, a new working-class party will emerge. It will generally force politics to take on an ideological and class-based character, an evolution that clearly occurred in Britain.

When the vote was extended to the working class at the end of the 19th century in Canada, some isolated labour, socialist, and communist political activity occurred, and by 1920 new class-based farmer and labour parties existed. But the newly enfranchised working class did not manage to create a successful class-based party because the Liberals and Conservatives did everything in their power to discourage such a development, using both seductive and coercive techniques. Eventually, the farmers' interest in politics declined, and the working class mostly supported the two old-line parties on ethnic/religious and regional grounds, rendered content by the occasional piece of social legislation.

The Depression represented the collapse of the capitalist system, and the CCF emerged to become the most sustained working-class, left-wing party to that point in time. As unionization expanded significantly in the 1940s, the CCF achieved its highest popular standing. Soon afterward, however, Liberal welfare initiatives helped to draw off working-class support. This decline led to the creation of the NDP in 1961, but even with the NDP's organic link to the labour movement, most working-class Canadians continued to vote Liberal or PC (or, later, for other parties).

Analysts have proposed many reasons for the lack of class consciousness among the Canadian working class.[4] Those who defend the lack of such consciousness argue that other divisions legitimately take precedence in Canada, that the system permits social mobility, that most people feel themselves to be middle class, that material benefits are widely shared, and that the Liberal and Conservative parties have accommodated working-class interests along with ethnic, religious, and regional interests in the broker system. Those who decry the lack of working-class consciousness contend that the Liberals and Conservatives were firmly entrenched when the franchise was extended to the working class and had already defined politics around social differences other than class. These two parties diverted attention from class-based issues either by appealing to one or more ethnic/religious and regional groups or by developing pan-Canadian appeals, such as the argument that national unity was the primary issue. These parties have been accused of deluding voters into the belief that they belonged to the middle class and of giving them the false impression of inclusion and social mobility.

Advocates of a class-based party system thus point out that the existing system is partially class-based—the upper and upper middle classes are conscious of their class position and vote accordingly; it is just that the working class does not vote appropriately. These advocates claim that a class-based system would provide ideological alternatives in elections that would make them more meaningful. Moreover, when the Liberals and Conservatives are unsuccessful as brokers, the separation of one or more ethnic-regional units is possible. In such circumstances, class and ideology could be the integrating ingredients, uniting the people of various regions and ethnic groups around nationwide poles of left and right.[5]

Class-based parties are one kind of ideological party, but it is possible for a party to be based on a set of principles of some other kind, such as nationalism (e.g., the PQ and BQ) or populism (part of the Reform/Alliance focus). It is also quite likely in real life that some—perhaps most—parties will combine elements of both the broker and class-based or ideological models.

What Do You Think?

Should political parties each establish a fairly clear-cut ideological approach, or should they broaden out and try to be nearly all things to all people? Would you prefer a two-party system with one party on the left and the other on the right?

One-Party Dominance

Until 1993, Canada basically possessed a two-party system, or a two-plus system, as mentioned above. H.G. Thorburn maintains, however, that the Canadian party system has really been dominated not by two major parties but by one—the Liberals—since about 1900.[6] The Liberals are the government party, power oriented rather than issue oriented, attracting "winners" and "successes" as supporters and candidates, and maintaining themselves in office with the help of public service expertise, public opinion polls, and the chance to choose election day. Writing before 1993, Thorburn saw the Conservatives as the opposition party, ordinarily having to settle for the role of critic and being elected to office only on those rare occasions when the people get thoroughly fed up with the Liberals. However, with their divisiveness, "opposition mentality," and lack of preparedness to govern, the Conservatives never remain in power very long. Finally, Thorburn termed the NDP the innovative party, not really having a chance to govern nationally but being responsible for introducing new left-wing ideas from beyond the range of current ideological conformity, often at the provincial level. The results of the 1993, 1997, and 2000 elections showed that the Liberals were more dominant than ever, but the PCs and NDP were eclipsed to a large extent by the Reform/Alliance, with its innovations from the right. Even though reduced to a minority government in the 2004 election, the Liberal Party was the only one with substantial support across the country.

Minor Parties

Because Canada has had more minor parties than other similar political systems, political scientists have developed several theories to account for them. Essentially, these parties can all be explained by the fact that at one time or another certain ethnic, regional, or class grievances have gone unsatisfied by the broker parties. Moreover, new minor parties are to be expected when party iden-tification is weak, and in the context of the ideological stagnation and oppor-tunism of the broker system. In particular, if the working class never managed to establish a major party in Canada, it is not surprising that minor working-class parties would be created. The principal factors responsible for the rise of the var-ious minor parties in Canada involve regional or ethnic alienation, class or ide-ology, a poor economy, and charismatic leadership. As shown in Table 9.1, more than one of these factors is often involved.

The Decline of Parties?

Some political scientists, including John Meisel, regretfully detect a decline of political parties.[7] Meisel suggests a number of reasons why this is the case and why traditional party functions have been taken over by other institutions. Perhaps because voters perceive that parties no longer serve their interests very well, people seem to prefer to participate directly in specialized voluntary associations.[8] The result is that interest groups have greatly increased in number and strength. As well, the quantity and complexity of information with which governments must deal have come to mean that generalist politicians can no longer cope with it, which leaves them increasingly dependent upon the bureaucracy. This culmi-nates in a situation in which interest groups confer with bureaucrats to work out policies that the politicians can neither understand nor alter, further reducing the role of political parties in the policymaking process. Federal–provincial confer-ences and committees have become the forum in which many public policies are ironed out, and once certain political and bureaucratic compromises have been made, there is little that other politicians or parties can do about them.

TABLE 9.1 FACTORS INVOLVED IN THE RISE OF MINOR PARTIES

	Region	Ethnicity	Class/Ideology	Economy	Leader
Progressives	*		*	*	
CCF			*	*	
Social Credit	*		*	*	*
Reconstruction			*	*	
Bloc Populaire	*	*			
NDP			*		
Créditistes	*	*	*	*	*
Libertarian			*		
Christian Heritage			*		
Green			*		
Confederation of Regions	*	*			
Reform/Alliance	*	*	*		*
Bloc Québécois	*	*			*

Meisel also notes that parties now gear most of their activity to the demands of the media, and to the extent that elections are dominated by leader images and leader debates, the need for traditional party organizations diminishes. Similarly, public opinion polls provide better feedback to politicians than their traditional discussions with party activists. Investigative journalism has reduced the role of the opposition in Parliament, direct-mail appeals have replaced traditional forms of party fundraising, and modern transnational corporations are beyond the control of any party or government. Other recent developments that have contributed to the decline of parties are the increasing power of the prime minister, the influence of election strategists and other specialist advisers, and the new role of the courts and the Charter of Rights and Freedoms.

Party Organization

A political party has been defined as an organized group, but the structure of such a group requires clarification. Two main components of each party can be identified: the parliamentary party or **party caucus**, that is, the party's elected representatives

Why the Green and Marijuana Parties remain minor parties. (Bruce MacKinnon/artizans.com)

in Parliament, and the **extra-parliamentary party** organization made up of party activists, the party staff, and ordinary party members.

Party Membership

All parties strive to sign up members, but most fall far short of their expectations. No more than 3 percent of Canadians actually carry a party membership card, and only a few make a small contribution of time or money at election time.

The NDP usually takes the concept of party membership more seriously than the other parties, often putting considerable effort into an annual membership drive. New members must take an oath that they support the party's principles, and strict rules apply with respect to the right to vote at nomination meetings. Constituency association representation at party conventions is based on the size of the local membership, and the party is unique in also having affiliated members, that is, members of trade unions that have voted to affiliate with the party.

The Liberals and Conservatives are normally more casual about the annual renewal of party memberships. For the most part, their members sign up in connection with a meeting to nominate a candidate for the next election or to choose delegates to a national convention. It is typical for aspiring Liberal candidates or delegates to recruit large numbers of new members (often from ethnic groups in large urban centres) just prior to the deadline.

Party Leadership

In the new millennium, there are essentially two methods of choosing party leaders in Canada. The traditional way is at a national convention, to which constituency associations elect delegates.[9] Amid a great abundance of speeches, socializing, and twisting of arms, delegates engage in several rounds of voting until one candidate has at least 50 percent of the votes. There is much to be said for a traditional leadership convention, such that it attracts free media attention, usually raises the morale of party members, and can have a unifying effect on the party as the delegates gradually come together around the successful candidate.

The more recent procedure for choosing party leaders has been to allow every card-carrying member of the party to cast a vote. This avoids much of the cost of holding a national convention; eliminates the unholy fighting among various candidates for delegates at the constituency level; and ensures that the decision is not left to the more affluent members of the party who can afford the travel costs. The Parti Québécois was the first party to move to a "one member–one vote" leadership selection process, and many provincial party leaders have now been elected on this basis. At the national level, the Progressive Conservative Party and the Canadian Alliance both used this system, in which party members could vote by telephone, by mail, or in person in local constituencies. Such procedures have potential problems of their own, however, including technological breakdowns, an unrepresentative electorate, and the involvement of voters who have no knowledge of the candidates or who actually support other parties. Many partisans also feel that the loss of the publicity value of a nationally televised convention carries a high cost; they suggest that by imposing spending limits on candidates and subsidizing delegates' expenses, some of the worst features of conventions can be avoided. Moreover, in the future, the new election legislation will regulate the financial aspects of leadership campaigns, making them much more modest events. Increasingly, parties try to combine the best of both worlds: giving every member a vote but also having a leadership convention.

Most parties also have **leadership review** mechanisms in their constitutions, although these vary in detail. The NDP opens nominations for the position of leader at its national convention every two years, so that an unsatisfactory leader can be immediately replaced. However, in the absence of a concrete challenger, no vote is needed. The other parties generally put the question "Are you in favour of having a leadership convention?" at the first convention following an election.

Party Policymaking

All political parties have difficulty designing their policymaking process. On the one hand, they want to give ordinary party members an opportunity to contribute to party policy. But on the other, every party worries that the issues are too complex to be guided exclusively by ordinary members' views, and no party wants to be saddled with unrealistic policy commitments. Thus, they all struggle to combine grassroots input with the influence of the party elite.

Liberal and Conservative national conventions or general meetings usually include a policy session and sometimes focus primarily on policy. But even if specific resolutions are debated and passed, party leaders or cabinets retain the right to determine official party policy. The Liberals' "Red Book," used as the party platform in the 1993 election, drew substantially from party policy meetings over the previous two years but was not bound by them. As part of its rebuilding process after 1993, the PC Party designed a new policymaking process combining greater membership input with expert advice. A certain tension existed in the Reform/Alliance between its populist intentions and the dominance of its leader and elite, and it remains to be seen what role the party membership will have in formulating the policies of the new Conservative Party.

The NDP always claimed to be particularly distinctive in the realm of party policymaking. It has regular policy sessions every two years, which are the predominant item on the convention agenda. Constituency associations are invited to submit resolutions in advance, and resolutions passed by the convention are considered to be official and binding on the leader and the parliamentary party. Even in the NDP, however, constituency resolutions are now vetted by the party's policy committee with its considerable resources before being transmitted to the

Progressive Conservative leader Peter MacKay (left) and Canadian Alliance leader Stephen Harper shake hands in October 2003, following the official announcement of a merger deal between the two parties. (CP Photo/Fred Chartrand)

council and convention, and in an election campaign the leader has considerable discretion in deciding which issues to emphasize.

Party Conventions

All parties have constitutions that outline their objectives, structures, and procedures. In theory, at least, the ultimate power in each party is held by the convention that all parties try to hold at regular two-year intervals. The convention agenda normally includes the election of the party executive, constitutional amendments, and policy discussions, but such conventions also serve important social and morale-building purposes. In the Liberal and Conservative parties, each constituency association is entitled to an equal number of delegates, while in the NDP, representation is based on the size of the local membership. All parties include certain ex-officio delegates such as MPs; in the NDP, affiliated labour unions also send delegates. Women's, youth, campus, Aboriginal peoples', and ethnic groups may also send delegates to certain party conventions.

Federal–Provincial Party Links

The federal nature of Canada and the existence of two levels of government at which political parties seek to influence policy and personnel raises the question of the relationship between national and provincial party organizations. To over-simplify the situation somewhat, the federal and provincial Progressive Conservative parties were essentially independent. There was virtually no formal organizational or financial link between the two wings of the party, and there was no provincial PC at all in Quebec. Thus, federal and provincial party member-ships were usually separate, and a complete set of federal riding associations and executives coexisted with provincial party organizations at the grassroots level.

By contrast, the NDP could be called an "integrated" party because, with the exception of Quebec, one joins the NDP at the provincial level and automatically becomes a member of the national party. Provincial offices of the party serve the needs of both federal and provincial parties, and the two levels of the party are integrated financially. In Quebec, however, federal and provincial wings of the party are quite separate.

The Liberal Party is characterized by two different federal–provincial rela-tionships. In Quebec, Ontario, Alberta, and British Columbia, the party is split into federal and provincial wings, each with separate finances, memberships, con-stituency associations, executives, conventions, and offices. In the other provinces and territories, the party is more "unitary." Where the federal and provincial wings of the Liberal Party are organizationally separate, there is less inclination to be ideologically compatible or to be helpful to each other in their respective election campaigns.

Preston Manning wanted to concentrate all of Reform's attention at the national level and persuaded his members to back his objection to provincial party branches. When Reform transformed itself into the Canadian Alliance, it retained the same policy with respect to provincial branches of the party, hoping to cultivate close relations with provincial Conservative organizations, especially in Alberta and Ontario. When the Alliance and PCs merged, the new Conservative Party of Canada inherited a lack of formal links to provincial par-ties from both of its parents, but it developed good relations with the parties that had retained the "Progressive Conservative" label in the provinces.

Party Ideology

For the purposes of this discussion, **ideology** can be defined as a coherent set of ideas or principles about how a society ought to function, with particular reference to the role of the state. If Canadian politics has been dominated by broker parties, one would not expect the role of ideology to be of fundamental importance. Nevertheless, it can be argued that genuine ideological differences do exist in Canada, and that such ideologies as liberalism, conservatism, and social democracy can be found to differentiate the three traditional parties.[10] The ideological continuum can be sketched in diagrammatic form as in Figure 9.1, based on the contending principles of collectivism and individualism on the one hand and egalitarianism and inequality on the other.

This perspective suggests that the overwhelming ideology in Canada is **liberalism**, but that traces of **social democracy** and **conservatism** also exist and that each of the ideologies is represented by a corresponding party. Liberalism seeks to liberate the individual and maximize each individual's freedom and potential, something that almost all Canadians would support. The differences that emerge essentially centre on the role of the state.

Social democracy seeks to liberate the individual from the inequalities and exploitation of the capitalist system; it believes in striving toward equality of condition, not merely equality of opportunity; and it prescribes a large element of state action or **collectivism** in order to achieve such liberation and equality.

In discussions of political ideology, these views are generally referred to as being on the **left**. In particular, social democracy emphasizes government planning, regulation, ownership of some of the major industries of the country, progressive taxation, and redistribution of income via social programs. Adherents are

Figure 9.1 The Ideological Continuum in Canada

	LEFT	CENTRE	RIGHT	
Collectivism				Individualism
	NDP	Liberal Party	Conservative Party	
Egalitarianism				Inequality

sometimes subdivided between "democratic socialists" and "social democrats," depending on the extent to which they wish the state to intervene and the extent of equality they wish to effect. Canada's social democratic parties, the CCF and the NDP, take credit for introducing public hospital and medical insurance after forming the government of Saskatchewan, pressing for other social programs, advocating a more progressive taxation system, creating a variety of Crown corporations in the provinces where they held power, and supporting the establishment of new government bodies in Ottawa.

Liberalism, too, has a dual personality and can be subdivided into "welfare" and "business" variants. Business liberals believe that the state inhibits individual self-fulfillment and that its role should therefore be minimized so that individualism can prevail. Welfare liberals, on the other hand, take the view that the state can be a positive agent in liberating individuals from the constraints of other forces, including the private enterprise economy. Welfare liberals therefore stand for a combination of individualism and collectivism and a combination of equality and inequality that they usually label "equality of opportunity." The Liberal Party is composed of business and welfare liberals, which places it in the centre of the Canadian ideological continuum. While Liberals obviously hold the private enterprise system in greater esteem than does the NDP, Liberal governments introduced old age pensions, family allowances, and many other social welfare programs over the years, although many observers saw a rightward shift after 1993.

Conservatism also has two variants. On the one hand, conservatives seek to liberate the individual from the restrictions of the state. Reducing the role of the state to a minimum and allowing capitalistic market forces to determine the distribution of power and wealth is often labelled **individualism**. If this results in inequalities, conservatives are generally unconcerned; inequalities are both natural and deserved—some people are more talented and work harder than others. These attitudes are labelled as being on the **right**, and these conservatives can be called "business liberals." Business liberals in the Conservative Party generally took a more extreme position on these issues than their counterparts in the Liberal Party. The second wing of the Canadian Progressive Conservative Party was the "progressive" element, people who were sometimes called **Red Tories**. These Conservatives combined beliefs in privilege and collectivism, seeing society as an organic whole, emphasizing community values as well as individualism, and standing for order, tradition, and stability. They believed in hierarchy—that everyone should occupy his or her place—but they also had a paternalistic concern for the condition of all the people. This aspect of conservatism is not unique to Canada, being found quite commonly in Britain and the rest of Europe; it stands out only in contrast to a lack of such sentiment within American conservatism.

Thus, the ideology of the Progressive Conservative Party was divided as much as that of the other two parties. Furthermore, the Red Tory element overlapped to some extent with welfare liberalism and even social democracy. While the Mulroney government pursued a fairly consistent business-liberal agenda—privatization, deregulation, deficit reduction, and cutting of social programs—its Progressive Conservative predecessors sometimes exhibited a Red Tory touch, such as in the creation of the RCMP, CBC, CNR, the National Energy Board, the Bennett New Deal, and the Stanfield proposal for government controls on wages and prices.

If liberalism in the United States lacks the collectivist aspect, how does one account for its presence in all three of the traditional Canadian party ideologies? One explanation focuses on the United Empire Loyalists, who removed most of the collectivist tendencies from the U.S. political culture when they migrated to Canada and left behind undiluted business liberalism in that country. The United Empire Loyalists legitimized ideological diversity in Canada and, because of their early predominance, made collectivism a respectable and important element in the Canadian political culture. In fact, they added to the collectivist approach already found in the feudal background of French Canada, that is, the ideas of hierarchy, order, stability, and community. Collectivism was reinforced by subsequent waves of British immigrants, whose intellectual baggage included both Red Tory and socialist views, along with the influence of the Social Gospel movement. Such collectivist tendencies were discussed in Chapter 6.

Over the past 20 years, the whole ideological spectrum has shifted to the right. In Canada, this began with the Mulroney government, which pursued a business-liberal, **neoconservative**, or **neoliberal** agenda in which renewed reliance was placed on market forces and the extent of government intervention was reduced. For the first time in Canadian history, social programs were cut back rather than expanded; Crown corporations were privatized rather than created; regulations were repealed rather than promulgated; public debts and deficits were reduced rather than increased; and public servants were fired rather than hired. The whole phenomenon could be called the "dismantling of the state." The new ideology went beyond one or two parties; it affected governing parties of all ideological persuasions: PCs, Liberals, the Parti Québécois, and even the NDP in Saskatchewan.

What's in a Name?

The terms "neoliberalism" and "neoconservatism" have been commonly applied to the ideology of certain contemporary political parties, especially the Canadian Alliance and perhaps the new Conservative Party of Canada. While the two terms are often used to mean the same thing, a distinction can be made between them. Both neoliberalism and neoconservatism advocate that government withdraw from the private market economy, but sometimes neoconservatism is taken to include a belief in a strong state that can promote certain traditional social values and regulate behaviour in areas such as abortion, same-sex relationships, and freedom of expression.

The Reform Party was very much part of this shift to the right, and it exerted great influence at both federal and provincial levels, even though it did not form the government. The other leaders of this right-wing crusade, Conservatives Ralph Klein in Alberta and Mike Harris in Ontario, also followed the Reform lead. Reform/Alliance believed in reducing the role of government, reducing taxes, reducing regulation, privatizing Crown corporations, laying off public servants, reducing the debt and the deficit, and cutting back social programs. This is all consistent with a belief in individualism, which is unconcerned about whether it leads to socioeconomic inequalities. What distinguished the Reform/Alliance from other Canadian parties was therefore an almost complete absence of the collectivist value. In this respect, it was a clone of the U.S. Republican Party, with which it maintained contact.

A second strand of Reform/Alliance ideology was social conservatism, such as in its opposition to abortion and same-sex rights and its promotion of traditional "family values." This bundle of issues led to internal divisions within the party in the 2000 leadership race and election because to some extent this neoconservative position contradicts the neoliberal one. Social conservatism advocates a strong role for the state in moral regulation by maintaining law and order and upholding conventional values.

A third aspect of Reform/Alliance ideology was its populist streak. It was against political elitism and professed to value the wisdom of ordinary people, giving them direct participation in decisionmaking via referendums, for example. This emphasis on direct participation, too, is an Americanism, as opposed to the traditional Canadian belief in **representative democracy**. The final main concern of the Reform/Alliance was a territorial rather than ideological issue—that the West was getting shortchanged within Confederation.

With the recent merger of the Progressive Conservative and Canadian Alliance parties, it is not yet completely clear where the party stands ideologically. Leader Stephen Harper came from the far-right of the spectrum, embodying the essence of neoliberalism, while former PC leader, Joe Clark, denounced the union, as many former Progressive Conservatives abandoned the new party. Harper tried to present a platform in the 2004 election that was somewhat more moderate than that of the Alliance, but he was dogged daily by candidates' espousal of extreme social conservative (neoconservative) positions, which he did not always disavow. Harper endorsed greater funding for medicare, although he would allow the provinces maximum flexibility in its administration. He maintained the Alliance position on tax cuts, same-sex marriage, gun control, law and order, and increased spending on the military, but he downplayed referendums. To some extent, the partial shift in policy brings the party back from beyond the range of the Canadian political culture.

The other new party, the Bloc Québécois, has one main objective: Quebec sovereignty. The question of nationalism generally overwhelms the left–right ideological approach in Quebec, but the BQ and PQ have usually been placed on the left side of the continuum, somewhere between the Liberals and the NDP.

As a result of the general shift to the right, the NDP now occupies the previous position of the Liberal Party. The Chrétien government pursued the same kind of leaner government that it previously condemned under Mulroney, and Finance Minister Paul Martin dismembered many of the social programs that were largely the creation of his father, a long-time "welfare" Liberal cabinet minister. A crush occurred on the right-wing side of the spectrum, and the Progressive Conservative Party found it difficult to identify its own ideological space between the Chrétien Liberals and the Canadian Alliance. Finally, under new leader Peter MacKay, the PCs threw in the towel and merged with the Alliance in a new Conservative Party, in what was frequently depicted as an Alliance takeover.

SUMMARY

This chapter discussed political parties in Canada. It made the case that for all their faults, political parties are beneficial, indeed necessary, to the operation of the political system. It traced the evolution of the Canadian party system from two parties before 1921, through a series of additional parties until 1993, following which five parties were represented in Parliament, to the presence of four parties in 2004. The chapter then contrasted the advantages and disadvantages of broker and class-based parties, accounted for the rise of so many minor parties over the years, and asked whether political parties are in decline. The next section dealt with party organization and looked at differences in the concepts of membership, leadership, policymaking, and general operations. The last section of the chapter analyzed party ideologies, primarily in terms of individualism and collectivism and in terms of equality and inequality. It also described where Canadian political parties are situated in relation to three main ideologies: liberalism, conservatism, and social democracy.

DISCUSSION QUESTIONS

1. Is Canada likely to have a four-party system for the foreseeable future?
2. Is the new Conservative Party of Canada a broker party, a class-based party, or an ideological party?
3. Is it possible in this complex, information-driven age for ordinary party members to make useful policy suggestions within the political parties to which they belong?
4. How do you categorize yourself ideologically? Why?

KEY TERMS

Broker party A kind of political party that tries to appeal to many different interests and to "broker" compromises among them, rather than having any distinct ideology.

Class-based party A political party that appeals primarily to one socioeconomic class or another.

Collectivism As opposed to individualism, an ideology that holds that the public interest is enhanced by substantial collective action, normally via government.

Conservatism A political ideology generally characterized by a belief in individualism and a minimum of government intervention in the economy and society, as well as by tradition, elitism, and opposition to change.

Extra-parliamentary party That part of a political party beyond its members of Parliament—that is, party members, local and national executives, and party headquarters.

Ideology A coherent set of ideas or principles about how a society ought to function, with particular reference to the role of the state.

Individualism An ideology that holds that individuals should have maximum freedom or liberty to do as they please, especially in economic terms, and that governments should not get involved in taxation, regulation, redistribution, or ownership.

Leadership review A clause in the constitutions of political parties that allows party members or convention delegates to review the leader's performance.

Left That part of the ideological spectrum that believes in equality in society and the intervention of government via collectivist measures such as taxation, regulation, redistribution, and public ownership to effect such equality.

Liberalism An ideology based on a belief in the rationality of the individual and on maximizing individual freedom, liberty, and self-fulfillment. Before 1900, this was assumed to entail a minimal role for government; after 1900, liberalism usually advocated a larger role for the state and was placed on the centre-left of the spectrum.

Multiparty system Typically European in nature, a party system characterized by many parties, usually without any one having a majority in the legislature.

Neoconservatism An ideology originating in the 1980s calling on government to withdraw from its extensive intervention in the private market economy but perhaps still promote certain traditional social values.

Neoliberalism An ideology originating in the 1980s calling on government to withdraw from its extensive intervention in the private market economy—emphasizing privatization, deregulation, balancing of budgets, and trimming of social programs—as well as from regulating society in general.

One-party dominance A party system characterized by the dominance of a single party.

Party caucus The whole body of MPs of any party, together with such senators as choose to attend, who hold a regular weekly meeting to discuss parliamentary strategy and party policy.

Political party An organized group that makes nominations and contests elections in the hope of influencing the policy and personnel of government.

Red Tories A minority faction within the former Progressive Conservative Party that had collectivist leanings akin to many British and European conservatives, stressing order, tradition, stability, and a paternalistic concern for the condition of the working class.

Representative democracy A system of government based on the periodic election of representatives to Parliament, as opposed to more direct participation by voters in making public decisions.

Right That part of the ideological spectrum that cherishes individualism and believes in leaving the private sector to operate with minimal government intervention.

Social democracy A moderate leftist ideology that emphasizes the principle of equality and usually prescribes a large role for government to intervene in society and the economy.

Two-party system A type of party system in which two main parties are of approximately equal strength and alternate in office.

Two-plus party system A type of party system in which two main parties are of approximately equal strength and alternate in office but are accompanied by one or more minor parties of significant strength.

FURTHER READING

Campbell, Colin, and William Christian. *Parties, Leaders, and Ideologies in Canada*. Toronto: McGraw-Hill Ryerson, 1996.

Cross, William. *Political Parties*. Vancouver: UBC Press, 2004.

Flanagan, Tom. *Waiting for the Wave: The Reform Party and Preston Manning*. Toronto: Stoddart, 1995.

Jeffrey, Brooke. *Hard Right Turn: The New Face of Neo-Conservatism in Canada*. Toronto: HarperCollins, 1999.

Martin, Lawrence. *Iron Man: The Defiant Reign of Jean Chrétien*. Toronto: Viking Canada, 2003.

Thorburn, H.G., and Alan Whitehorn, eds. *Party Politics in Canada*. 8th ed. Scarborough: Prentice-Hall Canada, 2001.

Whitehorn, Alan. *Canadian Socialism: Essays on the CCF and the NDP*. Toronto: Oxford University Press, 1992.

Chapter 10

Pressure Groups, Social Movements, and Lobbying

Pressure groups, advocacy groups, or interest groups develop in almost every political system when individuals with common concerns band together in order to strengthen their cause. At least part of their effort involves interacting with government. This chapter will identify some of the leading Canadian pressure groups and social movements, outline their targets and methods, assess their resources, and then give an account of the activity of new lobbying firms.

Chapter Objectives

After you have completed this chapter, you should be able to:

Understand the prominence of pressure groups in the political system

Provide examples of leading pressure groups in a variety of fields

Distinguish between institutionalized and issue-oriented groups, public interest and self-interested groups, and social movements

Discuss how the structure of government affects the way pressure groups are organized

Enumerate the targets of pressure group activity and the methods used to reach them

Analyze the importance of different group resources

Discuss the rise of new forms of lobbying and enumerate the provisions of the Lobbyists Registration Act

Comment on unsavoury aspects of the professional lobbying scene

The Functions of Pressure Groups and Lobbying

An **advocacy group**, **interest group**, or **pressure group** (terms are used interchangeably here) can be defined as any group that seeks to influence government policy without contesting elections, that is, without putting forward its own candidates. Alternatively, pressure groups have been defined as organizations whose members promote their common interest by acting together to influence public policy.[1] The term **lobbying** is generally used to refer to any organized attempt to influence the decisionmakers, an activity that is most commonly undertaken by pressure groups but could also be done by individuals, companies, or other political actors. Increasingly, however, pressure groups have been joined by professional lobbying firms in this activity.

Pressure groups are involved primarily in the function of "interest articulation"; they normally have a narrow focus and are organized around a single interest that they try to impress upon those in authority. As society becomes more complex, Canadians increasingly demonstrate a preference to form or join such specialized, functional groups in order to transmit their demands to government, rather than rely on the broader and largely territorial representation of parties and elections. Thus, in the promotion of interests, pressure groups provide a supplementary kind of "functional" representation, especially between elections.[2]

The Array of Canadian Pressure Groups

The number of advocacy groups operating in Canada is in the thousands. If a distinction can be made between pressure groups and interest groups, it could be said that an interest group *becomes* a pressure group when it actively pursues an objective with government. Thus only some of the largest and most influential pressure groups are listed in Table 10.1.

Business Groups

In the case of business, nothing prevents individual companies from lobbying on their own behalf for grants, subsidies, tariff protection or free trade agreements, loan guarantees, tax write-offs, government contracts, or policy changes, and many firms do so on a regular basis.[3] In addition, the firms within almost every

TABLE 10.1 LEADING NATIONAL PRESSURE GROUPS

Business	Canadian Council of Chief Executives
	Canadian Manufacturers and Exporters
	Canadian Chamber of Commerce
	Canadian Federation of Independent Business
	Canadian Bankers' Association
	Canadian Home Builders Association
	Canadian Association of Broadcasters
	Canada's Research-Based Pharmaceutical Companies
Agriculture	Canadian Federation of Agriculture
Labour	Canadian Labour Congress
Professions	Canadian Bar Association
	Canadian Medical Association
	Canadian Federation of Students
Ethnic	Assembly of First Nations
	Canadian Ethnocultural Council
	National Congress of Italian Canadians
Religious	Canadian Council of Churches
	Canadian Conference of Catholic Bishops
	Canadian Jewish Congress
	United Church of Canada
Causes	John Howard Society
	Canadian Civil Liberties Association
	National Action Committee on the Status of Women
	Pollution Probe
	Mothers Against Drunk Driving
	Non-Smokers' Rights Association
	Council of Canadians
	Canadian Council on Social Development

industry have organized a common pressure group to promote the interests of the industry as a whole. It is estimated that more than 600 business groups are active in Canadian politics.[4] Superimposed upon these industrial groupings are such "peak" organizations as the **Canadian Council of Chief Executives**, the Canadian Manufacturers and Exporters, the Canadian Chamber of Commerce, and the

Canadian Federation of Independent Business. They each represent a wide range of business interests. In agriculture, nearly 100 active organizations vie for influence, the leading group being the Canadian Federation of Agriculture.

Profile

The Canadian Council of Chief Executives: A Business Pressure Group

The Canadian Council of Chief Executives, formed as the Business Council on National Issues (BCNI) in 1976, comprises the chief executive officers of the 150 leading Canadian corporations. With over $2.3 trillion in assets, it bills itself as "the senior voice of Canadian business on national and global issues." The president and chief executive is Tom d'Aquino, who manages its day-to-day affairs. Both the council and its observers give it credit for setting the agenda for all recent Canadian governments. First, it promoted the idea of free trade between Canada and the United States, then pressured the government to balance the budget, and then advocated tax cuts. Each of these high-pressure campaigns resulted in a reduction in the size and role of the state. For more information on the council, go to http://www. ceocouncil.ca.

Nonbusiness Groups

The **Canadian Labour Congress** (CLC) functions as a common voice for organized labour, but only about 65 percent of union members in Canada belong to unions affiliated with the CLC. Another 6 percent belong to the Quebec-based Conseil des syndicats nationaux, while most of the rest have not joined any central labour organization. The CLC maintains a link to the New Democratic Party, as do many of its individual unions, a unique relationship among Canadian pressure groups.

Many of the ethnic groups in Canada have their own organized associations, such as the National Congress of Italian Canadians. Most of these have been brought together, with government support, in the umbrella organization called the Canadian Ethnocultural Council. The largest of several Aboriginal groups is the **Assembly of First Nations**. The English and French are organized only where they are minorities—the anglophone Alliance Quebec and the Fédération des communautés francophones et acadienne du Canada, incorporating provincial units such as the Association canadienne-française de l'Ontario (ACFO). Religious denominations in Canada also function as pressure groups from time to time, with the Canadian Conference of Catholic Bishops, the United Church of Canada, the Canadian Council of Churches, and the Canadian Jewish Congress probably being most influential. Most professions have organizations that speak for their members on relevant issues, the Canadian Medical Association and Canadian Bar Association being two of the oldest and most important. A large proportion of postsecondary students belong to the Canadian Federation of Students.

Other Categorizations of Pressure Groups

However much any of the previously mentioned groups claim to be pursuing the public interest, they can be generally categorized as "self-interested" groups because in most cases their principal concern is to improve their own, usually economic, position. The true "public interest" group exists to promote causes that it sees as beneficial to society as a whole and that do not directly benefit its own members, such as the John Howard Society (improving prison conditions and the lot of ex-inmates), the Canadian Council on Social Development (promoting better social policy), the Canadian Civil Liberties Association (protecting civil liberties from government infringement), and a variety of environmental groups.

With some exceptions, those named above and many others are called **institutionalized pressure groups** because they are permanent, well-established, formal organizations. Almost all maintain a head office in Ottawa with a full-time staff, a sizable budget, and a reasonably stable membership. Most have developed continuous links with the authorities and represent their members' interests on a daily basis, year after year.

In contrast, some groups spring up spontaneously around a specific issue, and once the issue is resolved, they fade away. Such **issue-oriented pressure groups** lack the institutionalized groups' permanence, office, staff, budget, membership, and access to the authorities. Instead, they more likely resort to attracting public attention to their cause through media coverage of such actions as demonstrations. Examples of issue-oriented groups include the Stop Spadina group that opposed extension of the Spadina Expressway in Toronto in the early 1970s and "Bread Not Circuses," which objected to Toronto's bid to host the 1996 (and 2008) Olympic Games. Rural Dignity was another spontaneous national group that sprang up to fight against the deterioration of rural and small-town life in general, and of its mail service in particular. If their issue is not resolved, or if they anticipate further challenges, such groups may become a more permanent fixture.[5]

Political scientists often find it useful to distinguish between pressure groups and social movements. Many of the issue-oriented groups referred to are, in fact, part of larger unstructured social movements, of which the environmental, women's, and peace movements have been most prominent historically. More recent examples include the Aboriginal, gay, animal rights, anti-poverty, and anti-globalization movements. A **social movement** has been defined as an informal network of organizations and individuals who on the basis of a collective identity and shared values engage in political and/or cultural struggle and undertake collective action designed to affect both state and society.[6] Social movements begin at the margins of the political system, possess an alternative vision of "the good life," and usually consist of coalitions of small local groups that have not yet hardened into a cohesive national group.

The National Action Committee (NAC) on the Status of Women is a somewhat institutionalized coalition of some 700 women's groups, while the Canadian Environmental Network is a looser coalition of hundreds of environmental groups. The Council of Canadians is a citizens' movement that provides a critical voice on key national issues such as safeguarding social programs, promoting economic justice, renewing democracy, asserting Canadian sovereignty, preserving the environment, and promoting alternatives to corporate-style free trade. It is part of and is backed by the Solidarity Network, which is, in turn, a broad coalition of labour, women's, anti-poverty, health, peace, farming, cultural, environmental, Aboriginal, student, faith, youth, and seniors groups. Also allied with these groups is the Canadian Centre for Policy Alternatives.

The Council of Canadians and its allies also put much effort into stopping the Multilateral Agreement on Investment (MAI), working successfully with similar grassroots groups around the world. The Internet facilitates both national and international grassroots political campaigns, and such social movements and networks are often seen as one of the few counterweights to corporate globalization in the modern world.[7] In fact, opposition to globalization via new free trade agreements that primarily benefit transnational corporations is the very issue that increasingly inspires social movements.

Such movements run into much bureaucratic and political party resistance because of a reluctance to consider radical new ideas, and they often do not achieve immediate success. In the long run, however, they widen the scope of public discourse, and parties and other mainstream political institutions eventually respond. Take recent improvements in legislation with respect to women and the environment, for example, and changes in public attitudes toward war, Aboriginal peoples, gays and lesbians, and the treatment of animals.

Other categorizations are also sometimes useful in discussing pressure groups. Most groups are "autonomous" in the sense that they develop without government initiative, although they may later seek government financial support. But politicians or bureaucrats are sometimes involved in the creation of interest groups, whether for personal gain or in the hope of promoting a certain public policy objective. In the late 1960s, for example, the federal government began to fund anti-poverty, women's, minority official language, Aboriginal, and other ethnic groups to ensure that these interests would be heard in the political marketplace.[8] The Trudeau and Mulroney governments cut back on grants to Aboriginal, women's, and poor and disabled people's groups both for fiscal and ideological reasons or when a particular group became too critical of the hand that fed it. Canada has been something of a world leader in government support of critical interest groups, but such grant reductions reveal the dangers that arise if a group becomes too critical and too dependent.

Profile

The Council for Canadians: A Social Movement

The Council of Canadians is a citizens' movement that provides a critical voice on key national issues. It has been active on such issues as free trade, public pensions, bank mergers, concentrated media ownership, the use of growth hormones in cattle, and other aspects of genetically modified food. One of the Council's priorities is to persuade federal and provincial governments to prohibit the bulk export of Canadian water. The Council is part of the Solidarity Network and the Alternative Federal Budget (AFB) movement, along with the Canadian Federation of Students (CFS), CLC, NAC, National Anti-Poverty Organization (NAPO), unions, and environmental groups. The AFB hammers out a detailed and sophisticated alternative federal budget each year, which is published by the Canadian Centre for Policy Alternatives, one of the few think tanks on the left. For more information on the Council of Canadians, go to http://www.canadians.org.

Pressure Group Structures

As far as the structure of pressure groups is concerned, issue-oriented groups can burst forth anywhere an issue arises—at the international, federal, provincial, or municipal level. Institutionalized groups, on the other hand, tend to be organized wherever government decisions regularly affect them. The federal nature of the country means that authoritative decisions are made at two or more levels of government, and most institutionalized groups parallel the federal structure of government. They find it advantageous to be organized at both levels because the division of powers between the federal and provincial governments is so blurred. The Canadian Medical Association is composed of 10 autonomous provincial divisions (such as the Ontario Medical Association); the Canadian Chamber of Commerce has strong provincial branches (such as the Alberta Chamber of Commerce), as does the Canadian Labour Congress (for example, the Nova Scotia Federation of Labour). These latter two groups in particular also maintain municipal organizations—local chambers of commerce or boards of trade in every sizable community and local labour councils across the country.

Many pressure groups, including those representing the interests of teachers, nurses, and students, are actually more strongly organized at the provincial level than in Ottawa. This is because they are more affected by decisions of provincial governments than by federal ones. Some, such as the medical and legal professions, are even delegated powers by provincial governments to regulate themselves.

Already vocal in dealing with national and provincial governments, students may even organize protests at the campus level to try to change university or college decisions. In recent years, such protests have often focused on increases in tuition fees or exclusive rights contracts granted to individual corporations (like Coke or Pepsi) to advertise or provide a service on campus.

Targets and Methods of Pressure Group Activity

Besides being affected by federalism, Canadian interest groups are very much influenced in their operations by the fact that they exist in a parliamentary system. This system, despite its name, places most of the decisionmaking power in the hands of the bureaucracy and the cabinet. Pressure groups that understand this basic truth direct most of their attention to these two branches of government.

In this connection, Paul Pross's conception of **policy communities** should be mentioned.[9] This concept is based on the premise that each field of public policy is discrete and specialized, with its own constellation of participants. Each policy community consists of a grouping of government agencies, politicians, pressure groups, corporations, institutions, media people, and individuals who have an interest in that particular policy field and attempt to influence it. These actors initially attempt to establish their legitimacy with the lead government agency, and if they achieve such recognition and status, they may be made part of the agency's information flow. Once such groups are given the privilege of consultation and access to strategic information, they normally behave quite cooperatively, and the whole policy community becomes cohesive and mutually supportive. All the actors involved, including the lead agency, prefer to keep the issues that concern them within the "community" and have a strong incentive to resolve any problems there rather than open the issues up to cabinet discussion or, even worse, public debate and confrontation.

The Bureaucracy

As discussed in Chapter 14, the bureaucracy advises the cabinet on almost all of its decisions. It drafts legislation and regulations according to the cabinet's general instructions; it proposes budgets and spends government money; and it implements policies and programs once they have been given cabinet and/or legislative approval. All of these areas hold considerable scope for bureaucratic discretion. It is for this reason that institutionalized groups in particular direct the bulk of their messages at the bureaucratic target. Many pressure group demands involve technical matters that only the bureaucracy understands and that it may be able to satisfy without reference to the politicians.

Such groups try to cultivate close relationships with senior public servants, hoping to be able to contact these officials on an informal, direct, day-to-day basis via telephone calls, faxes, meetings, letters, and business lunches. Although bureaucrats may be suspicious of these groups' motives, the relationship between a pressure group and its most relevant government department may ultimately become a reciprocal one, as desirable for the public service as it is for the group.

Thus, what is called a **clientele relationship** often develops between such groups as the Canadian Federation of Agriculture and the Department of Agriculture, the Canadian Medical Association and the Department of Health, the petroleum and mining associations and the Department of Natural Resources, and big business organizations and the Department of Finance. The relations between such a department or agency and its allied pressure groups may even become so close that it is difficult to tell them apart. The department or agency almost becomes an extension of the pressure group, making policy in the interest of the group and promoting the interest they both represent within the higher councils of government. The minister, deputy minister, and Department of Finance speak for the business community, while the minister, deputy minister, and Department of Agriculture speak for the farming community, and so on.

In return for the various ways in which the bureaucracy responds to group demands, the group may pass on information that the department needs or desires in order to do its work. Many problems become too complex for politicians—ministers or MPs—to understand, especially as larger numbers of issues, constituents, and obligations eat up their time. As a consequence, legislation is increasingly drafted in skeletal form with the specifics delegated to the bureaucracy to be added later in the form of **regulations** or "delegated legislation." Bureaucrats regularly consult institutionalized pressure groups as they draft legislation, design programs, and draw up regulations. The group may also be a valuable ally in persuading other bureaucratic agencies or ministers to do what the department wants.

Although pressure groups are usually seen in terms of their "input" function of making demands, they also perform various "output" functions. A group may be better equipped to inform its specialized membership about new laws, regulations, or programs than a department that is restricted to the media or other regular channels of communication. In addition, the cooperation of the group might be indispensable to the successful execution of a program. In some cases, as noted, certain groups are even delegated powers of self-regulation.

When public servants themselves are members of interest groups, it naturally assists the group in maximizing its influence. For example, medical bureaucrats often belong to the Canadian Medical Association and legal bureaucrats to the Canadian Bar Association. In fact, considerable movement of personnel takes place between interest groups and the higher levels of the public service: officials often move from pressure group jobs to the bureaucracy or vice versa.

The Cabinet

The cabinet is the second most frequently targeted branch of government because it makes the major governmental decisions in a parliamentary system. Since it is now virtually impossible to meet the prime minister and cabinet as a whole, groups often find it productive to submit single-issue representations to individual ministers, who spend much of their time in meetings with such groups. If a minister stays in one position long enough, a pressure group may be able to construct a more personal, informal relationship, as the Canadian Federation of Agriculture did with Jimmy Gardiner, who served as minister of agriculture for 22 years. The social scene in Ottawa should also be mentioned, for parties and receptions provide excellent opportunities for cabinet ministers, deputy ministers, and established pressure group representatives (especially corporate ones) to meet and mingle.

The Trudeau government established the precedent of encouraging various groups to meet with the minister of finance prior to the preparation of the annual budget, a practice that was even more widespread under Mulroney's first finance minister, Michael Wilson. As noted below, pressure groups are now invited to appear before the House of Commons Standing Committee on Finance, but that does not preclude a private meeting with the minister.

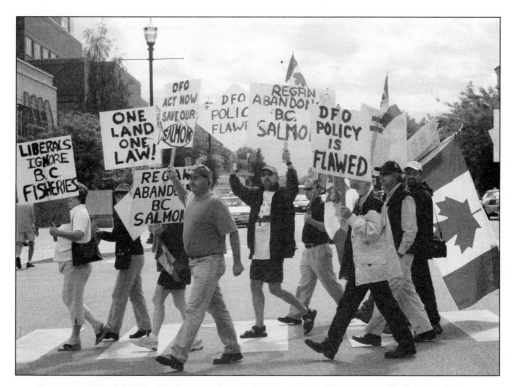

Protesters in Kelowna, B.C., take advantage of a rare cabinet meeting outside Ottawa to make their views known.
(CP Photo/Chuck Stoody)

It is sometimes claimed that most public decisions in Canada emerge from the interaction of three agents: the cabinet, the senior public service, and pressure groups, especially in the business field.[10] The individuals who occupy the top positions in these sectors are elites in two senses. First, they are small numbers of people with disproportionate amounts of power, compared to ordinary citizens. Second, they have exclusive socioeconomic backgrounds, coming from families of higher social class, higher incomes, and higher educations. Robert Presthus thus postulates that the common backgrounds and values of political, bureaucratic, and corporate leaders help to facilitate agreement among them. Commanding the heights of these sectors of society, they easily accommodate each other in the working out of public policies. Lobbyists from professional lobbying firms also fit perfectly into this arrangement.

Parliament

The third main branch of the government is the legislature or Parliament, but as discussed in Chapter 15, it largely legitimizes decisions previously taken by the executive. That being the case, the House of Commons is not as often the target of interest group activity, but it does remain the object of considerable attention, especially for groups lacking access to the executive branch. One of the main reasons that a bill is usually sent to a legislative committee during its passage is to allow interest groups to make representations on it. The Standing Committee on Finance, with its pre-budget hearings, is now integrated into the expenditure management system and provides an excellent opportunity for pressure groups to make their case.

Especially in a majority government situation, however, ministers have traditionally been reluctant to accept amendments proposed at the legislative stage, so that groups are better advised to make their case at the executive level before the bill is made public. It has even been said that the sight of a pressure group at the legislative level in Canada is a sign that the group already failed at the level of the bureaucracy and the cabinet. Nevertheless, groups often converge on MPs in their offices or inundate them with letters, e-mails, or postcards. For example, although not ignoring the cabinet and bureaucracy, the Canadian Chamber of Commerce is particularly adept at applying pressure on MPs through its base in almost every constituency across the country. Pressure groups sometimes meet with individual party caucuses, and certain MPs may already belong to a group, in which case they can be expected to speak on its behalf.

The upper chamber of Parliament, the Senate, is also involved in the lobbying process. Because many senators have close corporate connections and function regularly as lobbyists for big business, the Senate has been called "a lobby from within."[11] During passage in that chamber, much legislation is considered by the Senate Committee on Banking, Trade and Commerce, many of whose members hold directorships in Canadian banks and other large corporations. Such holdings have not deterred committee members from active consideration of questions relating to financial institutions in what many observers see as a classic case of conflict of interest.

Other Targets

Pressure groups have many targets beyond these three main branches of government. If they can find a legal or constitutional angle to their demand, for example, such groups may take cases to the courts. Corporations have sometimes challenged federal or provincial legislation in the courts as a violation of the division of powers; francophone groups have used the courts to uphold constitutionally guaranteed minority language rights; and Aboriginal groups are increasingly using the courts to uphold or broaden the meaning of treaty and other Aboriginal rights. The Charter of Rights and Freedoms provides added potential for targeting the courts by actually inviting individuals and groups to challenge federal or provincial legislation that they consider to be discriminatory. The tobacco industry, for example, was temporarily successful in arguing that the law banning tobacco advertising violated the companies' freedom of expression.

As mentioned, only the Canadian Labour Congress has seen fit to attach itself formally to a political party—but this strategy may have reduced the group's impact on Liberal and Conservative governments. Other groups remain scrupulously nonpartisan so that they can exert equal influence on whatever party is in power, which is not to say that business groups in particular have any difficulty in gaining access to any party.

Another target of pressure group activity is the royal commission. These elaborate investigations of public problems normally invite pressure groups and experts to submit briefs in public hearings, supplementing whatever original research the commission itself undertakes.

Besides their direct representations to government, pressure groups and corporations increasingly try to influence public opinion in what is called **advocacy advertising** in the hope that the authorities will respond to a clear message from the public. In 1991, for example, both the Pharmaceutical Manufacturers Association and the rival Canadian Drug Manufacturers' Association took out media advertisements to make their case on opposite sides of the question of patent protection for new drugs, and since then, other groups have used this device regularly.

Many pressure groups increase their public profile once an election has been called. This phenomenon, discussed in Chapter 8, is usually called **third-party advertising**. Pressure groups often seek the response of parties and candidates to questions of concern to the group and then indicate their support or opposition in media advertising. The National Citizens Coalition was especially active in this respect, while the Canadian Alliance for Jobs and Trade Prospects and its anti–free trade counterpart, the Pro-Canada Network, were particularly visible in 1988. As noted, though, limits on third-party advertising during election campaigns have recently been upheld by the Supreme Court. In addition, national or local pressure groups sometimes target particular politicians, especially ministers, for defeat.

If all else fails, a group may resort to demonstrations, protest marches, tractor parades, sit-ins, and road and bridge blockades. Some of these are peaceful and legal, such as the orderly demonstrations that are an almost daily occurrence on Parliament Hill and frequently greet prime ministers on their travels. But the frustration of Aboriginal, environmentalist, anti-poverty, and other issue-oriented groups and movements increasingly takes the form of civil disobedience. The 1990 armed standoff at Oka, Quebec, was one of the rare occasions in which a group resorted to violence, but only after governments failed to respond to the Mohawks' verbal protests.

In recent years, globalization and free trade agreements that are claimed to benefit only transnational corporations have attracted much violent protest. At the World Trade Organization (WTO) Summit in Seattle in late 1999, at the Summit of the Americas in Quebec City in April 2001, and at the G7/G8 summit in Genoa three months later, hundreds of protesters took to the streets. While most protesters acted in a nonviolent fashion, some were intent on shutting the meetings down. Such demonstrations attract much media and public attention and may be the only way to make a point about certain issues. On the other hand, demonstrations should not be seen as the most common form of pressure group activity, and in some instances they may be counterproductive.

Group Resources and Determinants of Success

It is hard to determine why some groups are successful and others are not; however, factors accounting for success and failure include the following:

- Members
- Cohesion
- Money
- Information
- Sympathy of the government and popularity of the cause
- Financial position of government
- Absence of opposition

The size of the group is usually important, considering that numbers represent votes. The authorities feel comfortable ignoring very small groups, for example, because the electoral consequences would be minimal. In this respect, the Canadian Labour Congress and the National Action Committee on the Status of Women should be regularly successful in having the authorities respond to their demands because, with millions of members, they are the largest pressure groups in Canada.

The fact that the CLC is not overly influential points to the equal importance of the cohesiveness of the organization. First, as previously mentioned, the labour movement as a whole is not very cohesive, and even among those who are members of the CLC, unity, commitment, and militancy are notoriously lacking. Moreover, on those occasions when the CLC "declared war" on the government, the bulk of its members continued to vote for parties other than the NDP. Liberal and Conservative governments apparently feel that the CLC is so incapable of mobilizing its members behind the demands issued by its leadership that it can often be ignored. In recent years, NAC has also been seriously divided in its priorities and has become a basket case financially. In contrast, the Royal Canadian Legion and the Canadian Chamber of Commerce are able to mobilize their members to inundate the authorities with regular demands for concerted action.

As in other aspects of politics, money is an important resource. In the case of pressure groups, money can buy staff, offices, organization, expertise, publicity, and other useful weapons with which to get the group's message across. The Canadian Council of Chief Executives, the Canadian Manufacturers and Exporters, and the Canadian Chamber of Commerce are all financially strong, which gives them the capacity both to generate information to strengthen their case and to transmit it to relevant targets. Except for those representing big business or highly paid professions, however, most groups have financial problems.

Information is a fourth crucial resource in pressure group politics. Especially at the bureaucratic level, where much of this politics takes place, any vital information that is lacking as the public service drafts technical laws and regulations will be eagerly accepted. Even at the political level, the group may be able to present data and alternative analyses of policy that will lead ministers to rethink their proposals. Closely associated with information is the professional expertise of the pressure group's staff, and in this connection, the large business groups are able to produce mounds of well-researched and glossy documents. The Canadian Bar Association makes frequent representations to parliamentary committees, royal commissions, and government departments, and because of its expertise both in the substance of many issues and in the drafting of legislation, it is often asked for advice.

The sympathy of the government and the popularity of the cause are also important. If a basic correspondence exists between the demands of the group and the government's stated objectives or the prevailing public opinion, the pressure group will have greater success than if there is a vast gap in ideological perspective between the group and the values of the government or society in general. It is not surprising, for example, that the CLC would be virtually ignored by the business-oriented Mulroney government. Similarly, the minister responsible for the status of women in that cabinet repeatedly refused to meet the National Action Committee on the Status of Women because of the group's intense criticism. The government even cut NAC's annual grant and gave the first federal grant to the small rival organization, REAL Women (Realistic, Equal, Active for Life). A related point is the sharing of a professional orientation between group leaders and the bureaucracy. Many examples could be given of the success of a group because its officials shared the professional norms of the relevant public servants in their reciprocal relationship.

Since many pressure group demands relate to the spending of public money, the financial position of the government will often influence a group's success. As a result, requests for funds were more likely to be fulfilled in the prosperous and free-spending 1960s and 1970s than in the era of government restraint since 1985.

Finally, a group will be more influential if it has no organized opposition. One of the reasons for the success of the Canadian Medical Association over the years, for example, was that it had medical politics almost all to itself.[12] Contrast that situation with the abortion issue, where for many years the two vehemently opposing sides were evenly divided.

Lobbying in Canada

The tendency of the rich and powerful, including big business, to benefit from pressure group politics and elite accommodation can only be enhanced by recent developments in the practice of lobbying in Canada. If lobbying is the activity of trying to influence the authorities, it is, of course, a perfectly legitimate activity for anyone to undertake in a democracy. Traditionally, individuals, companies, unions, and pressure groups of all kinds have done their own lobbying, but in recent years Canada has seen the mushrooming of professional lobbying—consultant or government relations firms that lobby on behalf of an individual, company, or pressure group in return for a fee.

Those engaged in the new lobbying industry justify their existence largely in terms of the increasing size and complexity of government. The federal government grew enormously in the 1960s and 1970s, and the policymaking process was restructured such that corporations and interest groups could no longer find their way around Ottawa. The early 1980s constituted a period in which new means of

Malcolm Mayes/artizans.com

influence were being sought, and an expansion of such firms appeared to take place about the time the Mulroney government was elected in 1984. Many of the leading figures in the establishment of first wave of professional lobby firms were old cronies of the prime minister.

Given that the bureaucracy can satisfy many of the corporations' needs, ex-bureaucrats have also joined or formed lobbying firms in order to capitalize on their inside knowledge and connections. Federal conflict-of-interest guidelines preclude senior government employees from dealing with their former departments for one year after their departure from public employment, but these rules are sometimes broken.

Some of the largest consultant lobbying firms and a sample of some of their principal clients are given in Table 10.2. The table reveals that some companies engage the services of more than one lobbying firm.

TABLE 10.2 LARGE CONSULTANT LOBBYING FIRMS AND A SAMPLE OF THEIR CLIENTS, 2004

Global Public Affairs Inc.: Sun Life, Irving Oil, Inco, McCain Foods
Capital Hill Group: Canadian Tire, Molson Canada, Canadian National, Cineplex Odeon
Hill & Knowlton Canada: Bombardier, Alcan, Province of P.E.I., Microsoft
GPC International: Bombardier Aerospace, Power Financial, Canadian National
Grey, Clark, Shih & Associates, Ltd.: Magna, Maple Leaf Foods, Cameco, Hong Kong
SAMCI (S.A. Murray Consulting Inc.): Pepsi-Cola, Hudson's Bay Co., Visa
Earnscliffe Strategy Group: Microsoft, Canadian Pacific, Labatt Breweries, AT&T Canada

Source: Prepared by the author on the basis of the Public Registry of Lobbyists, available on the Industry Canada website at http://strategis.ic.gc.ca/cgi-bin/sc_mrksv/lobbyist/bin/lrs.e/view_search.phtml? (Retrieved 15 June 2004). Reproduced with the permission of the Minister of Public Works and Government Services Canada, 2004.

Registration of Lobbyists

After the emergence of such professional lobbying firms, a consensus developed among politicians that legislation, registration, and regulation were necessary. The registration idea was part of the Mulroney government's ethics package unveiled after its early troubled record of cabinet resignations due to conflicts of interest and numerous legal charges against Tory backbenchers.[13] Parliament consequently passed the Lobbyists Registration Act in 1989. According to that act, a lobbyist is an individual *who, for payment, on behalf of any person or organization ... undertakes to arrange a meeting with a public office holder or to communicate with a public office holder in an attempt to influence*

(a) the development of a legislative proposal ...

(b) the introduction, passage, defeat or amendment of any bill or resolution ...

(c) the making or amending of any regulation ...

(d) the development or amendment of any policy or program ...

(e) the awarding of any monetary grant or contribution or other financial benefit ... or

(f) the awarding of any contract.

The law divided lobbyists into two categories: Those who work for any client for a fee are classified as "Tier I" lobbyists, while "Tier II" lobbyists include those who engage in traditional pressure group or corporate lobbying—that is, in-house employees of an organization whose duties involve communicating with public officeholders on behalf of the organization.

The legislation acknowledged that lobbying public officeholders is a legitimate activity, but required lobbyists to register because it is desirable that officials and the public know who is attempting to influence government and because paid lobbyists should not impede free and open access to government. With certain exceptions, lobbyists had to file a return including the name and address of the lobbyist and the lobbying firm, the name and address of the client, and the subject matter of the solicitation.

Many critics felt that the 1989 legislation was very weak and contrasted it with the U.S. law on this subject adopted in 1946.[14] Some lobbyists did not register, and even when they did, the disclosure provisions in the Canadian law were

---

What Do You Think?

Do you think professional lobbyists are a positive or negative force in Canadian politics? Do you think their activities are sufficiently regulated? Do they make government more or less democratic?

minimal. The law did not even require revelation of the specific object of the representations; moreover, the act was almost totally lacking an effective enforcement mechanism.

The whole procedure provided a lucrative living to those who claimed to be intimates of ministers or ministries, and it favoured those who could afford to hire such professional lobbyists. In what John Sawatsky calls "one of the most odious lobby campaigns in the history of Canada," the fight of the Pharmaceutical Manufacturers Association to extend drug patent protection, "Gerry Doucet handled the PMAC file in GCI's [Government Consultants International's] office; his brother Fred handled the issue in the Prime Minister's Office."[15]

A parliamentary committee reviewed the Lobbyists Registration Act in 1993 and made many recommendations to strengthen the act. Not surprisingly, the lobbyists lobbied ferociously against greater transparency in their operations, and the amendments that were finally adopted in 1995 were a pale imitation of what had been recommended by the committee and promised by the Liberals during the 1993 election campaign. The new act recognized three categories of lobbyists: Tier I (consultant lobbyists who lobby for clients) and two types of Tier II lobbyists, in-house lobbyists (corporate), and in-house lobbyists (organization)—that is, employees of corporations or interest group organizations for whom lobbying was a significant part of their duties. On March 31, 2003, there were 908 Tier I lobbyists registered, collectively employed by 504 firms, and 294 and 311 lobbyists respectively in the Tier II categories.

As well, the new legislation required coalitions and grassroots lobbying to be registered and was somewhat more rigorous in what else had to be reported. The specific legislative proposal, bill, resolution, regulation, policy, program, or contract in question now has to be identified, along with the name of each department or other governmental institution lobbied. Contingency fees (fees based on the successfulness of the lobbying effort) are not outlawed, but any such fees must be disclosed to the registrar, as must the source and amount of any government funding of the client. As for enforcement, the registrar may audit information contained in any return or other document submitted and issue interpretation bulletins and advisory opinions. The six-month limitation of proceedings on contraventions was extended to two years. The ethics counsellor previously appointed by the Liberal government to administer the Conflict of Interest Code for cabinet ministers was required to work with interested parties to develop a code of conduct for lobbyists. The code came into effect in 1997, and lobbyists had a legal obligation to comply with it. The ethics counsellor was to investigate and publicly report on breaches of the code and could report publicly the fees, disbursements, and expenses paid to a lobbyist relating to any lobbying activity. Unfortunately, this official reported only to the prime minister, rather than to Parliament. Perhaps the most positive aspect of the 1995 changes therefore was the electronic registration of required information and public accessibility to the registry through the Internet.

While this revised law was an improvement on the original, it remained highly defective. "By leaving vague the definitions of lobbying, and by excluding any lobbying associated with a consultative exercise, the government ... left much room for those sincerely wishing to avoid disclosing their activities or their aims to do so."[16] In other words, much lobbying is simply not recorded. The law did not require lobbyists to disclose positions currently or recently held in national political parties, ministers' offices, or the federal public service; it did not actually prohibit the use of contingency fees; and it did not require disclosure of the global cost of each lobbying campaign. At the same time, the industry was invaded by associates of the Liberal Party.

It was not until 1999 that the RCMP for the first time looked into a potential violation of the act in connection with a Liberal activist close to the prime minister. This activist did not register as a lobbyist but allegedly met civil servants on behalf of a Shawinigan hotel owner who received a $100 000 government cheque to expand his operation. After the investigation, the RCMP found insufficient facts to support filing a criminal charge. Two later cases were reviewed by the Registrar of the Lobbyists Registration (LR) Branch but not referred to the RCMP for further investigation. The scandal-plagued Chrétien government made a minor change to the definition of lobbying in 2003, and when the Martin government replaced the ethics counsellor with the more independent ethics commissioner, it shifted enforcement of the Lobbyists' Code of Conduct to the Registrar for Lobbyists, a bureaucrat rather than an officer of Parliament.

While he was minister of finance, Paul Martin developed very close ties to one lobbying firm in particular, Earnscliffe Strategy Group. A specific criticism of this relationship was that Earnscliffe both lobbied the department of behalf of its clients and received contracts from the department to do public relations work. Later, many professional lobbyists, especially from Earnscliffe, were central to Martin's campaign for the Liberal leadership, as well as being the core of his subsequent transition team as he set up his new government. Several then became part of his Prime Minister's Office (PMO), although at that point such people had to cease their professional lobbyist functions. About the time Martin took over as prime minister, Earnscliffe split into two, with its communications wing sold off to a major international PR firm. While this move overcame one criticism, those intimates who returned to Earnscliffe would be able to tout to their clients their close connections to the PM and to their former colleagues now in the PMO.

The reports of the LR Branch are not particularly revealing, so it is fortunate that two external organizations keep their eye on lobbying activity in Ottawa: the Advocacy Research Centre (ARC) and Democracy Watch. ARC publishes a biweekly *Lobby Monitor*, which reveals the major lobbying efforts currently in progress, the techniques being used, and the people involved. Democracy Watch is more critical; it conducts a continuing campaign to clean up the lobbying business, with recommendations such as the following:

- Make the Lobbyists Registration Branch an independent office of Parliament
- Disclose lobbyists' connections to politicians and political parties
- Increase transparency about who is lobbying whom over what
- Embark on a more committed enforcement of the act
- Reveal the overall cost of a lobbying campaign.[17]

SUMMARY

This chapter discussed pressure groups (also called interest groups or advocacy groups), social movements, and lobbying. Since pressure groups are not an official part of the political system, their importance is often overlooked, but the first part of the chapter showed how prominent and significant they are. The chapter then listed examples of some of the principal pressure groups in various fields, provided different categorizations that are often useful, and differentiated pressure groups from social movements. The chapter also demonstrated how the federal structure of government in Canada affects the organization of pressure groups—usually requiring their presence at both levels of government. The targets of pressure group activity were outlined, including the four institutions of government: bureaucracy, cabinet, Parliament, and the courts. The next section tried to account for the relative success of pressure group efforts in terms of the different resources possessed by such groups, especially size, cohesion, money, information, government sympathy, and the tenor of the group's message. The final part of the chapter dealt with lobbying. It identified certain lobbying firms, their clients, and their modes of operation; it discussed the attempt to regulate lobbying activity via legislation; and it revealed continuing problems in this area that the political system should address.

DISCUSSION QUESTIONS

1. Why do business groups have more influence than other kinds of groups?
2. Why are student pressure groups so consistently ignored by federal and provincial governments?
3. Would groups that lack close links with the authorities (for example, anti-poverty, anti-globalization, and Aboriginal groups) be better advised to work through regular political channels or to opt for more confrontational tactics in order to try to influence public policy?
4. How democratic is the sort of lobbying that goes on, often behind closed doors? Does the Lobbyists Registration Act provide adequate transparency?

KEY TERMS

Advocacy advertising Advertising that advocates a political point of view rather than trying to sell a good or service.

Advocacy group/interest group/pressure group Any group seeking to influence government policy without contesting elections; an organization whose members promote their common interest by acting together to influence public policy.

Assembly of First Nations The largest interest group representing status and non-status Indians (who now prefer to be called First Nations peoples).

Canadian Council of Chief Executives The most powerful peak business pressure group in Canada, representing the 150 largest firms in the country.

Canadian Labour Congress The largest labour pressure group in Canada; the political voice of over 2.5 million members.

Clientele relationship The intimate and mutually advantageous relationship that sometimes develops between a government department or agency and the interest group with which it most frequently interacts.

Institutionalized pressure group A kind of pressure group characterized by permanence, resources, governmental recognition and acceptance, and well-developed links with the authorities.

Issue-oriented pressure group A kind of pressure group that springs up around an issue and disappears once that issue has been resolved.

Lobbying Any organized attempt to influence the authorities, now often performed by professional lobbyist firms.

Policy communities Loose communities that form for the purpose of shaping public policy, taking the form of discrete and specialized clusters of government departments and agencies, pressure groups, politicians, corporations, and interested individuals.

Regulations The detailed rules drafted by the bureaucracy under the authority of laws passed by Parliament that are too voluminous and technical to put into the legislation itself.

Social movement An informal network of organizations and individuals who on the basis of a collective identity and shared values engage in political struggle intended to expand the boundaries of the existing system, such as the women's and environmental movements.

Third-party advertising Advertising by advocacy groups, as opposed to political parties, during an election campaign.

FURTHER READING

Ayers, Jeffrey M. *Defying Conventional Wisdom: Political Movements and Popular Contention against North American Free Trade*. Toronto: University of Toronto Press, 1998.

Coleman, William. *Business and Politics: A Study of Collective Action*. Montreal: McGill-Queen's University Press, 1988.

———, and Grace Skogstad. *Policy Communities and Public Policy in Canada*. Mississauga: Copp Clark Pitman, 1990.

Conway, Janet M. *Contesting Globalization: Social Movements, Identity, Place and Knowledge*. Black Point, N.S.: Fernwood Publishing, 2004.

Pal, Leslie. *Interests of State: The Politics of Language, Multiculturalism, and Feminism in Canada*. Montreal: McGill-Queen's University Press, 1993.

Phillips, Susan. "Competing, Connecting, and Complementing: Parties, Interest Groups, and New Social Movements." In A. Brian Tanguay and Alain-G. Gagnon, eds. *Canadian Parties in Transition*. 2nd ed. Scarborough: Nelson Canada, 1996.

Pross, Paul. *Group Politics and Public Policy*. 2nd ed. Toronto: Oxford University Press, 1992.

Sawatsky, John. *The Insiders: Government, Business, and the Lobbyists*. Toronto: McClelland and Stewart, 1987.

Young, Lisa, and Joanna Everitt. *Advocacy Groups*. Vancouver: UBC Press, 2004.

PART 3

The Constitutional Context

If "politics" and "government" can be separated, the first half of this text dealt with politics and the second half considers government. Chapter 1 provided an overview of government, but this second half goes into more depth and is itself divided between the constitutional context and the process of governing. The Constitution forms the framework of the whole political system, and is analyzed in the following two chapters. Chapter 11 outlines the historical development of the Canadian Constitution, its ingredients and principles, and the addition of the Charter of Rights and Freedoms in 1982. Since one of the most important aspects of the Constitution is the relationship between the federal and provincial governments, Chapter 12 examines all aspects of Canadian federalism.

Chapter 11

The Canadian Constitution and the Charter of Rights and Freedoms

This chapter begins with an overview of Canadian constitutional history and the road to Canadian Confederation. It then proceeds to examine the basic ingredients and principles of the Canadian Constitution. The final section of the chapter provides a more detailed treatment of the Charter of Rights and Freedoms, which was added to the Constitution in 1982.

Chapter Objectives

After you have completed this chapter, you should be able to:

Explain the main principles of the pre-Confederation constitutional documents

Enumerate the reasons for and outline the process leading toward Confederation

List the various ingredients of the Canadian Constitution

Recount the main provisions of the Constitution Act, 1982

Enumerate the six basic principles of the Canadian Constitution

Distinguish among various methods of protecting rights and freedoms

Enumerate the rights and freedoms included in the Charter and provide examples of prominent cases involving judicial interpretation thereof

Discuss how the reasonable limits and notwithstanding clauses modify the guarantees of the Charter

Discuss how the Charter has judicialized politics and politicized the judiciary and whether this is a positive change in the political system

Early Political Institutions

The territory that is now called Canada was first occupied by Aboriginal peoples. France and Britain colonized parts of this territory in the 1500s and 1600s and periodically fought over them for nearly 200 years. After the 1759 Battle of the Plains of Abraham, part of the Seven Years' War between these traditional European rivals, the 1763 Treaty of Paris transferred Quebec, Prince Edward Island, Cape Breton, and New Brunswick to British control. Interaction between the new British power and the Aboriginal peoples is discussed in Chapter 4.

The **Royal Proclamation of 1763**, the first distinctively Canadian constitutional document, created the colony of Quebec.[1] Apart from Aboriginal peoples, Quebec at the time was largely made up of French-speaking farmers, clergy, and seigneurs. The British-appointed government was English-speaking, but it resisted the idea of imposing the English language and Protestant religion on such a homogeneous French-Catholic population.

In 1774, the **Quebec Act** provided for a new set of government institutions. The governor appointed a council to advise him, but there would be no elected assembly in the colony. Roman Catholics were allowed freedom of religion and could be appointed to the council, and the colony combined British criminal law with French civil law. Meanwhile, the first elected assembly in the "Canadian" part of British North America had been summoned in Nova Scotia in 1758, followed by Prince Edward Island in 1773.

When the residents of the 13 "American" colonies revolted against British rule in 1776, French Canadians essentially remained neutral. Thousands of ex-Americans loyal to Britain—the United Empire Loyalists—migrated to "Canada." This influx led to the severing of New Brunswick from Nova Scotia in 1784, together with the creation of its own assembly, since the Loyalists were accustomed to operating with such elected offices. Then, in response to pressure from those Loyalists who migrated to what is modern-day Ontario, as well as to reward the loyalty of the French in Quebec, Britain passed the **Constitutional Act** of 1791. It divided the colony into two—Upper and Lower Canada—each with a governor, an appointed executive council, an appointed legislative council, and a locally elected assembly. In Upper Canada (Ontario), which was almost exclusively English, the Constitutional Act provided for British civil law, while Lower Canada (Quebec) retained the French civil law system. The executive council gradually evolved into the cabinet, while the legislative council was the forerunner of the Senate. Thus, by 1791, all the colonies had achieved **representative**

government, that is, a set of political institutions including an elected legislative assembly (see Figure 11.1).

Discord subsequently developed between the locally elected assembly and the executive, composed of the governor and his appointed executive council. The assembly represented the people and could articulate their views, but it had no real power over the appointed councils. This situation was complicated by the cultural division in Lower Canada—a French assembly and an English executive—with "two nations warring in the bosom of a single state."[2] Reformers demanded **responsible government**, in which the members of the executive council would come from and reflect the views of the elected assembly. This problem eventually erupted into the Rebellions of 1837 in both Upper and Lower Canada, led by William Lyon Mackenzie and Louis-Joseph Papineau respectively. The British government put them down by force and then appointed Lord Durham to investigate the situation.

The 1839 **Durham Report** recommended that the principle of responsible government be implemented, so that the executive branch would govern only as long as it retained the confidence of the assembly. Durham outlined a division of powers between local and imperial authorities such that in local matters the governor would follow the advice of colonial authorities, but in matters of imperial concern he would act as an agent of the British government. Overcoming British resistance, responsible government was adopted in Nova Scotia, New Brunswick, and the colony of Canada in 1848, and three years later in Prince Edward Island. Thus, by 1851, all the pre-Confederation colonies operated on the basis that the

Figure 11.1 Evolution of Canadian Pre-Confederation Political Institutions

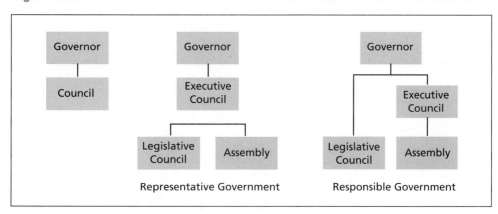

cabinet or executive council had to resign if it lost the confidence of the elected legislative assembly.

Durham also recommended that Upper and Lower Canada be united into a single colony of Canada, partly as one last attempt to submerge and assimilate the French. The colonies were amalgamated by the 1840 **Act of Union**, but when it became clear that the objective of assimilation would not be achieved, French was recognized as the second official language of the legislature. Moreover, most governments of the period had joint English and French leaders.

The Road to Confederation

Economic, political, and military factors soon drove the British North American colonies to consider uniting.[3] Because the British had discontinued colonial trading preferences, and because a reciprocity treaty with the United States had expired, the colonies hoped to establish a new free trade area among themselves. This large internal market would be enhanced by a railway link between the Maritimes and central Canada, also providing the latter with a winter Atlantic port. The future prospect of annexing and developing the West was seen as a further source of economic prosperity.

Meanwhile, the colony of Canada had experienced political deadlock between its two parts, then called Canada East (Quebec) and Canada West (Ontario), as well as between French and English component groups. Public decisions had to be made in one combined set of governmental institutions, yet the needs and demands of the two parts were often quite different. This led to the practice of requiring a "double majority" (a majority of members from each part of the colony) for the passage of bills. Confederation would grant greater autonomy to the two parts because provincial governments would handle distinctive internal matters on their own, while a central government would deal with common problems. Such a two-tier structure also appealed to the Maritime provinces, which did not wish to turn all decisions over to a distant central government.

The individual colonies also felt vulnerable in a military sense. The United States had a powerful army on their doorstep, and the British government no longer seemed interested in providing military protection. By joining together, the colonies would make American aggression more difficult.

In the 1860s, Nova Scotia, New Brunswick, and Prince Edward Island began to consider forming a Maritime union and called the Charlottetown Conference of 1864 for this purpose. When delegates from the colony of Canada arrived, however, the idea of a larger union was put up for debate. The essentials of the **Confederation** scheme were agreed upon at the Quebec Conference later that year, and the London Conference of 1866 fine-tuned the agreement, leaving Prince Edward Island temporarily on the sidelines. Thus, the four provinces of Nova Scotia, New Brunswick, Quebec, and Ontario were officially united on July 1, 1867, by the **British North America Act (BNA Act)**, later renamed the **Constitution Act, 1867**.

Components and Principles of the Canadian Constitution

The Canadian Constitution would be easier to comprehend if it consisted of a single document by that name. In the absence of such a document, we can define a **constitution** as the whole body of fundamental rules and principles according to which a state is governed. Canada's Constitution provides for the basic institutions of government and relations between them, relations between national and provincial governments, and relations between governments and citizens.[4] Such a comprehensive definition suggests that the final product may not be neat and tidy and that some of it may not be written down at all.

In the search for the components that fit the definition of a constitution provided above, it will be seen that the Canadian Constitution is a great hodgepodge. It essentially consists of the following:

- Constitution Act, 1867, and its amendments
- British and Canadian statutes
- Constitution Act, 1982, principally the Charter of Rights and Freedoms
- Judicial decisions
- Constitutional conventions

The Constitution Act, 1867, and Its Amendments

We turn first to the formal, legal documents, the most important of which is the Constitution Act, 1867, as mentioned above. That act provided much of the basic machinery and institutions of government and established a federal system.

Part III of the act deals with the executive power, for example, and section 9 declares that the executive authority over Canada is vested in the Queen. Subsequent clauses refer to the governor general and to the Canadian Privy

Council, which is "to aid and advise in the Government of Canada." Section 13 observes that the "governor general in council" refers to the governor general acting by and with the advice of the Canadian Privy Council. Note that the prime minister and cabinet are not explicitly mentioned.

Part IV establishes the legislative power—the Senate and House of Commons. The act requires that money bills (bills that involve the raising or spending of money) originate in the House of Commons, and within it, from members of the executive branch.

Part V concerns provincial constitutions, including the position of lieutenant governor. Since the 1867 act created the provinces of Ontario and Quebec, it had to establish their legislatures, whereas the legislatures of Nova Scotia and New Brunswick continued in their pre-Confederation form.

Part VI, the "Distribution of Legislative Powers" or **division of powers** between the central and provincial governments, is probably the most important part of the document. The core of Canadian **federalism** in a constitutional sense consists of section 91, the federal powers; section 92, provincial powers; section 93, education; and section 95, concurrent powers.

Part VII is concerned with the judiciary. It is a short section that gives the governor general the power to appoint superior, district, and county judges. It also provides for judges' retirement and removal, and it allows Parliament to set up a general court of appeal. Note that the 1867 act does not explicitly establish the Supreme Court of Canada.

Part VIII deals with the division of provincial revenues, debts, and assets at the time of Confederation. It makes clear that the provinces have possession of their own lands, mines, and minerals. Part IX is a miscellaneous collection, including section 132, the treaty power, and section 133, regarding English and French languages. The final section provides for the admission of other colonies.

The Constitution Act, 1867, was thus very brief on the executive and judicial branches of government and included virtually nothing about limiting the powers of government in relation to the people. The act also lacked any mention of the means to amend it, but since it was a statute of the British Parliament, most formal changes to the act until 1982 were made by that Parliament at Canadian request.

Such formal amendments to the 1867 act are also part of the Canadian Constitution, some more important than others. They were often termed "British North America Acts," of whatever year in which they were passed, but in 1982, they were mostly renamed "Constitution Acts" of the appropriate year. For example, the BNA Act, 1940, which is now called the Constitution Act, 1940, transferred jurisdiction over unemployment insurance from the provincial to the federal level of government.

British and Canadian Statutes

The second major component of the Canadian Constitution is a collection of British statutes and orders-in-council and Canadian statutes. Chief among acts passed by the British Parliament that are of constitutional status for Canada is the **Statute of Westminster, 1931**, which declared Canada to be totally independent of Britain. Henceforth, no British law would apply to Canada unless (as in the case of constitutional amendments) Canada requested it. The Northwest Territories, British Columbia, and Prince Edward Island were British colonies added to Canada by means of British orders-in-council, that is, decisions of the British cabinet, as distinct from acts of Parliament. Therefore, they must be considered another ingredient of the Canadian Constitution.

So are the Canadian statutes that carved provinces out of the Northwest Territories, the Manitoba Act of 1870, and the Saskatchewan and Alberta Acts of 1905. Other Canadian statutes of constitutional significance include the Supreme Court Act, an ordinary law that fleshes out the provisions of the 1867 act with respect to the judicial branch of government, the Federal Court Act, the Parliament of Canada Act, the Bill of Rights, the Canada Elections Act, the Citizenship Act, the Emergencies Act, the Canadian Human Rights Act, the Yukon Act, and the Nunavut Act.

The Constitution Act, 1982

Although the **Constitution Act, 1982,** was in a sense the last amendment to be passed by the British Parliament to the Constitution Act, 1867, it is worthy of separate mention. Canada was completely self-governing after 1931, but most amendments to the 1867 act still had to be made by the British Parliament, because no formula had been developed to do so in Canada. The Constitution Act, 1982, contained such a domestic **constitutional amending formula**, and the Canada Act passed by the British Parliament at the same time finally terminated all British authority over Canada. Part V of the act provided five different amending formulas, depending on the subject matter of the amendment:

- Unanimous consent of federal and provincial legislatures
- Consent of Parliament and seven provincial legislatures representing at least 50 percent of the population

- Consent of Parliament and one or more provinces affected
- Consent of Parliament alone
- Consent of a provincial legislature alone

Because of subsequent dissatisfaction with this formula, Parliament passed a law in 1996 to the effect that in the case of amendments falling in the second category above, the federal government would not agree to any constitutional amendment that did not have the consent of Ontario, Quebec, British Columbia, Alberta, and a majority of Atlantic provinces.

The second main part of the Constitution Act, 1982, was the Charter of Rights and Freedoms, a significant addition to the Canadian Constitution discussed in detail later in the chapter. The 1982 act also contained statements on Aboriginal peoples' rights and equalization payments to have-not provinces. As far as the division of powers was concerned, a new section, 92A, was added to clarify and extend provincial powers over natural resources. The 1982 document did not alter the position of the monarchy in Canada, however; Elizabeth II continues to be recognized as Queen of Canada, having no connection to the British government in this role.

Judicial Decisions

The fourth ingredient of the Canadian Constitution consists of judicial decisions that have clarified or altered provisions of the 1867 act or other parts of the Constitution. The largest body of such decisions consists of the judgments of the British **Judicial Committee of the Privy Council**, Canada's final court of appeal until 1949. It was John A. Macdonald's intention to create a strong central government, but the Judicial Committee interpreted the 1867 act in such a way as to minimize federal powers and maximize those of the provinces. The court decisions that effected such a wholesale transformation of the federal nature of the country must be considered a part of the Constitution alongside the actual provisions of the original act. The very power of the courts to invalidate legislation in this manner—**judicial review**—is a basic principle of the Constitution.

Constitutional Conventions

Thus far, all the ingredients listed can be found in written form, although not in one place. The final component of the Constitution, on the other hand, has never been committed to paper. It consists of **constitutional conventions**, that is, unwritten rules of constitutional behaviour that are considered to be binding by and upon those who operate the Constitution but that are not enforceable by the courts.[5] Constitutional conventions develop from traditions, and through constant recognition and observance they become as established, rigid, and sacrosanct as if they were written down. Many of these informal rules have been inherited from Britain, some have been modified in the Canadian environment, and others are unique to Canada. Many relate to the operation of the executive branch of government, given such slight attention in the 1867 act. The dominant position of the prime minister and cabinet, the subordinate place of the governor general, and the principle of responsible government are three of many conventions that are part of the Constitution.

Principles of the Constitution

The preceding discussion has identified three basic principles of the Canadian Constitution: responsible government, federalism, and judicial review. At least three other fundamental principles are also embedded in the Canadian Constitution: constitutional monarchy, the rule of law, and democracy.[6]

In terms of its head of state, Canada is a **constitutional monarchy**. This is not a principle that attracts much attention, largely because the monarch herself lives in another country and because her actual power, as well as that of her Canadian representative, the governor general, is not extensive. Nevertheless, the monarchical system underlies a great deal of the operation of government in Canada, largely in the form of the Crown, as discussed in Chapter 13.

The **rule of law** is another constitutional principle inherited from Great Britain that rests largely on convention and judicial precedent. In essence, it means that all government action must be based on law and that governments and government officials must obey the law. In other words, the law is supreme, and no one, including the lawmakers, is above it. Courts in Canada as well as in Britain have had occasion to overturn government decisions and actions that were not based on law. The sixth principle, democracy, was analyzed fully in Chapter 6.

The Charter of Rights and Freedoms

In the eyes of some observers, the pre-1982 Canadian Constitution was deficient in lacking a statement of **civil liberties**, that is, the rights and freedoms that individuals enjoy beyond the reach of the government or the state. Such rights and freedoms are an integral part of a democratic political system and represent territory into which the government is not allowed to enter. In typical British manner, however, the fact that they were not written down did not mean that they did not exist.

Political systems that value civil liberties have adopted two principal methods to protect them. The British approach is to make Parliament supreme, but on the presumption that neither the legislature nor the executive would infringe such rights and freedoms because both branches of government are held in check by public opinion, tradition, the political culture, and self-restraint. In such a system, civil liberties are so deeply ingrained in the values of the people and politicians alike that they do not need to be written down, and the authorities would never think of infringing them—even though, in theory, Parliament could do so. While the courts cannot overturn legislation in Britain—that is, they do not have the power of judicial review—they have wide **judicial discretion** in the interpretation of laws, and many safeguards of civil liberties have been introduced into the law as canons of interpretation. Thus, even in the British system, judicial precedents accumulated into the **common law** offer some protection against arbitrary government action. So does the basic constitutional principle, the rule of law.

The American approach, derived in reaction to an imperial government that *did* encroach upon colonial liberties, is to provide for a written statement of civil rights in the constitutional Bill of Rights. Then, if legislation is passed or the executive takes action that is felt to violate a person's rights, such acts can be challenged in the courts. It is up to the courts to determine whether the government has infringed rights and freedoms as defined in the Constitution. The courts thus have the power of judicial review, and they can overturn offensive legislation or executive actions.

In Canada, federal and provincial politicians occasionally violated civil liberties, such as in the case of the Quebec Padlock Law and the Alberta Press Bill, which blatantly interfered with such freedoms as speech, press, and assembly. Such actions persuaded Prime Minister Diefenbaker to enact the **Canadian Bill of Rights** in 1960. The bill's apparent intention was to allow the courts to invalidate legislation that they found to conflict with the Bill of Rights, but this aim was not clearly articulated. Other serious gaps in the bill were that it applied only to the federal government, not to the provinces; that it allowed legislation to be passed that overrode the bill, as long as this was acknowledged (that is, a notwithstanding clause); that as an ordinary piece of legislation, the bill could be amended in the routine way; and that it was superseded by the War Measures Act, at the very time when it might be needed most.

Not surprisingly, the courts made very limited use of the Bill of Rights. In only one case, the *Drybones* case of 1970, did they decide that a clause of an act violated the Bill of Rights and was therefore inoperative. The bill was more useful in clarifying legal rights and was referred to in several cases to fill in gaps in definitions of such concepts as "right to counsel," the "right to an interpreter," and the "right to a fair hearing."

Prime Minister Trudeau recognized the limitations and ambiguities of the Canadian Bill of Rights and wanted to incorporate new kinds of rights into the Constitution. Finally, in 1982, with the adoption of the **Charter of Rights and Freedoms**, he accomplished his objective. The Charter was entrenched in the Constitution, and it is increasingly the task of the judiciary to determine if and when governments have encroached upon the following rights and freedoms:

- Fundamental freedoms
- Democratic rights
- Mobility rights
- Legal rights
- Aboriginal rights
- Equality rights
- Language rights
- Minority language education rights

Among other things, Trudeau was determined to protect official minority language education rights across the country in an effort to undercut Quebec's claim that it alone represented French Canada. Moreover, he hoped to counter centrifugal forces throughout the land and pressures for decentralization to the provinces by creating an instrument that the courts could use to cut down self-serving provincial laws. As a new national symbol, the Charter would also serve to increase the allegiance of all citizens to the national government.

The Charter is generally a much stronger document than its predecessor. Besides being broader in scope, the Charter applies equally to both federal and provincial governments. Being entrenched into the Constitution, it is difficult to amend. It also states very clearly that the courts are to invalidate any legislation that they find to conflict with the provisions of the Charter. We will briefly examine the provisions of the Charter and note some of the prominent court decisions it has inspired.

Pierre Elliott Trudeau, father of the Charter of Rights and Freedoms. (CP Photo)

Reasonable Limits on Rights and Freedoms

It must first be said that the rights articulated in the Charter are not absolute. Section 1, the **reasonable limits clause**, indicates that these rights are subject to "such reasonable limits, defined by law, as can be demonstrably justified in a free and democratic society." The courts are thus allowed to find that while a piece of legislation violates certain rights, it is still acceptable according to their definition of reasonable limits. In order to decide which restrictions can be justified in a free and democratic society, the Court developed guidelines in the *Oakes* case that have come to be called the **Oakes test**. The objective of the government in limiting a Charter right must be pressing and substantial, and the means adopted must be proportional to that objective. That is, the means must be rationally connected to the objective; they must impair the right as little as possible; and the benefits of the restriction must exceed its costs. In fact, the Supreme Court has made extensive use of section 1, upholding many laws that it considered to be in violation of Charter rights but that were saved because the infringements were reasonable.

Fundamental Freedoms

At least from a political point of view, section 2 of the Charter is probably most important. It lists the following **fundamental freedoms**: freedom of conscience and religion; freedom of thought, belief, opinion, and expression, including freedom of the press and other media of communication; freedom of peaceful assembly; and freedom of association.

With respect to freedom of religion, the Supreme Court threw out the Lord's Day Act as an infringement of freedom of religion because its restrictions on Sunday activities were clearly related to the Christian sabbath and discriminated against other religions. On the other hand, the Court upheld Ontario's Retail Business Holidays Act, an act designed to limit Sunday shopping and preserve Sunday as a day of rest on a secular rather than a religious foundation. The courts also decided that public schools may no longer hold a compulsory and exclusively Christian school prayer. Ontario's publicly funded Roman Catholic separate school system was upheld as a pre-Charter constitutional right, and it does not discriminate against other private religious schools for which public funding is not guaranteed.

Freedom of expression has brought a wide range of issues before the courts. Perhaps most controversial was the Supreme Court's rejection of the French-only sign provision of Quebec's Bill 101, which also violated Quebec's own Charter of Rights. The Court decided that freedom of expression not only included the freedom to express ideas but also the freedom to choose the language in which to express them. Moreover, the concept of freedom of expression incorporated "commercial expression," such as a company's right to erect a sign or engage in advertising. Thus, the federal government's first attempt at prohibiting tobacco advertising was also deemed a violation of tobacco companies' freedom of expression. But a majority of the Court concluded that a partial ban on such advertising as well as prohibiting the dissemination of hate literature were both acceptable as reasonable limits on freedom of expression.

Obscenity also falls into the category of freedom of expression. In the *Butler* case, the Court divided pornography into different categories, saying that portrayal of sex with violence and sex that is degrading or dehumanizing can be restricted by the authorities, but that portrayal of explicit sex that is neither violent nor degrading is generally acceptable unless children are involved. In later cases, an artist's depiction of children in various sexual activities was deemed to be art rather than pornography, and customs officers were instructed not to differentiate in the standards they applied to homosexual and heterosexual materials. In the 2001

Sharpe case, the Supreme Court unanimously upheld the provisions of the Criminal Code that prohibit the possession of child pornography as a reasonable limit on freedom of expression. As for prostitution, the Court similarly upheld the prohibition on communicating for the purposes of sidewalk solicitation.

Case Study
Use of Reasonable Limits in the *Sharpe* Case Regarding Child Pornography

In the *Sharpe* case, in 2001, the Supreme Court ruled that the law prohibiting the possession of child pornography infringed Robin Sharpe's freedom of expression. But the Court went on to uphold the law as a reasonable limit on his Charter right because:

- The objective of the law that criminalized the possession of child pornography was pressing and substantial
- The means chosen by Parliament were rationally connected to the objective
- Allowing minor and reasonable exceptions (e.g., innocent photographs of a baby in the bath) showed that the law was a minimal impairment of the Charter right
- The benefits of prohibiting such materials outweighed any costs to the right of freedom of expression

Freedom of expression and freedom of the press in connection with election campaigns have also fostered several constitutional cases. The Supreme Court decided that the three-day blackout period before election day in which newspapers could not publish public opinion polls was too long. As mentioned in Chapter 8, repeated efforts by Parliament to restrict third-party advertising during election campaigns were thwarted by the lower courts in Alberta but ultimately upheld by the Supreme Court in 2004.[7]

In another controversial decision (with two prominent members dissenting), the Supreme Court ruled that freedom of association includes the right to join a trade union but does not guarantee the right of a union to go on strike. In other words, freedom of association does not prevent federal or provincial legislatures from passing back-to-work legislation or otherwise interfering in the collective bargaining process.

Democratic and Mobility Rights

Under **democratic rights** in sections 3 to 5, the Charter guarantees that every citizen of Canada has the right to vote in federal and provincial elections; that no Parliament can continue for more than five years, except in time of real or apprehended war, invasion, or insurrection; and that Parliament must sit at least once every year. Section 3 has been used in several cases dealing with federal and provincial electoral laws that denied the vote to certain categories of people. One of the most controversial decisions in this respect stated that all prisoners have the right to vote in federal elections; another established that the privilege of listing a candidate's affiliation on the ballot cannot be restricted to parties running 50 candidates or more. Rather unexpectedly, the democratic rights section has also been used to assess the validity of electoral maps that determine the size of constituencies.

Under section 6, **mobility rights**, every citizen of Canada has the right to enter, remain in, and leave Canada, and every citizen or permanent resident has the right to take up residence and pursue a livelihood in any province. On the other hand, laws establishing reasonable residency requirements for receiving public services are acceptable, as is giving preference to local residents if the unemployment rate in that province is higher than the national rate. Trudeau included mobility rights because of his concern that some provinces were restricting the entry of residents of other provinces, as in the case of cross-border employment, but these clauses have not featured frequently in judicial interpretation.

Legal Rights

Legal rights are contained in sections 7 to 14. In section 7, everyone has the right to life, liberty, and security of the person and the right not to be deprived thereof except in accordance with the principles of fundamental justice. "Security of the person" was used to invalidate the abortion provision of the Criminal Code in the famous *Morgentaler* case in 1988. A majority of the Court ruled that the law, with all its arbitrary and bureaucratic procedures, violated the security of the person of the woman concerned and constituted a "profound interference with a woman's body." Sue Rodriguez, dying of Lou Gehrig's disease, was not so fortunate in arguing that security of the person provided her with the right to assisted suicide—only a minority of judges agreed with her.

In the *Singh* case, "security of the person" required that the Immigration Department provide an oral hearing for refugee claimants when their lives could be in danger if deported. "Fundamental justice" also necessitated giving such claimants an opportunity to state their case and to know the case against them. In cases of sexual assault, the Supreme Court has grappled with the right of the accused to use evidence about the victim's previous sexual activity against the right of the victim not to be unnecessarily hounded on the subject on the witness stand. To some extent, the result of several such cases was to tighten up the concept of consent in sexual matters: "no means no." The Supreme Court has upheld the existing Criminal Code provisions with respect to the moderate spanking of children and the criminalization of the possession of marijuana against claims that they violated fundamental justice and/or security of the person.

Section 8 establishes the right to be secure against unreasonable search and seizure. In dismissing the charge of collusion between the Southam and Thomson newspaper chains, the Court extended this right to corporations and decided that the search of Southam's offices by anti-combines officials had indeed been unreasonable because it had not been authorized by a judge. This section has also come into play in cases involving police officers making spot checks, taking blood or DNA samples, or entering houses; customs officers performing strip searches at border points; guards frisking prisoners; and police officers frisking people on the street.

Section 9 grants the right not to be arbitrarily detained or imprisoned, and section 10 states that on arrest or detention, everyone has the right to be informed promptly of the reasons therefor, as well as the right to contact a lawyer without delay and to be informed of that right. The Court has ruled that random police spot checks are a reasonable limit on the right not to be arbitrarily detained and that roadside breath tests do not include the right to retain counsel. However, a person who fails that test and is asked to accompany the police officer to a police station has a right to retain counsel before the breathalyzer test is conducted there. Moreover, the Court has ruled that a person has the right to be told of his or her right not only to a lawyer but also to legal aid and must have a reasonable opportunity to exercise these rights.

Section 11 includes a variety of rights available to a person charged with an offence. "To be tried within a reasonable time" has been extremely controversial after the *Askov* decision found that a delay of almost two years between a preliminary hearing and a trial had been excessive. The lower courts took this to mean that everyone had a right to a trial within six to eight months of being charged, and some 34 500 cases were thrown out in Ontario alone.

Persons charged cannot be compelled to testify against themselves, cannot be denied reasonable bail without just cause, and are presumed innocent until proven guilty according to law in a fair and public hearing by an independent and impartial tribunal. The presumption of innocence was addressed in the *Oakes* case. Under the "reverse onus" clause of the Narcotics Control Act, a person proven to be in possession of a narcotic was also presumed to be guilty of trafficking, and it was up to the person charged with possession to prove his or her innocence on the trafficking charge. The *Oakes* case invalidated this clause as an unreasonable limit on the presumption of innocence. Persons charged with an offence are guaranteed a trial by jury if the maximum punishment for the offence is imprisonment for five years or more; as well, whether they are finally acquitted or found guilty and punished, they cannot be tried for the offence again.

Everyone has the right not to be subjected to any cruel and unusual treatment or punishment. In the 2001 *Latimer* case, the Supreme Court rejected the claim that the minimum mandatory sentence of 10 years in jail constituted cruel and unusual punishment in the case of a father who took the life of his severely disabled daughter because he could not bear to see her in such pain. Section 14 stipulates that a party or witness in any proceeding who does not understand or speak the language in which the proceeding is conducted or who is deaf has the right to the assistance of an interpreter.

Equality Rights

Equality rights are contained in section 15, which reads as follows:

> *Every individual is equal before and under the law and has the right to the equal protection and equal benefit of the law without discrimination and, in particular, without discrimination based on race, national or ethnic origin, colour, religion, sex, age or mental or physical disability.*

In the *Andrews* case, the Supreme Court laid down a two-step process for interpreting equality rights. The Court first determines if there has been a violation of the equality rights listed in section 15 (or of others analogous to them), and then whether there has been a harmful or prejudicial effect. In other words, inequalities and distinctions are permitted if no negative discrimination is involved. According to Ian Greene, the Court made it clear that "it intends to interpret section 15 to help clearly disadvantaged groups in society."[8] Moreover, the second part of the section permits **affirmative action** programs that give preference to those who have been discriminated against in the past. Equality rights are, of course, subject to reasonable limits, and on this basis the Supreme Court has allowed several kinds of discrimination to continue. In the case of mandatory

Reprinted with permision from *The Globe and Mail*.

retirement at age 65, for example, the Court ruled that such laws and policies were a violation of equality rights and did involve discrimination but could be allowed as reasonable limits.

Perhaps the most innovative use of section 15 has been in connection with sexual orientation and same-sex rights.[9] In 1995, the Supreme Court ruled unanimously that the Charter prohibited discrimination on the basis of sexual orientation, even though this was not explicitly listed in section 15. After "reading in" this addition to the list in section 15, the Court made the same order with respect to the Individual's Rights Protection Act in Alberta. Then, in 1999, the Court moved on to same-sex partnerships, finding that in most situations, laws could not discriminate between same-sex and opposite-sex couples. This prohibition on discrimination eventually included both adoption and marriage.

Language Rights

Sections 16 to 22 of the Charter constitutionalize the federal and New Brunswick Official Languages Acts. These sections guarantee that certain government agencies will operate on a bilingual basis, as discussed in Chapter 3. Section 23 constitutionalizes **minority language education rights**, and some would argue that this was the only part of the Charter with which Pierre Trudeau was truly concerned. The clause guarantees these rights to Canadian citizens who constitute English- and French-language minorities in all provinces in areas "where numbers warrant." The Supreme Court can decide when the number of francophone students warrants a French-language school, and it has also ruled that such a school must have a "distinct physical setting" and that French-language parents must have a say in the "management and control" of it. The Supreme Court struck down the provision in Quebec's Bill 101 that limited access to the English-language school system in Quebec to the children of parents who were themselves products of that system (the "Quebec clause"). Indeed, section 23 (the "Canada clause") was deliberately drafted so that it would conflict with Bill 101, in order that Canadian citizens who moved to Quebec could also send their children to the English-language schools.

Other Provisions

Section 24 makes clear, where the Bill of Rights did not, that the courts have the power to interpret the Charter and to invalidate laws that conflict with it. The Charter does not actually bar illegally obtained evidence, as in the United States; the admission of such evidence is acceptable as long as it does not bring the administration of justice into disrepute.

Sections 25 through 30 relate to specific groups in society. Section 25 reads that the rights and freedoms in the Charter shall not be construed so as to abrogate or derogate from any Aboriginal, treaty, or other rights or freedoms that pertain to the Aboriginal peoples of Canada, including any rights or freedoms that have been recognized by the Royal Proclamation of 1763 and any others that may be acquired by the Aboriginal peoples of Canada by way of land claims settlements.

Section 27 asserts that the Charter shall be interpreted in a manner consistent with the preservation and enhancement of the multicultural heritage of Canadians, and section 28 ensures that the rights and freedoms referred to in the Charter are guaranteed equally to male and female persons. The women's movement considered the addition of section 28 to be essential in order that governments would not be able to use the notwithstanding clause (section 33) to override the gender-equality provision of section 15. According to section 29, nothing in the Charter abrogates or derogates from any rights or privileges guaranteed by or under the Constitution of Canada in respect of denominational schools. This section thus protects section 93 of the 1867 Constitution Act, which guaranteed existing Protestant and Roman Catholic separate schools.

Section 32 clarifies that the Charter applies to the Parliament and government of Canada, to the legislature and government of each province, and to the Northern territories. By implication, it also applies to the municipal level of government. Thus all legislation in Canada must be consistent with the Charter, as must all actions of government executives, including ministers, public servants, and police officers. The Charter is not intended to apply to the private sector, but certain institutions occupy an ambiguous position. The Charter has been applied to community colleges, for example, but more autonomous semi-public institutions such as hospitals and universities are exempt. Federal and provincial human rights codes are intended to prevent discrimination in the private sector, but since such codes take the form of laws, they must also remain consistent with the Charter.

The Notwithstanding Clause

As mentioned above, the "reasonable limits" clause in section 1 allows the courts to exempt certain laws from the application of the Charter. The second limitation on Charter rights revolves around the **notwithstanding clause** in section 33. In the areas of fundamental freedoms, legal rights, and equality rights, either level of government is allowed to pass legislation contrary to the Charter. On the other hand, the legislation cannot be used to circumvent democratic rights, mobility rights, or linguistic rights. The notwithstanding clause would normally come into play when legislation was introduced to override a judicial decision regarding a Charter right. Such a bill can be exempted from the provisions of the Charter only for a five-year period, however, after which it becomes inoperative if not passed again.

Despite the number of times the Supreme Court has invalidated federal or provincial legislation since 1982, governments have rarely re-enacted such provisions under section 33. Over the first 23 years, it was used only in Saskatchewan and Quebec. The Saskatchewan government used section 33 (unnecessarily, as it turned out) to pass back-to-work legislation to end a public service strike in 1986. The first Parti Québécois government in Quebec (1976–85) routinely applied the notwithstanding clause, as a matter of principle, to all new legislation. The next Liberal government discontinued that practice, but when the Supreme Court ruled that French-only store signs violated their owners' freedom of expression, Premier Bourassa invoked section 33 (and the equivalent clause in the Quebec Charter of Rights) and then passed what he considered to be a compromise law that allowed certain bilingual signs inside the store. While this incident in particular gave the notwithstanding clause a negative reception in most of English

Canada, section 33 is often defended as a general principle. It allows democratically elected legislators, if they choose, to have the final say in many areas.

What Do You Think?

In cases like restricting abortion, discriminating on the basis of sexual orientation, or denying same-sex marriage, do you think the federal Parliament or a provincial legislature should use the notwithstanding clause to override a Supreme Court decision if a majority of legislators disagree with it?

Provincial politicians in Alberta have occasionally threatened to invoke the notwithstanding clause. That province probably contains the leading critics of judicial activism in the defence of minority rights, and federal members of the Alberta-based Reform/Canadian Alliance also advocated the use of section 33 on occasion.[10]

Implications of the Charter for the Political System

The Charter of Rights and Freedoms has attracted both passionate support and opposition. Both sides agree, however, that the adoption of the Charter has significantly changed the operation of the Canadian political system. The courts have become involved in almost all of the most difficult political issues that have arisen over the past 23 years: Aboriginal rights, abortion, assisted suicide, euthanasia, French-only signs, gender equality, impaired driving, mandatory retirement, minority language schools, official bilingualism, political rights of public servants, pornography, prostitution, redistribution of constituency boundaries, the right to strike, same-sex relationships, separate schools, sexual assault, sexual orientation, Sunday shopping, testing the cruise missile, and tobacco advertising. Such cases have enmeshed the courts in considerable political controversy and, as Peter Russell says, the Charter has "judicialized politics and politicized the judiciary."[11] Table 11.1 (page 276) shows how the public feels about legislatures or courts having the final say.

While most Canadians seem pleased with the courts' involvement (some of them ignorant of the fact that most rights and freedoms were equally enjoyed before 1982), representatives of both the left and the right have made scathing attacks on the "legalization of politics" in Canada. Michael Mandel, for example, argues that judges make highly political decisions but disguise this fact through

TABLE 11.1 COURTS VERSUS LEGISLATURES: WHO SHOULD HAVE THE FINAL SAY?

	Percentage of Respondents
Courts	59.6
Legislatures/government	26.5
Don't know/refused	13.9

Source: Adapted from Paul Howe and David Northrup, "Strengthening Canadian Democracy: The Views of Canadians," *Policy Matters* 1, no. 5 (July 2000), 100. Reprinted by permission of Institute for Research on Public Policy, Montreal. www.irpp.org

legal interpretations and abstract principles that are unintelligible to the general public. Mandel challenges the generally accepted view that politicians make decisions that are popular, political, and self-serving, while judges' decisions are impartial, objective, technical, rational, and in the public interest. Their invocation of the reasonable limits clause, for example, has been highly discretionary.[12]

Mandel's second argument is that while the Charter has been sold as enhancing democracy and the power of the people, it has really reduced the degree of popular control over government. It has transferred power from representative, accountable legislatures and politicians to unrepresentative, unaccountable, and unrestrained judges, courts, and an elitist legal profession.

Third, legalized politics enhances individual and corporate rights against the collective welfare of the community. The adoption of individualistic American values in the Charter, as opposed to traditional Canadian collectivism, is strengthened by the tendency of the courts to cite American precedents when making their decisions.

Mandel's fourth point is that legalized politics is conservative, class-based politics that defends existing social arrangements and undermines popular movements. For a variety of reasons—including the cost of litigation, the background and attitudes of judges, and the biases in the law and the Charter—the socially disadvantaged and labour unions were better off without it.

The attack from the right focuses on the claim that women and minorities have benefited from Charter decisions at the expense of the majoritarian views of elected legislatures and the general public.[13] It is true that an implication of adopting the Charter is that minority groups increasingly ignore the usual political processes—legislatures, cabinets, and bureaucracies—and take their demands to the courts instead. To some extent this happened when such groups were unable to accomplish their goals through traditional political activity, in which case it could be argued that this alternative avenue is advantageous. The Charter does serve to protect certain minority rights against the tyranny of the majority. On the other hand, few observers would welcome a general transformation of political activity into legal activity with the attendant loss of political skills and organization that traditionally characterize a democracy. Seymour Martin Lipset fears that the Charter will remove one of the last traits that distinguish Canadians from Americans by increasing the litigious character of citizen–state relations, and that it will bring about a "rights-centred" political culture.[14]

The main nonpolitical effect of the Charter has been to restrict the behaviour of police officers and others engaged in law enforcement. The manner in which they deal with those suspected or accused of committing an offence is subject to rigid Charter rules. Many apparent cases of guilt have been thrown out because according to a judge, police officers' collection of evidence brought the administration of justice into disrepute. This was commonly because the accused gave a confession in unusual circumstances; because the accused was denied the right to retain and instruct counsel without delay; or because police (or anti-combines) officers did not comply with a judge's interpretation of Charter restrictions on search and seizure. Thus, law enforcement officers often complain that they are expected to do their job with their hands tied behind their backs.

Greg Hein has shown that it is corporations, not women or minority groups, that are the single biggest interest in taking Charter cases to the courts.[15] But if we focus on winners rather than users, it is more difficult to generalize. Official-language minorities, criminals, the gay and lesbian communities, and corporations would probably top the list.

In any case, such analysts and critics at least offer a salutary reminder to question the face value of court decisions; to refrain from glorifying the Charter, judges, lawyers, and courts; and to remember traditional ways of making public decisions and of protecting rights and freedoms. Parliament and the courts each have their own understandable and legitimate perspectives on Charter issues, and the best approach is to hope for some kind of dialogue between them.[16]

Reflecting the fact that it was born of political compromise, the Charter retains one main limitation on judicial interpretation, the notwithstanding clause. Any legislature may pass an act violating certain aspects of the Charter, as long as it says explicitly that it is doing so. Canadians are left with a strange system under which the courts can overrule the legislatures but the legislatures can overrule the courts. Canadian political compromise that it is, this system of protecting rights and freedoms may turn out to be superior to either total legislative supremacy or exclusive judicial review. The truth of the matter, however, is that politicians are now afraid to use the clause because of an anticipated public backlash.

SUMMARY

This chapter focused on the Canadian Constitution and an important recent addition thereto, the Charter of Rights and Freedoms. The first part of the chapter outlined the evolution of Canadian constitutional development up to Confederation. It showed that the Canadian Constitution is not a single document, but rather consists of many different documents—British and Canadian statutes and judicial decisions—and unwritten constitutional conventions. It enumerated the basic provisions of the Constitution Act, 1867, and the Constitution Act, 1982, and the six basic principles of the Canadian constitution. Turning to the Charter of Rights and Freedoms, the chapter demonstrated that a written charter is not the only way to protect civil liberties. It then discussed the major parts of the Charter together with examples of definitive judicial decisions relevant to each clause. Charter rights are not absolute, and the two loopholes in the document, the reasonable limits and notwithstanding clauses, were both examined. At the end, the chapter considered the major impact that the Charter has had on the operation of Canadian politics and looked at its pros and cons.

DISCUSSION QUESTIONS

1. Would it be possible or advisable to incorporate all the ingredients of the Canadian Constitution into a single document?
2. What were the symbolic, legal, and political consequences of adopting the Constitution Act, 1982?
3. Is the increase in judicial power in the Canadian political system as a result of the adoption of the Charter of Rights and Freedoms an asset or a liability?

KEY TERMS

Act of Union The 1840 act that united the colonies of Upper and Lower Canada into the colony of Canada and that was partly designed to assimilate the French.

Affirmative action A law or program that provides preference in the hiring or promotion process to individuals with certain characteristics.

British North America Act (BNA Act) The 1867 act of the British Parliament that created Canada by uniting the four original provinces, that provided some of the essential elements of the new country's Constitution, and that in 1982 was renamed the Constitution Act, 1867.

Canadian Bill of Rights An act of the Canadian Parliament passed in 1960 that outlined basic civil liberties but whose defects caused judicial confusion and limited the bill's effectiveness.

Charter of Rights and Freedoms Part of the Constitution Act, 1982, that guaranteed fundamental freedoms and legal, democratic, linguistic, mobility, and equality rights.

Civil liberties Freedoms or rights, including the freedoms of speech, press, religion, and assembly, that citizens enjoy and that cannot be infringed upon by government.

Common law The basis of the British and Canadian legal systems that consists of the accumulation of judicial precedents, which guide judges in the absence of a legislature-made law.

Confederation The foundation, in 1867, of Canada with the union of four provinces.

Constitution The whole body of fundamental rules and principles according to which a state is governed.

Constitution Act, 1867 The new name for the British North America Act, 1867, which united the four original provinces.

Constitution Act, 1982 The act sponsored by Prime Minister Trudeau that contained a made-in-Canada constitutional amending formula and a Charter of Rights and Freedoms.

Constitutional Act The 1791 British law that divided Canada into two separate colonies—Upper and Lower Canada—each with a governor, executive and legislative councils, and assembly.

Constitutional amending formula The process for amending the Constitution.

Constitutional conventions Unwritten rules of constitutional behaviour that are considered to be binding by and upon those who operate the Constitution but that are not enforceable by the courts.

Constitutional monarchy The official designation of the Canadian form of government, characterized by a monarch who is head of state but who rules according to the Constitution, which confides almost all governmental power into other hands.

Democratic rights A category of rights in the Charter of Rights and Freedoms that, among other things, guarantee the vote to every Canadian citizen.

Division of powers The distribution of legislative powers between the federal and provincial governments, largely contained in sections 91 and 92 of the Constitution Act, 1867.

Durham Report The 1839 report by Lord Durham that recommended the union of Upper and Lower Canada and the granting of responsible government to the colony of Canada.

Equality rights A category of rights in the Charter of Rights and Freedoms that prohibit governments from discriminating against certain categories of people.

Federalism (federation) A system of government characterized by two levels of authority (federal and provincial) and a division of powers between them, such that neither is subordinate to the other.

Fundamental freedoms Political freedoms—of religion, speech, press, assembly, association, etc.—that governments are not supposed to encroach upon and that are guaranteed by the Charter of Rights and Freedoms.

Judicial Committee of the Privy Council A committee of the British Parliament that functioned as Canada's final court of appeal until 1949.

Judicial discretion The leeway inevitably bestowed on the courts when they interpret laws, even when they do not, or have no power to, overturn them.

Judicial review The power of the courts to overturn legislation or actions of the executive branch of government.

Legal rights The rights of a person suspected or accused of committing a crime, now listed in the Charter of Rights and Freedoms.

Minority language education rights Rights established in section 23 of the Charter of Rights and Freedoms whereby French-speaking Canadians can send their children to French-language schools wherever their numbers warrant, a principle also extended to English-speaking Canadians where they are a minority.

Mobility rights A category of rights in the Charter of Rights and Freedoms guaranteeing the freedom to move from one province to another and seek employment there.

Notwithstanding clause Section 33 of the Charter of Rights and Freedoms that allows federal or provincial governments to pass laws that violate certain sections of the Charter.

Oakes test The strategy outlined in the *Oakes* case for interpreting the reasonable limits clause of the Charter of Rights and Freedoms.

Quebec Act The 1774 British law that provided for a system of government for the colony of Quebec that included certain privileges for the French-language, Roman Catholic majority.

Reasonable limits clause Section 1 of the Charter of Rights and Freedoms, which allows the courts to uphold a law even if it violates a Charter right.

Representative government A form of government including an assembly elected by the citizens but not necessarily incorporating the principle of responsible government.

Responsible government A form of government in which the political executive must retain the confidence of the elected legislature and resign or call an election if and when it is defeated on a vote of nonconfidence.

Royal Proclamation of 1763 The British policy enunciated after conquering Quebec that in a large area called Indian Territory forbade the purchase or settlement of land without a treaty between the Crown and the Indian people concerned.

Rule of law The constitutional principle that all government action must be based on law and that governments and government officials must obey the law.

Statute of Westminster The 1931 British law that declared Canada and the other Dominions to be fully independent.

FURTHER READING

Borovoy, Alan. *When Freedoms Collide: The Case for Our Civil Liberties*. Toronto: Lester & Orpen Dennys, 1988.

Greene, Ian. *The Charter of Rights*. Toronto: Lorimer, 1989.

Heard, Andrew. *Canadian Constitutional Conventions*. Toronto: Oxford University Press, 1991.

Hiebert, Janet. *Charter Conflicts: What Is Parliament's Role?* Montreal: McGill-Queen's University Press, 2002.

Mandel, Michael. *The Charter of Rights and the Legalization of Politics in Canada*. Rev. ed. Toronto: Wall and Thompson, 1994.

Morton, F.L., and Rainer Knopff. *The Charter Revolution and the Court Party*. Peterborough: Broadview Press, 2000.

Reesor, Bayard. *The Canadian Constitution in Historical Perspective*. Scarborough: Prentice-Hall Canada, 1992.

Romanow, Roy, J. Whyte, and H. Leeson. *Canada … Notwithstanding: The Making of the Constitution, 1976–1982*. Toronto: Methuen, 1984.

Russell, Peter. *Constitutional Odyssey*. 2nd ed. Toronto: University of Toronto Press, 1993; 3rd ed., 2004.

Sharpe, Robert J., et al. *The Charter of Rights and Freedoms*. 2nd ed. Toronto: Irwin Law, 2002.

Chapter 12

The Provinces and the Federal System

The adoption of a federal system was one of the crucial decisions taken in the creation of Canada, and the shape of the federal–provincial relationship remains at the heart of contemporary Canadian politics. After introducing the role of the provinces, this chapter outlines the federal system in Canada at its creation and then traces the evolution of that system, especially through changes in the division of powers and federal–provincial financial relationships. The chapter concludes with a discussion of Canadian federalism today and an enumeration of recent developments.

Chapter Objectives

After you have completed this chapter, you should be able to:

Define federalism and distinguish it from other forms of intergovernmental relations

Enumerate the ingredients of the Confederation Settlement

Distinguish between the intended division of powers between federal and provincial governments and the actual judicial interpretation of these sections

Discuss the evolution of federal–provincial finance, including taxation agreements; conditional, unconditional, and block grants; and equalization payments

Explain how the centralized federation of 1867 became the decentralized Canada of today

Identify the characteristics of cooperative federalism, discuss the concepts of executive and bureaucratic federalism, and outline the major features of Canadian federalism today

The Provincial Political Systems

Canada is composed of 10 provinces and 3 territories (see Figure 12.1). The provinces are autonomous within the powers given them by the Constitution, but the powers of the territories could theoretically be revoked. Unlike the provinces, therefore, the territories are constitutionally subordinate to the federal government.

Each of the provinces can be considered a separate political system. Each one has a full complement of governmental institutions, a somewhat distinctive political culture, party system, and array of pressure groups. The distinctiveness of each province is the principal reason for establishing Canada as a federation, yet their governmental operations bear a striking resemblance to those at the federal level.

Each province is formally headed by the lieutenant governor, the equivalent of the governor general, who represents the Queen and performs primarily ceremonial and social functions. The effective head of the provincial government is

Figure 12.1 Canada's Provinces, Territories, and Capitals

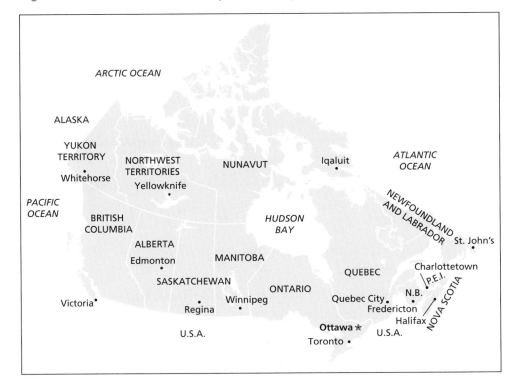

the premier, analogous to the prime minister, along with the cabinet, who are officially called the executive council. As in Ottawa, the provincial cabinet typically sets priorities, especially financial; determines policies; gives direction for the preparation of legislation; oversees departmental administration; and makes order-in-council appointments.

The provincial legislatures consist of the elected representatives of the people, called MLAs (members of the Legislative Assembly) except in Newfoundland and Labrador, Quebec, and Ontario. Each provincial legislature has only one chamber, which is divided between government and opposition members, and functions quite similarly to the House of Commons. A number of provinces have opted for fixed election dates every four years.

Given the expansion of provincial government operations, at least until 1990 or so, provincial politicians are increasingly dependent on the bureaucracy or public service to advise them on their decisions and the implementation of their programs. The most important provincial responsibilities are health and education, and those two departments consume the largest share of each province's finances. Provinces have their own sources of revenue, but as noted later in this chapter, they also depend heavily on transfers from the federal government. In fact, despite the division of powers between the two levels of government, there is a great deal of interaction between them, especially at the ministerial and bureaucratic levels.

Each province also establishes its own hierarchy of courts and its own system of municipal government. The province determines the structures, responsibilities, and financial powers of its local governments; in other words, municipal governments are constitutionally subordinate to the province. In theory, there is no connection between municipal authorities and the federal government—those two levels of government communicate via the provinces. In practice, however, actions of the federal government often have serious consequences for municipalities. More and more observers are recommending that large cities in particular be somehow brought into the ambit of Canadian federalism.

Federalism and the Confederation Settlement

In a formal sense, **federalism** can be defined as a system of government characterized by two levels of authority, federal and provincial, and a division of powers between them, such that neither is subordinate to the other. This definition distinguishes the relationship between provincial and national governments from that between municipal and provincial governments, for in the latter case the municipalities are clearly subordinate entities. This federal–provincial equality of status is provided for in the constitutional division of powers between the two levels of government that is found primarily in sections 91 and 92 of the Constitution Act, 1867. Other aspects of federalism are also important, however, such as federal–provincial financial relations and joint policymaking mechanisms. The recent tendency of federal and provincial governments to download their responsibilities illustrates both the subordinate and the increasingly significant role of municipalities.

The fundamentals of Canadian federalism, often called the **Confederation Settlement**,[1] were incorporated into the **Constitution Act, 1867**. As noted in Chapter 1, the principal architect of Confederation was Sir John A. Macdonald, who intended the new country to be a highly centralized federation, with Ottawa retaining most of the power. In fact, the Confederation Settlement was not consistent with the modern definition of federalism because in certain respects the provinces were made subordinate to the central government.

The Confederation Settlement consisted of five principal components:

- Division of powers between federal and provincial governments
- Division of financial resources
- Federal controls over the provinces
- Provincial representation in central institutions
- Cultural guarantees

The Fathers of Confederation gave the provinces 16 specific **enumerated powers** in section 92 (e.g., hospitals and municipal institutions) and then left everything else—the **residual powers**—to Ottawa in section 91. For greater certainty, however, they also listed 29 federal powers such as trade and commerce and national defence. Two **concurrent powers**—agriculture and immigration—were listed in section 95, and the treaty power in section 132 gave the federal government the power to implement Empire treaties, regardless of their subject matter (see Table 12.1).

In the division of financial resources, federal dominance was even more apparent. The settlement gave Ottawa the power to use any mode or system of taxation, including both direct and indirect taxes. Since the only tax widely used at the time was the customs duty, an indirect tax, the provincial power over direct taxation was not considered to be significant. Instead, the provinces were

TABLE 12.1 THE CORE OF THE FEDERAL–PROVINCIAL DIVISION OF POWERS

Federal Powers	Provincial Powers
• Trade and commerce	• Direct taxation within the province
• Any form of taxation	• Public lands
• National defence	• Hospitals and health care
• Banking	• Municipal institutions
• Indians	• Education
• Criminal law	• Property and civil rights
• Interprovincial transportation and communication	• Administration of justice

expected to raise their revenues from the sale of shop, saloon, tavern, and auctioneer licences, as well as to rely on federal subsidies. The federal government was to pay each province an annual per capita grant of 80 cents plus a small subsidy to support its government and legislature. The act also stated that the federal government would assist the provinces by assuming their pre-Confederation debts. It should be added that the provinces were authorized to raise revenues from their natural resources, but this source was not taken seriously at the time because few such resources had yet been discovered.

In addition, in a clear departure from what is now regarded as the federal principle, Ottawa was given several means of controlling the provinces. As an alternative to granting royal assent, the lieutenant governor, a federal appointee, was permitted to reserve provincial legislation for the consideration of the federal cabinet, which could then approve or reject it. Even if the lieutenant governor gave assent to a piece of provincial legislation, however, the federal cabinet could subsequently disallow it. As well, the federal government could declare any local work or undertaking to be for the general advantage of Canada and unilaterally place it within federal jurisdiction. These three controls are respectively referred to as reservation, disallowance, and the declaratory power.

Given the highly centralized nature of the division of powers, the limited financial resources of the provinces, and the federal controls, it is clear that the Confederation Settlement of 1867 placed the provinces in a subordinate position, somewhat akin to municipalities, rather than giving them the equal or coordinate status provided for in the modern definition of federalism.

In the light of the federal government's dominant position, it is not surprising that the smaller provinces were concerned with their representation in Ottawa. The fourth aspect of the 1867 Settlement, therefore, was agreement on provincial representation in the House of Commons and the Senate, a question of much more concern at the time than the division of powers. The great compromise that allowed Confederation to go forward was agreement that the provinces would be represented according to population in the Commons but that regional equality would prevail in the Senate. Thus, each of the three original regions—the Maritimes, Quebec, and Ontario—was to receive 24 senators, appeasing smaller provinces that could be easily outvoted in the lower chamber.[2]

Confederation was more than just a union of provinces; it was also seen as a union of two cultural groups, English and French. Thus, the fifth aspect of the Confederation Settlement might be called cultural guarantees. Considering the anxiety of French Canadians about the preservation of their language and culture, these guarantees were surprisingly minor. Section 133 of the 1867 act made French and English official languages in the federal Parliament and federal courts as well as in the Quebec legislature and Quebec courts—but nowhere else. At the time, religion was probably of greater concern than language, so existing separate school systems in the provinces (especially Ontario and Quebec) were guaranteed by allowing the federal government to step in to restore them, if necessary. French Canada was also protected by giving power over property and civil rights to the provinces, so that Quebec could maintain certain cultural particularisms, including its civil law system.

John A. Macdonald, the architect of a centralized federal system. (William James Topley/Library and Archives Canada/PA-027013)

Of these five components of the Confederation Settlement, only three relate directly to the relationship between federal and provincial governments. This chapter will therefore proceed to track the development of the Settlement in these three aspects: the division of powers, financial resources, and federal controls. In discussing the evolution of Canadian federalism, it is critical to understand how the very centralized federation created in 1867 became the highly decentralized Canada of today. This trend is apparent in all three areas.

Division of Powers

If changes to the **division of powers** between federal and provincial governments have resulted in the provinces being more important today, there are two ways in which this could have happened. First, formal constitutional amendments could have altered the division of powers in the provinces' favour; second, judicial decisions interpreting sections 91 and 92 of the Constitution Act, 1867, could also have had this effect.

Since 1867, only four formal constitutional amendments have been adopted that directly affected the division of powers. In 1940, unemployment insurance was added to the list of federal powers in section 91 after the courts had earlier declared that it belonged to the provinces. In 1951, old age pensions were made a concurrent power, allowing the federal government into this area as well. In 1964, Ottawa's jurisdiction was enlarged to include widows' and survivors' benefits and disability pensions. In 1982, the new section 92A increased provincial jurisdiction over natural resources, while at the same time the Charter of Rights and Freedoms generally reduced the powers of both levels of government. Thus, in the first three cases, the net result was a slight increase in federal powers, but this increase was accomplished with the unanimous consent of the provinces. The 1982 amendment was the only formal constitutional amendment that in any way increased provincial powers at the expense of the federal government. Formal constitutional amendments, therefore, do little to explain the more powerful provinces of today.

Judicial interpretation of the federal and provincial powers in the 1867 act is a much more complicated and significant subject. Before 1949, the **Judicial Committee of the Privy Council** (JCPC) in London was Canada's final court of appeal, and its decisions had a major impact in transforming Canadian federalism from a centralized to a decentralized system. The most important JCPC decisions related to the federal peace, order, and good government clause as opposed to the provincial power over property and civil rights.

The **peace, order, and good government (POGG) clause**, one of two parts of section 91 in the 1867 act, says that all powers not given to the provinces in section 92 are left with the federal government. This clause is also known as the residual clause. The second part of section 91 provides, "for greater certainty," a list of 29 examples of federal powers. In the course of its judgments, the Judicial Committee drove a wedge between these two parts of section 91, deciding that the 29 enumerations were the *real* federal powers rather than just examples, and ignoring the peace, order, and good government clause except in cases of national emergency. But in times of national emergency, as determined by the JCPC, federal powers were almost unlimited. This became known as the **emergency doctrine**, and how the courts managed to transform the residual clause into an emergency power is a very long story. In normal times, on the other hand, the JCPC gave an extremely broad interpretation to section 92-13, property and civil rights in the province, finding that almost any matter that was the subject of a federal–provincial constitutional dispute could be incorporated within this provincial power.[3] That is why so little was left over for the federal residual clause.

The effect of the judicial interpretation of the peace, order, and good government clause, along with other clauses such as trade and commerce and treaty powers, was to reduce significantly the intended dominance of the federal government. The complementary broad interpretation of property and civil rights increased substantially the scope of provincial powers. This influence has been very controversial in political, judicial, and academic circles because it was clearly contrary to John A. Macdonald's conception of Canadian federalism and because it did not permit Ottawa to take initiatives that centralist advocates often wished.[4]

Other observers contend, however, that the Judicial Committee's line of interpretation was consistent with the increasing size and distances that characterized the country as time went on, as well as with societal forces and public orientations, at least outside Ontario. They argue that the provincial bias pervading so many of the JCPC's decisions was "in fundamental harmony with the regional pluralism" of the federal, decentralized, diversified nature of Canadian society. However desirable centralization may have seemed at the outset, it was inappropriate in the long run "for the regional diversities of a land of vast extent and a large, geographically concentrated, minority culture."[5]

What Do You Think?

Are you a centralist or a decentralist? Would you give more money and power to the federal or provincial level of government? What are the advantages and disadvantages of each approach to Canadian federalism?

Federal–Provincial Finance

In the Confederation Settlement, the federal government was given the power to levy any kind of tax, while the provinces were restricted to direct taxation.[6] The federal government was also committed to pay the provinces small annual grants. While the intention was thus to create a highly centralized federation, the financial factor also ultimately contributed to the increased power of the provinces. This situation came about because the provinces levied direct taxes that they were not expected to use, such as income taxes; because the provinces successfully lobbied for larger federal grants; and because some provincial revenues, such as those from natural resources, turned out to be more significant than anticipated.

Provincial revenues proved to be inadequate from the beginning, and it did not take long for the provinces to begin levying their own direct personal and corporate income taxes and to demand larger sums from Ottawa. With both levels of government taxing the same personal and corporate incomes, but in a totally uncoordinated fashion, and with provinces always lining up for more federal funds, the federal–provincial financial situation became very complicated. This muddied state of affairs worsened with the advent of the Depression, when even fewer funds were available to go around. As a result, Prime Minister Mackenzie King appointed the Rowell-Sirois Commission, officially the Royal Commission on Dominion–Provincial Relations, in 1937. Its only recommendation to be immediately implemented was that the costly responsibility for unemployment insurance be transferred to the federal government.

Before 1940, therefore, the two levels of government were relatively independent on both the taxation and expenditure sides of public finance. Since the Second World War, on the other hand, they have become intimately intertwined, and Ottawa has taken the lead (sometimes with provincial encouragement) in coordinating the various ingredients of the financial relationship. The complicated federal–provincial financial situation since 1940 might be simplified somewhat by considering three aspects separately: taxation agreements; conditional and block grants; and equalization payments.

Taxation Agreements

Between 1942 and 2001, the taxation side was characterized by a series of five-year federal–provincial taxation agreements. The name and terms of the agreements changed over the years, but the basic objective was the same: to effect a degree of coordination in the field of federal–provincial taxation. The main taxes in question were personal and corporate income taxes. While the federal personal income tax was standard across the country (except for Quebec), each province was able to determine its own rate as a percentage of the federal tax, so that the provincial portion varied widely. Except for Quebec, all personal income taxes have been collected by Ottawa in the first instance, after which the provincial portion was transferred back, an arrangement that until recently was found to be satisfactory to all concerned. Quebec has always collected its own personal income tax, so that its residents complete two separate income tax forms. By 2001, however, all provinces had separated their provincial income tax from the federal income tax system, meaning that the provincial tax is no longer necessarily calculated as a percentage of the federal tax.

Conditional and Block Grants

The second aspect of the federal–provincial financial picture was **shared-cost programs**. These expanded considerably after 1940 in the joint development of a welfare state. The most important shared-cost social programs were postsecondary education (1952), hospital insurance (1957), the Canada Assistance Plan (1966), and medical insurance (1968). Hospital and medical insurance were later combined. These programs are termed the "major" federal transfers to the provinces, but a large number of "small" transfer programs also exist.

Federal grants for postsecondary education have always been of a **block grant** variety, that is, a sum of money given to each province for the operating costs of universities and colleges but without any conditions or strings attached. Such a grant significantly helped to fund universities and colleges and allowed provinces to keep tuition fees relatively low. The other major shared-cost programs originally fell into the **conditional grant** category. The usual pattern here was for the federal government to pay approximately 50 percent of the cost of each program provided that the provinces met Ottawa's conditions. For example, Ottawa would fund half of any provincial health care program that was comprehensive (covering all necessary health services provided by hospitals and medical practitioners), universal (covering the whole population), portable (covering the costs of provincial residents while temporarily absent from the province), accessible (not impeding or precluding reasonable access to services by extra charges), and publicly administered. Under the Canada Assistance Plan, Ottawa similarly provided half the funding for almost any provincial or municipal program that provided social assistance and welfare services to persons in need. In this case, the main condition was that anyone in need had to be included, and no one could be forced to work for welfare. Without federal contributions to health and social assistance programs, many provinces would not have been able to finance them.

Most of these programs fell constitutionally within provincial jurisdiction, but Ottawa always maintained that its **spending power** allowed it to make payments to individuals, institutions, and other governments in fields over which Parliament did not necessarily have the power to regulate. The federal government even claimed that it could attach conditions to such spending and has often done so. In the exercise of its spending power, Ottawa was able to establish national standards in a number of social programs.

While a combination of provincial pressure and federal political and bureaucratic expansionism inspired most of these programs, the provinces often criticized the federal conditions attached to them as being out of place in areas of provincial jurisdiction. Quebec in particular took this point of view in the early 1960s. In response, the Pearson government allowed the provinces to opt out of certain conditional grant programs and continue to receive federal funding as long as they maintained an equivalent program. Then, in the 1970s, Ottawa became upset at the rapidly escalating costs of many of these programs and its commitment to finance 50 percent of whatever the provinces spent on them.

In 1977, therefore, the federal government passed the Established Programs Financing Act, which encompassed postsecondary education and health care. This act had two major implications. First, Ottawa removed the detailed conditions attached to the health insurance programs, as many provinces wished. But in return, the federal government no longer felt obliged to pay 50 percent of the provincial program costs. The federal grants now took the form of tax transfers (giving the provinces more room to levy their own taxes) as well as cash, and henceforth, Ottawa would increase its funding of such programs only by a certain annual percentage. Removing the conditions from health insurance grants, however, led to problems such as hospitals introducing user fees, doctors double- or extra-billing, and provinces using health care funds for other purposes.

Unhappy with these developments, the federal government consequently passed the **Canada Health Act** in 1984. The act resurrected the five earlier conditions connected to health care and penalized those provinces permitting extra charges. At the same time, the federal share of such programs fell below 50 percent, and the 1990s saw a progression of freezes and cuts in funding. For a time, the Canada Assistance Plan (CAP) remained a conditional grant program, with Ottawa continuing its 50 percent contribution, but the Mulroney government put a ceiling on its CAP contributions to the three richest provinces in the early 1990s, and the Liberals repealed the plan completely.

The 1994 federal budget brought in by Finance Minister Paul Martin announced a freeze on all major federal transfers except equalization payments, and the 1995 budget inaugurated a significant transformation of federal–provincial transfers. Beginning in 1996–97, Established Program Funding (postsecondary education and health insurance) and the Canada Assistance Plan (social assistance and welfare services) were combined into one block grant called the **Canada Health and Social Transfer (CHST)**.

The CHST was a combination of cash payments and tax points (federal withdrawal from joint tax fields), but it represented a significant reduction from previous amounts. It was at this time that postsecondary education fees began to skyrocket, as provinces in turn reduced university and college funding. As a block grant, the CHST did not contain the conditions of CAP, nor were Ottawa's expenditures driven by provincial costs. The only condition on welfare transfers was that provinces not impose a minimum residency requirement. As a result, many provinces reduced social assistance programs and/or brought in workfare. Despite the protests of almost all social reformers, who did not trust provincial governments to provide adequate social assistance programs, Ottawa felt that it could not retain such conditions when it was reducing its contributions. On the other hand, the federal Liberal government continued to defend the principles of the Canada Health Act and fought with Alberta over the funding of private health clinics that charged "facility fees." Ottawa later accepted Alberta's Bill 11, which most observers saw as a violation of the Canada Health Act, and was reluctant to enforce the act in a number of instances in other provinces.

Equalization Payments

The third aspect of federal–provincial finance consists of **equalization payments**. In 1957, the federal government began to pay these unconditional grants to have-not provinces based on provincial need, so that all could offer a relatively equal standard of services. The essence of equalization payments was to bring the have-not provinces up to the national average tax yield per capita. Typically, Ontario, British Columbia, and Alberta have been above the national average and have not received equalization payments, while the other seven provinces receive an annual payment based on the per capita shortfall of tax revenues multiplied by the province's population. By the beginning of this century, British Columbia also qualified.

Provincial Finances

In 2004, the Canada Health and Social Transfer was divided into two separate parts—Canada Health Transfer and Canada Social Transfer—and a supplementary Health Reform Transfer was also provided. As shown in Table 12.2, major federal transfers to the provinces reached $50 billion.

In addition to their grants from Ottawa, the provinces have levied over 30 forms of direct taxation that were unanticipated in 1867. The enormous natural resource revenues that some provinces (especially Alberta) receive on top of direct taxation and federal contributions are also significant. A comparison of federal transfers and the provinces' own revenues (taxes plus natural resource and other revenues) is shown in Table 12.3 (page 296).

Thus, the combination of unanticipated federal grants, direct taxes, and natural resource revenues has contributed significantly to the enhanced status of the provinces in the Canadian federal system. It should also be reiterated that the two

TABLE 12.2 MAJOR FEDERAL TRANSFERS TO PROVINCES, 2004–05 ($ MILLIONS)

	Canada Health Transfer	Canada Social Transfer	Health Reform Transfer	Equalization Payments	Total
Newfoundland and Labrador	409	243	24	726	1 304
Prince Edward Island	109	65	7	246	400
Nova Scotia	738	439	44	1 146	2 256
New Brunswick	592	352	35	1 155	2 015
Quebec	5 926	3 522	354	3 761	13 083
Ontario	9 745	5 792	582	–	16 119
Manitoba	920	547	55	1 341	2 722
Saskatchewan	783	465	47	462	1 622
Alberta	2 512	1 493	150	–	4 156
British Columbia	3 289	1 955	196	824	6 054
Total	25 106	14 922	1 500	9 660	49 866

Note: The CHT and CST figures include tax transfers as well as cash. Equalization associated with the CHT/CST tax transfer is included under both the CHT/CST and Equalization, but the total figures are adjusted to avoid double counting.

Source: Adapted from Department of Finance Canada, "Federal Transfers to Provinces and Territories" (March 2004), http://www.fin.gc.ca/FEDPROV/mtpe.html (Retrieved 20 June 2004). Reproduced with the permission of the Minister of Public Works and Government Services, 2004.

TABLE 12.3 ESTIMATED FEDERAL TRANSFERS AND PROVINCES' AND TERRITORIES' OWN REVENUES, 2002–03

	Federal Transfers ($ millions)	Provinces' Own Revenues ($ millions)	Total Provincial Revenues ($ millions)	Percentage of Total Provincial Revenues from Ottawa
Newfoundland and Labrador	1 756	2 945	4 701	37.4
Prince Edward Island	390	757	1 147	34.0
Nova Scotia	2 142	5 114	7 256	29.5
New Brunswick	2 019	4 103	6 122	33.0
Quebec	9 964	53 327	63 291	15.7
Ontario	9 661	70 425	80 086	12.1
Manitoba	2 436	7 005	9 441	25.8
Saskatchewan	1 178	6 815	7 993	14.7
Alberta	2 301	22 829	25 130	9.2
British Columbia	4 035	24 472	28 507	14.2
Nunavut	844	123	967	87.2
Northwest Territories	528	468	996	53.0
Yukon	483	137	620	77.9
Total	37 737	198 207	235 944	16.0

Source: Karen Treff and David B. Perry, *Finances of the Nation 2003*, Table A7, p.A: 11, 2004. Reprinted with permission of the Canadian Tax Foundation.

levels of government began by operating more or less independently of each other, taxing and spending in different areas, with federal grants being unconditional in nature. Then, for about 60 years, the federal and provincial governments became closely intertwined by taxation agreements on the revenue side and by conditional and block grant programs in terms of expenditures. At the beginning of the 21st century, however, the degree of integration declined, especially with the disengagement of federal and provincial personal income tax systems.

Some observers advocate new national programs such as pharmacare or daycare, while others warn about the deterioration and/or abandonment of existing national programs and standards. The richest and most autonomy-minded provinces continue to argue for greater decentralization of powers and more tax room, but the have-not provinces are not capable of increasing their own tax rev-

Provincial and federal governments do pharmacare logroll. (Malcolm Mayes/artizans.com)

enues, so they have a stake in keeping a strong central government that can act as a redistributive agency.

Federal Controls

As mentioned, the 1867 Constitution Act contained three specific federal controls over the provinces: reservation, disallowance, and the declaratory power. In the first 30 years after Confederation, all three controls were actively used, and this had the effect of keeping the provinces subordinate to Ottawa. Their use gradually declined and then ceased completely: the reservation and declaratory powers were last used in 1961, and disallowance, in 1943. As these were the federal powers that originally precluded Canada from being classified as a true federation, their disuse has meant that the provinces have shrugged off their subordinate status. Canada is now a genuine federation, and a highly decentralized one at that.

Canadian Federalism Today

Federal–provincial relations in Canada have gone through many different phases since 1867, depending on shifting attitudes of federal and provincial governments, states of war and peace, and variations in judicial interpretation. In fact, Canadian federalism has experienced pendulum-like swings between centralization and decentralization, and the evolution from a centralized to a decentralized federal system has not been a unilinear process.

Cooperative Federalism

The phase of Canadian federalism that began after the Second World War might be called **cooperative federalism**. The essence of this concept is that while neither level was subordinate to the other, the federal government and the provinces were closely intertwined rather than operating independently. Here the crucial variable was financial relations. As noted earlier, the post-1945 period has been marked by federal–provincial taxation agreements on the revenue side and a host of shared-cost programs in terms of expenditures.

Cooperative federalism resulted from several developments.[7] First, federal and provincial objectives often had to be harmonized if public policy was to be effective. Second, public pressure forced the federal government to establish minimum national standards throughout the country in certain public services even within provincial jurisdiction such as health care. Third, the two levels of government competed for tax revenues and needed to coordinate these efforts to some extent, at least for the convenience of taxpayers. Fourth, given a generally vague division of powers, federal and provincial ministers and bureaucrats usually sought to maximize their jurisdiction and the programs of the two levels of government eventually overlapped.

Cooperative federalism was made operational by hundreds of federal–provincial conferences at all levels—first ministers, departmental ministers, deputy ministers, and even lesser officials—who engaged in almost continuous consultation, coordination, and cooperation. Cooperative federalism can be conducted on a multilateral basis, involving the federal government and several or all provinces, or on a bilateral basis, in which Ottawa interacts with individual provinces. Since the ministers and bureaucrats involved are all part of the executive branch of government, cooperative federalism is sometimes called **executive federalism**. Two main implications of executive federalism are that legislatures, political parties, and the public at large are not given much role to play in decisions that emerge from the secrecy of such meetings and that federal–provincial conflicts are worked out in conferences or meetings rather than being referred to the courts.

Executive federalism can therefore be defined as "relations between elected and appointed officials of the two levels of government."[8] When it is practised at the level of first ministers, it is often called "federal–provincial summitry." The **first ministers' conference**—that is, a conference of premiers and the prime minister—is not provided for anywhere in the written Constitution and rests upon a conventional base. Nevertheless, especially since 1945, this institution has made many significant policy decisions with respect to constitutional issues, shared-cost programs, and taxation and fiscal arrangements. Some of these had to be ratified later by federal and provincial legislatures, but except on constitutional matters, legislative ratification was usually a formality. Such agreements could rarely be altered in any legislature because they would then have to be changed in all 11. First ministers' conferences became more elaborate and institutionalized over time. They were usually held in the Government Conference Centre in Ottawa, the refurbished old train station across from Parliament Hill. They could be televised, in whole or in part, but it was generally agreed that any serious negotiation had to take place behind closed doors. The prime minister functioned as chair, in addition to representing the federal government, and individual ministers from

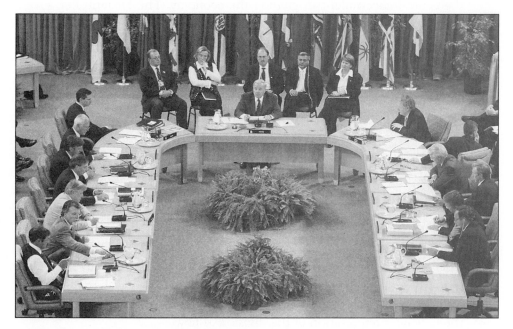

Prime Minister Paul Martin and his provincial and territorial counterparts participate in session at the First Ministers' Conference on Health in September 2004. (CP Photo/Fred Chartrand)

either level of government were usually allowed to speak as well. Every delegation brought along a host of advisers. After the collapse of the Charlottetown Accord, however, such first ministers' conferences fell into disrepute and were replaced by occasional first ministers' dinners at the prime minister's residence.

Executive federalism conducted at the level of departmental ministers and leading bureaucrats is sometimes labelled "functional" or "bureaucratic" federalism. This form of executive federalism is usually more successful than federal–provincial summitry, partly because the officials involved often share certain professional norms, and once they reach a consensus, these experts may be able to "sell" it to their departmental and first ministers.

The Decline of Cooperative Federalism

Canadian federalism between 1945 and 1960 may have been "cooperative" in the sense that the two levels of government were closely intertwined, but it continued to be highly centralized in the immediate postwar period. The ministers and bureaucrats in Ottawa who had almost single-handedly run the country during the Second World War were reluctant to shed their enormous power. Moreover, they had discovered **Keynesian economics**, which prescribed a leading role for the central government in guiding the economy. The Diefenbaker government after 1957 was more sensitive to provincial demands, and the whole picture was increasingly complicated from 1960 onward by the Quiet Revolution in Quebec. This period still manifested an intertwined, nonsubordinate relationship between the two levels of government, but with Quebec regularly rejecting federal initiatives, cooperation was sometimes harder to come by. The concept of "opting out" was a hallmark of this phase of federalism, which saw a significant degree of decentralization take place.

Between about 1970 and 1984, federal–provincial relations were racked with conflict. Quebec and the other provinces were more aggressive than ever, but the Trudeau government was not prepared for any further decentralization. Thus, taxation agreements were accompanied by more provincial unhappiness, and block funding replaced conditional grants in important areas, leaving the two levels less intertwined than before. Moreover, especially at the level of first ministers, federal–provincial conferences frequently failed to come to any agreement, and Ottawa often chose to act unilaterally. In this phase, federal–provincial conflicts were more frequently referred to the courts, resulting in a renewed emphasis on the judicial interpretation of the division of powers.

The Trudeau era was characterized by years of federal–provincial discord over resource and energy policies, especially the National Energy Program; conflict with Newfoundland over offshore oil; and conflict with Saskatchewan over the regulation and taxation of that province's oil and potash industries. When these disputes coincided with Trudeau's attempt to unilaterally amend the Constitution and entrench official bilingualism as a national policy, many Western Canadians began to re-examine their place in the federation. Some of the heat was reduced when Trudeau conceded the new section 92A of the Constitution Act, 1982, which recognized enhanced provincial jurisdiction over natural resources. He made this concession in order to secure federal NDP support for his constitutional package and as a peace offering to the West.

When Brian Mulroney came to power in 1984, he was determined to improve federal–provincial relations and embark on another period of decentralized, genuinely cooperative federalism. In this objective he was somewhat successful, for much of the federal–provincial animosity of the Trudeau years seemed to dissipate. Western and Eastern concerns about energy resources were respectively resolved to a large extent in the 1985 Western and Atlantic Accords. During its second term, however, the Mulroney government increasingly aroused provincial anger, especially as it became obsessed with deficit reduction and cut back on grants to the provinces. The Mulroney government even enforced the Liberals' Canada Health Act, imposing penalties on provinces that allowed doctors to extra-bill or permitted hospitals to charge user fees. The major federal–provincial dispute of the Mulroney years concerned the Goods and Services Tax (GST). To some extent it was just "good politics" for provincial premiers to jump on the anti-GST bandwagon because of widespread popular opposition. Most provinces refused to integrate their sales taxes with the new federal tax, even though many mutual advantages would have accrued from doing so.

The Chrétien Liberals were initially popular with provincial governments in offering funds under the national infrastructure program, and they were somewhat successful in negotiating a reduction in provincial barriers to the free movement of people, goods, services, and capital across the country in the Agreement on Internal Trade. They had only partial success in implementing their promise to replace the GST (in reality, harmonizing it with the provincial retail sales tax in a handful of provinces), and then they angered the provinces with reductions in their transfers, especially after 1995. The provinces' principal complaints included severe reductions in health, postsecondary education, and welfare transfers, although provinces also joined in to protest the cuts to almost every other aspect of federal government operations, such as a wide range of transportation subsidies. On the other hand, Ottawa did not cut equalization payments.

Federal–Provincial Conflict: Should Ottawa Tell the Provinces How to Spend Their Medicare Dollars?

The most persistent federal–provincial issue in recent times concerns health care. If the federal government makes substantial annual contributions to provincial health care programs, is Ottawa entitled to insist that they not be spent to finance health care services that are privately provided? Private MRI machines and private eye surgery clinics are often mentioned in the context of this debate. Some provinces contend that as long as people do not have to pay extra for privately provided services, that is, as long as these services are covered by the provincial medicare plan, this is acceptable. Other health care advocates argue that public funds should not leak out into the pockets of profit-making ventures. What do you think?

More harmoniously, the Chrétien government transferred responsibility for labour market training to the provinces via bilateral deals rather than constitutional amendment and replaced the Child Tax Benefit with a new integrated National Child Benefit system developed through federal–provincial cooperation. Most important, perhaps, was the 1999 **Social Union Framework Agreement** (SUFA), a framework on which to construct or modify federal, provincial, or joint social programs. Ottawa agreed to consult with and provide advance notice to provincial governments prior to renewing or significantly changing social transfers; it also agreed not to introduce new social programs involving transfers of money to the provinces without the support of a majority of provinces. On the other hand, Ottawa retained the right to use its spending power to make transfers directly to people, such as in the case of the Millennium Scholarship program.

The post-1985 period has been labelled "collaborative" but "disengaging" federalism.[9] While the two levels of government remained intertwined in a large number of areas (collaborative), both levels of government increasingly desired to extract themselves from joint programs (disengaging). One reason for the latter development was that provinces wanted to establish their own income tax systems. Another was that integration involved a certain amount of duplication that probably increased program costs. In some cases, when Ottawa was no longer funding programs so generously, it could not impose national standards on them;

in other cases, right-wing provincial governments rejected such standards. The net result was that the quality of social programs declined, with much discussion erupting over the issue of two-tier health care.

Canadian Federalism in the 21st Century

Despite all the talk about disengaging, in the early 21st century the federal and provincial governments continue to be intertwined in programs in almost every area. In fact, what is most striking is that while the formal Constitution lists only three concurrent powers, Canada is characterized by a large amount of de facto concurrent jurisdiction.[10] Moreover, an enormous degree of federal–provincial interaction will be required in the future to come up with solutions to many public problems.[11] While most of the interaction takes place at the ministerial and bureaucratic levels, Paul Martin began his regime by being much more open than his predecessor to talking individually and collectively to provincial premiers themselves.

Health care continues to be the hottest issue in federal–provincial relations. The Accord on Health Care Renewal in 2003 promised the provinces an increase of $35 billion over five years. Also in 2002–03, Ottawa agreed to set up a three-person panel to resolve federal–provincial disputes over the Canada Health Act, and most provinces agreed to join the Health Council of Canada, an independent body to advise Canadians on the performance of their health care system. In the 2004 election campaign, all parties promised to transfer more money to the provinces for health care, and at the September first ministers' meeting, Ottawa did just that. Prime Minister Martin's key priority was to use the money to reduce waiting times, and the provinces committed to establish and publish benchmarks and targets to monitor progress in meeting this goal. The 10-year plan allowed Quebec to implement its own plan, a recognition of the principle of asymmetrical federalism.

Other contentious issues in the new century include the formula for determining equalization payments, the Kyoto Protocol, and working toward more autonomous Aboriginal governments. Indeed, the very structure of Canadian federalism is complicated by two new developments: on the one hand, the need for direct communication between the federal government and the cities, and on the other, the desire of provinces to deal with external political systems, especially American states. Thus, just when it was expected that Canadian federalism was becoming disengaged and less complicated, it seems that new engagements are arising that make the subject more challenging than ever.[12]

Upon taking office, Quebec Premier Jean Charest persuaded his fellow premiers to establish a new Council of the Federation. Its objective is to speak with a strong, united voice for the provinces in their relations with the federal government. Then Prime Minister Paul Martin promised provincial premiers a closer relationship than that existing under his predecessor, including annual first ministers' meetings.

SUMMARY

This chapter examined the relationship between the provinces and the federal government. It began by defining federalism as a system in which neither level of government is subordinate to the other and by setting out the five main provisions of the Confederation Settlement. The heart of the chapter demonstrated how the provinces have become more powerful than originally intended, partly through judicial (mis)interpretation of the division of powers, partly though the enormous increase in provincial financial resources, and partly because the federal government no longer uses its means of controlling the provinces. The evolution of federal–provincial finance is particularly important, replete with taxation agreements, shared-cost programs, and various kinds of grants. The chapter showed that despite the division of powers, the two levels of government are closely intertwined, and that almost all powers, in practice, are concurrent. The chapter concluded with a description of developments in Canadian federalism in recent years and of future challenges.

DISCUSSION QUESTIONS

1. Should the federal government increase its financial transfers to the provinces, or should it give them increased taxation room instead?
2. Should the federal government be able to spend money for any purpose, even within provincial jurisdiction?
3. Should Ottawa be able to set conditions on provincial medicare programs?
4. Should Ottawa be able to deal directly with large cities, and should provinces be able to deal directly with neighbouring U.S. states?

KEY TERMS

Block grant A federal grant to the provinces that is given for a specific purpose, such as postsecondary education, but does not contain rigid conditions or standards.

Canada Health Act The 1984 act that reimposed conditions on federal grants to the provinces for health programs, especially to prevent extra-billing, privatization, or other moves toward a two-tier health system.

Canada Health and Social Transfer (CHST) The annual federal block grant to the provinces between 1996 and 2004 intended to be used for health, postsecondary education, and welfare, now replaced by the Canada Health Transfer and the Canada Social Transfer.

Concurrent powers Powers officially shared by the federal and provincial governments, namely agriculture, immigration, and old age pensions.

Conditional grant A federal grant to the provinces, usually in support of a shared-cost program within provincial jurisdiction, to which Ottawa attaches conditions or standards before the province receives the money.

Confederation Settlement The deal made among the Fathers of Confederation that entailed setting up a new federal system of government with a division of powers, including financial powers, federal controls over the provinces, provincial representation in federal institutions, and certain cultural guarantees.

Constitution Act, 1867 The new name for the British North America Act, 1867, which united the four original provinces.

Cooperative federalism A variant of Canadian federalism since the Second World War in which neither level of government is subordinate to the other and in which there is an extensive degree of interaction between them.

Division of powers The distribution of legislative powers between the federal and provincial governments, largely contained in sections 91 and 92 of the Constitution Act, 1867.

Emergency doctrine A constitutional doctrine invented by the Judicial Committee of the Privy Council that in times of national emergency, the peace, order, and good government clause became an emergency clause, increasing the powers of the federal government.

Enumerated powers The powers of the provincial governments that are explicitly listed in section 92 of the Constitution Act, 1867.

Equalization payments Large annual cash payments made by the federal government to have-not provinces to help them provide a satisfactory level of public services.

Executive federalism A variant of cooperative federalism characterized by extensive federal–provincial interaction at the level of first ministers, departmental ministers, and deputy ministers.

Federalism (federation) A system of government characterized by two levels of authority (federal and provincial) and a division of powers between them, such that neither is subordinate to the other.

First ministers' conference A federal–provincial conference consisting of the prime minister and provincial premiers (and, increasingly, territorial leaders).

Judicial Committee of the Privy Council A committee of the British Parliament that functioned as Canada's final court of appeal until 1949.

Keynesian economics An economic theory that to promote general economic stability, government should counterbalance the private sector, spending (running deficit budgets) in periods of unemployment when the private sector doesn't spend, and taxing (withdrawing money from the system) in periods of inflation when the private sector is spending too much.

Peace, order, and good government (POGG) clause The words in the opening sentence of section 91 of the Constitution Act, 1867, which states that the residual powers rest with the federal government but which has been often misinterpreted by the courts as dealing with an emergency power only.

Residual powers Those powers not given to the provinces in the Constitution Act, 1867, that were assigned to the federal government under the POGG clause in section 91.

Shared-cost programs Government programs whose cost is shared by the federal and provincial governments.

Social Union Framework Agreement An overall framework of federal–provincial relations agreed to in 1999 by all governments except Quebec that sought to end long-standing irritants on both sides.

Spending power The unofficial power of the federal government to spend money in any field, including those within provincial jurisdiction.

FURTHER READING

Bakvis, Herman, and Grace Skogstad, eds. *Canadian Federalism: Performance, Effectiveness, and Legitimacy*. Toronto: Oxford University Press, 2002.

Canadian Tax Foundation. *Finances of the Nation*. Toronto, biennial.

Hogg, Peter. *Constitutional Law of Canada*. Student edition. Toronto: Carswell, 2002.

Institute of Intergovernmental Relations. *Canada: The State of the Federation*. Kingston: Queen's University, annual.

Meekison, J. Peter, Hamish Telford, and Harvey Lazar. *Canada: The State of the Federation, 2002: Reconsidering the Institutions of Canadian Federalism*. Kingston: Institute of Intergovernmental Relations, 2002.

Mellon, Hugh, and Martin Westmacott, eds. *Challenges to Canadian Federalism*. Scarborough: Prentice-Hall Canada, 1997.

Milne, David. *Tug of War: Ottawa and the Provinces under Trudeau and Mulroney*. Toronto: Lorimer, 1986.

Rocher, François, and Miriam Smith, eds. *New Trends in Canadian Federalism*. 2nd ed. Peterborough: Broadview Press, 2003.

Russell, Peter. *Constitutional Odyssey*. 3rd ed. Toronto; University of Toronto Press, 2004.

———, et al. *Federalism and the Charter*. Ottawa: Carleton University Press, 1989.

Smiley, D.V. *The Federal Condition in Canada*. Toronto: McGraw-Hill Ryerson, 1987.

Smith, Jennifer. *Federalism*. Vancouver: UBC Press, 2004.

PART 4

Governing

Having examined the societal context of the political system and the means of linking people to government in the "politics" part of this book, and the constitutional context as the first part of the "government" section, we can now focus on governing itself. This part of the book, therefore, examines the individual institutions of government in detail. These institutions comprise the executive, including the Crown, the prime minister, and the cabinet; the bureaucracy or public service; Parliament, including the House of Commons and the Senate; and the judiciary. The functions and operations of each branch of government are outlined, as are the kinds of outputs or authoritative decisions each makes. Initially, however, these institutions are put into the context of the policymaking process to provide an overview of how they interact with each other in order to produce public policies.

PART A

Chapter 13

The Executive

The prime minister and cabinet constitute the political **executive** and are the key players in the Canadian policymaking process. Their decisions are sometimes overturned by the courts and occasionally even by Parliament, and they are based to a considerable extent on advice from the bureaucracy and other sources. But in the end, the prime minister and cabinet—often called the **government** of the day—are responsible for making the biggest political decisions in the country. This chapter begins with a brief discussion of the policymaking process and the Crown and then concentrates on the prime minister and cabinet.

Chapter Objectives

After you have completed this chapter, you should be able to:

Outline the policymaking process in its most comprehensive form

Appreciate the ways in which the monarchy or Crown is engrained in the political system

Understand the ceremonial and symbolic functions of the Crown and assess the rare use of the discretionary powers of that office

Comprehend the importance of the prime minister and cabinet in the policymaking process and in providing political leadership, as well as the sources of their power

Enumerate the factors that contribute to the pre-eminence of the prime minister

Discuss the factors that influence the composition of the cabinet

Discuss the principles and processes of cabinet operation

Enumerate the functions of the four main cabinet support agencies

The Policymaking Process

The analysis of the individual institutions of government that follows in this and subsequent chapters will be more meaningful if first put in the context of the policy-making process. This section provides an overview of that process, indicating in a general way how the institutions interact with each other in the making of public policy. **Public policy** can be defined as "a course of action or inaction chosen by public authorities to address a given problem or interrelated set of problems."[1]

Chapter 1 contained a model of the whole political system that included such components as demands, authorities, and outputs. If we magnify the "authorities" part of that model, the result would look something like Figure 13.1.

As this model suggests, the actual process can be divided into six phases: initiation, priority-setting, policy formulation, legitimation, implementation, and interpretation. Most policies and decisions do not involve such an elaborate process; indeed, many can be made unilaterally by the prime minister, the cabinet, the bureaucracy, or the courts. But the model shows the policymaking process in its broadest form, that is, a policy that requires the passage of a new law, or an amendment to an existing law, and that is later interpreted by the courts. Think of the evolution of the laws restricting tobacco advertising or establishing the gun registry.[2]

The authorities are bombarded daily with hundreds of demands. These demands emanate from many different sources, and most have no impact. But the policymaking process is set in motion when the prime minister and cabinet are struck by a particular demand being made and decide to look into it further. On a smaller scale, a single minister may also make such a decision. It is at this point that a demand is sometimes said to become an issue. An issue, therefore, is a demand that has made it onto the public agenda and that is under serious consideration by the authorities.

The second phase of the policymaking process involves the prime minister and cabinet again, this time in their priority-setting capacity. They decide which of the proposals they have previously selected for consideration are worthy of adoption. In other words, the prime minister and cabinet (or, on lesser issues, an individual minister) decide whether or not to take action on the issue, and if they decide to act, they determine the general lines of the new initiative. For example, they decide that they will restrict tobacco advertising or that they will require guns to be registered.

Figure 13.1 The Canadian Policymaking Process

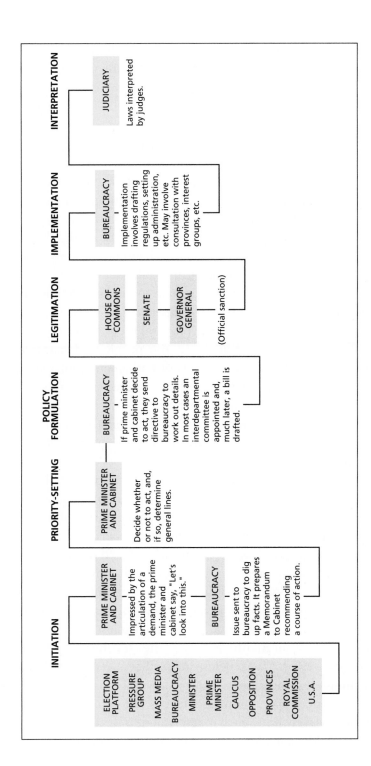

INITIATION

ELECTION PLATFORM
PRESSURE GROUP
MASS MEDIA
BUREAUCRACY
MINISTER
PRIME MINISTER
CAUCUS
OPPOSITION
PROVINCES
ROYAL COMMISSION
U.S.A.

PRIME MINISTER AND CABINET

Impressed by the articulation of a demand, the prime minister and cabinet say, "Let's look into this."

BUREAUCRACY

Issue sent to bureaucracy to dig up facts. It prepares a Memorandum to Cabinet recommending a course of action.

PRIORITY-SETTING

PRIME MINISTER AND CABINET

Decide whether or not to act, and, if so, determine general lines.

POLICY FORMULATION

BUREAUCRACY

If prime minister and cabinet decide to act, they send directive to bureaucracy to work out details. In most cases an interdepartmental committee is appointed and, much later, a bill is drafted.

LEGITIMATION

HOUSE OF COMMONS

SENATE

GOVERNOR GENERAL

(Official sanction)

IMPLEMENTATION

BUREAUCRACY

Implementation involves drafting regulations, setting up administration, etc. May involve consultation with provinces, interest groups, etc.

INTERPRETATION

JUDICIARY

Laws interpreted by judges.

The limited number of projects that have been given the green light by the cabinet in the priority-setting phase then enter the policy formulation phase. Once the cabinet has approved a proposal in principle, it sends a directive to the bureaucracy to work out the details. This is usually a time-consuming process requiring coordination among many federal government departments. It may also involve consultation with provincial governments, interest groups, and others. Questions may be referred back to the cabinet for further direction, but eventually a Memorandum to Cabinet is submitted, outlining the policy in detail. Assuming the proposal requires legislative action, the policy formulation stage culminates in a bill being drafted on the basis of the Memorandum to Cabinet.

The proposal then enters the legislative arena, as did the two bills mentioned above, regarding tobacco advertising and gun registration. The relevant minister may accept technical alterations to the bill as it proceeds through the House of Commons and the Senate, but the main intent or principle of the bill cannot be changed without approval from the cabinet. The legislative stage is referred to as "legitimizing" the bill because the proposal is put under the scrutiny of the democratically elected representatives of the people and made legitimate by their approval. The cabinet and members of Parliament contribute political expertise to the process, but given the shortage of time and limited technical expertise characteristic of the legislative branch, most such bills are passed in "skeletal" form, with details to be added later. The legitimation stage ends with the token approval of the governor general, signifying that the policy has been officially sanctioned.

Royal assent is by no means the end of the policymaking process. Few laws attain any significance just by sitting on the statute books; they must be implemented in order to be made effective. Implementation almost always involves the drafting of detailed **regulations** by the bureaucracy, to add meat to the skeleton of the statute. What wording or pictures will be used on cigarette packages, and how or which guns will be registered? Even though they have the same legal standing as if they were part of the enabling statute itself, the regulations that a law authorizes the executive to make are given only the scarcest scrutiny by either ministers or Parliament and thus are almost the exclusive preserve of the bureaucracy. Implementation normally requires the setting up of new administrative machinery—new staff, agencies, field offices, and operational manuals, among other things. It is therefore not surprising that most legislation does not automatically take effect upon royal assent; it is not "proclaimed" or made operational until the government is ready to implement it. It took more time and money than anticipated, for example, to set up the national gun registry.

The policymaking process may well end, at least for the time being, with the implementation phase. But if new legislation is involved, it is often subject to interpretation by the courts. Thus, it is appropriate to add a sixth phase to the policymaking process, that of judicial interpretation. Judges always have an impact on a law by means of how they interpret it, but in some cases the law's very constitutionality may be challenged in the courts. In such a case, the judiciary must decide whether the provisions of the law are contrary to the Charter of Rights and Freedoms or to the division of powers between federal and provincial governments. The gun control and tobacco advertising laws were both subject to such judicial interpretation.

The Crown

Canada is a **constitutional monarchy**, which essentially means that it is a democracy headed by a king or queen. In other words, the Queen is the Canadian head of state, but she reigns according to the Constitution. Canada is also said to have a dual executive, meaning that the formal and largely symbolic executive powers are given to the Queen, but the effective executive is made up of the prime minister and cabinet. The prime minister is called the head of government.

The concept of the **Crown** revolves around the head of state and can be defined as the collectivity of executive powers exercised by or in the name of the monarch. Although the Crown is largely irrelevant to the effective functions of government, many government operations are performed in the name of the Queen or governor general.[3] Moreover, the Crown provides useful functions in the political system that are largely of a symbolic and ceremonial nature.

The Crown is not only the collectivity of executive powers but also represents the entire state and embodies what belongs to the people collectively. This can be seen in **Crown corporations** (state-owned corporations) or Crown lands (state-owned lands). In addition, the Crown is central to the legal system. Crown attorneys prosecute crimes on behalf of society; court cases are initiated in the name of the Queen, for example, *R.* (for Regina) *v. Canadian Newspapers Co.*, or against the government *(Russell v. The Queen)*; branches of the judiciary may be called the Court of Queen's Bench; and lawyers are awarded the title of Queen's Counsel (QC). The term "royal" is also widely used in Canada to refer to institutions that function for the advantage of all in the name of the Queen: royal commissions, which investigate problems for the general good, and the Royal Canadian

Mounted Police, who are charged with capturing violators of society's laws. In another branch of government, three important aspects of Parliament reflect the existence of the monarchical system: royal assent, the Speech from the Throne, and Her Majesty's Loyal Opposition. "Loyal Opposition" demonstrates that criticism of the government has been legitimized and institutionalized in the name of the Queen.

The Queen of Canada, Elizabeth II, is also the queen of other countries and normally resides in Britain. That means that she needs a local representative in Canada, the **governor general**, who may, in her absence, perform any of her functions and exercise any of her powers. Until 1926, the governor was a double agent: besides being the representative of the monarch, he was an agent of the British government, and as long as Canada was a British colony, the governor general exercised authority over Canada on behalf of the British cabinet. Today, the governor general has no connection whatsoever to the British government. The Canadian prime minister nominates the governor general, who, upon appointment by the Queen, serves a term of approximately five years.

Queen Elizabeth II poses with Canadian veterans on Juno Beach, France, on the 60th anniversary of the D-Day landings.
(CP Photo/Mike Large)

Some of the powers of the Crown are provided for in the Constitution Act, 1867, while others, the **prerogative powers**, are left over from the era when the monarch really ruled. Despite this impressive theoretical list of powers, there is no doubt that in a democratic age almost all of them must be exercised on the advice of the government—the prime minister and cabinet—of the day. The most important prerogative power of the governor general is the appointment of the prime minister, but this must be performed on the basis of constitutional convention. In ensuring that the office of prime minister is never vacant, the governor general normally relies on the operation of political parties and elections, and he or she does not have far to look. On two occasions in the 1890s, however, the governor had to help find a prime minister—John Abbott in 1891 and Mackenzie Bowell in 1894. Political parties are better organized today, and they prefer to choose their own leaders. Thus, if the position should suddenly become vacant, such as through the death or unexpected resignation of the prime minister, the cabinet and/or government caucus would name an acting leader pending a leadership convention. But in a minority government scenario, the governor general might still be called upon to play a part.

The two most controversial discretionary acts of governors general occurred in 1896 and 1926, when the governors not only acted on their own initiative but also refused the advice of the prime minister and cabinet. The first occasion concerned the question of making government appointments. Many appointments, such as those of senators and judges, are made in the name of the governor general, even though they are decided upon by the cabinet. But the Charles Tupper government chose to retain office after it lost the 1896 election (awaiting defeat in the House of Commons) and during that interim period presented a list of several recommended appointments to the governor general, which he refused to endorse.

The second famous case of refusing government advice, the **King–Byng dispute**, involved the dissolution of Parliament. The governor general normally dissolves Parliament to precipitate an election on the advice of the prime minister, but in 1926 Lord Byng refused Mackenzie King's request to do so. In this case, the governor general was primarily influenced by the fact that a motion of censure against the government regarding a scandal in the Customs Department was under debate in the House of Commons. The request for a dissolution appeared to be an attempt to avoid defeat in the Commons. In addition, the opposition Conservatives actually had more seats than the governing Liberals (who had been kept in power with the support of the Progressives), and an election had been held only eight months before. Thus, it seemed logical to Lord Byng to try to avoid an election when an alternative government might be available.

Whether such discretionary action is appropriate today as a check on unconstitutional behaviour by prime ministers and cabinets remains an open question. Everyone agrees, however, that in normal circumstances governors general must act on the advice of the prime minister and cabinet. Before governors general invoke such emergency powers, "they must be sure they have reached the danger point, and that their actions will stand up to the subsequent judgment of other institutions and the people."[4] The governor general has been called a "constitutional fire extinguisher," whose emergency powers can be used only "when normal controls cannot operate and a crisis gets out of hand." Andrew Heard adds that "governors should intrude into the democratic process only to the minimum extent absolutely required for the basic functioning of Parliamentary government."[5] Since the governor general is intended to function as an impartial symbol of unity, any act that could be interpreted as remotely partisan must be avoided.

The Prime Minister and Cabinet
Powers of the Prime Minister and Cabinet

The prime minister and cabinet have the power to make the most significant governmental decisions. Given their importance, it is ironic that they are not provided for in the written parts of the Constitution, their functions and powers resting instead on custom and convention. What *is* provided for in the 1867 Constitution Act is a **Privy Council** to advise the governor general in the exercise of the powers of that office. In fact, the cabinet acts as a committee of the Privy Council, but rather than merely advising the governor general, it actually makes the decisions in question. With rare exceptions, the prime minister and cabinet exercise whatever powers are given to the Queen or the governor general in the Constitution. Such decisions, especially appointments, often take the form of **orders-in-council**.

Thus, after an election, the governor general calls upon the leader of the party with most members elected to the House of Commons to become prime minister and to form a government.[6] The prime minister assumes the title "Right Honourable" and selects the cabinet ministers, all of whom are sworn into the Privy Council, which allows them to use the title "Honourable" for life.

In normal circumstances, then, the prime minister and cabinet exercise the powers of the Crown. These powers include summoning and dissolving Parliament; the pardoning power; and the appointment of senators, judges, other officials, and royal commissions. The prime minister and cabinet recommend **money bills** to Parliament, and all international acts and the general conduct of foreign relations are the prerogative of the cabinet, including declaring war and peace, signing treaties, appointing ambassadors, and recognizing foreign governments. The cabinet may feel it politically advantageous to have Parliament debate declarations of war and may need to submit legislation to Parliament to make treaties effective, but unlike in the United States, such international acts are essentially within the purview of the executive branch of government, not the legislature.

Exercising the powers of the Crown is only a small part of the reason that the prime minister and cabinet are the centre of gravity in the Canadian political system, however. More importantly, and similar to the executive of any organization, they have the responsibility for providing political leadership and determining priorities. That is, the prime minister and cabinet decide which problems to deal with, establish the general thrust and direction of new policies, and determine the spending priorities of the government. In the British and Canadian systems, the responsibility for initiating legislation rests primarily with the cabinet. As seen in Chapter 15, opportunities do exist for other members of Parliament to introduce bills, but most of the time of the House of Commons is set aside for government business. The **Speech from the Throne** provides the cabinet with an opportunity to outline its legislative program at the beginning of the session. The cabinet's virtual monopoly over the passage of legislation should ensure coordination among government policies, while its total monopoly over financial legislation is designed to guarantee a close relationship between policies adopted and the funds to make them effective. Such strong executive leadership, based on tradition, necessity, and the Constitution Act, and backed up by vast resources and advice, has generally proven itself to be an effective way to run a country.

Beyond the powers of the Crown and this general leadership function, cabinet power is also derived from specific acts of Parliament. Almost every law delegates to a minister or the **governor in council** (i.e., the cabinet) the power to make decisions of many kinds. Similarly, it is largely on the basis of acts of Parliament that individual ministers are charged with supervising the administration of their departments. Ministers provide direction and leadership, establish priorities, and transmit their personal, party, and cabinet perspectives, all in an effort to ensure that the public servants in their departments remain accountable to democratically elected leaders and public opinion. As mentioned, ministers are also given quasi-legislative powers to issue regulations under a law, sometimes called delegated or subordinate legislation, which flesh out the bare bones of the statute. In addition, ministers are involved in Parliament, answering questions about the department's operations, defending departmental spending proposals, and piloting bills emanating from the department.

The principle of **individual ministerial responsibility** requires that each minister is responsible to Parliament for everything that goes on in his or her department. It was once thought to entail a minister's resignation over public servants' errors, even those the minister knew nothing about.[7] In an age of big government, however, the principle has lost most of its meaning. Ministers can still be criticized for departmental failures and are expected to correct them, but they rarely resign except for monumental personal mistakes and **conflicts of interest**. In the 1990s, for example, the lax administration of the Human Resources Development department attracted much criticism, but the principle of ministerial responsibility required only that the minister, Jane Stewart, clean up the mess, not resign. Accountability for the dramatic increase in the costs of the gun registry and for the 2003 sponsorship scandal in Quebec was even more elusive.

The Prime Minister

The system of government that Canada inherited from Britain has traditionally been called **cabinet government**, but such a label does not do justice to the modern pre-eminence of the prime minister. Most observers agree that cabinet government has been transformed into a system of **prime ministerial government**, and no one doubts that the prime minister has enormous power and should be singled out for special attention.[8] The pre-eminence of the prime minister over cabinet colleagues can be seen in 10 of the PM's principal powers, rights, or responsibilities. In many cases, these relate to the different arenas in which the prime minister must operate, such as cabinet, Parliament, party, media, federal–provincial relations, international diplomacy, and the economy:[9]

- Cabinet-maker
- Chair of cabinet meetings
- Party leader
- Chief policymaker
- Leading player in the House of Commons
- Chief personnel manager
- Controller of government organization
- Adviser to governor general
- Chief diplomat
- Public persuader

First, the prime minister is the cabinet-maker. Prime ministers select their own ministers, subject to certain conventions discussed below, and decide what portfolios to assign to each of them. Ministers thus owe allegiance to the prime minister, who also issues them "mandate letters" that inform them of the PM's policy expectations in their portfolio.[10] In addition, the prime minister promotes and demotes ministers, asks for their resignation, or, if necessary, dismisses them.

Chairing cabinet meetings is a second main source of the prime minister's power. To start with, the prime minister determines the agenda of such meetings, but in addition to the usual advantages of a chair, the prime minister benefits from the peculiar way in which cabinet decisions are arrived at. Rather than by motions and votes, the decision is reached when the PM summarizes the discussion and articulates the "consensus"—either by extracting a real consensus from the meeting or by imposing his or her own viewpoint. Ministers who do not agree with this interpretation either keep quiet or resign. Even though many decisions

Paul Martin has trouble building his cabinet. (Bado/artizans.com)

are now made by cabinet committees, the prime minister decides which commit-tees will be struck, who will chair them, who will sit on them, and which matters will be sent to them, so that this delegation of power from the full cabinet does not necessarily reduce the PM's control.

Third, the prime minister is the leader of the party, and the PM's pre-eminence has probably increased over the years as political parties have become more cohesive and as election campaigns have come to focus on party leaders. In fact, many ministers may have been elected on the leader's coattails. As leader, the prime minister can control party organization, personnel, strategy, and policy, and in exceptional circumstances impose or veto party candidates. Jean Chrétien and Paul Martin "appointed" a number of Liberal candidates in recent elections, for example, while Brian Mulroney refused to sign the nomination papers of Sinclair Stevens in order to improve his party's reputation in terms of integrity.

Fourth, the prime minister could be called chief policymaker. The PM has the last word on government policy, whether in personal interaction with individual ministers, within the cabinet chamber, in Parliament, or in other forums such as the media. Modern government, of course, is too complex for one person to have an active role in formulating all policies, but the prime minister "can play a crit-ical role in problem definition."[11] A recent example of prime ministerial power is the Clarity Act, which Jean Chrétien bulldozed through despite considerable opposition from cabinet colleagues and the Liberal caucus.

Fifth, the prime minister is the central player in the House of Commons. Even though control of the parliamentary agenda is now delegated to the government House leader, the PM is still expected to be there and speak for the government in the oral Question Period almost every day.

A sixth source of prime ministerial pre-eminence is an enormous power of appointment. This includes the appointment of ministers, senators, Supreme Court judges, deputy ministers, and heads of a wide range of government agencies.

Given the extent and power of the bureaucracy today, the prime minister's seventh power, control over government organization, is also significant. Subject to usually routine parliamentary approval, the PM can decide to create new departments and set out their mandates, reorganize government departments, abolish departments or agencies, or privatize Crown corporations. Prime Minister Martin, for example, established new ministries of state for Infrastructure and Communities and for Families and Caregivers.

Eighth, the prime minister personally advises the governor general on such matters as when to call the next election. Chrétien called the November 2000 election against the virtually unanimous advice of cabinet and caucus, and many Liberals had doubts about Martin's election call for June 2004.

In an era of summit diplomacy, the prime minister often overshadows the minister of foreign affairs on the world stage, functioning as Canada's chief diplomat. This role can be observed in annual bilateral meetings with the U.S. president, annual meetings of the Group of Eight leading industrialized countries, Commonwealth Conferences, meetings of the Francophonie, other summits, and occasional appearances at the United Nations.

The prime minister is also the chief "public relations officer" of the government, or "public persuader."[12] Television has become the main instrument for transmitting the prime minister's message to the party, the government, and the public. Survival in the battleground of media relations "threatens to become the key determinant of prime ministerial success."[13]

Given all these powers and a normally deferential majority in the House of Commons, the PM can usually succeed in controlling the policy and personnel of government. In many respects, in fact, the Canadian prime minister is more powerful than the American president, except of course in international clout. In order to get his agenda adopted, the latter must bargain with Congress in which party discipline is not strong, whereas prime ministers can usually count on a disciplined majority to back their measures. Indeed, the expansion of prime ministerial staff, the holding of prime ministerial news conferences, the making of televised addresses to the nation, luxurious travel arrangements, and other conspicuous trappings of power have led many observers to criticize the "presidentialization" of the office of prime minister.[14] And one potential constraint that prime ministers do not have to worry much about is cabinet revolts. However much ministers may resent the prime minister's dominance, internal attempts to overthrow the PM are rare, only two having occurred in Canadian history (against Mackenzie Bowell and John Diefenbaker).

Others continue to emphasize the restraints on the power of the prime minister. Theoretically these include the media, opposition parties, the Constitution, and the party, but more practically they involve financial constraints, opposition from the provinces, international influences, and the limits within which government policy of any kind can effect societal change. Of course, if the government is not supported by a majority in the House of Commons, that is, if it finds itself in a minority position, as was the case after the 2004 election, the prime minister loses much of this dominance. In such a situation, the PM may have to seek the approval of one or more opposition parties for many of the government's initiatives. Even with a majority, the prime minister is often at the mercy of events, which may bring about a fall in public support and a loss of much overall influence in turn.

Table 13.1, which contains a list of prime ministers ranked by length of tenure, reveals the variations in prime ministerial political fortunes.

TABLE 13.1 PRIME MINISTERS OF CANADA, RANKED BY LENGTH OF TENURE

Mackenzie King: 21 yrs., 5 mo.	Lester Pearson: 5 yrs.
John A. Macdonald: 19 yrs.	Alexander Mackenzie: 4 yrs., 11 mo.
Pierre Elliott Trudeau: 15 yrs., 5 mo.	John Thompson: 2 yrs.
Wilfrid Laurier: 15 yrs., 3 mo.	Arthur Meighen: 1 yr., 8 mo.
Jean Chrétien: 10 yrs., 2 mo.	John Abbott: 1 yr., 5 mo.
Brian Mulroney: 9 yrs., 9 mo.	Mackenzie Bowell: 1 yr., 4 mo.
Robert L. Borden: 9 yrs., 9 mo.	Joe Clark: 9 mo.
Louis St. Laurent: 8 yrs., 7 mo.	Kim Campbell: 133 days
John Diefenbaker: 5 yrs., 10 mo.	John Turner: 80 days
R.B. Bennett: 5 yrs., 3 mo.	Charles Tupper: 69 days

Composition of the Cabinet

In theory, all cabinet ministers are equal, although in practice this is far from being the case. All recent PMs, for example, designated one minister as deputy prime minister, although in some cases this title seemed to carry more prestige than any real power.

Below the deputy PM are the regular departmental ministers, each normally in charge of a single department. An informal ranking of these departments may result in variations in influence among this group of ministers, with finance, foreign affairs, justice, industry, health, international trade, Treasury Board, and human resources usually being among the key portfolios. The cabinet also contains some ministers who do not have full-fledged departments to administer, especially the government leaders in the House of Commons and the Senate. This category may also include junior ministers, variously called ministers without portfolio, ministers of state, or secretaries of state. They could be in charge of small agencies or assigned to assist a senior minister. With the exception of the Chrétien era, the Canadian tradition has been that all ministers, even these junior ones, were included in the cabinet.

Since the cabinet occupies such a central position in the Canadian policy-making process, every interest in the country would like to be represented in its deliberations. This desire alone creates pressure to expand its size. In general, the cabinet contained about 13 or 14 ministers before 1911, then rose to around 20 until about 1960, increasing to 30 under Trudeau, and to around 40 in the Mulroney period. Chrétien reduced the cabinet's size to 23 in 1993, supplemented by 9 junior ministers, called secretaries of state, who were part of the ministry but not invited to cabinet meetings. The secretaries of state each had a small staff and operating budget, and received 75 percent of a cabinet minister's pay. After the 2000 election, Chrétien's cabinet grew to 29, along with 8 secretaries of state in the ministry. Paul Martin had 39 cabinet ministers, including many ministers of state, but all receiving equal remuneration, and with a reserved seat at cabinet meetings.

Several conventions have developed to constrain the PM's prerogatives in the selection of ministers. In the first place, reflecting the fact that Canada is a democracy and that the ministers represent the people, all cabinet ministers must have a seat in Parliament. Ministers sit in the legislative branch of government at the same time as they form the executive. Almost all ministers therefore have a seat in the House of Commons. It is possible for the prime minister to name someone to the cabinet who has not won election to the Commons, but convention dictates that such a person run in a by-election as soon as possible in order to obtain a seat. This sometimes happens when a PM chooses to appoint a person of unusual qualifications from outside parliamentary life, rather than a sitting back-bencher, as Jean Chrétien did with Stéphane Dion and Pierre Pettigrew in 1996. The modern tradition is to include only one senator in the cabinet, usually serving as government leader in that chamber and having no departmental responsibilities.

The next constraint on the prime minister is the convention that each province be represented in the cabinet. This flows from the fact that Canada is a federation and that the Senate has never performed its intended role of representing provincial interests in Ottawa. Thus, with the occasional exception of Prince Edward Island, every province that has elected a member to the government side of the Commons has been awarded a cabinet position. This convention usually results in some ministers being appointed only because their province needs cabinet representation, rather than on their merits, leaving worthy MPs from other locations excluded. In both the Trudeau and Clark governments, the prime minister chose to appoint senators to the cabinet to represent provinces that had not elected any or enough government members (the three Western

NEL

provinces in the former case and Quebec in the latter). That such a practice breaks the modern convention of having only one senator in the cabinet attests to the importance of provincial representation. In 1997, Chrétien responded to the absence of Liberal MPs from Nova Scotia by choosing his one senator from that province.

It is not only that residents of a province feel more secure if one of their number is in the cabinet; it is also very useful for the cabinet itself to have such provincial representation.[15] In fact, ministers essentially wear two hats: they speak for their department as well as for their province. This arrangement is functional for patronage as well as policy purposes: appointments and contracts awarded on a partisan basis in any province will be the responsibility of the resident minister, often called the "political minister" for that province.

Larger provinces are not content with a single minister, of course, and in a cabinet of 30 or 40 members, Ontario and Quebec have sometimes exceeded 10. In such cases the ministers can be distributed so that each region within the province gains its own representative. Prior to 1984, however, Quebec was usually underrepresented in the cabinet when the Conservatives were in power, and the West was inadequately represented in the Pearson and Trudeau cabinets.

The next convention of Canadian cabinet-making is the need for a balance of ethnic representatives. A proper balance of anglophone and francophone ministers— that is, about one-third francophone and two-thirds anglophone—may result almost automatically from the carefully constructed provincial representation. French Canadians were underrepresented even in Liberal governments before 1963, however, and often grossly underrepresented in Conservative cabinets. It was only in the Pearson, Trudeau, and Mulroney cabinets that francophone ministers achieved or exceeded the one-third benchmark. Those of other ethnic origins were not proportionately represented in the past, except perhaps in the Clark and Mulroney cabinets, but now expect fairer cabinet representation.

As for other social divisions, religion was much more important in the pre-1900 period than it is today. Prime ministers are now more concerned with appointing women to the cabinet. Since it was difficult to include representatives of all social groups in his 1993 cabinet of only 23, Chrétien tried to appease some of the others in the appointment of the secretaries of state: three women, one member from P.E.I., one Aboriginal person, and one Asian.

The cabinet is therefore a principal locus of elite accommodation, and William Matheson writes of a representative cabinet as follows: "in the Canadian context the cabinet has filled a dual role, for in addition to exercising the usual functions of executive leadership, the cabinet has provided an arena in which the elites may counter the dysfunctional and unstabilizing effects of cultural, regional, and religious fragmentation."[16]

Once the PM has chosen the people who will form the cabinet, they must be assigned portfolios, that is, departmental responsibilities. It is not normally expected that ministers will be expert in the fields to which they are appointed, partly because the electorate is not likely to furnish the prime minister with members of Parliament having such credentials. Indeed, an argument can be made that a semi-expert is more dangerous than a total amateur, since the latter will have enough sense to listen to the real experts within the department, while the former might try to substitute his or her limited knowledge for theirs. Thus, apart from the minister of justice's normally being a lawyer, there is no necessary relationship between ministers' training or pre-political occupation and their departmental assignment.

What Do You Think?

Is the Canadian system of appointing a minister to head a department that he or she knows virtually nothing about a good way to run a government? Is the concept of "amateur ministers" really sound, or is there just no alternative?

Operation of the Cabinet

CABINET SOLIDARITY AND CABINET SECRECY

The cabinet is usually considered to be a collective decisionmaking body. Exceptions to this notion include the prime minister's penchant to make decisions single-handedly and decisions taken by cabinet committees or by individual ministers. Regardless of which or how many ministers are involved in the making of such decisions, however, the cabinet operates on the principle of **cabinet solidarity**, meaning that all ministers must publicly defend all cabinet policies or else resign. Ministerial resignations because of policy differences are rare in Canada, perhaps only 28 since 1867,[17] suggesting that the thought of giving up the perks of office engenders considerable flexibility in ministers' principles. The most extreme manifestation of cabinet solidarity can be seen in terms of the annual budget, which is usually the most important government policy statement of the year. Only the finance minister and PM know much about it until the budget is delivered in Parliament, yet all ministers must support it. Cabinet solidarity is related to the principle of collective ministerial responsibility to Parliament. If the government loses the confidence of the legislature, it must collectively resign or call an election.

Cabinet solidarity is also linked to the principle of cabinet secrecy or confidentiality. Cabinet operations are shrouded in secrecy, and ministers are not supposed to disclose information about its deliberations. Such confidentiality protects state secrets, protects the cabinet against opposition and media exploitation of ministerial discord, and protects senior civil servants from identification and public criticism. Cabinet documents are not normally made public for 20 years, and, as a result, we do not know as much about how the cabinet operates as about decisionmaking bodies that meet in public. In fact, this exception from the Access to Information Act frustrates everyone who wants to understand why the cabinet makes the decisions it does. On the other hand, clever ministers are conscious that information represents power and that a well-timed "leak" can sometimes be of benefit when involved in a battle within cabinet.

CABINET BEHAVIOUR

At the time of Confederation, many cabinet ministers retained positions as corporate directors or other business connections. It is only since about 1960 that ministers have been required to divorce themselves from their former corporate relationships under various versions of conflict-of-interest guidelines. The problem continued to arise from time to time with individual ministers, however, and became critical during the Chrétien era. The prime minister himself was implicated in a dubious business operation in his constituency, while Finance Minister Paul Martin received regular briefings on the activities of his company, Canada Steamship Lines. Chrétien was forced to tighten the rules regarding prime ministerial and ministerial corporate relationships at the end of his tenure, and under Martin the long-promised independent ethics commissioner was appointed. This commissioner is now an officer of Parliament, no longer reporting to the prime minister, and has a stricter set of conflict-of-interest rules to apply to members of Parliament both inside and outside the cabinet.

CABINET PROCEDURE

Before 1960 or so, perhaps especially in the Mackenzie King and St. Laurent eras, ministers and departments were largely autonomous. Each developed its own policies and programs with little regard for central coordination and with only minimal prime ministerial interference. Strong ministers could make many decisions and policies without consulting their colleagues, and such ministers tended to remain in charge of a single department for long periods of time. Such autonomous departmental ministers often doubled as strong regional ministers, who were also allowed to handle regional responsibilities on their own. In addition, senior bureaucrats usually served their careers within a single department and became "carriers of the interests, traditions, skills and memories of these particularized bureaucratic organizations."[18]

Despite what has been said previously about collective cabinet decision-making, the change from autonomous ministers to collegial cabinet decisions is really a product of the post-1960 period and the enormous expansion of government activity in the following 25 years. As society and its problems became more complex, individual ministers and departments could no longer make decisions and policies in isolation; the policies of one department almost inevitably affected those of another. More consultation and coordination were required, with the result that ministerial collegiality replaced departmental autonomy. To some extent the need for policy coordination coincided with the view that cabinet ministers should have greater control over the bureaucracy; another stimulus was the concern for more rational government decisionmaking. The Pearson era was transitional in this respect, and the major change was adopted in the Trudeau period.

Prime Minister Trudeau attempted to increase the rationality of government policymaking in a variety of ways.[19] First, the PM and cabinet gave more attention to setting the overall priorities of the government. Second, the four central agencies—Prime Minister's Office, Privy Council Office, Department of Finance, and Treasury Board Secretariat—were expanded and strengthened so as to provide policy analysis to the prime minister and cabinet independent of other government departments. Third, to avoid cabinet overload and to enhance specialization and policy coordination within it, most of the cabinet's work was done in committees. Fourth, cabinet procedures were rigidly adhered to, including agendas, advance notice of issues, and advance circulation of background documents. All of these measures tended to render cabinet decisions more coordinated, organized, and disciplined, hence the term institutionalized cabinet.[20]

The cabinet as a whole normally meets for about three or four hours once a week. An agenda is prepared by the Privy Council Office (PCO) under the prime minister's supervision. It is circulated in advance, together with background documents—largely **Memorandums to Cabinet** from individual departments—and cabinet committee decisions and recommendations. The Privy Council Office will also have prepared a briefing note to help the PM get through the meeting successfully, most PMs preferring that ministers and departments sort out their differences beforehand.[21] Rather than resolving questions by a formal vote, the prime minister sums up the discussion on each item and articulates the consensus arrived at. If this bears little resemblance to the actual tenor of the meeting, ministers who do not agree with this interpretation either keep quiet or resign, as noted previously. A handful of senior officials on hand take note of the discussion and decisions and circulate minutes afterward. They are rarely asked to speak, but may pass notes to the PM. Given the demands on the time of those involved, meetings are conducted in a very businesslike manner.

The first item on the agenda is "General Discussion," which includes whatever is on the PM's mind. The second item is "Presentations," in which ministers may be invited to brief the cabinet on various issues. The third item is a list of "Nominations" or government appointments to be confirmed. The fourth item is cabinet committee decisions, attached to the agenda as appendices. A prime minister usually finds it annoying if any minister challenges a cabinet committee decision at this point.

As mentioned, since the mid-1960s, more and more such work has been done by cabinet committees rather than by the full cabinet, each committee also normally meeting once a week. Unlike in full cabinet meetings, ministers may bring advisers along to cabinet committees, so they are less reliant on their own personal resources. Between the Pearson and Mulroney regimes, the Priorities and Planning Committee was clearly the most important cabinet committee. Its special functions included setting priorities, allocating budgets, reviewing other committee decisions, making many important decisions itself, and supervising federal–provincial relations. Being chaired by the prime minister and containing the most important ministers (including the chairs of other cabinet committees) also added to its significance.

Jean Chrétien hoped to revert to the St. Laurent model of a cabinet operation, in which individual ministers and departments were allowed to look after their own affairs. The maze of cabinet committees was reduced, leaving five after the 2000 election: Economic Union, Social Union, Treasury Board, Government Communications, and the Special Committee of Council.[22] Chrétien curtailed the scope of many other coordinating central agencies, and departments were allowed more leeway in moving funds from one program to another. Even in an era of government downsizing, however, many observers felt that the complexity of issues required greater coordination and consultation, and that the 40-year-old model was no longer adequate. The Department of Finance began to fill the gap, as it dominated the **Expenditure Management System**. This was partly because the budget and the deficit were the driving forces of the day, but also because some kind of coordinating device was needed. The PCO also remained a significant coordinating mechanism. After the 2004 election, Paul Martin established eight cabinet committees, two of which he personally chaired.

Cabinet committees function much like cabinet as a whole. Working with the chair and the PM, the PCO develops and distributes an agenda that is largely composed of Memorandums to Cabinet from various departments. Much interdepartmental discussion and negotiation takes place in advance, but if the committee cannot come to a consensus, the memorandum is returned for further work. If it is approved, it is attached to the agenda of the next meeting of the full cabinet.

Cabinet Support Agencies

As mentioned, the following four main central agencies exist to support the prime minister and/or the cabinet as a whole:

- Prime Minister's Office
- Privy Council Office
- Department of Finance
- Treasury Board Secretariat

The **Prime Minister's Office (PMO)** handles the prime minister's correspondence, media relations, partisan appointments, public appearances, and speeches, and it briefs the PM on legislative proceedings. The office contains nearly one hundred people who monitor political developments and offer policy advice from a partisan point of view. The PM usually meets daily with the head of the PMO to be briefed on developments from a partisan perspective. Under every recent prime minister, the PMO has had a powerful influence on virtually all government decisions.

The **Privy Council Office (PCO)** has served several unique purposes since it was recognized as the cabinet secretariat and since cabinet meetings became more businesslike in 1940 due to the pressures of war. First, it provides logistical support for the cabinet—organizing meetings, preparing agendas, writing and distributing background material, taking and circulating minutes, and communicating cabinet decisions. In these ways, the PCO is engaged in the coordination of overall government policy. The PCO also performs the same services for cabinet committees. PCO officials brief cabinet committee chairs and the prime minister even on the strategy of conducting their meetings. All these functions help the PCO obtain the kind of decisions that it considers best. Another example of its influence is in its detailed strategy notes for the prime minister when he or she meets important people or makes critical telephone calls.

Other sections of the Privy Council Office have responsibility for the machinery of government, the appointment of senior public service personnel, and federal–provincial relations. The head of the PCO, the **Clerk of the Privy Council and Secretary to the Cabinet**, is regarded as the government's highest-ranking public servant. The Clerk meets daily with the prime minister to review problems and render nonpartisan advice and could be called the lynchpin of the government of Canada. Being the closest adviser to the PM, the Clerk has his or her hands on almost everything that really counts: drafting the Speech from the Throne, working with the Department of Finance on the budget, organizing the machinery of government, writing mandate letters for ministers and deputy ministers, appointing and evaluating deputy ministers, chairing the coordinating committees of deputy ministers, keeping an eye on Memorandums to Cabinet, helping to strategize cabinet and cabinet committee meetings, and keeping track of federal–provincial relations. The prime minister may be the most important player in the actual making of government decisions, but the Clerk advises on almost every one.

The **Department of Finance** and the Treasury Board Secretariat primarily supply financial information to the cabinet, and they have historically exercised a cautioning, restraining influence on new program proposals. The role of the Department of Finance is to look at the government's overall revenue and expenditure situation, including its accumulated debt, and to advise on allocations among departments. Under the powerful deputy minister, it is also the chief adviser on taxation policy and on transfer payments to the provinces. While reporting directly to the minister of finance and in that sense being an ordinary department of government, the Department of Finance has a special responsibility of advising the cabinet collectively on such matters, being incorporated into the process of developing Memorandums to Cabinet, as well as preparing the budget. In an age of government restraint and retrenchment, its influence necessarily increases, and in the first part of the Chrétien regime, that department basically determined the government's whole agenda.[23]

The **Treasury Board** is a committee of cabinet chaired by the minister called President of the Treasury Board, who is in turn in charge of a full-fledged government department, the **Treasury Board Secretariat** (TBS). This secretariat has the overall responsibility for controlling regular departmental spending, being involved in the development of detailed departmental budgets—the **Estimates**—and overseeing the actual expenditure of funds. The TBS is also in charge of labour relations in the public service and issues policies on personnel, administration, and finance. Prime Minister Martin transferred some of its human resources functions to a new agency, so that the TBS could concentrate on enhancing financial accountability within the public service. Although its perspective is more detailed than that of the Department of Finance, the two agencies usually see things in a similar light, and the Treasury Board Secretariat's influence also increases when a government is obsessed with its deficit.

Figure 13.2 illustrates how these central agencies, as well as other relevant departments, have to be persuaded to support any departmental initiative before it can appear on the agenda of a cabinet committee en route to the cabinet as a whole.

Figure 13.2 Flow of Departmental Initiative to Cabinet

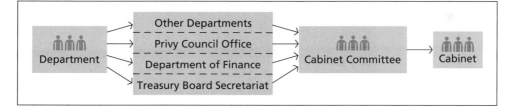

SUMMARY

This chapter examined the executive branch of government. It began by outlining the six phases of the policymaking process—initiation, priority-setting, policy formulation, legitimation, implementation, and interpretation. The second part dealt with the Crown—the place of the monarch and governor general—and claimed that they have an important symbolic and ceremonial role to play. The chapter then explained the important decisionmaking functions of the prime minister and cabinet and sought to discover the sources of their powers. It separated out the prime minister for special attention, enumerating 10 roles that establish the PM's pre-eminence over the whole political system, including the cabinet. The next section revealed the factors that influence a prime minister in the construction of a cabinet and was followed by a discussion of the principles and processes of the cabinet's operation. In particular, the increased use of cabinet committees and the heightened concern with ethical behaviour were highlighted. Finally, the chapter considered the important influence on the prime minister and cabinet of four main cabinet support agencies: the Prime Minister's Office, the

Privy Council Office, the Department of Finance, and the Treasury Board Secretariat.

DISCUSSION QUESTIONS

1. What are the advantages and disadvantages of recognizing the Queen as the Canadian head of state?
2. Does the prime minister have too much power in the Canadian system of government?
3. Should individual departments and ministers have more power at the expense of collective decisionmaking processes and central agencies?

KEY TERMS

Cabinet government A system of government in which the major political decisions are made by the cabinet as a whole, as opposed to one in which the prime minister acts with considerable autonomy or dominance.

Cabinet solidarity A convention that all cabinet ministers publicly support whatever decisions the cabinet has taken, regardless of their personal views.

Clerk of the Privy Council and Secretary to the Cabinet The head of the Privy Council Office and head of the federal public service; the chief nonpartisan adviser to the prime minister and cabinet.

Conflict of interest A situation in which any public officeholder places personal benefit (usually financial) before the public interest.

Constitutional monarchy The official designation of the Canadian form of government, characterized by a monarch who is head of state but who rules according to the Constitution, which confides almost all governmental power into other hands.

Crown The collectivity of executive powers exercised by or in the name of the monarch.

Crown corporation A corporation owned by the government that assumes a structure similar to that of a private company and that operates semi-independently of the cabinet.

Department of Finance The government department that has overall responsibility for the government's finances and its role in the economy and that has a powerful influence on all government policy.

Estimates The annual spending plans of government departments and agencies.

Executive That branch of government that provides leadership and makes the major decisions.

Expenditure Management System The process for determining government financial priorities and the annual distribution of public funds.

Government The set of authorities, centred around a prime minister, cabinet, and party, that currently occupy the executive offices of the state and provide political leadership.

Governor general The representative of the Queen in Canada who normally performs her head-of-state functions.

Governor in council The prime minister and cabinet (but *not* the governor general) exercising powers of the Privy Council.

Individual ministerial responsibility The principle that cabinet ministers are individually responsible to the House of Commons to answer for everything that happens in their department.

King–Byng dispute The 1926 dispute between Prime Minister Mackenzie King and Governor General Lord Byng over King's request for a dissolution of Parliament, which Byng denied.

Memorandum to Cabinet The formal written document that a minister submits to the cabinet seeking to initiate or change a government policy.

Money bill A bill to raise money for government purposes or to spend public funds.

Order-in-council A formal, legal decision made by the prime minister and cabinet (governor in council), including regulations and appointments.

Prerogative powers That small number of residual powers of the Crown that remain from the era of an all-powerful monarch that the Queen or governor general can still exercise on rare occasions at his or her own discretion.

Prime ministerial government The notion that the prime minister is now so pre-eminent that the label "cabinet government" no longer accurately describes how decisions are made in the political executive.

Prime Minister's Office (PMO) The office that supports and advises the prime minister in partisan terms.

Privy Council A body established by the Constitution Act, 1867, to advise the governor general in the exercise of the powers of that office but effectively taken over by the prime minister and cabinet.

Privy Council Office (PCO) The office that supports and advises the prime minister, cabinet, and cabinet committees in nonpartisan terms.

Public policy A course of action or inaction chosen by public authorities to address a given problem or interrelated set of problems.

Regulations The detailed rules drafted by the bureaucracy under the authority of laws passed by Parliament that are too voluminous and technical to put into the legislation itself.

Speech from the Throne The document prepared by the prime minister and cabinet and read by the governor general at the opening of each session of Parliament that outlines the government's legislative proposals for the session.

Treasury Board A cabinet committee whose primary responsibility is to restrain government spending.

Treasury Board Secretariat The government department that advises the Treasury Board in its deliberations and that functions as a restraining influence on departmental spending.

FURTHER READING

Bakvis, Herman. *Regional Ministers*. Toronto: University of Toronto Press, 1991.

Campbell, Robert M., et al., eds. *Real Worlds of Canadian Politics: Cases in Process and Policy*. 4th ed. Peterborough: Broadview Press, 2004.

Dunn, Christopher, ed. *The Handbook of Canadian Public Administration*. Toronto: Oxford University Press, 2002.

Greenspon, Edward, and Anthony Wilson-Smith. *Double Vision: The Inside Story of the Liberals in Power*. Toronto: Doubleday Canada, 1996.

Heard, Andrew. *Canadian Constitutional Conventions: The Marriage of Law and Politics*. Toronto: Oxford University Press, 1991.

Milne, Glen. *Making Policy: A Guide to the Federal Government's Policy Process*. Ottawa: Glen Milne, 2000.

Robertson, Gordon. *Memoirs of a Very Civil Servant: Mackenzie King to Pierre Trudeau*. Toronto: University of Toronto Press, 2000.

Savoie, Donald J. *Governing from the Centre: The Concentration of Power in Canada*. Toronto: University of Toronto Press, 1999.

Simpson, Jeffrey. *The Friendly Dictatorship*. Toronto: McClelland and Stewart, 2001.

Smith, David E. *The Invisible Crown*. Toronto: University of Toronto Press, 1996.

Chapter 14

The Bureaucracy

Most citizens encounter public servants as providers of services, but the **bureaucracy** is probably even more significant in its advisory role. Modern government is so pervasive and complex that the prime minister and cabinet ministers hardly make a move without the advice of their permanent, expert staff. In fact, the bureaucracy has become so large and indispensable that many observers wonder whether it can be kept under political control. This chapter begins by examining the functions and powers of the bureaucracy and then deals in turn with the three main kinds of bureaucratic organization. It concludes with a discussion about controlling the bureaucracy and the recent attempts to reform it.

Chapter Objectives

After you have completed this chapter, you should be able to:

Identify the role of the bureaucracy in the phases of the policymaking process

Describe the structure of a government department, the roles of the minister and deputy minister, and the principle of ministerial responsibility

Discuss the links between government departments and central agencies, their provincial counterparts, and pressure groups

Discuss the merit system and assess the attempts to make the public service more representative of society

Outline the purposes, structures, and operations of Crown corporations

Outline the purposes, structures, and operations of administrative agencies and regulatory tribunals

Enumerate the methods of controlling the bureaucracy

Discuss recent attempts to reform the bureaucracy

Functions and Powers of the Bureaucracy

As Glen Milne, a veteran of the federal policy process, observes, "only major decisions require cabinet approval and fewer still require new legislation or amendments. In practice, the vast majority of federal government decisions are made at the bureaucratic level within a hierarchical framework of policies decided by cabinet and individual ministers."[1] But even when the other institutions of government are involved, the bureaucracy is usually there too.

Thus, the significance of the bureaucracy can be demonstrated by examining its presence in the model of the policymaking process presented in Figure 13.1 (page 313). First, the bureaucracy plays a crucial part in the initiation phase. The bureaucracy may be a source of demands, since administrators of any program may be among the first to recognize its inadequacies. Even if a demand reaches the cabinet from other sources, once the politicians decide to look into an issue further, the public service will be asked to provide additional information and advice.

If the cabinet decides to take action at the priority-setting stage, it is rarely without advice from the public service, and the bureaucracy is then centrally involved in the policy formulation phase. With its concentration of technical information and experience, the public service spends a great deal of its time formulating policies, since the details of such policies are usually beyond the grasp of the politicians. Once the policy, program, or law has received political authorization by cabinet and/or Parliament, implementation is almost exclusively a bureaucratic responsibility. In today's complex society, the politicians are forced to leave wide discretionary powers to the public service to carry out their general, abstract goals.[2]

Because of the time and informational constraints on Parliament, most bills are passed in rather general or skeletal form, and the real meat or substance of the law is expressed in the **regulations** issued under it. These are published under the authority of the minister or cabinet in the *Canada Gazette*. A considerable lag often exists between the political approval of a law and its effective implementation, during which time the public service drafts such regulations, sets up new administrative machinery, and hires new personnel. The implementation phase may involve time-consuming negotiations with the provinces or with relevant interest groups. Once the date arrives for the start of a new program, it is the bureaucracy again that actually provides the service, does the regulating, or performs whatever other functions are involved. Implementation also requires the bureaucracy to disseminate information to the public about new policies or programs, and it may even involve exercising quasi-judicial powers.

Given its role in almost all phases of the policymaking process, reference to "bureaucratic power" in political science or contentions that the bureaucracy is more powerful than the legislature or even the prime minister and cabinet should not be surprising. While it is more conventional to say that the prime minister and cabinet make the most important decisions in the political system and that they theoretically control the bureaucracy, this is not to deny the extent of bureaucratic power in the modern state. The most common forms of bureaucratic operations are government departments (185 000 employees, including about 60 000 armed forces personnel), Crown corporations (70 000 employees), and administrative agencies and regulatory tribunals (120 000 employees, including about 21 000 RCMP personnel).

Government Departments

Most of the government of Canada's operations are organized into **government departments**. Although each is created by an act of Parliament that sets out its responsibilities, the cabinet can determine the internal structure of the department and can even transfer responsibilities from one department to another.

A major consolidation of departments took place in 1993, reducing the overall number from 25 to about 20. Minor modifications have been made since, such that, as of 2005, the departments were as follows:

- Agriculture and Agri-Food
- Canadian Heritage
- Citizenship and Immigration
- Environment
- Finance
- Fisheries and Oceans
- Foreign Affairs
- Health
- Human Resources and Skills Development
- Indian and Northern Affairs
- Industry
- International Trade
- Justice
- National Defence
- Natural Resources

- Public Safety and Emergency Preparedness
- Public Works and Government Services
- Social Development
- Transport
- Treasury Board Secretariat
- Veterans Affairs

It should be added that another 10 or so ministers of state hover around these full-fledged departments.

The government department assumes a pyramidal shape, with the minister at its apex. Since ministers in this system are chosen from among the politicians elected to Parliament, it is too much to hope that they will be experts in the work of the department. All that is expected is that they have intelligence, ideas, common sense, and an ability to relay government priorities and public opinion to departmental experts as well as to relate expert advice from the department to Parliament and the public. Ministers will naturally develop some expertise if they stay in one cabinet position for any length of time, but they are often shuffled to another department just as they are getting the hang of it.

Ministers are responsible for their department in the sense that they are expected to provide overall direction and to accept criticism for its faults. In other words, ministers take most of the credit or blame for what the department does, whether or not they know what is going on within it. As pointed out in Chapter 13, the principle of **individual ministerial responsibility** was once thought to mean that ministers had to resign for serious mistakes made by their public servants. But no cases of this occurring have ever been recorded since 1867, and in this age of big government, it is not a realistic proposition.[3] What does ministerial responsibility mean today? First, ministers occasionally resign over their personal mistakes or conflicts of interest. Second, they must take political responsibility and answer to Parliament for all actions of their officials. The minister must explain and defend the actions of the department in Parliament, especially during Question Period, and when a bureaucratic error is made, the minister must apologize and promise to correct the mistake. Third, although ministers may discreetly discipline the offender, they should not violate the traditions of public service anonymity.[4] The lax accounting of job-creation funding at Human Resources Development Canada (HRDC) in 2000 is a recent illustration that this is all that ministerial responsibility means.

In the aftermath of the HRDC case and others, the Auditor General wrote in 2001 that "Canada has never modernized its doctrine to distinguish between a minister's area of public responsibility and that of his senior public servants. To

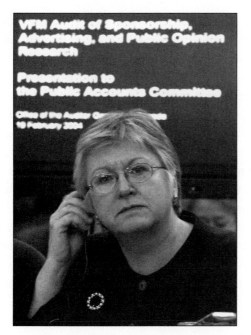

Auditor General Sheila Fraser appears before the
House of Commons Public Accounts Committee during
its 2004 investigation of the sponsorship deals of the
federal government. (CP Photo/Tom Hanson)

me, there is a certain lack of realism in holding ministers ultimately accountable for everything."[5] In a similar vein, Donald J. Savoie notes that bureaucrats have increasingly come to dominate the policymaking process without being responsible for their actions, and he questions whether ministers should be held accountable instead.[6] During the 2004 election campaign, the public was understandably angry that it could not determine who was responsible for the escalating costs of the gun registry or for the sponsorship scandal in Quebec.

The more permanent head of the department is the **deputy minister**. Even though they are appointed by the prime minister (on the advice of the Clerk of the Privy Council and Secretary to the Cabinet), "deputies" or "DMs" are usually career public servants. Deputy ministers have two principal roles: they act as chief policy advisers to the minister and function as managers of the department. Such officials used to spend a lifetime working their way toward the top of a single department and became great experts in its subject matter. Over the past 35 years, however, emphasis in the appointment of deputy ministers has switched to managerial skills that can be applied in any administrative setting. Even though DMs are now frequently shuffled from one department to another, they are usually in place longer than the minister and are thus likely to develop greater knowledge of the department's work. Deputy

What Do You Think?

How can we raise the level of accountability or responsibility for serious errors in the operation of government departments, such as the HRDC mess, the gun registry overspending, or Quebec sponsorship scandal? Make the minister resign? Make the deputy minister resign? Make the Auditor General even more vigilant?

ministers also interact regularly with DMs in other federal departments, provincial DMs in corresponding departments, and the heads of pressure groups particularly interested in the department's work.

The relationship between the minister and the deputy minister is of great interest and concern to political science and public administration.[7] Ideally, the minister sets the priorities for the department, while the DM provides a number of options among which the minister can choose. The deputy should give the minister advice based on administrative, technical, and financial considerations, but the advice must also be sensitive to the political context. Evidence exists that the reality of the relationship sometimes approaches this theoretical ideal. On the other hand, weak ministers may be mere puppets of their bureaucratic advisers. Even strong ministers may be presented only with alternatives favoured by the department, and it has been said that officials in the Department of Finance imposed their ideological bias on one of their most able ministers, Paul Martin.[8] Ministers may encounter bureaucratic resistance to new initiatives, such as in being denied relevant information, having it delayed, or having new policies implemented without enthusiasm.

It is not easy for a single, solitary, temporary, amateur minister to impose his or her will on thousands of expert, permanent public servants who have established departmental attitudes, values, policies, and procedures. Ministers are allowed to appoint a small personal, partisan staff, but these people are engaged primarily in promoting the image and reputation of the minister. In the Mulroney regime, ministers set up large offices headed by a powerful chief of staff, and these were, among other things, the target of most lobbying efforts. Chrétien reverted to an earlier era by reducing the size and significance of ministerial offices and eliminating the chief of staff position, replacing it with the position of executive assistant. Nevertheless, the minister's political staff is significant.[9] Staff members manage the minister's agenda, correspondence, travel, appointments, media liaison, public appearances, and meetings with lobbyists and pressure groups. While they may also provide partisan policy advice and bargain with their counterparts in other ministers' offices, any effort to interfere in the administration of the department is strongly resented by the deputy minister.

Under the deputy minister, the department is typically divided into several branches, each headed by an assistant deputy minister (ADM), and the hierarchy broadens out below them. Those divisions of a department that actually carry out services and interact with the public are said to be performing "line" functions. Except for the top managerial posts, most of the line positions in any department are located in the "field"—in local offices in communities across the country. But every department also has "staff" divisions serving internal needs: policy development and research, personnel, financial, information, and legal divisions. The people working for these divisions, as well as the heads of the line divisions, are normally located in Ottawa.

Hundreds or thousands of public servants in the department are ranged in descending levels of authority under the deputy minister and share four basic characteristics: they are expert, permanent, impartial, and anonymous. First, they are chosen on their merits—ability, knowledge, training, and/or experience—for the duties their position entails. Second, they are career public servants, normally remaining within the public service until retirement. Third, they are nonpartisan and expected to serve whichever party comes to power with equal loyalty and enthusiasm. Fourth, bureaucrats are not normally identified in public; instead, the minister speaks for the department and takes responsibility for its performance. Figure 14.1 illustrates an organizational chart of a hypothetical government department.

The federal public service is divided into six main occupational categories: management or executive; scientific and professional; administrative and foreign service; technical; administrative support; and operational. The first four categories are called "officer" categories, generally requiring postsecondary education, and the last two are called "support." University graduates are normally hired in the administrative and foreign service or scientific and professional groups and

....

Figure 14.1   Organizational Chart of a Hypothetical Government Department

work their way up from there. Within each group are many levels or steps that determine one's salary level.

Relations with Other Departments and Central Agencies

The operation of a government department is complicated by the necessity of interacting with other departments as well as by the authority of various central bureaucratic agencies to intervene in its affairs. Since almost any law, policy, or program affects a variety of departments, many interdepartmental committees exist. Among the permanent ones are two Coordinating Committees of Deputy Ministers, one on management and the other on policy. In addition, whenever any new policy is under active consideration, an ad hoc interdepartmental committee is appointed to look into it. The problem must be examined from a number of departmental perspectives and is also subject to considerable bureaucratic politics and territorial claims.

The central agencies that regularly complicate the life of a department include the Public Service Commission (PSC), the Treasury Board Secretariat (TBS), and the Privy Council Office (PCO). The **Public Service Commission** is a three-member board theoretically in charge of all hiring, promotions, and dismissals. It polices the merit system and prevents appointments and promotions from being made on partisan or discriminatory grounds. In practice, however, the PSC delegates much of its authority to individual departments. The **Treasury Board Secretariat**'s responsibility for financial and expenditure management was outlined in Chapter 13. The TBS scrutinizes departmental plans, performance, and spending; aims to enhance the financial accountability within the public service; and represents the employer in the collective bargaining process. It is responsible for the preparation of the Estimates, and it issues all sorts of administrative policies such as those on purchasing, contracts, and travel. The Department of Finance is normally allied with the TBS as an opponent of new departmental spending programs.

Relations between the Privy Council Office and government departments primarily arise in connection with policy development and coordination, reallocation of programs between departments, reorganization of departments, and senior management appointments. The PCO drafts the prime minister's mandate letter to the minister of the department and takes a great interest in any new policy proposals emanating from it. Moreover, under Paul Martin, some of the human resources functions of the TBS have been moved to the Public Service Human Resources Management Agency, which is attached to the PCO.

Bears try to cross picket line of striking National Park employees. (Malcolm Mayes/artizans.com)

Staffing the Bureaucracy

The Canadian public service originally operated on the spoils system, under which the party that won an election replaced those holding civil service positions with its own friends and supporters. One of the main motives for entering the political arena in that era was to reward family and friends with **political patronage**—government jobs and contracts.[10] Such partisan, amateur personnel proved to be increasingly inadequate as government operations grew more complex after 1900, leading to the creation of the Civil Service Commission, predecessor to the Public Service Commission, in 1908. Henceforth, public servants in

Ottawa were supposed to be hired on merit—that is, on the basis of their qualifications, training, and experience, rather than on partisanship or nepotism. And after passage of the 1918 Civil Service Act, field positions were also to be based on merit. Politicians were reluctant to give up their traditional right to reward their supporters with government jobs, however, and the foundations of the modern merit system in Ottawa were not really laid until the 1930s.[11]

Even if patronage was virtually eliminated in the public service, there remained considerable scope for partisan appointments in other areas. Senators, lieutenant governors, certain types of diplomats, citizenship judges, and some real judges were still often appointed on a partisan basis, as were those appointed to the boards of Crown corporations, administrative agencies, and regulatory tribunals and those working in the PMO and ministers' offices. The Liberals accused Brian Mulroney of excessive patronage, but the Chrétien government was no more restrained.[12]

Almost as soon as the **merit system** was fully effective, people began to demand that the bureaucracy be more representative of the society that it served. Given the power of the public service, many critics argued that the bureaucracy could be responsive to all parts of society only if it included a proportional representation of various groups in the population. The senior levels of the public service had always overrepresented males, anglophones, the middle and upper classes, the well educated, and Ontarians. Thus it was claimed that policy recommendations and implementation reflected an insensitivity to women, the working class, the poor, francophones and other ethnic groups, and the peculiarities of hinterland regions.

The first main concerns in this connection were the small number of francophones in the higher reaches of the bureaucracy and the virtual absence of the French language at policymaking levels. The passage of the **Official Languages Act** in 1969 essentially bilingualized the executive branch of government. It gave both English- and French-speaking citizens the right to deal with head offices of government departments (as well as with local offices where numbers warranted) in either official language. It also expanded language-training programs, made recruitment and promotion of francophones a higher priority, and designated certain positions as bilingual. It was fortunate that the Quebec educational system had improved by this time so that the new policy involved little or no loss of quality in government appointments and promotions. The policy did, however, ignite a backlash against the preference given to French Canadians and to bilingualism. As of 2003, 38 percent of public service positions had been designated as bilingual,

51 percent as English-essential, 5 percent as French-essential, and 6 percent as requiring either official language. As for the people who occupied these positions, about 69 percent were anglophones and 31 percent francophones. Compared to countrywide census statistics, francophones were actually overrepresented in the administrative and foreign service and administrative support categories.[13]

Women were targeted for increased representation in the higher levels of the public service in the 1960s and 1970s.[14] In addition, the pay equity program of the 1980s and 1990s was designed primarily to ensure that women received equal pay for doing work having the same value as that done by men. It is not easy to compare dissimilar jobs for purposes of compensation, but many occupational groups comprising largely women have argued that their work was undervalued just because they were women. Many have subsequently had their salaries increased under the pay equity program; for example, a $3.6 billion pay equity settlement was negotiated in 1999 for some 200 000 secretaries and clerks.

The next stage in creating a more **representative bureaucracy** came in 1983, when an explicit affirmative action program was adopted for women, Aboriginal peoples, and people with disabilities, and two years later visible minorities were added to the list. Once again, this did not necessarily result in a decline in the quality of appointments and promotions, but it sparked opposition from those who did not fall into the designated categories, such as able-bodied, anglophone, white males. A stronger Employment Equity Act in 1995 required the adoption of policies and practices that would ensure that people in the four designated groups achieved a degree of representation in each occupational group proportional to their numbers in the Canadian workforce. Table 14.1 (page 348) provides 2003 figures by equity categories. The Public Service Modernization Act passed in that year sought to sustain the merit principle but add flexibility to the staffing process in order to permit managers to appoint people more quickly.

The Estimates System

Beyond staffing, a major concern of government departments is determining their budgets. As noted earlier, the authorities spend a great deal of their time discussing the expenditure of public funds. Members of Parliament want money allocated to their constituencies, premiers and federal ministers press to get funds allocated to their priorities and provinces, and bureaucrats seek funding for their programs and departments. In addition, much of the pressure from interest groups and corporations consists of demands for federal funds. In earlier eras, such

TABLE 14.1 PUBLIC SERVICE BY EMPLOYMENT EQUITY CATEGORIES, 2003

	Women		Aboriginal Peoples		People with Disabilities		Visible Minorities		
	Number	%	Number	%	Number	%	Number	%	Total
Executive	1 424	33.8	114	2.7	193	4.6	177	4.2	4 209
Scientific and Professional	9 212	40.3	541	2.4	831	3.6	2 633	11.5	22 880
Administrative and Foreign Service	39 798	59.1	2 690	4.0	3 963	5.9	4 951	7.3	67 389
Technical	5 445	31.0	502	2.9	759	4.3	880	5.0	17 557
Administrative Support	27 074	83.1	1 612	4.9	2 499	7.7	2 741	8.4	32 586
Operational	3 209	17.2	967	5.2	910	4.9	676	3.6	18 693
Total	86 162	52.8	6 426	3.9	9 155	5.6	12 058	7.4	163 314

Source: Adapted from Treasury Board of Canada Secretariat, *Employment Equity in the Public Service, 2002–2003*, Figures 11, 12, 13, and 14, http://www.tbs-sct.gc.ca/report/empequi/2003/ee05_e.asp (Retrieved 2 Nov. 2004).

spending was the prerogative of individual politicians or governing parties and was carried out on a patronage basis. Nowadays, the spending process has been highly bureaucratized, and it is the function of the **Estimates** system to decide how such funds will be allocated in any fiscal year. Of course, partisan considerations have not been entirely eliminated.

On the advice on the Department of Finance, the Treasury Board, and the Privy Council Office, the cabinet decides what the government's financial priorities and overall levels of government revenue and expenditure will be and approves any new spending initiatives. The preparation of the Estimates involves projections of the cost of new and existing programs at the departmental level within these limits and guidelines. A great deal of interaction takes place between departments and the Treasury Board Secretariat as deputy ministers and ministers try to maximize their departmental allocations while Treasury Board personnel engage in cutting them back. At the end of the process, the Estimates are consolidated for cabinet approval and introduced into Parliament by the president of the Treasury Board before the beginning of the next fiscal year.

Interaction with Provinces and Pressure Groups

Much of the interaction between federal and provincial governments takes place at the bureaucratic level. Because the division of powers is rather vague and because both federal and provincial personnel usually try to maximize their jurisdiction, the two levels end up operating programs in the same fields. Limitations on provincial finances have in some cases prompted the provinces to request federal financial assistance. When Ottawa agreed to such demands, it usually attached conditions to the expenditure of the funds, making the two levels of government even more intertwined. At the height of cooperative federalism, federal and provincial program administrators would often interact harmoniously in the design and operation of such integrated programs as the Canada Assistance Plan.[15] Despite the more recent trend toward "disengagement," line officials in many federal departments still interact regularly with their provincial counterparts.

The close relationship between pressure groups and the bureaucracy was discussed in Chapter 10. Groups wishing to influence either the formulation or the implementation of policies and programs are active in taking their message to the relevant government department. Sometimes public servants resist the efforts of self-interested groups, but generally the department is more receptive if the group has vital, reliable information that may lead to the development of a more effective program or can help muster support for the departmental initiative among other key players in the policymaking process.

These mutually advantageous contacts between a group and a department may result in a symbiotic, **clientele relationship**. It is generally in the interest of both the department and the group to keep their relationship somewhat confidential so that they can present a united front in case central agencies and cabinet committees become involved. Such relationships may or may not serve the broader public interest.

Crown Corporations

The second most important form of bureaucratic organization is the **Crown corporation**. Crown corporations are government-owned operations that assume a structure similar to that of private corporations. There are about 50 major Crown corporations at the federal level, including:

- Atomic Energy of Canada Ltd. (AECL)
- Bank of Canada
- Business Development Bank of Canada
- Canada Mortgage and Housing Corporation
- Canada Post Corporation
- Canadian Broadcasting Corporation
- Marine Atlantic Inc.
- VIA Rail Canada Inc.

The largest in terms of employees are Canada Post (45 612), the Canadian Broadcasting Corporation (7422), AECL (3334), and VIA Rail (3054).

One major difference between a Crown corporation and a regular government department is its organizational structure. A Crown corporation includes a board of directors, president, vice presidents, etc. The cabinet appoints the president as well as the board of directors, who theoretically set the general policy of the corporation. Many Crown corporation presidents have been appointed on a patronage basis, but after ridding itself of several of them for various reasons, including the sponsorship scandal in Quebec, the Martin government pledged that their replacements would be selected on the basis of merit.

A second distinguishing feature of the Crown corporation is that it is not subject to day-to-day political direction. The statute that creates it sets out its objectives to some extent, and while the cabinet may issue general policy guidelines, the corporation otherwise operates more or less independently. The cabinet minister to whom the Crown corporation is attached acts largely as a channel of communication between it and Parliament, passing on answers to parliamentary inquiries but not being held responsible for the corporation in the same way as for a regular department. On the other hand, because the government creates the Crown corporation, appoints its leading personnel, and usually provides some of its funds, the minister and cabinet cannot avoid complete responsibility for its actions. A government obsessed with its deficit can make deep cuts in a Crown corporation's budget, as the CBC found throughout the Mulroney and Chrétien periods.

Third, Crown corporations are freer of bureaucratic controls relating to personnel and finance than ordinary government departments. As a general rule, the greater the financial self-sufficiency of the corporation, the greater its autonomy. Crown corporations can therefore operate more flexibly than government departments, especially if they are in competition with private firms.

The Crown corporation is thus a logical structure for a governmental operation of a commercial or industrial nature. It may also be used in politically sensitive areas such as broadcasting, and/or if the operation has private sector competition. More specifically, Crown corporations have been created to promote national integration (VIA Rail, Canada Post, and Marine Atlantic), national identity (CBC and Canada Museums), a particular industry (Canadian Wheat Board), and business in general (Business Development Bank).

Like other government operations, then, Crown corporations have a public policy purpose. They are created where, for one reason or another, the private sector has not met public needs. The basic objective of Crown corporations is to provide a public service, not to make a profit, but because most Crown corporations need annual public subsidies, they are often criticized for being inefficient. In fact, however, they may be just as efficient as private companies; the subsidies are necessary because many Crown corporations operate in areas where no profit is feasible.

The 1980s witnessed a worldwide trend toward the **privatization** of public enterprises, led by Margaret Thatcher in Britain, and the Mulroney government happily jumped on the bandwagon. Privatizations were made largely for two ideological reasons: the government had an instinctive preference for the private sector, and the sale of Crown corporation shares helped to reduce the national

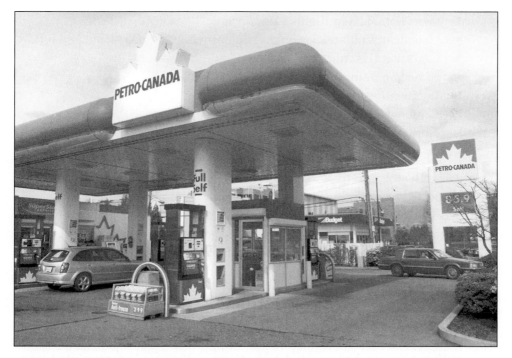

In March 2004, the federal government announced the sale of its final 19 percent stake in Petro-Canada that could mean a windfall of $3 billion for the federal treasury. (CP Photo/Chuck Stoody)

deficit. Privatizers also argued that such Crown corporations no longer served a public policy purpose and that they would operate more efficiently as private companies. The Chrétien government also did its share of privatization, such that by the beginning of the 21st century, the following major Crown corporations were no longer owned by government: Air Canada, Canadian National Railway, Eldorado Nuclear, Fishery Products International, Petro-Canada, Teleglobe Canada, and Telesat.

Administrative Agencies and Regulatory Tribunals

Administrative agencies and **regulatory tribunals** are the third basic form of bureaucratic organization. Such agencies regulate many aspects of our daily lives. Some of the most important among them are:

- Canadian Nuclear Safety Commission
- Canadian Food Inspection Agency
- Canadian Human Rights Commission
- Canadian Radio-television and Telecommunications Commission (CRTC)
- Canadian Revenue Agency
- Canadian Transportation Agency
- Immigration and Refugee Board
- National Energy Board
- National Parole Board

In structure, administrative agencies and regulatory tribunals bear considerable resemblance to Crown corporations. They comprise a chair and board appointed by the cabinet and are advised by a permanent, expert staff. The incidence of partisanship in appointments to the chair and board is unfortunately quite large; indeed, these remain one of the last refuges of patronage in the political system. Such agencies and tribunals typically receive policy guidelines from the cabinet, but as with Crown corporations, ministers are kept at arm's length from their day-to-day operations.

Administrative agencies and regulatory tribunals may make quasi-legislative rules and regulations, such as in the case of the Canadian-content regulations of the CRTC. A typical regulatory agency also makes quasi-judicial decisions based on the cabinet's policy guidelines and its own regulations. Among other things, regulatory agencies decide contentious immigration cases (Immigration and Refugee Board), review transportation rates (Canadian Transportation Agency), approve exports of natural gas and electricity (National Energy Board), and allow prisoners out of jail (National Parole Board).

These functions could presumably be performed by regular government departments, but they are given to semi-independent agencies in order to divorce them from political and partisan considerations. Such adjudicative functions could also be performed by the courts, but these kinds of decisions demand a technical expertise not expected of judges. Moreover, given the backlog in the court system, it is hoped that the decisions of administrative agencies and regulatory tribunals will be made more quickly and more cheaply than those of the courts.

At the same time, however, regulatory agencies are expected to provide an impartial, court-like hearing, and in many cases lawyers are present in the same capacity as in court. Decisions of such agencies are normally appealable to the courts on procedural grounds but not on the substance of the case; some are appealable to the cabinet.

Many observers have argued that there are too many regulatory agencies with too much power. Hence, **deregulation** was a companion ingredient to privatization in the neoconservatism (or neoliberalism) of the past 20 years. The Canadian transportation industry in particular was deregulated to a large extent.

***

Not all government operations fall into the three categories discussed above. Others include central agencies (e.g., PCO), royal commissions, advisory councils (e.g., National Council of Welfare), funding bodies (e.g., Social Sciences and Humanities Research Council), and agents of parliament (Auditor General, Elections Canada, the Information Commissioner, and the Commissioner of Official Languages). One-of-a-kind agencies include Statistics Canada, the RCMP, the Correctional Service, and the Canadian Security Intelligence Service.

Royal commissions are formal, in-depth inquiries set up by the cabinet to investigate some difficult problem for which the resources of the regular public service are considered inadequate. Royal commissions may be headed by up to 10 commissioners, usually people of stature and expertise, and normally involve extensive public hearings and an elaborate research program. They are often regarded somewhat cynically because of their cost and because of the length of time it takes them to produce a report. Cynics also point out that governments have not had a good record of implementing royal commission recommendations; indeed, such commissions often seem to be appointed to take the heat off a particular issue on which the government has no intention of taking action. Sometimes they are also seen as devices to generate support for a policy that the government already had in mind. For example, their terms of reference may exclude alternatives that the government has already rejected. Nevertheless, many royal commissions have served a useful purpose, and many public policies—such as equalization payments, medicare, official bilingualism, and free trade—owe their existence, at least in part, to royal commission reports.

Controlling the Bureaucracy

Given the enormous influence and considerable power of the bureaucracy in the modern state, democracies are understandably concerned about keeping the public service under control. Means of doing so are identified in Figure 14.2.

First, individual ministers and the cabinet as a whole are supposed to provide political control of the bureaucracy. The minister gives direction to the public service and has the power to veto any of its proposals. Ministers have provided varied accounts of what happens in practice: some argue that they do control their departments, while others feel that they are manipulated by their public servants. In a more specialized context, civilian control of the military and police is an important principle in a democratic society.

Second, the power of some bureaucrats is controlled by other bureaucrats. This includes the financial control of the Treasury Board Secretariat and the Department of Finance, the personnel control of the Public Service Commission, and the policy control of the Privy Council Office.

Figure 14.2 Means of Controlling the Bureaucracy

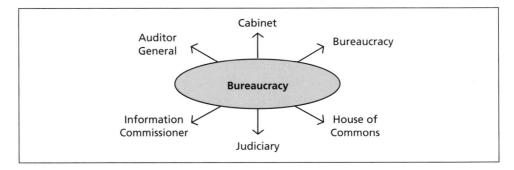

The third line of defence against bureaucratic power is the House of Commons. One principle of parliamentary government is that the executive (cabinet or bureaucracy) is not allowed either to raise or to spend money without Parliament's approval. In practice, proposals for tax changes as well as spending proposals all originate with the executive. They are rarely altered in the legislative process, and the taxing and spending usually begin before Parliament has given its consent. Examining the Estimates, however, gives the House of Commons an opportunity to question and criticize ministers and deputy ministers about all aspects of their departmental spending, programs, and policies. Furthermore, once the money has been spent, an official of Parliament, the **Auditor General**, inspects the Public Accounts and informs Parliament of instances where funds were misspent.[16] The **Public Accounts Committee** of the House (chaired by an opposition member) goes through the Auditor General's reports and calls onto the carpet those ministers or deputy ministers who have committed the worst financial faults.

The Auditor General's staff function something like spies within the public service, recording any decisions or practices that are illegal, immoral, wasteful, or otherwise ill advised. Considerable controversy raged in the 1980s over the size of this staff, their ability to gain access to cabinet documents, and the question of whether they should function narrowly as auditors or make broader policy recommendations. They now perform "legislative audits," which go well beyond traditional financial auditing. In the light of the Auditor General's revelation of financial improprieties in the Human Resources Development department, the firearms registry, and the sponsorship scandal in Quebec, the office of the Auditor General—and the incumbent, Sheila Fraser—have now been accorded heroic status. Especially in the absence of other devices to ensure accountability in the spending of public funds, almost everyone is now prepared to give the Auditor General all the resources she asks for.

The House of Commons has several other means of exercising some control over the bureaucracy, the first being the daily oral Question Period. In this case, the Commons criticizes the minister, who is theoretically responsible for everything the department does. Although the minister is expected to take the blame for bureaucratic errors, public servants seek to avoid bringing such embarrassment or disrepute upon their minister and department. In addition, members of Parliament receive requests on a daily basis from their constituents to intervene on their behalf to speed up or correct bureaucratic decisions. MPs and their staff normally handle such problems with a telephone call or a letter to the public servant or minister concerned. Another aspect of parliamentary control of the bureaucracy is exercised by the Standing Joint Committee on the Scrutiny of Regulations, which attempts to review the reams of regulations that the bureaucracy produces annually. On the other hand, as the Auditor General pointed out in 2001, Parliament needs more information about the government's use of resources and about the results of government programs.

A fourth kind of control of the bureaucracy is provided by the judiciary. The power of the courts to overturn decisions of bureaucrats in regular government departments is essentially restricted to cases of breaches of the law or actions taken beyond the public servant's jurisdiction. The Charter of Rights provides more scope for this kind of judicial review than has existed in the past. In the *Singh* case, for example, the Supreme Court ruled that the Immigration Department had to provide an oral hearing for all refugee claimants rather than deport such claimants on the basis of written documents alone, as was previously done. The *Little Sisters* case involved a bookstore complaining that customs officers routinely rejected, merely on the basis of sexual orientation, books and magazines that the store had ordered. The Supreme Court told customs officers that they must not discriminate against gay or lesbian material; all sexually oriented material must be judged by the same criteria. Police officers are a special category of bureaucrats who have also had their professional behaviour severely restricted by judicial interpretation of the legal rights section and/or section 24 of the Charter, as noted in Chapter 11.

In the Words of the Court
Customs Officials and the *Little Sisters* Case

"The Customs treatment was high-handed and dismissive of the appellants' right to receive lawful expressive material which they had every right to import.... [I]t is fundamentally unacceptable that expression which is free within the country can become stigmatized and harassed by government officials simply because it crosses an international boundary.... A large measure of discretion is granted in the administration of the Act, from the level of the Customs official up to the Minister, but it is well established that such discretion must be exercised in accordance with the Charter."

Source: *Little Sisters Book and Art Emporium v. Canada (Minister of Justice)*, [2000] 2 S.C.R. 1120.

Regulatory agencies are usually expected to operate in a court-like manner, and their decisions can be overturned by the courts for procedural abuses as well as for exceeding their jurisdiction. The Federal Court of Canada, discussed in Chapter 16, specializes in hearing appeals from such regulatory agencies.

Finally, of several independent watchdog agencies, the most important next to the Auditor General is the **Information Commissioner**. Canadian governments have traditionally functioned under a cloak of secrecy at both the cabinet and bureaucratic levels. This tradition prevented the opposition and the public from knowing what alternative policies had been considered, what kind of public opinion polling was done, or what advice was actually offered by the bureaucracy. The 1983 **Access to Information Act** considerably improved the situation, although the many exemptions in the act mean that it is not entirely effective. If a citizen, journalist, company, or pressure group is denied access to a desired piece of government information, that person or organization can appeal to the Information Commissioner, who can overrule the department in the matter. The government can, however, appeal to the Federal Court, and in recent years that court has frequently sided with the government, especially the PMO, when the Information Commissioner supported more openness.

Reform of the Bureaucracy: The New Public Management

Apart from the problem of keeping the bureaucracy under some kind of democratic control, three other problems or dysfunctions are often identified. First, from the public's perspective, the bureaucracy is accused of being bound up in "red tape." This generally includes a collection of sins that characterize the behaviour of all large organizations, not only governmental ones, including delays, a multitude of forms, excessive rules and regulations, difficulty in finding the appropriate official to solve a problem, and lack of helpful, personal attention. If these dysfunctions are more characteristic of government than of large private firms, it is primarily because governments are required to operate according to the law and the regulations issued under the law. Government must treat everyone in exactly the same way, and unlike private firms it cannot show favouritism or make individual exceptions. Delays may be the result of public servants wanting to be certain that their decision is absolutely right, because mistakes may be criticized in Parliament or in the media.

A second general criticism of bureaucracy is that it is inefficient because it lacks the profit motive of the private sector. Officials in private firms are said to move more quickly because they are in greater danger of losing their jobs and because minimizing costs is a higher priority. To some extent this is true, or at least may once have been. Given that the essential difference between the public and private sectors is that the bureaucracy is charged with providing a public service, however, it should be judged primarily on the adequacy of that service. Nevertheless, the widespread belief that there is much "fat" and inefficiency within the bureaucracy led both the Mulroney and Chrétien governments to impose severe financial restraints on government departments and Crown corporations, leading them to make across-the-board cuts, terminate programs, lay off staff, freeze hiring, charge user fees, and contract out certain services.[17] As a result, those public servants left often report higher levels of stress.

From a management point of view, the main dysfunction of the public service is that deputy ministers and other managerial personnel are too hemmed in by rules and regulations and their authority is too limited by central agencies. Several recent reforms have been introduced to provide more autonomy and managerial flexibility to deputy ministers by relaxing some of the detailed rules and reporting requirements.

The reforms mentioned previously—the increased autonomy of managers, privatization of Crown corporations, deregulation, and the restructuring of government departments in 1993—were merely part of a major transformation of the Canadian federal public service over the past 15 years that has parallels around the world and that is often called the **New Public Management** (NPM). General factors leading to such public service reform included concern with debts and deficits, changing public and private sector expectations, globalization, new technologies, growing doubts about the capacity of state institutions to fulfill their mandates, and citizen demands for direct political participation.[18]

The 1994 and 1995 federal budgets inaugurated a process generally labelled Program Review. This involved a fundamental rethinking of what government did and how it did it—or redefining the role of government.[19] Through this process, the federal government determined which activities it could continue to deliver or support within a much reduced budget. It also identified which activities it could cease providing, scale back, devolve, or deliver or finance differently. The process involved significant reductions in subsidy programs, increased user fees, and the provision of many government activities on a commercial basis. In the 1995 budget, the minister of finance ensured that real Program Review would happen when he declared his intention to eliminate 45 000 public service jobs by 1998 to help the government reduce its deficit.

Another part of New Public Management was called Alternative Service Delivery (ASD). ASD is a generic term covering a variety of innovative means of providing government services that involve reducing the size and expense of government, making government more citizen-oriented, involving users in service delivery, providing more flexibility in service delivery, enhancing employee motivation, and incorporating new developments in information technology. ASD consists primarily of special operating agencies and developing partnerships with provinces or commercial or nonprofit organizations outside government.

Special operating agencies (SOAs) are units that function with relative autonomy within government departments. In most cases, they have the potential to become self-financing, and their objective is to deliver a service along private sector lines, that is, in a manner that is more sensitive to client requirements, that promotes a more creative entrepreneurial working environment, and that brings savings to government. The Passport Office and the Translation Bureau are examples of the 19 SOAs in existence.

The first kind of partnership involves the provinces, and the two main initiatives in this category were the Canadian Food Inspection Agency and the Canada Revenue Agency (CRA). The former combines the food inspection services previously provided by three separate federal departments and opens the way for provincial government involvement. The CRA is a transformation of the Revenue Canada department into an agency responsible for collecting federal taxes, as well as provincial taxes upon request.[20]

The federal government may enter other kinds of partnerships with private firms (sometimes called public–private partnerships or P3s), nonprofit, noncommercial, or volunteer organizations. The government–private company relationship behind the construction and operation of the Confederation Bridge between Prince Edward Island and New Brunswick and the creation of local authorities to operate Canadian airports are prominent examples. Another is NAV CANADA, the agency created to replace the government's air traffic control system. Its board of directors includes representatives of the airlines, government, and employee unions, and it sets its rates so that it breaks even. In some cases, government employees have been encouraged to quit their jobs and set up their own companies to provide the same services in the private sector.

It should be said, however, that not everyone thinks the reality of NPM matches its rhetoric, and many observers do not believe it to be a good idea at all.

For example, the whole movement stems from a preoccupation with cutting government expenditures, which involved the elimination of thousands of government jobs. Beyond the fact that fewer public servants are now delivering fewer public services is a troubling question of democratic accountability. It can certainly be argued that with semi-independent partners of various kinds supplying public services, any semblance of democratic ministerial responsibility has been lost.

The latest innovation in government operations is "e-government," that is, making government information "electronic" and putting it online. Ottawa intends to be more electronically connected to its citizens than any other government in the world, with Canadians being able to access all government information and services on the Internet.

SUMMARY

This chapter began by showing that bureaucracy plays a major part in almost every phase of the policymaking process. Even when the prime minister and cabinet actually make decisions, the bureaucracy provides advice, and on most lesser occasions the bureaucracy makes decisions on its own. The chapter then analyzed the operation of the government department, distinguishing the roles of the minister and deputy minister and trying to clarify the principle of individual ministerial responsibility. It showed that the minister, deputy minister, and lower bureaucrats are in regular contact with other departments and central agencies of the federal government as well as provincial departments and pressure groups. It also discussed a major concern in staffing the bureaucracy: selecting the best people for the job while trying to accurately represent the society at large. The chapter then considered Crown corporations, administrative agencies, and regulatory tribunals, distinguishing their purposes, structures, and operations from those of regular government departments. The next section dealt with the methods of keeping the bureaucracy under some degree of democratic control. The chapter concluded with a discussion of the New Public Management and other recent bureaucratic reforms.

DISCUSSION QUESTIONS

1. How can financial accountability in the public service be brought to an acceptable level?

2. To what extent should Canada establish a "representative bureaucracy"?
3. Given the necessity of the bureaucracy in the modern state, are the democratic controls on its power sufficient?
4. How do you feel about downsizing of the public service, privatization of Crown corporations, deregulation, and the various initiatives involved in the New Public Management?

KEY TERMS

Access to Information Act The 1983 act that gave citizens, journalists, and others the right to gain access to government documents, with certain exceptions, and established the office of Information Commissioner.

Auditor General The official of Parliament whose staff audit the expenditures of government departments and who reports on instances of funds being unlawfully or unwisely spent.

Bureaucracy The permanent officials employed by the government, also known as the public service.

Clientele relationship The intimate and mutually advantageous relationship that sometimes develops between a government department or agency and the interest group with which it most frequently interacts.

Crown corporation A corporation owned by the government that assumes a structure similar to that of a private company and that operates semi-independently of the cabinet.

Deputy minister The public servant who heads each government department, manages the department, and advises the minister.

Deregulation A government policy that removes previous regulations, especially those affecting the corporate sector.

Estimates The annual spending plans of government departments and agencies.

Government department A government organization headed by a minister who is politically accountable for its operations and a deputy minister who is in charge of its hierarchical administrative apparatus.

Individual ministerial responsibility The principle that cabinet ministers are individually responsible to the House of Commons to answer for everything that happens in their department.

Information Commissioner The official of Parliament who encourages government to operate on a more open basis and makes judgments in cases where departments withhold information under the Access to Information Act.

Merit system A system of hiring and promoting public servants on the basis of their merits (education, experience, etc.) rather than on party preference or other considerations.

New Public Management A movement within public administration since about 1990 that involved the downsizing of government operations, alternative service delivery, and partnerships with private sector agencies.

Official Languages Act The 1969 federal act that established official bilingualism in Canada and gave citizens the right to deal with certain offices of the federal government in either English or French.

Political patronage Making appointments to public offices or awarding government contracts on a partisan basis.

Privatization Transferring a government program, agency, or Crown corporation to the private sector.

Public Accounts Committee The House of Commons committee that examines the Public Accounts and the Auditor General's reports and criticizes government officials for illegal or unwise expenditures.

Public Service Commission The central personnel agency of government designed to police the merit system and ensure that partisanship is kept out of the regular public service.

Regulations The detailed rules drafted by the bureaucracy under the authority of laws passed by Parliament that are too voluminous and technical to put into the legislation itself.

Regulatory tribunal A government agency established to regulate an area of public policy, such as transportation or communications, that operates at arm's length from the cabinet.

Representative bureaucracy A public service that reflects the composition of the population, with the most usual concerns being gender, ethnicity, and region.

Royal commission An elaborate investigation set up by the cabinet to research a significant policy problem, to listen to and educate the public, and to make recommendations to the government.

Treasury Board Secretariat The government department that advises the Treasury Board in its deliberations and that functions as a restraining influence on departmental spending.

FURTHER READING

Auditor General. *Reflections on a Decade of Serving Parliament, Report of the Auditor General of Canada*. February 2001. http://www.oag-bvg.gc.ca/domino/reports. nsf/html/01cap_e.html.

Clerk of the Privy Council and Secretary to the Cabinet. *Annual Report to the Prime Minister of Canada*. http://www.pco-bcp.gc.ca/default.asp?Language=E &Page=Report&doc=annual-report_e.htm.

Dunn, Christopher H., ed. *The Handbook of Canadian Public Administration*. Toronto: Oxford University Press, 2002.

How Ottawa Spends. Toronto: Oxford University Press annual.

Inwood, Gregory J. *Understanding Canadian Public Administration: An Introduction to Theory and Practice*. 2nd ed. Scarborough: Prentice-Hall Canada, 2004.

Kernaghan, Kenneth, and David Siegel. *Public Administration in Canada: A Text*. 4th ed. Scarborough: Nelson Canada, 1999.

Osbaldeston, Gordon. *Keeping Deputy Ministers Accountable*. Toronto: McGraw-Hill Ryerson, 1989.

Pal, Leslie A. *Beyond Policy Analysis: Public Issue Management in Turbulent Times*. 3rd ed. Scarborough: Thomson Nelson, 2005.

Peters, B. Guy, and Donald Savoie. *Taking Stock*. Montreal: McGill-Queen's University Press, 1998.

Savoie, Donald J. *Breaking the Bargain: Public Servants, Ministers, and Parliament*. Toronto: University of Toronto Press, 2003.

Chapter 15

Parliament

Although the term theoretically also includes the Queen and the Senate, the word **"Parliament"** is popularly synonymous with the House of Commons, by far its most important part. Hence, those elected to the House of Commons are called members of Parliament or MPs. The House of Commons is the central link between the public and the government in Canadian democracy; it is where the elected representatives of the people meet in daily, open, verbal combat. This chapter examines the House of Commons from a number of perspectives and later explores the role of the other branch of the legislature, the Senate.

Chapter Objectives

After you have completed this chapter, you should be able to:

Discuss the functions of the House of Commons and of its individual members within and beyond the policymaking process

Comment on the extent to which MPs are representative of the population

Outline the weekly and yearly parliamentary timetables

Evaluate the advantages and disadvantages of strict party discipline

Identify the different stages and kinds of legislation

Identify the various officers of the House of Commons

Discuss the committee system of the House

Comment on the various roles that MPs perform and on members' services

Discuss the balance between government and opposition, distinguishing between majority and minority situations

Enumerate the intended functions of the Senate and assess its performance

Discuss possible avenues of Senate reform

Functions and Powers of the House of Commons

The **Westminster model** of government employed by Canada begins with a bicameral **legislature**—an elected lower house, the House of Commons, with primary legislative powers and answerable to the people through elections, and an appointed upper house, the Senate, with limited legislative powers. The executive is part of the Commons and, through the cabinet, drives or "energizes" the legislative process. The **government** or cabinet is in charge of and is responsible for the conduct of parliamentary business, while an institutionalized opposition has the right and duty to criticize the government. This model therefore promises potent government and political stability through the cabinet, along with political accountability through open debate. MPs can thus be divided into three main groups: those who serve as cabinet ministers, those who support the cabinet (government **backbenchers**), and those who oppose the government (the **opposition**).[1]

Historically, the sovereignty or **supremacy of Parliament** has been a basic principle of Canadian government. Apart from interfering in provincial jurisdiction and with other minor exceptions, Parliament could pass laws that were virtually beyond review by any other organ of government, including the courts. With the adoption of the Charter of Rights and Freedoms in 1982, however, this principle was considerably transformed. The courts' power of **judicial review** has been greatly extended and now includes the right to examine both federal and provincial legislation in terms of the Charter and to invalidate such legislation to the extent of any contradiction. On the other hand, rather than throw out a law, the courts have often suggested that the legislation be redrafted to fit within the boundaries of the Charter. As a last resort, the notwithstanding clause allows for the reassertion of Parliamentary sovereignty on many points.

In discussing the functions of the House of Commons, it is instructive to examine its role in the chart of the policymaking process illustrated in Figure 13.1 (page 313). First, Parliament may be involved in the initiation phase by raising issues in the daily Question Period and in general debates, in criticizing existing spending programs, or by means of private members' bills. It is then virtually nonexistent in the priority-setting and policy-formulation phases. However, the Commons dominates the legitimation stage. Whether or not bills are refined in the process, cabinet proposals are made legitimate by their passage through the formal, authorized, democratic channels of the Commons. The House may not make many significant changes, but it does subject bills to extended debate and publicizes their advantages and disadvantages before converting them into laws or statutes. The legislative stage serves to inform the public of the content of new policies, and out of this "prolonged warfare," consent or acceptance is eventually obtained. This debate essentially prepares the electorate for its decision on how to vote in the next election.

Composition of the House of Commons

The basic principle of representation in the House of Commons is that each province is represented in proportion to its population. Chapter 8 outlined how the 308 seats in the Commons are distributed among the provinces, as shown in the accompanying box.

Seats in the House of Commons			
Ontario	106	New Brunswick	10
Quebec	75	Newfoundland and Labrador	7
British Columbia	36	Prince Edward Island	4
Alberta	28	Nunavut	1
Manitoba	14	Northwest Territories	1
Saskatchewan	14	Yukon	1
Nova Scotia	11	**Total**	**308**

Even if members of Parliament other than cabinet ministers have only a limited role in the policymaking process, the social background characteristics of ordinary members merit examination. To the extent that MPs are not representative of the population, certain issues are not likely to be addressed.

Since they are elected to represent territorial units and usually live in or near their constituencies, MPs almost automatically become representative of the population in a geographic sense. MPs are also fairly representative in terms of English and French ethnic backgrounds. The Constitution Act, 1867, required from the beginning that all House documents be printed in English and French, but the absence of simultaneous interpretation until 1958 and the unilingualism of most MPs served to limit interaction between the two linguistic groups.

On the other hand, members of Parliament do not reflect the population very well in terms of other ethnic origins, education, occupation, class, or gender. Although not as exclusive in these respects as cabinet ministers, MPs have higher educational levels and higher-status occupations than the general population. Historically, the legal profession has furnished the largest single group in the Commons, but since 1984 those with a business background have predominated. Educators are now usually second, often exceeding lawyers, and administrators are a close fourth. This change still leaves a gross underrepresentation of the working class.[2] Relatively few women have been elected to the House of Commons, although the number has increased in recent years, reaching 53 of 295 in 1993, 62 of 301 in 1997 and 2000, and 65 of 308 in 2004—just over 20 percent.

What is probably most striking about Canadian MPs, especially compared to members of other legislatures around the world, is their rapid turnover in office. There are relatively few **safe seats** in Canada, so that the proportion of new members after each election averages 40 percent, and the typical MP serves less than 10 years.[3] This is partly a reflection of the low degree of party identification among the electorate, and it means that few members remain in Parliament long enough to develop an understanding of the institution or to stand up to a long-serving prime minister. The 1993 turnover was over 75 percent, as a result of the decimation of the Conservatives and NDP; in 1997, it was over 30 percent; in 2000, 15 percent; and in 2004, 35 percent.

The Parliamentary Timetable

Perhaps the best way to get an overview of the work of the House of Commons is by examining the parliamentary timetable—the agenda of a typical session and a typical week.

The Typical Session

The normal practice is to have each session of Parliament last about one year. A session begins with the **Speech from the Throne**, prepared by the prime minister and read by the governor general. Its function is to outline the government's legislative plans for the session, and it introduces the Throne Speech debate, a six-day debate in which MPs can talk about anything that comes to mind. Party leaders and cabinet ministers may use the occasion to articulate their priorities, while backbenchers often expound on the wonders or troubles of their constituency.

The second major event of the session is the **budget** and the budget debate. The minister of finance delivers the budget, a statement chiefly concerned with tax changes (the revenue side of the government's books) but also dealing with government finances in general. Among other things, the budget usually fleshes out the promises of the Speech from the Throne. The budget sets the stage for a four-day freewheeling debate and provides the opposition with a second opportunity to try to defeat the government. Legislation incorporating the specific tax changes mentioned in the budget comes along later, although the changes usually take effect as of budget night.

A third part of the session consists of the government's spending proposals for the next fiscal year, the **Estimates**. Once tabled, however, the Estimates are transmitted to standing committees of the House for scrutiny, so that they occupy little time of the Commons as a whole.

A fourth element of the session consists of the 21 **opposition days**, when the opposition parties choose the subject of debate and the government in turn responds. These are divided proportionally among the opposition parties and distributed throughout the session.

Other than these four components, the time of the House of Commons is taken up with the discussion of bills, and most of that time with bills introduced by the government. Indeed, it is partly because of the volume of government legislation that some sessions of Parliament exceed a year in length. Since bills that have not passed die at the end of the session, governments are tempted to allow sessions to continue beyond one year until all current legislation is disposed of.

The Commons sits for about 135 days per year. When the government wishes to take a break within a session, it adjourns the House. When it wants to bring a session to an end, it prorogues the Commons, setting the stage for a new Speech from the Throne to initiate a new session. Finally, an election call results in the **dissolution of Parliament**.

The Typical Week

The House begins its sessions at 11:00 a.m. on Monday and meets at 10:00 a.m. on the other four weekdays. The weekly schedule is shown in Figure 15.1 (page 370).

The most exciting part of the day is the 45-minute oral **Question Period**. It is this period that offers the opposition its best opportunity to criticize and embarrass the government, as it grills cabinet ministers about their deficiencies and faults. Ministers are not given notice of such questions, but before going into the

Figure 15.1 **Daily Order of Business**

HOURS	MONDAY	TUESDAY	WEDNESDAY	THURSDAY	FRIDAY	HOURS
10:00–11:00		Routine Proceedings		Routine Proceedings	Government Orders	10:00–11:00
11:00–11:15	Private Members' Business (3)				Members' Statements	11:00–11:15
11:15–12:00					Oral Questions	11:15–12:00
12:00–1:00					Routine Proceedings (1)	12:00–1:00
1:00–1:30	Government Orders	Government Orders (2)	Review of Delegated Legislation (4)	Government Orders (2)	Government Orders (2)	1:00–1:30
1:30–2:00					Private Members' Business	1:30–2:00
2:00–2:15	Members' Statements	Members' Statements	Members' Statements	Members' Statements		2:00–2:15
2:15–2:30	Oral Questions	Oral Questions	Oral Questions	Oral Questions		2:15–2:30
2:30–3:00						2:30–3:00
3:00–5:30	Routine Proceedings (1) Government Orders (2)	(1) Government Orders (2)	Routine Proceedings (1) Notices of Motions for the Production of Papers Government Orders (2)	(1) Government Orders (2)		3:00–5:30
5:30–6:30		Private Members' Business (3)	Private Members' Business (3)	Private Members' Business (3)		5:30–6:30
6:30–7:00	Adjournment Proceedings (2)	Adjournment Proceedings (2)	Adjournment Proceedings (2)	Adjournment Proceedings (2)		6:30–7:00

(1) Possible extension of Routine Proceedings to complete Introduction of Government Bills pursuant to Standing Order 30(4).
(2) Possible extension or delay pursuant to Standing Order 33(2) respecting Ministerial Statements.
(3) Possible delay or rescheduling pursuant to Standing Order 30(7) to compensate for a delay or an interruption of more than 30 minutes, and pursuant to Standing Order 33(2) respecting Ministerial Statements.
(4) If required, House to sit at 1:00 p.m. for the review of Delegated Legislation pursuant to Standing Order 128(1).

Source: Daily Order of Business, 2002, http://www.parl.gc.ca/information/about/process/house/DOB/dob-e.htm. Reproduced with permission of the House of Commons.

chamber they are briefed by aides who try to anticipate what questions might be asked. Even greater daily effort goes into the preparation and rehearsal of questions by opposition party leaders and their staff. The **Leader of the Opposition** and the leaders of any other recognized parties begin the attack, and the Speaker of the House distributes the opportunity to ask questions to various opposition parties in a rough proportion to their numbers. Since ministers often respond in a deliberately vague manner, several supplementary questions are allowed, but the objective of the opposition is not so much to elicit information as to portray the government in a negative light. Such exchanges, along with corridor interviews and hallway "scrums" based on Question Period, find their way onto the television news and form the backbone of media reporting on the House. Government backbenchers are also allowed to participate, but they usually ask "planted" questions to which relieved ministers give prepared and self-serving replies.

Immediately before Question Period, 15 minutes are set aside for members' statements, during which individual MPs have 60 seconds to get something off their chests. After Question Period, unless the House is involved in one of the special events—the Throne Speech or budget debates or an opposition day—the regular business is the discussion of government orders, usually government bills. Government bills are those introduced by a cabinet minister with the full backing of the cabinet, and these debates are the basic routine of Commons life. At this point in the day most of the **parliamentary press gallery** and MPs leave the chamber in search of more pressing or more interesting activity. The speeches in these debates are generally dull and boring—the public and media can hardly be blamed for paying so little attention to them when MPs themselves rarely listen to each other. The few members assigned to make up quorum on any day are more likely to be answering their mail or reading the newspaper.

Only five hours a week are reserved for private members' bills and motions, at the normal rate of one hour per bill. These bills and motions, introduced either by government supporters who are not in the cabinet or by opposition members, are usually of little interest to anyone else. They are virtually assured of being dropped to the bottom of the pile when their hour on the stage has elapsed.

Finally, the adjournment proceeding is a half-hour opportunity at the end of the daily sitting (6:30 to 7:00 p.m.) four times a week for opposition MPs to pursue issues that they feel were inadequately answered in the Question Period. Ministers usually send their **parliamentary secretary**—an MP assigned to help them in any way they see fit—to fill in for them when called to account so late in the day.

Given the sharply adversarial nature of Question Period and the dullness of the rest of the parliamentary day, television coverage of the House of Commons does little to enhance the public's support of the government or politicians in general. On the other hand, "the all-consuming ritual of adversarial combat completely dominated by political parties"[4] has its defenders: it serves the functions of keeping government conduct under constant surveillance and presents a clear-cut picture to the electorate of which party is responsible for everything that has been done. In an ideal situation, it also identifies an alternative government.

Party Discipline and the Caucus

The most significant aspect of the operation of the House of Commons is probably that everything is organized along party lines and that **party discipline** is so rigid. Almost all members belong to one party or another, and with rare exceptions, the MPs of each party vote together. Why is it that members of Parliament so consistently toe the party line?

The most obvious reason for party discipline, at least on the government side of the House, is the system of **responsible government**. It is commonly believed that if the cabinet is defeated on a major measure, it must resign or call an election; therefore, its backbenchers must always ensure that cabinet proposals are passed. Until such time as the principle of responsible government is interpreted more flexibly, government supporters will always be pressured to put party loyalty ahead of their own views or those of their constituents. That kind of reform could be accomplished by regarding a limited number of nonconfidence motions as really critical, and then allowing the cabinet to carry on in spite of the occasional defeat of a piece of legislation, a mode of operation that is more characteristic of Britain.

Several other reasons can also be cited to explain why MPs stick together with party colleagues in parliamentary votes. One is the tendency of people who belong to a political party to see things in a similar light—a natural cohesiveness common to most organized groups. Related to this cohesiveness is an equally natural deference to the leadership of the party and a desire to present an image of party unity to the public. In addition, MPs are encouraged to support the party line because of the prospects of promotion. Government backbenchers who are well behaved can become committee chairs, parliamentary secretaries, or cabinet ministers, while even opposition party members can be moved up to more important responsibilities, such as into their party's "shadow cabinet." Members also want to participate in the distribution of perks available in parliamentary life, especially opportunities to travel at public expense, which are generally in the control of the party whips. Another inducement is to receive full support of the party organization in the next election, including campaign funds and a visit by the party leader. Moreover, given the high turnover rate, many MPs depend on the government to provide them with employment if they suffer defeat. The ultimate sanctions for disloyal behaviour are expulsion from the party caucus and denial of the party label in the next election. For all these reasons, parties vote as blocs and a government with a majority of seats in the Commons feels confident that it can get parliamentary approval for almost anything it wants.

Jean Chrétien took a hard line on party discipline.
(CP Photo/Adrian Wyld)

In modern times, Jean Chrétien took a particularly hard line on party discipline. For example, despite concessions made to Liberal dissenters and other opponents of his government's gun control bill, three backbenchers voted against it due to pressure from their constituents. The PM quickly retaliated by removing them from their committee assignments. When veteran MP Warren Allmand voted against the 1995 budget because it dismantled historic Liberal social programs, the prime minister removed him from his committee chair position. Chrétien even threatened not to sign the nomination papers of Liberal candidates in the next election if they had voted against government measures. When John Nunziata did so, based on the claim that the government had violated its "Red Book" campaign promise to replace the GST, he was quickly booted out of the party. He ran successfully in 1997 as an independent candidate but was defeated in 2000.

As Chrétien moved closer to retirement, his power over the Liberal caucus declined. In an unprecedented and humiliating revolt in 2002, 55 Liberal backbenchers broke with the government to ensure the passage of an opposition motion to allow standing committees to elect their own chairs by secret ballot rather than have them imposed by the PMO. This was actually part of a package of proposals to reduce the "democratic deficit" in the operation of the House of Commons put forward by Chrétien's rival, Paul Martin. When Martin became prime minister in 2003, he introduced a new approach toward party discipline in Canada, which consisted of three alternatives for voting in the Commons. A three-line vote indicates that Liberal MPs must support the government; a two-line vote tells MPs how the government wants them to vote, but private members are allowed to dissent; and a one-line vote is a **free vote**, even for ministers. The assumption was that most bills would fall into the second category, with only votes of confidence and a limited number of matters of fundamental importance to the government being considered three-line votes.

Martin's reforms reflected increased pressure to allow greater opportunity for MPs to represent the interests of their constituencies rather than slavishly following the dictates of the party. Rare free votes have been held on such subjects as capital punishment and abortion, and few would argue against a little more autonomy and freedom for the individual MP. On the other hand, free-vote advocates and opponents of party discipline sometimes fail to appreciate the merits of an executive-centred system. Forcing MPs to toe the party line has allowed the executive to pursue a collectivist public interest beyond the narrow interests of constituencies, provinces, and other pressures, and it has permitted Canadian governments to be more activist and welfare-oriented than legislature-centred systems such as that of the United States.[5] Party discipline protects MPs individually and collectively from the blandishments and threats of single-interest pressure groups and lobbyists, and it promotes the accountability of the government party to the electorate. It also frees the prime minister from time-consuming negotiations with individual MPs. Given the Canadian tradition, it is unlikely that party discipline will ever be loosened excessively, despite Martin's initiatives.

To balance the public display of party discipline, MPs are allowed to speak their mind in the secrecy of the **party caucus**.[6] The caucus consists of all the elected members of each party (and such senators who choose to attend) who meet behind closed doors on Wednesday mornings. In a typical government caucus meeting of over 150 MPs, the opportunity to make an effective contribution is obviously limited. As in the case of cabinet secrecy, however, members occasionally "leak" caucus information for their own benefit. Provincial and regional caucus meetings of each party are held before the general caucus meeting, and caucus committees are often appointed. In the case of the government party, the prime minister and cabinet ministers attend such meetings, unlike in Britain.

Stages and Kinds of Legislation

The great bulk of legislation introduced takes the form of **public bills**. These are general legislative proposals, such as the Income Tax Act or the Employment Insurance Act, that affect all Canadians. Most public bills (and all **money bills**, that is, the bills involving the raising or spending of money) are sponsored by the government and introduced by a cabinet minister, thereby being titled **government bills**. As noted earlier, most of the weekly and yearly agenda is taken up with such government business.

However, a certain amount of time (now normally five hours per week) is set aside for members who are not in the cabinet to introduce legislation and motions of their own. Since these MPs (on whichever side of the House) are private members, their proposals are called **private members' bills**. These bills are still of a general nature, such as those attempting to restore capital punishment, but they almost never reach the statute books. That is because the government arranges to have them "talked out." It ensures that a backbencher is still talking when the time for consideration of the bill expires and they therefore do not come to a vote. Historically, the most that private members could hope for was that the cabinet might incorporate their ideas into a government bill. Since 1992, however, provision has been made for a more in-depth examination of a random sample of 30 private members' bills and motions per session. A House committee decides which ones are "votable," and up to 10 of these get expanded debate and can come to a vote. Then, if successful, they can continue in the regular legislative channels. Lynn McDonald's 1988 private member's bill on nonsmokers' rights was a rare example of one that made it to the statute books; others included the earlier bill to change the name of Trans-Canada Airlines to Air Canada, the bill that recognized the beaver as a symbol of Canadian sovereignty, and Svend Robinson's bill to classify anti-homosexual propaganda as a hate crime.[7]

Private bills, on the other hand, refer to a specific person or corporation. Certain divorces used to be effected by act of Parliament and took the form of private bills, although today this category consists mostly of bills incorporating companies or other organizations. Private bills now originate in the Senate and occupy very little of the Commons' time.

Turning to the stages of the legislative process, the first requirement is for three readings in each chamber. Most government bills originate in the Commons, although—with the exception of money bills—they may be first introduced in the Senate. First reading simply means that a bill has been introduced—it is tabled, printed, and made public—and may be briefly explained. Some days later, the bill comes up for second reading. This stage involves a debate on the principle of the bill and may last several days, or even weeks if it is controversial. A favourable vote at the end of the second-reading debate means that the bill has been approved in principle.

Even if the opposition has little chance of defeating a bill, it may hope that prolonged exposure of the flaws in the legislation will persuade the government to amend it. Failing that, public opinion can be aroused via media coverage so that the electorate will remember the debate when the next election occurs. Excessive opposition debate is called a **filibuster**, but government and opposition rarely agree on what is excessive. The counterpart of the filibuster is **closure**, a rule allowing a majority government to cut off debate. Although the closure rule has been used quite routinely in recent years, a more civilized procedure is for the government to negotiate with the opposition over the time to be allocated to debating various issues.

After second reading, a bill goes to committee, where it is examined in detail. In the small, informal confines of a Commons committee, the bill is scrutinized and voted on clause by clause, while ministers, public servants, interest groups, and other experts may be called upon for explanations or criticisms. After being approved, sometimes with amendments, the bill is reported back to the House in what is called the Report stage. This gives all members of the House, not just those on the committee, an opportunity to propose amendments. In recent years, the moving of hundreds of amendments at the Report stage of a bill (for example, by the Bloc Québécois in the case of the Clarity Act) has resulted in the creation of a new delaying tactic. Once a bill has been approved at the Report stage, it goes to third reading for a final, overall appraisal.

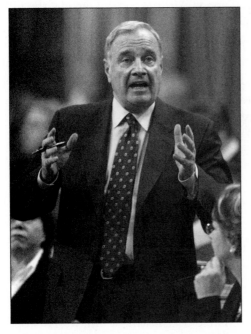

Prime Minister Paul Martin responds to questions regarding the sponsorship program during Question Period in the House of Commons in May 2004. (CP Photo/Jonathan Hayward)

As part of his package of Commons reforms, Paul Martin promised to send most two- and one-line vote bills to committee after first reading, rather than after they had been approved in principle. To allow the committee to debate the principle of the bill would allow more scope for both government backbenchers and opposition MPs to contribute to the shape of the legislation.

Assuming that the bill started in the Commons, it must then go through the same procedure in the Senate. In the rare case that the Senate amends a bill already approved by the Commons, the bill will have to go back to the lower house to see if it is acceptable in its amended form. Once a bill is passed in identical terms by both houses, it is given royal assent by the governor general or a Supreme Court judge acting as "deputy governor general." It then becomes a law or statute, although it may not be immediately proclaimed.

This may seem like an overly complicated process, but each stage has a distinctive purpose, and most bills must be debated for some time before the media and public begin to pay attention to them. Besides being necessary to engender eventual public knowledge of and consent to the law, reasonably lengthy consideration of the merits and faults of the bill serves to help the electorate gradually make up its mind about whether to re-elect the government that introduced such legislation or to opt for an opposition party that criticized it effectively.

Officers and Procedure of the Commons
The Speaker

The leading official of the House of Commons is the presiding officer, the **Speaker**, for whom deputy or acting speakers can substitute in the chair. The Speaker interprets and enforces the written rules of the Commons, called the **Standing Orders**,[8] plus unwritten traditions, practices, and conventions. The powers of the Speaker include recognizing which member can speak and ruling on whether motions are in order, whether debate is relevant, whether questions are urgent, and whether an unruly MP should be expelled. It is therefore important for the person selected to be competent and impartial. Unfortunately, Speakers used to be chosen by prime ministers from among their party's MPs and thus carried the suspicion of being biased in favour of the government. In seeking eventual reward beyond the Speakership, such as promotion to the cabinet, some also feared displeasing the prime minister. In 1986, a major change was adopted that allowed MPs to choose their own Speaker by secret ballot. Two years later, the Speaker was given new authority to "name" (i.e., suspend) a member for the rest of the day and for a period of five days for a second breach of the rules.

The Speaker can vote only in the case of a tie and cannot articulate the needs of his or her constituency or constituents in the Commons as such. In compensation for this silence, ministers and bureaucrats are especially sensitive to the concerns that the Speaker discusses with them outside the Chamber.

House Leaders, Party Whips, and Clerks

From within their ranks, each party selects a House leader and a party whip. The government **House leader** is a cabinet minister who manages the government's business in the Commons. This minister seeks to work out an agenda for House business with the opposition party House leaders, who function as procedural strategists for their parties and often speak for them if their leaders are absent. It is a credit to the House leaders that the Commons has functioned as well as it has, seeing that it has been occupied by four or five official parties since 1997.

Party whips are responsible for ensuring that their party's members are present for important votes and that they vote the right way.[9] Whips must therefore know the whereabouts of all their party's MPs at all times. Whips also distribute members' offices, assign members to parliamentary committees, and line up the order of party speakers in Question Period and debates. It is largely through the whips that party leaders impose discipline on their members. Members' opportunities to speak, to serve on the committee of their choice, and to travel as part of parliamentary delegations are largely influenced by their degree of party loyalty. In return, whips seek out backbench opinion on various matters and transmit it to the party leadership. Given the power of the party whips and House leaders to organize the business of the House, independent MPs and those belonging to parties with fewer than 12 members find little opportunity to participate.

The chief permanent official of the Commons is the Clerk of the House, a position analogous to a deputy minister in a government department. As chief procedural adviser to the Speaker and manager of the support staff attached to the Commons, the Clerk is also required to act in a totally nonpartisan manner. The Clerk is assisted at the table by the deputy clerk and several principal clerks. Figure 15.2 shows the layout of the Commons chamber.

Procedure in the Commons

Votes in the Commons are taken orally when the Speaker invites members to say "aye" or "nay." When either side wants a formal recorded vote, it requests a **division**. In this case, the division bells ring until the government and official opposition party whips agree that all their available members have arrived, at which time a standing, recorded vote is conducted. It used to be that if either whip refused to give the go-ahead, the bells could ring indefinitely, but after the two-week "bell-ringing incident" of 1982, a 30-minute limit was adopted in 1986. A new procedure in 1994 allowed for deferred divisions with all-party consent.

Figure 15.2 **The Layout of the House of Commons Chamber**

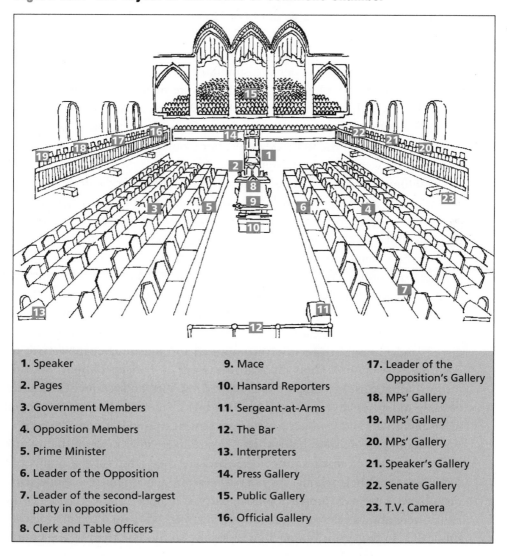

1. Speaker	**9.** Mace	**17.** Leader of the Opposition's Gallery
2. Pages	**10.** Hansard Reporters	
3. Government Members	**11.** Sergeant-at-Arms	**18.** MPs' Gallery
4. Opposition Members	**12.** The Bar	**19.** MPs' Gallery
5. Prime Minister	**13.** Interpreters	**20.** MPs' Gallery
6. Leader of the Opposition	**14.** Press Gallery	**21.** Speaker's Gallery
7. Leader of the second-largest party in opposition	**15.** Public Gallery	**22.** Senate Gallery
8. Clerk and Table Officers	**16.** Official Gallery	**23.** T.V. Camera

Source: Reproduced with permission of the Library of Parliament/Bibliothèque du Parlement.

The length of MPs' speeches has been severely curtailed over the past 20 years. The 1982 reforms generally shortened them from 40 minutes to 20, but this depends on who is speaking, in what debate, and at what stage of the debate. As a debate drags on, the maximum length is reduced to 10 minutes.

The Committee System

Much important legislative work of the House takes place outside the Commons chamber in a variety of committees. Committees allow a small number of people to develop expertise in a particular field and to examine proposals in depth; moreover, if several committees operate simultaneously, a greater volume of business can be accomplished. Committees allow private members to make constructive contributions to the governing of the country and to do so in a consensual rather than adversarial atmosphere. The Canadian Commons committee system did not function well during the first 100 years after Confederation, but repeated reforms since 1968 have made it more significant.

Standing committees are set up more or less permanently in most of the substantive areas of government policy, such as health and finance, largely paralleling government departments. They have two principal functions: to peruse the Estimates, that is, the government's spending proposals, and to examine legislation at the committee stage. The Estimates of the Department of Health, for example, are scrutinized by the Standing Committee on Health. In studying bills clause by clause after second reading, committees question ministers, public servants, pressure groups, and other expert witnesses. Standing committees are also authorized to investigate any aspect of the department with which they are associated, and Prime Minister Martin promised to increase their powers to review government appointments. Committees have a budget (which Martin also pledged to increase) to hire a clerk, supporting staff, and researchers and thus to develop independent expertise. The Standing Committee on Finance is perhaps most important, and it now engages in extensive pre-budget consultations.

Standing committees have varied in size over time, most of them currently being composed of about 12 members. Because they often have a number of different issues on their agenda, they may also set up subcommittees. Representation on all committees is proportional to party standings in the House. Although chairs were always elected by committee members, they used to be preselected by the PMO, so that most retained more loyalty to the PM than to the committee itself. As mentioned, in 2002, a procedural change allowed committees to elect their chairs by secret ballot, although in a majority situation they still come from the government side. The main exception to this is the **Public Accounts Committee**, which normally has a government majority but has been chaired by an official opposition MP since 1958. It has the important function of examining the report of the **Auditor General**, the official of Parliament who audits the government's accounts.

Special committees are set up temporarily for some specific, special purpose. They usually have an investigatory function—to examine an issue before the government has determined how to deal with it.

In addition to the standing and special committees of the House of Commons alone, the Commons and Senate sometimes work together in joint committees. Joint committees avoid duplication and give senators a chance to get involved at an earlier stage of the process than is usually the case. The most important joint standing committee is that on the Scrutiny of Regulations. It has the vital but unenviable responsibility of scrutinizing the mounds of regulations and other subordinate legislation issued by the executive branch each year, and it can recommend that offensive delegated legislation be rescinded.

Finally, there is the committee of the whole. This is simply the entire Commons membership sitting in the chamber as a committee. In such a case, the Speaker is replaced in the chair by the deputy speaker, and the rules are somewhat relaxed. This committee is used only to debate appropriation bills (once the Estimates have been approved) and certain noncontroversial bills, preference otherwise being given to smaller committees that can meet simultaneously in rooms outside the Commons chamber.

The transformation of the committee system in recent years has enhanced the position of backbench MPs in the legislative process. Committees that are small and stable in their membership become more expert in their field, and as their members develop greater collegiality, they can shed a good deal of their partisanship. After 1986, for example, many committees developed a consensus on the issues before them that cut across party lines, becoming newly independent sources of power in the legislative system. This led to the acceptance of an unprecedented number of amendments to government bills. After 1993, unfortunately, standing committees increased in size again, and it was more difficult to gain a consensus among four or five different parties. After 2004, especially in minority government situations, committees should be stronger than ever.

Members' Roles and Services

The roles that members of Parliament perform can be seen in two different lights. First, in terms of how they vote, MPs can be classified as trustees, constituency delegates, or party delegates. "Trustees" are MPs who feel obliged to vote according to their own conscience, their own understanding of the issue in question, or their own conception of the national interest. "Constituency delegates," on the other hand, are MPs who vote the way they think a majority of their constituents want them to. "Party delegates" are those who vote as directed by the party leader and party whip.

Backbenchers sometimes face the dilemma of opposing the party and risking discipline or opposing their constituents and risking electoral defeat. Historically, MPs have rarely deviated from the party line: if the party's position conflicted with either their own views or those of their constituents, MPs have almost always been obliged to put the party position first. As mentioned, however, Paul Martin promised to be more lenient in imposing party discipline in the future.

The other way to examine the roles of MPs is in terms of how they spend their time or determine their priorities. The first role in this respect is the "lawmaker"—devoting attention to the legislative process by introducing, amending, and debating legislation. MPs are supported in these tasks by the Research Branch of the Library of Parliament.[10] Since this role is almost irrelevant to their constituents, MPs are more likely to spend time promoting their constituency to bring it public favours in what could be called a "representational" role. These members lobby ministers and public servants for new public buildings, roads, wharves, and other job-creation facilities, so that they will have something "concrete" to show for themselves by the time of the next election. Finally, MPs function as "ombudsmen" or social workers for their individual constituents, intervening with ministers or public servants to hasten administrative decisions, correct bureaucratic errors, and repair governmental injustices. There will always be constituents with passport, immigration, employment insurance, pension, and many other kinds of problems. This "caseload" of MPs is now so heavy that they are provided with considerable administrative assistance in their Ottawa and constituency offices.

In 2001, MPs received a pay raise, which increased their salaries to $141 000 by 2004. On top of this basic income, a large number of MPs received additional payments for supplementary responsibilities. Combining these two payments, the leading figures in the House of Commons now receive the following:

- Prime minister: $282 000
- Speaker, cabinet ministers, and Leader of the Opposition: $208 000
- Leaders of other recognized parties: $189 000

In addition to their basic pay, MPs receive many benefits and services at public expense: They are provided with parliamentary and constituency offices, together with equipment and supplies; they have an annual staff allowance of approximately $225 000; and they have virtually unlimited telephone, mailing, and travel privileges. Recognized parties in the House—that is, groups of at least 12 members—receive substantial annual funding for research purposes, the loss of which was a major blow to the Conservatives and NDP between 1993 and 1997.

The MPs' pension plan has raised much controversy. Although the plan is contributory, many observers felt that it was too generous because it was indexed to the cost of living and because, regardless of age, members became eligible for the pension immediately upon leaving the Commons after at least six years of service. Moreover, those subsequently appointed to a government position continued to receive the pension on top of their new salary. In 1995, some of these provisions for newly elected MPs were removed: They would have to wait until age 55 to collect, they could not "double-dip," and those who thought the plan was too generous could opt out entirely. Few did!

What Do You Think?

How much should members of Parliament be paid? And how should the amount be determined? Should their pay be equivalent to that of truck drivers, professors, nurses, judges, or public servants?

The Government–Opposition Balance and Parliamentary Reform

An objective look at Parliament reveals a basic dilemma: The government wants legislation passed expeditiously, but the opposition must have the time to criticize government proposals in order to make the public aware of their defects, as well as to articulate constituency needs.

When the government has a majority of seats in the Commons, the cabinet operates as a virtual dictatorship until it has to face the electorate again some four or five years down the road. The opposition can do little more than criticize and delay government legislation, taking advantage of Question Period, media scrums, and the introduction of amendments. The imbalance of resources between government and opposition is dramatic, and the rules of the Commons are stacked in the government's favour. As the Auditor General reported in 2001, the government does not even provide Parliament with enough information to evaluate the results of public programs.

Many observers who deplore the arrogance of a **majority government** and regret that so much opposition talent and so many opposition ideas ordinarily go to waste prefer a **minority government**. In this situation—where the government is outnumbered by opposition members—it may have to negotiate with opposition parties to some extent, such as to amend government proposals, abandon them, or even accept opposition initiatives. Between 1867 and 2002, there were eight minority governments in Canada; few of these could have been called weak and indecisive. Many were more active and courageous than the majority governments that preceded or followed them. Some were exceptionally bold and decisive, especially the Pearson governments (which was responsible for the Canada Pension Plan, the flag, medicare, and cooperative federalism) and the Trudeau minority, the latter being particularly sensitive to opposition demands with respect to regulating election finance, screening foreign investment, and creating Petro-Canada. Although minority governments admittedly did not last as long as majority governments, not all of them ended in defeat; some ceased when the prime minister decided to call an election with the hope of obtaining a majority. After the 2004 election, Canada experienced its ninth minority government, under Paul Martin.

Because of the imbalance between government and opposition in a majority situation, and because the legislative role of ordinary MPs has been so ineffective, parliamentary reform is never far from the minds of political scientists and politicians alike. Reform proposals are designed to remedy excessive partisanship, cabinet domination, and private members' lack of influence. These proposals commonly take the form of reducing party discipline, allowing more free votes, and giving greater powers to committees, all at the core of Martin's initiatives.

The questions of operating in a minority government situation and reforming the House of Commons lead to a discussion of the principle of responsible government, which declares that the cabinet must have the confidence of the Commons or call an election or resign. But it is not always clear whether the cabinet is required to take such drastic action. In a majority situation, the problem is most unlikely to arise, but when the government is in a minority position, does it have to resign or call an election over any and every defeat? The Standing Orders are silent on this point, and any doubts about it were probably resolved by the 1968 incident in which the Pearson government was defeated on a piece of financial legislation. Pearson argued that the defeat was a fluke and that his government should be able to carry on. In that case, the matter was decided when the cabinet subsequently survived an explicit **nonconfidence motion**. Any other case of dispute about whether or not a government has been defeated should probably be settled in the same manner.[11] In Britain, a majority government carries on despite the occasional defeat of a piece of its legislation, as long as it retains the confidence of the House on its overall performance.

The Senate
Purposes and Powers

The ideal of democracy was still not enthusiastically accepted in the 1860s. The Fathers of Confederation thus felt it advisable to provide for an appointed body that would exercise "sober second thought" with respect to measures emanating from the popularly elected House of Commons. The Senate was therefore to be the equivalent of the British House of Lords, an older, conservative influence, with a minimum age of 30, appointment for life, and a relatively high property qualification.[12]

Additionally, the smaller provinces would agree to join Confederation and accept representation by population in the House of Commons only if they were overrepresented in the Senate. The Fathers settled on a chamber that would be based on equal regional representation. Such a system gave the Maritimes and Quebec (and later, the West) a limited amount of protection against the voting power held by Ontario in the House of Commons. It followed that senators were supposed to represent their regions and provinces within the national policy-making system.

A third function of the Senate, not explicitly provided for in 1867 but that can also be seen as part of the concept of sober second thought, is to improve legislation from a technical point of view. The Senate often acts as a routine revising chamber, picking up on flaws in legislation that have not been noticed during its passage through the busy Commons.

As far as powers were concerned, the Senate was given a veto over all legislation, a power not subsequently restricted as in the case of the British House of Lords. The only point of Senate inferiority to the Commons was that money bills had to be introduced in the lower chamber. Nevertheless, nothing in law prevented the Senate from delaying, amending, or vetoing any bills, whether or not they involved money.[13]

It was not until 1982 that the Senate's power was in any way reduced, and that had to do only with constitutional amendments, not ordinary legislation.

According to the Constitution Act, 1982, the Senate can delay a constitutional amendment for only 180 days. If the Senate has defeated the constitutional amendment or not approved it by then, it can be repassed by the Commons, and then it will bypass the Senate in the process of ratification.

Composition of the Senate

Ontario, Quebec, and the Maritimes originally received 24 senators each. When Prince Edward Island joined Confederation, it received 4 of the 24 Maritime senators, reducing Nova Scotia's and New Brunswick's share to 10 each. In a general reform in 1915, the West was designated as a senatorial region with 24 senators (6 per province), preserving the principle of equal regional representation. In 1949, Newfoundland was awarded 6 senators in addition to the 96 already allotted, so as to leave the Maritime contingent intact. Finally, in 1975, the Yukon and Northwest Territories were given 1 senator each, as was Nunavut in 1999, so that the total became 105.

Current Provincial and Territorial Representation in the Senate

Ontario	24	Saskatchewan	6
Quebec	24	Newfoundland and Labrador	6
Nova Scotia	10	Prince Edward Island	4
New Brunswick	10	Nunavut	1
Alberta	6	Northwest Territories	1
British Columbia	6	Yukon	1
Manitoba	6	**Total**	**105**

The 1867 Constitution Act gives the governor general the power to appoint senators, but by convention this is done on the advice of the prime minister. Prime ministers have almost always chosen partisan supporters, such as sitting MPs seeking a safer haven, defeated MPs or candidates, those who have served the party organization well, retired premiers or other provincial politicians, and federal cabinet ministers who have outlived their usefulness. Hence, almost all of those appointed could be called "party hacks." In addition to rewarding faithful service to the party in the past, many appointments were made on the assumption that the new senator would continue to promote the party in the future. Such senators carried on as party fundraisers, party presidents, organizers, election campaign strategists or managers, or in other partisan capacities. Besides the partisan basis of their appointment, many senators have been held in low esteem because of their absenteeism and their corporate connections; occasional convictions for abusing their powers have also occurred.

The Constitution Act, 1867, speaks of "qualified persons" being eligible for appointment to the Senate, language originally understood to include only men. In one of the most famous court cases in Canadian history, however, an enterprising group of women challenged this interpretation of "persons," and in 1929, the Judicial Committee of the Privy Council decided that "persons" did include women![14] Thus, in recent years, increased consideration has been given to the appointment of women, as well as representatives of various ethnic communities.

Senators originally served for life, and many lived to a ripe old age before they died. Lester Pearson had a constitutional amendment passed in 1965 to the effect that incumbent senators could stay until death (all of them gone by 1997) or retire at 75 with a pension; all subsequent appointees have had to retire at 75, but they do receive a pension at that point.

Operation of the Senate

If the original intentions of the Senate are archaic or have not been fulfilled, today's senators justify their existence on other grounds. First, they point to the routine revision of bills in which Senate engages, and some observers support the validity of their claim.[15] In addition to this function, the Senate sometimes undertakes protracted examination of complex legislation, such as the Bankruptcy Act or the Criminal Code. Similarly, bills are occasionally introduced simultaneously in both chambers, so that the Senate can engage in an unhurried "pre-study" of the bill rather than waiting until it has passed three readings in the Commons.

Senators also seek to emphasize other important aspects of their work, such as their consideration of private bills. These concern individuals, companies, churches, professional associations, and other institutions and are a nuisance to a busy House of Commons. Since 1934, almost all private bills have been introduced in the Senate, where the background work can be done so that the Commons can approve them routinely at a later date. This practice does help the Commons, but private bills are not numerous and do not absorb much of anyone's time.

Another kind of work not originally provided for is the study of various public problems by Senate committees in what Colin Campbell calls "social investigations."[16] Senators often have the expertise and certainly the time to conduct inquiries that relieve the pressure on the House of Commons and are cheaper than royal commissions. Among the issues investigated by the Senate over the years were poverty, aging, unemployment, the mass media, science policy, land use, national defence, fisheries, Canadian–American relations, the Canadian Security Intelligence Service, medical care, and the legalization of marijuana. Many of these committee reports have been very useful to government policymakers.

Graham Harrop/artizans.com

Finally, the Senate reviews regulations issued by various government departments. The Standing Joint Committee on the Scrutiny of Regulations has the responsibility of reviewing the great quantity of subordinate legislation issued every year.

Even with all these activities, the Senate timetable is very lax, and a small group of does most of its work. There is no doubt, however, that the institution performs more useful functions than in the past, and many of its members deserve their annual paycheque, which was $116 000 in 2004.

The Senate is often considered less partisan than the Commons; however, when it has exercised its veto power, it has been motivated by partisanship: a Liberal majority in the Senate has obstructed a Conservative majority in the Commons, or vice versa.[17] Brian Mulroney had considerable difficulty with the Senate between 1984 and 1991, when a Liberal majority in that chamber coincided with a Conservative majority in the Commons. The Senate's changes to the Meech Lake Accord, for example, had to be overridden by the Commons after the expiry of the 180-day limit on constitutional amendments. Then, in mid-1988, at John Turner's direction, the Liberal majority in the Senate held up the

Canada–U.S. Free Trade Agreement until the electorate had a chance to express its will on this important measure. After the 1988 election, the Senate bowed to the popular will and passed the Free Trade Agreement, but it later dug in its heels on other measures, especially the Goods and Services Tax (GST). At this point, Mulroney invoked an obscure clause in the 1867 Constitution Act that allowed him to appoint eight additional senators (two for each of the four senatorial regions) to tip the balance in favour of the Conservatives.[18] After the GST passed in an atmosphere of great bitterness, the Senate defeated the government's compromise abortion bill (on a tie vote). This became the first measure in 30 years that the Senate actually defeated, but some cabinet ministers were probably secretly relieved that the Senate had exercised its rare veto.

By the time the Liberals came to power in 1993, the Conservatives had established a clear majority in the Senate, so positions were reversed, and the Liberals began to pay for their earlier intransigence. The Conservative majority in the Senate was particularly incensed about the Liberal bill cancelling the privatization of Toronto's Pearson Airport, and the bill was defeated (on another tie vote). The PC-controlled Senate then stalled or amended several other Chrétien government bills. Shortly after the 1997 election, a Liberal majority in the chamber was restored, but by then senators of all political persuasions were inclined to play a more active role than previously. Between 2001 and 2004, the Senate amended 11 bills that the Commons accepted in amended form; the Senate backed down on one amended bill that the Commons would not accept; and the two chambers were stalemated on two bills when the 2004 election was called.

Senate Reform

Given the limited value of the Senate as it traditionally operated, its reform has always been on the political agenda. All sorts of reform proposals have been made, primarily with respect to how senators are chosen and what they should do. The former range from abolition, to election, to having provinces choose some or all of its members. There is an increasing consensus that senators should be elected, to legitimize the Senate's existence in a democratic age. With respect to its functions and powers, many reformers have advocated reactivating the Senate's role of representing regional and provincial interests at the federal level.

In the 1980s, Alberta began pushing its **Triple-E Senate** proposal: elected, effective, and equal.[19] The government of Alberta felt so strongly about an elected Senate that it held a "senatorial election" in 1989 when, in the spirit of the Meech Lake Accord, Brian Mulroney asked for a list of provincial nominees to fill a vacancy. The Reform Party candidate won the provincewide contest, and Premier Don Getty forwarded his name to the prime minister, who after some delay reluctantly complied. Alberta held a second senatorial election in 1998 and a third in 2004, but nobody outside that province paid much attention. Triple-E advocates also want each province rather than each region to have an equal number of senators and want to give the Senate powers to protect smaller, hinterland provinces.

If the Senate is unlikely to be reformed through formal, constitutional amendments, the best that can be hoped for is that it will engage in informal self-reform. To some extent, this has been evident in recent years.[20] Younger, often female senators from a wider diversity of backgrounds are usually prepared to put in more effort than their predecessors. Its more vigorous members want the Senate to become the "think tank of the Canadian government." Although the lack of democratic accountability will always cloud the Senate's work, its members' considerable accumulated political experience can be something of an asset.

SUMMARY

This chapter discussed the two institutions make up the legislative branch of government—the House of Commons and the Senate—with the former being far more important. The chapter emphasized that, to a large extent, the legislative branch merely ratifies decisions and bills proposed by the executive, although this is less the case in a minority than a majority situation. But even if the government has a majority in the House of Commons, the chamber's role in the policymaking process is significant in many ways, not the least of which is in helping to educate the public about what the government is doing and holding it somewhat accountable. Moreover, MPs have other important functions apart from policymaking, including representing their constituencies and taking care of their constituents. An examination of the background of MPs revealed that they are closely representative of the population in some respects (especially geography) and less so in others (notably gender and class). The chapter then outlined the weekly and yearly timetables of the Commons, emphasizing that most of its time is taken up in the debate of government bills. In discussing the pros and cons of party discipline, the chapter indicated that it is likely to be less rigid in the post-Chrétien era. The next sections dealt with the various stages that a bill goes through en route to enactment; the different kinds of bills involved; the key officials in the House, especially the Speaker, the House leaders, and the party whips; and the committee system, in which backbench MPs often play a more meaningful role than in the chamber itself. The section on the House of Commons concluded with a discussion of the roles MPs perform, the services available to them, and the relationship between the legislature and the executive in majority and minority situations. The shorter section on the Senate pointed out that the original intentions for the Senate have been replaced with others and that the institution has recently become a much more useful part of the parliamentary system.

DISCUSSION QUESTIONS

1. If Parliament does not play a significant part in the policymaking process, what are its basic functions?
2. What are the advantages and disadvantages of rigid party discipline in the Commons?
3. Have Paul Martin's reforms made any difference?
4. Does the Senate do enough to justify its existence? If not, how should it be reformed, or should it be abolished?

KEY TERMS

Auditor General The official of Parliament whose staff audit the expenditures of government departments and who reports on instances of funds being unlawfully or unwisely spent.

Backbencher A member of Parliament, whether on the government or opposition side, who sits on the back benches and does not have a cabinet post or equivalent position in other parties.

Budget The annual financial statement of the government issued by the minister of finance that introduces tax changes and gives an overview of government finances for the next fiscal year.

Closure A rule in the House of Commons in which a cabinet minister introduces a motion to cut off debate.

Dissolution of Parliament The ending of a Parliament, usually after four or more years, by calling an election, an act normally in the hands of the prime minister but one that formally requires the approval of the governor general.

Division A formal standing, roll-call vote in the House of Commons in which members' names are recorded in Hansard.

Estimates The annual spending plans of government departments and agencies.

Filibuster An organized attempt by the opposition in the House of Commons to prolong debate and delay adoption of government measures.

Free vote A rare vote in the House of Commons in which members are not required to abide by the party line.

Government The set of authorities, centred around a prime minister, cabinet, and party, that currently occupy the executive offices of the state and provide political leadership.

Government bill A bill introduced by a cabinet minister on behalf of the whole government.

House leader The person appointed by each party in the House of Commons to deal with counterparts in other parties with respect to scheduling Commons business.

Judicial review The power of the courts to overturn legislation or actions of the executive branch of government.

Leader of the Opposition The leader of the main opposition party in the House of Commons.

Legislature That branch of government whose function is to represent the people and make laws.

Majority government A situation in which the party in power has over 50 percent of the seats in the House of Commons.

Minority government A situation in which the government party has fewer than 50 percent of the seats in the House of Commons.

Money bill A bill to raise money for government purposes or to spend public funds.

Nonconfidence motion A motion in the House of Commons, moved by the opposition, inviting MPs to demonstrate a lack of confidence in the government, which, if successful, would require the cabinet's resignation or the calling of an election.

Opposition Those members of Parliament who do not support the government of the day.

Opposition days Twenty-one days per session of Parliament set aside for the opposition parties to determine the topic of debate.

Parliament Theoretically, the Queen, the House of Commons, and the Senate, functioning collectively, such as in the approval of legislation, but often used to refer to the Commons and Senate or Commons alone.

Parliamentary press gallery Those members of the media who are registered to sit in the press gallery in the House of Commons and who report on its proceedings or on government in general.

Parliamentary secretary A government MP who has been given addition responsibilities to assist a cabinet minister.

Party caucus The whole body of MPs of any party, together with such senators as choose to attend, who hold a regular weekly meeting to discuss parliamentary strategy and party policy.

Party discipline The convention that all MPs within any party vote together on every occasion, as predetermined by the leader or in the party caucus meeting and as enforced by the party whip.

Party whip An official of each party in the House of Commons whose function is to enforce party discipline and ensure that members are present for all votes.

Private bill A bill introduced in Parliament that affects only a specific individual, company, organization, or group.

Private member's bill A public bill introduced in Parliament by an MP who is not in the cabinet.

Public Accounts Committee The House of Commons committee that examines the Public Accounts and the Auditor General's reports and criticizes government officials for illegal or unwise expenditures.

Public bill A bill introduced in Parliament that affects society in general.

Question Period The daily 45-minute period in the House of Commons in which opposition members spar with the prime minister and cabinet ministers.

Responsible government A form of government in which the political executive must retain the confidence of the elected legislature and resign or call an election if and when it is defeated on a vote of nonconfidence.

Safe seat A constituency that a single party can be assured of winning, election after election.

Speaker The presiding officer of the House of Commons.

Speech from the Throne The document prepared by the prime minister and cabinet and read by the governor general at the opening of each session of Parliament that outlines the government's legislative proposals for the session.

Standing committees Those committees of the House of Commons that are set up semi-permanently and that parallel government departments.

Standing Orders The written rules of the House of Commons.

Supremacy of Parliament The principle that no other organ of government can overrule Parliament or its laws.

Triple-E Senate A proposal for Senate reform in which each province would have an equal number of senators who would be elected and who would be given effective powers.

Westminster model The model of government developed in Britain in which the political executive is given extensive power to provide effective leadership.

FURTHER READING

Bejermi, John. *Canadian Parliamentary Handbook*. Ottawa: Borealis Press, annual.

Campbell, Colin. *The Canadian Senate: A Lobby from Within*. Toronto: Macmillan, 1978.

Docherty, David C. *Legislatures*. Vancouver: UBC Press, 2004.

———. *Mr. Smith Goes to Ottawa: Life in the House of Commons*. Vancouver: UBC Press, 1997.

Franks, C.E.S. *The Parliament of Canada*. Toronto: University of Toronto Press, 1987.

Heard, Andrew. *Canadian Constitutional Conventions*. Toronto: Oxford University Press, 1991.

Joyal, Serge. *Protecting Democracy: The Senate You Never Knew*. Montreal: McGill-Queen's University Press, 2003.

Robertson, James R. *House of Commons Procedure: Its Reform*. Ottawa: Library of Parliament Current Issue Review 82-15E, 2002.

Chapter 16

The Courts and the Administration of Justice

The **judiciary** or the court system was traditionally of little interest to political science—usually only in terms of its interpretation of the federal–provincial division of powers. Now that the Charter of Rights and Freedoms has catapulted the courts into the midst of many heated political issues, however, political scientists are giving this fourth branch of government much more attention. This chapter examines the judiciary as an institution of government, discussing the function of adjudication, categories of laws, the structure of the courts, the operation of the Supreme Court of Canada, and the appointment, removal, and independence of judges. The chapter ends with a brief account of policing and the correctional system in Canada.

Chapter Objectives

After you have completed this chapter, you should be able to:

Discuss the role of adjudication as exercised by the courts

Distinguish between the powers of judicial discretion and judicial review

Assess the equality of access to the judicial system

Distinguish between various categories of laws

Outline the structure of the Canadian court system

Describe the jurisdiction of the Federal Court of Canada

Discuss the powers and operations of the Supreme Court of Canada

Discuss the appointment of judges in Canada

Understand the principle of judicial independence and how it relates to the removal of judges

Discuss the function of policing in Canada and the operation of the correctional system

Functions and Powers of the Courts

The judiciary has always been associated with the "adjudication" function in the political system. Adjudication can be defined as interpreting the law in case of dispute, settling disputes by applying the law to them, or making a judgment based on the law. Peter Russell defines the term as "providing authoritative settlements in disputes about the law."[1]

The function of the judiciary therefore is to render formal, impartial, authoritative judgments in the case of legal disputes between two parties that cannot be settled otherwise. The judicial process generally relies on the adversarial system, with lawyers representing each side. The judge, clothed with the authoritative powers of the state, acts as an independent referee and decides which of the disputants is legally right. As a result, the process usually culminates in the designation of a winner and a loser rather than in the achievement of some acceptable middle ground, which is more characteristic of political conflicts.

Apart from the civil law system in Quebec, the Canadian legal system operates in the tradition of the English **common law**. The basis of that system is the accumulation over the centuries of judicial precedents, both in England and more recently in Canada. Thus, in a typical court case, the two sides seek to find precedents—previous court decisions—favouring their respective points of view. The judge (and sometimes the jury) has to decide which precedents most closely resemble the case currently before the court. The principle that precedents are binding on successive decisions is called **stare decisis**.

If the law were always comprehensive and crystal clear, and if the situations to which it applied were always simple and straightforward, adjudication would be fairly routine, and the potential for **judicial discretion** would be limited. The real world is more complex, however, and the law is unlikely to be clear on all points or to provide for every conceivable situation. Russell refers to the "inescapable generality of the law" such that, while judges theoretically settle disputes according to pre-existing law, they actually shape and develop the law in the very process of settling disputes about it. Judges at least establish priorities among competing legal rules and principles, and in this process they "put flesh on the bare skeleton of the law and shape its substance."[2]

Thus, rather than taking place subsequent to policymaking, the judiciary and the function of judicial interpretation were included in the chart of the policy-making process in Figure 13.1 (page 313). Unlike Americans, Canadian observers have not previously given much recognition to the concept of judicial involvement in this process. Russell argues that this omission "wrongly assumes that all important public policies are expressed in statutes passed by legislatures ... and

Beverley McLachlin, the first female Chief Justice of Canada.
(CP Photo/Jonathan Hayward)

overlooks the extent to which [such] policies ... are shaped through the process of being applied in particular cases by judges and administrators."[3] In the course of adjudicating disputes, the courts are inherently involved in policymaking.

Rather than meaning merely the interpretation of laws with discretion, **judicial review** is the power of the courts to declare them invalid. The original Constitution Act, 1867, did not contain any such provision, although the courts soon appropriated this power in one respect. Chapter 12 of this book detailed the extent to which the courts invalidated federal and provincial legislation as violations of the division of powers. In rendering federal or provincial legislation void if either encroached on the jurisdiction of the other, the decisions of the courts had a significant effect on the shape of Canadian federalism. The courts' power of judicial review was greatly enhanced with the adoption of the **Charter of Rights and Freedoms** in 1982, and the effects of the first 23 years of that review were discussed in Chapter 11. Peter McCormick writes:

> We should recognize that judges have always had power, have always affected our society by the decisions they make ... The Charter has simply made a longstanding reality more immediately visible and directed us belatedly to an assessment of the implications of judicial power.[4]

Thus, especially since 1982, the courts are active players in the policymaking process. Whether judges leave a law intact or declare it unconstitutional, their interpretation of any law has a major bearing on its effect. Judicial review also entails overturning executive decisions that the courts find to violate the law or the Constitution.

Access to and Costs of Justice

Many people cannot afford to hire a lawyer to defend themselves in a criminal or civil case, yet the objective of the court system must be the search for truth and the obtaining of justice, goals that have traditionally rested on the adversarial system. To ensure that those without the financial resources have a fairer chance to achieve justice, legal aid programs financed jointly by the federal and provincial governments have been established. These go some way to meet the fairness objective, but they vary in detail from one province to another, do not cover every kind of legal work, and have been cut back by governments intent on balancing their budgets. Community legal clinics and publicly paid duty counsel serve a similar function.

Related means of reducing the costs of the administration of justice are the practices of plea bargaining and pretrial conferences. Plea bargaining involves discussions between defence and Crown attorneys with the aim of achieving agreement on charges to be pursued, typically by having the accused plead guilty to one charge when the Crown drops other charges. This practice is routine at the provincial court level and avoids a lengthy, costly trial. In the higher trial courts, it is increasingly common for the judge to hold a pretrial conference with the lawyers for each side. Such conferences can result in a negotiated settlement or at least a time-saving clarification of the issues involved. Pretrial conferences have also proven useful in family and small claims courts. Although plea bargaining and pretrial conferences must not be allowed to subvert justice (as many observers feel was the case with Karla Homolka), they are valuable devices that cut costs for everyone involved (including the public) and reduce the workload of the usually congested court system. Some provinces have tried to save money and remove the adversarial nature of small claims or other civil cases by instituting various mediation services, such as Alternative Dispute Resolution (ADR).

Categories of Laws

The law can be defined as "society's system of binding rules."[5] Laws are commonly divided into different categories, one distinction being between "civil" and "criminal." A **civil law** regulates relationships between two private parties such as individuals or corporations; if private agreement cannot be reached in the case of dispute, one party may take the other to court. Most aspects of civil law in Canada are within provincial jurisdiction, largely based on the provincial power over property and civil rights. Civil cases often involve disputes over commercial contracts or property, and such cases are normally resolved by the court's ordering one party to pay damages to the other. Civil cases are decided on the basis of the "balance of probabilities" of the merits of each side.

Criminal law, on the other hand, is primarily a federal responsibility; it is thus more or less uniform throughout the country and has been consolidated in the **Criminal Code**. In this case, the commission of a crime such as murder, sexual assault, or theft is considered to be a wrong against society as a whole, and the state takes the initiative to bring the suspect to justice by means of the police and Crown attorneys. In criminal cases, judges may impose fines or prison sentences if the accused is found guilty. Such guilt must be proven "beyond a reasonable doubt," which is a considerably higher standard than just a balance of probabilities.

One of the many peculiarities of Canadian federalism is that although criminal law is within federal jurisdiction, it is usually the provincial attorneys general and their agents, the Crown attorneys, who are responsible for initiating proceedings against the person who is charged. This situation has come about because the provinces have jurisdiction over the administration of justice. Sometimes a case contains both civil and criminal elements, such as when a drunken driver does damage to another person's car. The state pursues the violation of the Criminal Code, but the victim's insurance company would have to take the initiative to sue for property damage.

Instead of this basic division between civil and criminal law, a distinction is sometimes made between public and private law.[6] Private law is essentially the same as civil law described above, that is, law that primarily involves private interests. Beyond the contracts and property mentioned, private law includes torts, wills, company law, and family law. Public law, involving the public interest or the government, goes beyond criminal law to include constitutional, administrative, and taxation law. Constitutional law has traditionally involved questions about federal or provincial jurisdiction, and governments themselves have often been the parties to a constitutional case. With the adoption of the Charter of Rights and Freedoms, a whole new aspect of constitutional law in Canada has emerged. Administrative law concerns the operation of government departments, agencies, and tribunals, and as government activity expanded over the years, this branch of law has also increased in significance. (Note the later discussion of the Federal Court of Canada.)

By giving the provinces jurisdiction over property and civil rights, the Fathers of Confederation allowed the province of Quebec to retain its distinctive private or civil law system called the **Code Civil du Québec**. The private law system in the other provinces is based on the English common law tradition. The theoretical distinction between the two systems in terms of form is that while the common law consists of a hodgepodge of judicial precedents, the Code Civil is a single comprehensive document. As Gerald Gall puts it, "in a common law system, the courts extract existing principles of law from decisions of previous cases, while in the civil law system, the courts look to the civil code to determine a given principle and they then apply the facts of an instant case to that principle."[7]

Structure of the Courts

Because the provinces that formed Confederation in 1867 already possessed a court system, and because the Judicial Committee of the Privy Council continued to function as a court of appeal for the whole British Empire, it was not necessary to devote much attention to the judiciary in the Constitution Act, 1867. The provinces were given responsibility for the establishment of a provincial court system, and the federal government was allowed to establish a general court of appeal. McCormick describes the logic of the court structure as follows:

First	Identify the more routine cases and those that involve less serious possible outcomes and assign them to an accessible high-volume, low-delay court, preferably one that sits in many different centres (provincial courts).
Second	Assign the less routine and more serious cases to a lower-volume court that can devote more time and more focused attention to each individual case (superior trial courts).
Third	Establish a court of appeal to correct simple errors and to promote uniformity in the application of the law within each province (provincial courts of appeal).
Fourth	Establish a "general court of appeal" to promote uniformity in the application of the law within the country as a whole and to provide judicial leadership (Supreme Court of Canada).
Fifth	Create a system of federal courts for cases directly involving the federal government as a party or raising issues concerning the administrative law applied by federal departments (Federal Court of Canada).[8]

Source: Excerpt from Peter McCormick, *Canada's Courts*, 1994, 23. Used with permission of James Lorimer & Company Ltd., Publishers.

As shown in Figure 16.1, the court systems within each province developed into a reasonably uniform three-level hierarchy. At the top are two "superior"

Figure 16.1 **The Court Structure of Canada**

courts—the superior trial court and the court of appeal—although they go by different names from province to province. At the bottom are "inferior" or provincial courts.

Because of the assumption that provinces could not be trusted to make worthy appointments to the two levels of superior courts in the province, the Fathers of Confederation provided that the judges of these courts would be appointed by the governor general, conventionally meaning the federal cabinet or minister of justice. Such judges are also paid by the federal government. Thus, in another peculiarity of Canadian federalism, each province determines how many superior court judges it needs, but they are appointed and paid by Ottawa. Since these courts and their judges are provided for in section 96 of the 1867 document, they are often called section 96 courts and section 96 judges. Judges of the lower provincial courts, on the other hand, are appointed by the provincial cabinet.

Provincial Courts

Whatever their structure or name, provincial courts generally are responsible for:

• Summary offences (less serious crimes and provincial and municipal offences)
• Most aspects of indictable offences, some mandatory and others optional
• Preliminary hearings for most serious crimes
• Bail hearings

- Youth criminal offences
- Family law, except divorce and proceedings flowing from divorce
- Small civil cases

Provincial courts have a monopoly on summary offences except in provinces where this responsibility has been given to lower tribunals such as justices of the peace. Summary offences, as noted, include violations of municipal bylaws, provincial offences, and the least serious Criminal Code offences, such as common assault. More serious crimes, called indictable offences, can be subdivided into three categories. Some, such as murder, are reserved for superior courts in the provinces; others, such as theft, are assigned to provincial courts; and those in an intermediate category can be tried in either section 96 or provincial courts. The federal Youth Criminal Justice Act covers offences committed by those aged 12 to 18, and in some provinces these offences are tried in special youth courts.

Family law is another area of great federal–provincial complexity. Since divorce is a federal responsibility, divorces are dealt with in section 96 courts, and any proceedings flowing from the divorce must also be dealt with there. On the other hand, if divorce is not involved, such matters as custody, access, maintenance, alimony, adoption, guardianship, and protection of children are handled in provincial courts, sometimes called family courts. Several provinces have tried to overcome the problem of the fragmentation of family law with a "unified family court" presided over by a section 96 judge.

Provincial courts, sometimes in a civil division and sometimes called small claims courts, also have jurisdiction over disputes involving small amounts of money. Each province determines the monetary limit for cases that can be considered at that level, with disputes involving larger sums being initiated at the section 96 court level.

Superior Trial Courts

The superior trial court in the province, whatever its name, is responsible for:

- Some mandatory and other elective indictable offences
- Civil matters over a given monetary amount
- Divorces and proceedings flowing therefrom
- Appeals from lower courts regarding summary convictions, juvenile cases, and family cases
- Administrative law cases

Provincial Courts of Appeal

Provincial courts of appeal hear criminal, civil, and other appeals. Although some of these courts' judgments can be appealed to the Supreme Court of Canada, decisions of the provincial courts of appeal are usually final, adding to the significance of this level of court.[9] The basic function of an appeal court is to correct errors or injustices that were made in a lower court, so that an appeal court is primarily interested in legal rather than factual issues.

The second function of the appeal court is to render an opinion in a **reference case**, that is, on a constitutional issue referred to it by the provincial cabinet. Russell thus speaks of the "lawmaking" role of appeal courts because their legal interpretations have a "creative legislative dimension."[10] Decisions of the court of appeal are binding on all courts below it in the same province and are "strongly persuasive" for trial courts in other provinces. Courts of appeal normally sit in banks of three judges, but these panels can be increased to five for very important cases. Each side of a case submits a brief or "factum" in advance that summarizes its arguments, and lawyers then engage in oral argument.

The Federal Court of Canada

The **Federal Court of Canada** was established in 1971, with trial and appeal divisions. It was intended to relieve the Supreme Court of Canada of routine appeals from certain federal administrative tribunals and to strengthen judicial review of federal administration by developing a more unified and cohesive body of federal administrative law.[11] The main areas of responsibility of the Federal Court are as follows:

- Citizenship, immigration, and refugee appeals
- Intellectual property cases, including copyright, trademark, and patent disputes
- Appeals from other federal administrative tribunals
- Civil cases involving the federal government
- Cases involving bills of exchange, promissory notes, admiralty law, aeronautics, and interprovincial works and undertakings
- Prerogative writs (e.g., injunctions) applying to agencies of the federal government
- Appeals relating to the Access to Information and Privacy Acts
- Issuance of Canadian Security Intelligence Service warrants
- Aboriginal law

Although the Federal Court deals with cases in all the above categories every year, it is dominated by those involving the Immigration and Refugee Protection Act and the Immigration and Refugee Board. It has recently seen a growth in Aboriginal cases dealing with monetary and constitutional issues, land entitlements, and natural resources. The Federal Court also hears appeals regarding the Access to Information Act and the Privacy Act and decides on requests for warrants from the Canadian Security Intelligence Service in order to plant bugs, open mail, and engage in other surreptitious activities.

The Federal Court consists of a chief justice and 12 other judges on its appeal division and the associate chief justice and 32 other full-time and assorted part-time judges on its trial division. The appeal division judges sit in panels of at least three members, and the individual judges of the trial division sit in cases all across the country.

The Supreme Court of Canada

The **Supreme Court of Canada** sits at the apex of the Canadian court system. The Supreme Court hears appeals from the provincial courts of appeal in civil and criminal cases and from the appeals division of the Federal Court of Canada in administrative law matters. The part of its work of most interest to political science involves constitutional law, whether in terms of the division of powers or the Charter of Rights and Freedoms. Besides hearing appeal cases from lower courts, the Supreme Court can be asked by the federal cabinet to give opinions, usually on constitutional matters, in reference cases. A recent example was the case regarding Quebec's right to make a unilateral declaration of independence. Although the Supreme Court hears fewer cases per year than any lower court, it is interested almost exclusively in questions of law. Thus, of all courts, it is the most heavily engaged in a "lawmaking" role, and its decisions are binding on all lower courts.

Until 1949, the Supreme Court was a seriously deficient institution. First, its decisions could be appealed to Canada's pre-1949 final court of appeal, the **Judicial Committee of the Privy Council** (JCPC) located in London, and it was bound by JCPC precedents. But even more humiliating, appeals could go directly to that Empire court from provincial appeal courts, completely bypassing the Supreme Court of Canada. This weakness in authority was exacerbated by the generally poor quality of judges appointed to it in that earlier period, with some notable exceptions.[12]

The Supreme Court of Canada. (CP Photo)

Canada could have cut off appeals to the Judicial Committee after obtaining complete independence in 1931, but it was unclear whether the provinces would have to agree to this measure, since their appeals could already go directly to the JCPC. By the late 1940s, it was determined that Ottawa could unilaterally curtail all such appeals, and it promptly did so. The Supreme Court of Canada has not been formally bound by Judicial Committee decisions since 1949 and has explicitly overruled them on occasion.

The Supreme Court used to have little discretion in deciding which cases it heard, but since 1974 it has basically controlled its own agenda. Such discretion considerably enhances the stature of the institution. Today, only two categories of cases have an automatic right of appeal to the Supreme Court: provincial reference cases and murder cases in which the provincial court of appeal was split on a question of law. Applications for leave to appeal discretionary cases are normally handled in writing by a panel of three judges, but sometimes the panel hears them live. Public law cases, especially criminal and constitutional, now clearly predominate over private law disputes on the Supreme Court docket.

Although an increasingly important institution of government, the Supreme Court rests primarily on the Supreme Court Act rather than being embedded in any constitutional document as such. That act provides for a nine-member court, three of whom must come from Quebec with its distinctive civil law system. Convention dictates that of the other six, three normally come from Ontario, two from the West, and one from Atlantic Canada. The act requires that at least five judges constitute a quorum, with the result that civil law cases from Quebec can be heard by a five-member panel including a majority from the civil law system. The position of Chief Justice normally alternates between francophone and anglophone members, simultaneous interpretation is available, and Supreme Court judges are now expected to be at least functionally bilingual. The judges hold office during good behaviour until the age of 75.

The Court holds three sessions of about two months' duration each per year, and then adjourns to write up its decisions.[13] As much as possible, the Court tries to hear cases with a full complement of nine. Judges study the lower court proceedings and judgments in advance, along with the written arguments of the lawyers for each side. Oral arguments normally last only two hours, during which time the judges often ask trenchant questions. In some instances, the Court also grants "intervenor status" to provincial governments and interest groups that are concerned about a case but not directly party to it. Once the arguments are completed, the judges usually "reserve judgment" and meet in private conference to discuss the case. Each gives his or her tentative conclusion, and one or more draft opinions are prepared. These are later circulated and evoke comments before being revised. Each Supreme Court judge is assisted by a number of outstanding new law school graduates called law clerks. They help the busy judges search for and sift through precedents and other relevant material on the issues involved. So much effort is put into the process of preparing their opinions that a decision is typically not issued until about six months after the Court hears the case, and it has occasionally taken over a year for all members of the Court to make up their mind. The Court tries to come to a unanimous decision, but if this is not possible, majority and minority opinions are issued. Members of the Supreme Court of Canada as of 2005 are listed in Table 16.1.

The Appointment of Judges

As has already been established, judges of the Supreme and Federal Courts of Canada as well as judges of the provincial superior trial courts and courts of appeal are appointed by the federal cabinet, and provincial court judges are appointed by

TABLE 16.1 MEMBERSHIP IN THE SUPREME COURT OF CANADA, 2005

Year of Appointment	Name
1989	Beverley McLachlin (Chief Justice)
1992	John C. Major
1997	Michel Bastarache
1998	Ian Binnie
2000	Louis LeBel
2002	Marie Deschamps
2003	Morris Fish
2004	Rosalie Abella
2004	Louise Charron

provincial cabinets. There are approximately 1000 judges in each category. All of the first group must be qualified lawyers of at least 10 years' standing, as must provincial court judges in Ontario and Quebec. Elsewhere, provincial court judges have to be members of the bar for a minimum of five years.

In a high proportion of cases over the years, Canadian cabinets at both federal and provincial levels have used judicial appointments to reward faithful party supporters, often defeated candidates.[14] Such **political patronage** raises three main problems: Unsuitable individuals are appointed because of their partisan connections; well-qualified candidates are overlooked because of their lack of service to the party in power; and partisan judges may favour their former political colleagues.[15] This patronage system of appointing judges is still alive, although it is not as blatant as it once was.

At the federal level, Pierre Trudeau as minister of justice instituted an informal practice of submitting names of potential judicial appointments to the National Committee on the Judiciary of the Canadian Bar Association (CBA). Trudeau sullied his own government's record in this field in 1984, however, with the appointment of six high-profile Liberal partisans, several to the Federal Court of Canada. After an even more partisan record of judicial appointments during its first term,[16] the Mulroney government established a somewhat more satisfactory appointment system in 1988 for all "federal" judges except those on the Supreme Court of Canada and then modified it slightly in 1991. An independent Commissioner for Federal Judicial Affairs now maintains a record of those interested in federal judicial appointments—to the Federal Court of Canada, the Tax

Court of Canada, and provincial and territorial superior courts. This official then submits such names to one of 16 seven-member advisory committees, each including a section 96 judge; one nominee of each of the provincial law society, the provincial branch of the CBA, and the provincial attorney general; and three nominees of the federal minister of justice. This committee ranks each candidate as "highly recommended," "recommended," or "not able to recommend," and the minister makes the final decision, even being entitled to choose from those not recommended.[17] While it is regrettable that partisanship still plays a role in this process, party service or legislative experience should not automatically disqualify a worthy candidate from a judicial appointment.[18]

The prime minister chooses the chief justice in each province, almost always from the existing bench, as well as new members of the Supreme Court of Canada. Prime ministers consult widely before making such appointments and have managed to overcome their penchant for partisanship in this one area. Patronage has therefore not been much of a problem on the Supreme Court for nearly 50 years.

Given the significant lawmaking potential of Supreme Court judges, many observers have proposed that nominees be subject to public hearings, such as appearing before a parliamentary committee, before being appointed. In this forum, they could be grilled about their views on a wide variety of issues. This is despite the fact that, without a formal consultation process, Supreme Court appointments have rarely generated much controversy. Jacob Ziegel has proposed an alternative to public confirmation hearings: a Supreme Court nominating commission. It would consist of nine people representing a variety of constituencies who would, after interviewing or studying the record of prospective candidates, present the prime minister with a shortlist from which one would be chosen. The Standing Committee of the House of Commons on Justice made a somewhat similar proposal in May 2004.[19] Both proposals rejected public hearings.

What Do You Think?

Historically, new appointees to the Supreme Court of Canada have been the product of extensive behind-the-scenes consultation by the prime minister, but Paul Martin himself proposed that Parliament have some say in the appointment of Supreme Court judges. How much public and/or parliamentary input should be added to the process? Should prospective judges be grilled in public before being appointed so that the public knows their views on controversial issues?

At the provincial court level, the attorney general now usually consults with the provincial judicial council or equivalent in making such appointments. A central nonpartisan nominating commission consisting largely of nonlawyers was established in Ontario in 1988, originally headed by political scientist Peter Russell. It screens judicial applicants on their merits and ranks the candidates from which the attorney general chooses. Few Canadians support the concept of elected judges.

Another controversial aspect of judicial appointments concerns the Supreme Court of Canada alone. Because this court must adjudicate federal–provincial disputes, concern has been expressed that all of its members are federally appointed. In theory, once chosen, judges act with total impartiality and their independence is protected in various ways. Nevertheless, it may not appear as if justice has been done in such a situation. The ill-fated Meech Lake and Charlottetown Accords provided for Ottawa to make Supreme Court of Canada appointments from lists provided by the provinces. The latter accord also proposed federal and provincial consultation with Aboriginal peoples in the appointment process.

Even though judges are expected to perform their duties in an unbiased manner, they naturally bring their personal predilections and prejudices to the post. This realization leads us to investigate whether they are representative of Canadian society. Partly as a consequence of equitable geographic representation, judicial appointments have balanced francophone and anglophone origins at both federal and provincial court levels, especially in recent years as provinces have made more French-language court services available. Those of other origins used to be excluded, but judges such as Laskin (Jewish), Sopinka (Ukrainian), and Iacobucci (Italian) have been appointed to the Supreme Court of Canada—and increasingly to lower courts as well. Thus, the most serious aspects of judicial underrepresentation relate to women and the working class.[20]

Just as in the case of different ethnic groups, however, more female and working-class law school graduates are becoming available for judicial appointments, and governments have at least begun to recognize the necessity of appointing greater numbers of female judges. The Supreme Court finally saw its first female member in 1982, and it now has a total of four women out of nine, including Beverley McLachlin, the first female Chief Justice. Such female judges have sometimes used their position to point out the male bias in legislatures, judiciaries, and laws.

As noted in Chapter 4, Aboriginal peoples have even more serious reservations about the Canadian judicial system, feeling that it discriminates against them at every turn. Many argue that an increase in the number of Aboriginal judges would not substantially improve this situation and therefore advocate the establishment of a parallel justice system to deal with Aboriginal defendants (at least where they did no harm to non-Aboriginals), reflecting their own distinctive concepts of guilt and of healing and rehabilitation rather than punishment. While it seems unlikely that a separate system will be created in the near future, the regular courts are increasingly recognizing traditional Aboriginal concepts in cases involving Aboriginal people. These include sentencing circles (involving a judge, police, elders, peers, family, and victims), elder sentencing panels, and community mediation processes.

Retirement, Removal, and the Independence of Judges

Whatever the process involved in making judicial appointments, judges are expected to abide by the principle of **judicial independence** or impartiality once they are on the bench. They are supposed to adjudicate without fear or favour with respect to private or political interests and without any incentive to give preference to the government side where it is involved.

The independence of judges is based primarily on security of tenure, and it is difficult for the government to remove judges before their scheduled date of retirement. Judges on the Supreme and Federal Courts of Canada and provincial superior courts have a mandatory retirement age of 75 years, and provincial court judges must retire at 65 or 70. The general rule is that they serve on "good behaviour"— that is, they cannot be removed unless they have been guilty of misbehaviour. Although the meaning of these terms has never been definitively established, judges are certainly removable for serious criminal acts and possibly for reasons of infirmity or incapacity, failure to execute their duties, or bringing the judicial system into disrepute.[21] On the other hand, they cannot be removed merely because the government regards a decision as erroneous or contrary to government policy, nor because they ruled against the Crown.

The process of removing a judge varies with the level of the position, the degree of difficulty increasing with the court's ranking in the hierarchy. Except in Ontario, where legislation is required, provincial court judges can be removed by an order-in-council of the provincial cabinet, but only after an inquiry has been conducted by one of the judge's peers or by the provincial judicial council. It is even more difficult to remove judges of the provincial superior courts and the federal courts. In that situation, the Canadian Judicial Council conducts an inquiry and reports to the minister of justice, after which the passage of a joint address of both houses of Parliament is required.

The **Canadian Judicial Council** was created in 1971 and consists of all the chief justices and associate chief justices of courts staffed by federally appointed judges. It is chaired by the Chief Justice of the Supreme Court of Canada. Like the provincial judicial councils, its primary purpose is to deal with complaints raised against individual judges, but it also has a role in the continuing education of judges, provides a forum for developing consensus among its members, and makes representations to government with respect to judicial salaries and benefits.

While a number of judges have been reprimanded by judicial councils, the issue of judicial removal has rarely arisen at the federal level. Several provincial court judges have been removed over the years, a practice that is increasingly common as the public becomes less tolerant of their faults. But only four judges of the old county and district courts met this fate, and not a single superior court judge has been removed from office. Such proceedings were initiated in five cases, but the judges either died or resigned during the removal process.

Besides security of tenure, judicial independence involves financial, administrative, and political independence.[22] Salaries and pensions are fixed in such a way that neither individually nor collectively can judges be intimidated by government threats to reduce them. Some judges did go to court, however, to challenge freezes or reductions in their salaries as part of provincial government restraint programs in the 1990s and again in Ontario in 2004. Superior court judges have seen their salaries increased substantially in recent years yet still asked for a 17 percent raise in 2004. In addition, judges are increasingly in control of the administration of the court system. Judges must also be able to function without political pressure—from cabinet ministers, legislators, bureaucrats, or other judges—whether in public or in private. At both federal and provincial levels, many cases have occurred of cabinet ministers contacting judges, but however innocent their questions might seem, this must not be done.

It is sometimes thought that the prospect of promotion from one court to another might bias a judge's decisions, but no evidence has been found to justify this fear. On the other hand, judges are not supposed to make public speeches that could compromise their impartiality. For example, when Tom Berger of the B.C. Supreme Court publicly criticized the 1982 Constitution Act for its omission of Quebec and virtual neglect of Aboriginal peoples, certain highly placed opponents of his views brought him before the Canadian Judicial Council. Although its recommendation was not to dismiss him, he resigned to protest the process employed.[23]

Policing and the Correctional System in Canada

Policing in Canada

In Chapter 14, police officers were categorized as a special kind of public servant. Police can be employed by the federal, provincial, or municipal governments. The Royal Canadian Mounted Police (RCMP) is the national police force with many appropriate central functions, such as operating a criminal information system and a forensic laboratory and maintaining international policing linkages. Ontario and Quebec possess their own provincial police forces, Newfoundland and Labrador retains the Royal Newfoundland Constabulary for certain purposes,

Graham Harrop/artizans.com

and larger municipal governments have local police services. Eight provinces, three territories, about 200 municipalities, and nearly 200 First Nations communities—all jurisdictions without their own police forces—have signed contracts with the RCMP to provide policing functions. But even where separate provincial and municipal police forces exist, and where they enforce the Criminal Code, the RCMP enforces federal non–Criminal Code statutes such as the Narcotics Control Act.

The basic functions of police officers of any kind are to prevent crime, to maintain order in the community, and to detect and apprehend offenders. In order to perform these important functions, police officers are given special powers, such as to question suspects, conduct searches, make arrests, and carry guns. On the highways alone, where the bulk of Canadians are most tempted to break the law, police officers can use concealed or unmarked patrol cars, photo radar or radar traps, and spot checks and Breathalyzer tests for impaired driving. As mentioned in Chapter 11, however, judicial interpretation of the Charter of Rights and Freedoms has served to restrict such police powers in many circumstances and to augment the rights of a person suspected of or charged with committing a crime.

Besides being subject to Charter restrictions, police forces must obey civilian authorities. While police forces are deliberately designed to operate at arm's length from politicians, police officers are subject to the general supervision of provincial or municipal civilian police commissions or, in the case of the RCMP, the minister of Public Safety and Emergency Preparedness.

The Canadian Correctional System

Since it is judges and the courts that put people into correctional institutions, it is appropriate to add a final word about the Canadian correctional system. As in many other aspects of the judicial system in Canada, there is an important federal–provincial dimension to this subject. Those adult offenders sentenced to two years or more are sent to federal penitentiaries, while those serving less than two years find themselves in provincial prisons or reformatories. In other words, both levels of government maintain correctional institutions, and the distinction between the two is based on the length of the sentence, not on whether the offender broke a federal or provincial law.

Federal legislation also requires the provinces to establish facilities such that young offenders are kept separate and apart from adult offenders. Youth crime is yet another complicated issue of federal–provincial relations, leading the provinces to make frequent criticisms of federal policy.

The Corrections and Conditional Release Act provides that an individual who has served a portion of his or her sentence may be released early (and conditionally) on parole. Three provinces have set up parole boards to review inmates of their own prisons or reformatories for this purpose, while the National Parole Board performs this function for federal institutions as well as for the other provinces.

SUMMARY

This chapter dealt with the judicial branch of government. It began by discussing its function of adjudication—providing authoritative settlements in disputes about the law. It then distinguished between judicial discretion (interpreting laws) and judicial review (overturning them). It noted the problem of access to the courts and outlined less than satisfactory ways of reducing that difficulty. The chapter went on to distinguish between civil and criminal law, as well as private and public law, and then addressed the structure of the court system in Canada. It discussed, in turn, lower provincial courts, superior trial courts in the provinces, provincial courts of appeal, the Federal Court of Canada, and the Supreme Court of Canada. After outlining the jurisdiction and operation of the two national courts, the chapter focused on the appointment of judges to different levels of courts and on the debate about whether the appointment process for the Supreme Court of Canada should be reformed. The chapter then turned to the principle of judicial independence and the deliberate intention to make it difficult to remove judges. The chapter ended with a note on the function of policing and corrections.

DISCUSSION QUESTIONS

1. Is judicial discretion in the interpretation of laws just as important as the power of judicial review?
2. How can fairness in the judicial system be guaranteed for Aboriginal peoples, the poor, women, and minorities?
3. If the current procedure for appointing judges is less than ideal, how should we reform it?
4. How would you improve the operation of police forces and the correctional system?

KEY TERMS

Canadian Judicial Council An agency composed of the federal and provincial chief justices that disciplines federally appointed judges and provides leadership and coordination among federal and provincial judicial systems.

Charter of Rights and Freedoms Part of the Constitution Act, 1982, that guaranteed fundamental freedoms and legal, democratic, linguistic, mobility, and equality rights.

Civil law A branch of law dealing with relations between private parties, such as individuals and corporations, that do not involve government.

Code Civil du Québec The unique system of civil law used in Quebec that is based on the Napoleonic Code.

Common law The basis of the British and Canadian legal systems that consists of the accumulation of judicial precedents, which guide judges in the absence of a legislature-made law.

Criminal Code A federal document that codifies most of the criminal law in the country.

Criminal law That branch of law dealing with wrongs committed against others that are considered to be offensive to society as a whole, for which the state takes the initiative to investigate, and for which perpetrators can be fined or jailed.

Federal Court of Canada A court established by the federal government dealing with cases involving that government and other specialized subjects within its jurisdiction.

Judicial Committee of the Privy Council A committee of the British Parliament that functioned as Canada's final court of appeal until 1949.

Judicial discretion The leeway inevitably bestowed on the courts when they interpret laws, even when they do not, or have no power to, overturn them.

Judicial independence The constitutional principle that the courts should function independently of the rest of the government apparatus, especially the politicians, with implications for security of tenure and remuneration of judges.

Judicial review The power of the courts to overturn legislation or actions of the executive branch of government.

Judiciary The court system.

Political patronage Making appointments to public offices or awarding government contracts on a partisan basis.

Reference case A case referred to the courts by a provincial or federal cabinet usually to obtain a ruling on the constitutionality of a law.

Stare decisis The legal principle that precedents are binding on similar subsequent cases, which forms the basis of the common law system.

Supreme Court of Canada The highest court in Canada and the final court of appeal since 1949.

FURTHER READING

Anderson, Ellen. *Judging Bertha Wilson: Law as Large as Life*. Toronto: University of Toronto Press, 2002.

Gall, Gerald. *The Canadian Legal System*. 4th ed. Toronto: Carswell, 1995.

Green, Ian, et al. *Final Appeal: Decision-Making in Canadian Courts of Appeal*. Toronto: Lorimer, 1998.

McCormick, Peter. *Canada's Courts*. Toronto: Lorimer, 1994.

———. *Supreme at Last: The Evolution of the Supreme Court of Canada, 1949–1999*. Toronto: Lorimer, 2000.

———, and Ian Greene. *Judges and Judging: Inside the Canadian Judicial System*. Toronto: Lorimer, 1990.

Russell, Peter. *The Judiciary in Canada: The Third Branch of Government*. Toronto: McGraw-Hill Ryerson, 1987.

Sharpe, Robert J., and Kent Roach. *Brian Dickson: A Judge's Journey*. Toronto: University of Toronto Press, 2003.

Ziegel, Jacob S. *Merit Selection and Democratization of Appointments to the Supreme Court of Canada*. Montreal: Institute for Research on Public Policy, 1999.

Glossary[1]

Numbers in parentheses refer to the chapter(s) containing the main discussion of the term.

Aboriginal self-government. A demand made by Aboriginal groups that they be able to govern themselves. (4)

Aboriginal title. The Aboriginal claim to land based on traditional occupancy and use rather than treaty. (4)

Access to Information Act. The 1983 act that gave citizens, journalists, and others the right to gain access to government documents, with certain exceptions, and established the office of Information Commissioner. (14)

Act of Union. The 1840 act that united the colonies of Upper and Lower Canada into the colony of Canada and that was partly designed to assimilate the French. (3, 11)

Advocacy advertising. Advertising that advocates a political point of view rather than trying to sell a good or service. (6, 10)

Advocacy group/interest group/pressure group. Any group seeking to influence government policy without contesting elections; an organization whose members promote their common interest by acting together to influence public policy. (1, 10)

Affirmative action. A law or program that provides preference in the hiring or promotion process to individuals with certain characteristics. (4, 11)

Assembly of First Nations. The largest interest group representing status and non-status Indians (who now prefer to be called First Nations peoples). (4, 10)

Auditor General. The official of Parliament whose staff audit the expenditures of government departments and who reports on instances of funds being unlawfully or unwisely spent. (14, 15)

Backbencher. A member of Parliament, whether on the government or opposition side, who sits on the back benches and does not have a cabinet post or equivalent position in other parties. (15)

Bandwagon effect. The notion that if and when they know which party or candidate is going to win the election, voters will move en masse in that direction. (7)

Bill 101. The 1977 Quebec language law that made French the official language of Quebec and put restrictions on the use of English in the public and private sectors, including French-only signs. (3)

Block grant. A federal grant to the provinces that is given for a specific purpose, such as postsecondary education, but does not contain rigid conditions or standards. (12)

British North America Act (BNA Act). The 1867 act of the British Parliament that created Canada by uniting the four original provinces, that provided some of the essential elements of the new country's Constitution, and that in 1982 was renamed the Constitution Act, 1867. (5, 11)

Broker party. A kind of political party that tries to appeal to many different interests and to "broker" compromises among them, rather than having any distinct ideology. (9)

Budget. The annual financial statement of the government issued by the minister of finance that introduces tax changes and gives an overview of government finances for the next fiscal year. (15)

Bureaucracy. The permanent officials employed by the government, also known as the public service. (1, 14)

By-election. An election held between general elections in a specific electoral district due to the death or resignation of the MP or a tie on election night. (8)

Cabinet government. A system of government in which the major political decisions are made by the cabinet as a whole, as opposed to one in which the prime minister acts with considerable autonomy or dominance. (13)

Cabinet solidarity. A convention that all cabinet ministers publicly support whatever decisions the cabinet has taken, regardless of their personal views. (13)

---

[1] A fuller definition of many of these terms can be found in John McMenemy, *The Language of Canadian Politics: A Guide to Important Terms and Concepts*, 3rd ed. (Waterloo: Wilfrid Laurier University Press, 2001).

Canada Health Act. The 1984 act that reimposed conditions on federal grants to the provinces for health programs, especially to prevent extra-billing, privatization, or other moves toward a two-tier health system. (12)

Canada Health and Social Transfer (CHST). The annual federal block grant to the provinces between 1996 and 2004 intended to be used for health, postsecondary education, and welfare, now replaced by the Canada Health Transfer and the Canada Social Transfer. (12)

Canada–U.S. Free Trade Agreement. The agreement signed by Canada and the United States in 1987 and taking effect in 1989 that gradually eliminated tariffs between the two countries and otherwise prohibited governments from interfering in the private marketplace. (5)

Canadian Bill of Rights. An act of the Canadian Parliament passed in 1960 that outlined basic civil liberties but whose defects caused judicial confusion and limited the bill's effectiveness. (11)

Canadian Broadcasting Corporation (CBC). The large national Crown corporation with radio and television divisions whose mandate is to promote meaningful communication among all parts of the country. (5, 7)

Canadian Council of Chief Executives. The most powerful peak business pressure group in Canada, representing the 150 largest firms in the country. (2, 10)

Canadian Judicial Council. An agency composed of the federal and provincial chief justices that disciplines federally appointed judges and provides leadership and coordination among federal and provincial judicial systems. (16)

Canadian Labour Congress. The largest labour pressure group in Canada; the political voice of over 2.5 million members. (2, 10)

Canadian Radio-television and Telecommunications Commission (CRTC). The regulatory agency established to police the communications industry, including radio, television, telephones, and telecommunications. (5, 7)

Charlottetown Accord. The 1992 constitutional agreement that responded to Quebec's demands for distinct society status, Aboriginal demands for self-government, and the West's demand for a Triple-E Senate, but was defeated in a national referendum. (3)

Charter of Rights and Freedoms. Part of the Constitution Act, 1982, that guaranteed fundamental freedoms and legal, democratic, linguistic, mobility, and equality rights. (1, 11, 16)

Chief electoral officer. The independent and impartial official who is in charge of the operation of the whole electoral system. (8)

Civil law. A branch of law dealing with relations between private parties, such as individuals and corporations, that do not involve government. (16)

Civil liberties. Freedoms or rights, including the freedoms of speech, press, religion, and assembly, that citizens enjoy and that cannot be infringed upon by government. (11)

Clarity Act. The 2000 act that specified the conditions under which the federal government would recognize a referendum result in Quebec on the issue of independence. (3)

Class consciousness. An awareness of the social class to which one belongs. (2, 8)

Class-based party. A political party that appeals primarily to one socioeconomic class or another. (9)

Clerk of the Privy Council and Secretary to the Cabinet. The head of the Privy Council Office and head of the federal public service; the chief nonpartisan adviser to the prime minister and cabinet. (13)

Clientele relationship. The intimate and mutually advantageous relationship that sometimes develops between a government department or agency and the interest group with which it most frequently interacts. (10, 14)

Closure. A rule in the House of Commons in which a cabinet minister introduces a motion to cut off debate. (15)

Code Civil du Québec. The unique system of civil law used in Quebec that is based on the Napoleonic Code. (16)

Coercion. Power based on authorized physical force, including police, armed forces, and jails, on which government has a near monopoly. (1)

similar to that of a private company and that operates semi-independently of the cabinet. (5, 13, 14)

Deference to authority. A value considered to be part of the Canadian political culture in which citizens are respectful of government authority and accept its word and orders with little question. (6)

Democracy. A political system characterized by popular sovereignty, political equality, political freedom, and majority rule. (6)

Democratic rights. A category of rights in the Charter of Rights and Freedoms that, among other things, guarantee the vote to every Canadian citizen. (11)

Department of Finance. The government department that has overall responsibility for the government's finances and its role in the economy and that has a powerful influence on all government policy. (13)

Deputy minister. The public servant who heads each government department, manages the department, and advises the minister. (14)

Deregulation. A government policy that removes previous regulations, especially those affecting the corporate sector. (14)

Dissolution of Parliament. The ending of a Parliament, usually after four or more years, by calling an election, an act normally in the hands of the prime minister but one that formally requires the approval of the governor general. (8, 15)

Distinct society clause. A controversial clause in the Meech Lake Accord, and slightly modified in the Charlottetown Accord, claiming that Quebec constituted, within Canada, a distinct society. (3)

Division. A formal standing, roll-call vote in the House of Commons in which members' names are recorded in Hansard. (15)

Division of powers. The distribution of legislative powers between the federal and provincial governments, largely contained in sections 91 and 92 of the Constitution Act, 1867. (11, 12)

Durham Report. The 1839 report by Lord Durham that recommended the union of Upper and Lower Canada and the granting of responsible government to the colony of Canada. (11)

Egalitarianism. As opposed to elitism, the philosophy or practice of providing everyone with an equal amount of power and/or treating everyone more or less equally. (6)

Emergency doctrine. A constitutional doctrine invented by the Judicial Committee of the Privy Council that in times of national emergency, the peace, order, and good government clause became an emergency clause, increasing the powers of the federal government. (12)

Employment equity. A policy that seeks to guarantee complete fairness in hiring, promotion, or remuneration, regardless of gender, ethnicity, or disability. (4)

Enumerated powers. The powers of the provincial governments that are explicitly listed in section 92 of the Constitution Act, 1867. (12)

Equality rights. A category of rights in the Charter of Rights and Freedoms that prohibit governments from discriminating against certain categories of people. (4, 11)

Equalization payments. Large annual cash payments made by the federal government to have-not provinces to help them provide a satisfactory level of public services. (2, 12)

Estimates. The annual spending plans of government departments and agencies. (13, 14, 15)

Executive. That branch of government that provides leadership and makes the major decisions. (1, 13)

Executive federalism. A variant of cooperative federalism characterized by extensive federal–provincial interaction at the level of first ministers, departmental ministers, and deputy ministers. (12)

Expenditure Management System. The process for determining government financial priorities and the annual distribution of public funds. (13)

Extra-parliamentary party. That part of a political party beyond its members of Parliament—that is, party members, local and national executives, and party headquarters. (9)

Federal Court of Canada. A court established by the federal government dealing with cases involving that government and other specialized subjects within its jurisdiction. (16)

Federalism (federation). A system of government characterized by two levels of authority (federal and provincial) and a division of powers between them, such that neither is subordinate to the other. (1, 11, 12)

Filibuster. An organized attempt by the opposition in the House of Commons to prolong debate and delay adoption of government measures. (15)

First ministers' conference. A federal–provincial conference consisting of the prime minister and provincial premiers (and, increasingly, territorial leaders). (12)

First Nations. A term that came into common usage in the 1970s that can refer to the Indian peoples of Canada, both status and non-status, or that can replace the word "band." (4)

First-past-the-post system. The kind of single-member electoral system used in Canada in which the candidate with the most votes wins the constituency, regardless of whether it is over 50 percent. (8)

Free vote. A rare vote in the House of Commons in which members are not required to abide by the party line. (15)

Front de libération du Québec (FLQ). The terrorist wing of the Quebec separatist movement in the 1960s and 1970s. (3)

Fundamental freedoms. Political freedoms—of religion, speech, press, assembly, association, etc.—that governments are not supposed to encroach upon and that are guaranteed by the Charter of Rights and Freedoms. (11)

Globalization. The modern phenomenon of nation-states declining in stature and power by giving way to the demands of transnational corporations via comprehensive free trade agreements, by massive diffusion of technological change, and by worldwide corporate competition or megamergers. (1, 5)

Government. (a) The set of institutions that make and enforce collective, public decisions for a society. (1) (b) The set of authorities, centred around a prime minister, cabinet, and party, that currently occupy the executive offices of the state and provide political leadership. (13, 15)

Government bill. A bill introduced by a cabinet minister on behalf of the whole government. (15)

Government department. A government organization headed by a minister who is politically accountable for its operations and a deputy minister who is in charge of its hierarchical administrative apparatus. (14)

Governor general. The representative of the Queen in Canada who normally performs her head-of-state functions. (13)

Governor in council. The prime minister and cabinet (but *not* the governor general) exercising powers of the Privy Council. (13)

Horse-race effect. The notion that election campaigns have degenerated into a "horse race" where everyone, especially the media, is concerned with which party is ahead, not with how parties would tackle serious public issues. (7)

House leader. The person appointed by each party in the House of Commons to deal with counterparts in other parties with respect to scheduling Commons business. (15)

Ideology. A coherent set of ideas or principles about how a society ought to function, with particular reference to the role of the state. (9)

Indian Act. The act that governed almost all aspects of Aboriginal life in Canada after the 1870s, giving extensive authority to government bureaucrats and minimal discretion to Native people themselves. (4)

Individual ministerial responsibility. The principle that cabinet ministers are individually responsible to the House of Commons to answer for everything that happens in their department. (13, 14)

Individualism. An ideology that holds that individuals should have maximum freedom or liberty to do as they please, especially in economic terms, and that governments should not get involved in taxation, regulation, redistribution, or ownership. (6, 9)

Information Commissioner. The official of Parliament who encourages government to operate on a more open basis and makes judgments in cases where departments withhold information under the Access to Information Act. (14)

Institutionalized pressure group. A kind of pressure group characterized by permanence, resources, governmental recognition and acceptance, and well-developed links with the authorities. (10)

Interest group. *See* Advocacy group/interest group/pressure group.

Issue-oriented pressure group. A kind of pressure group that springs up around an issue and disappears once that issue has been resolved. (10)

James Bay Agreement. The 1975 deal signed by the government of Quebec and its northern Aboriginal residents that gave the latter land, cash, and hunting rights in return for surrendering land for the James Bay hydroelectric project. (4)

Judicial Committee of the Privy Council. A committee of the British Parliament that functioned as Canada's final court of appeal until 1949. (11, 12, 16)

Judicial discretion. The leeway inevitably bestowed on the courts when they interpret laws, even when they do not, or have no power to, overturn them. (11, 16)

Judicial independence. The constitutional principle that the courts should function independently of the rest of the government apparatus, especially the politicians, with implications for security of tenure and remuneration of judges. (1, 16)

Judicial review. The power of the courts to overturn legislation or actions of the executive branch of government. (1, 11, 15, 16)

Judiciary. The court system. (1, 16)

Keynesian economics. An economic theory that to promote general economic stability, government should counterbalance the private sector, spending (running deficit budgets) in periods of unemployment when the private sector doesn't spend, and taxing (withdrawing money from the system) in periods of inflation when the private sector is spending too much. (12)

King–Byng dispute. The 1926 dispute between Prime Minister Mackenzie King and Governor General Lord Byng over King's request for a dissolution of Parliament, which Byng denied. (13)

Leader of the Opposition. The leader of the main opposition party in the House of Commons. (15)

Leadership review. A clause in the constitutions of political parties that allows party members or convention delegates to review the leader's performance. (9)

Left. That part of the ideological spectrum that believes in equality in society and the intervention of government via collectivist measures such as taxation, regulation, redistribution, and public ownership to effect such equality. (9)

Legal rights. The rights of a person suspected or accused of committing a crime, now listed in the Charter of Rights and Freedoms. (11)

Legislature. That branch of government whose function is to represent the people and make laws. (1, 15)

Liberalism. An ideology based on a belief in the rationality of the individual and on maximizing individual freedom, liberty, and self-fulfillment. Before 1900, this was assumed to entail a minimal role for government; after 1900, liberalism usually advocated a larger role for the state and was placed on the centre-left of the spectrum. (9)

Lobbying. Any organized attempt to influence the authorities, now often performed by professional lobbyist firms. (10)

Majority government. A situation in which the party in power has over 50 percent of the seats in the House of Commons. (1, 8, 15)

Majority rule. An element in the definition of democracy that in any decisionmaking setting involving a difference of opinion, the larger number should carry the day. (6)

Mandate. The concept that the winning party has an obligation to enact policies it promised during the election campaign. (8)

Mass media. Sources of information for the mass public—principally radio, television, and newspapers. (1, 7)

Meech Lake Accord. The 1987 package of constitutional reforms intended to bring Quebec back into the constitutional fold that was turned down in 1990. (3)

Memorandum to Cabinet. The formal written document that a minister submits to the cabinet seeking to initiate or change a government policy. (13)

Merit system. A system of hiring and promoting public servants on the basis of their merits (education, experience, etc.) rather than on party preference or other considerations. (14)

Minority government. A situation in which the government party has fewer than 50 percent of the seats in the House of Commons. (1, 8, 15)

Minority language education rights. Rights established in section 23 of the Charter of Rights and Freedoms whereby French-speaking Canadians can send their children to French-language schools wherever their numbers warrant, a principle also extended to English-speaking Canadians where they are a minority. (3, 11)

Mobility rights. A category of rights in the Charter of Rights and Freedoms guaranteeing the freedom to move from one province to another and seek employment there. (11)

Money bill. A bill to raise money for government purposes or to spend public funds. (13, 15)

Multiculturalism. A policy of encouraging ethnic and cultural groups to maintain their customs and traditions, often with public financial assistance. (4)

Multiparty system. Typically European in nature, a party system characterized by many parties, usually without any one having a majority in the legislature. (9)

National Energy Program. The 1980 policy associated with Pierre Trudeau designed to skim off petroleum tax revenue for Ottawa, keep the price of petroleum below world levels, encourage conservation, and Canadianize the industry, which met with great opposition in Western Canada. (2, 5)

National Policy. A broad nation-building 1879 policy of John A. Macdonald that included tariff protection for central Canadian manufacturing, massive immigration, and the construction of a national transportation system. (2, 5)

Neoconservatism. An ideology originating in the 1980s calling on government to withdraw from its extensive intervention in the private market economy but perhaps still promote certain traditional social values. (9)

Neoliberalism. An ideology originating in the 1980s calling on government to withdraw from its extensive intervention in the private market economy—emphasizing privatization, deregulation, balancing of budgets, and trimming of social programs—as well as from regulating society in general. (9)

New middle class. A term from class analysis describing salaried professionals such as teachers, public servants, and nurses. (2)

New Public Management. A movement within public administration since about 1990 that involved the downsizing of government operations, alternative service delivery, and partnerships with private sector agencies. (14)

News management. A variety of techniques used by politicians and governments to ensure positive media coverage. (7)

Nisga'a Treaty. The 2000 treaty signed by the Nisga'a First Nation and the governments of Canada and British Columbia that incorporated a land claim settlement and powers of self-government, considered the first modern-day Aboriginal treaty. (4)

Nomination. The act of becoming a candidate in an election, normally entailing being selected to represent a party at a nomination meeting and then completing official nomination papers. (8)

Nonconfidence motion. A motion in the House of Commons, moved by the opposition, inviting MPs to demonstrate a lack of confidence in the government, which, if successful, would require the cabinet's resignation or the calling of an election. (15)

North American Free Trade Agreement (NAFTA). The 1994 extension of the Canada–U.S. Free Trade Agreement to Mexico. (5)

Notwithstanding clause. Section 33 of the Charter of Rights and Freedoms that allows federal or provincial governments to pass laws that violate certain sections of the Charter. (11)

Nunavut. The eastern half of the Northwest Territories that was established as a separate, Inuit territory in 1999. (4)

Oakes test. The strategy outlined in the *Oakes* case for interpreting the reasonable limits clause of the Charter of Rights and Freedoms. (11)

Official Languages Act. The 1969 federal act that established official bilingualism in Canada and gave citizens the right to deal with certain offices of the federal government in either English or French. (3, 14)

One-party dominance. A party system characterized by the dominance of a single party. (9)

Opposition. Those members of Parliament who do not support the government of the day. (15)

Opposition days. Twenty-one days per session of Parliament set aside for the opposition parties to determine the topic of debate. (15)

Order-in-council. A formal, legal decision made by the prime minister and cabinet (governor in council), including regulations and appointments. (13)

Parliament. Theoretically, the Queen, the House of Commons, and the Senate, functioning collectively, such as in the approval of legislation, but often used to refer to the Commons and Senate or Commons alone. (15)

Parliamentary government. A form of government, distinct from the U.S. congressional system, characterized by parliamentary supremacy. (1)

Parliamentary press gallery. Those members of the media who are registered to sit in the press gallery in the House of Commons and who report on its proceedings or on government in general. (7, 15)

Parliamentary secretary. A government MP who has been given addition responsibilities to assist a cabinet minister. (15)

Party caucus. The whole body of MPs of any party, together with such senators as choose to attend, who hold a regular weekly meeting to discuss parliamentary strategy and party policy. (9, 15)

Party discipline. The convention that all MPs within any party vote together on every occasion, as predetermined by the leader or in the party caucus meeting and as enforced by the party whip. (15)

Party identification. The tendency of a voter to feel attached to a particular political party over an extended period of time. (8)

Party whip. An official of each party in the House of Commons whose function is to enforce party discipline and ensure that members are present for all votes. (15)

Pay equity. An element of employment equity programs designed to ensure that all employees are paid equally for work of equal value and are not discriminated against on the basis of gender or other factors. (4)

Peace, order, and good government (POGG) clause. The words in the opening sentence of section 91 of the Constitution Act, 1867, which states that the residual powers rest with the federal government but which has been often misinterpreted by the courts as dealing with an emergency power only. (12)

Policy communities. Loose communities that form for the purpose of shaping public policy, taking the form of discrete and specialized clusters of government departments and agencies, pressure groups, politicians, corporations, and interested individuals. (10)

Political culture. The sum total of the politically relevant values, beliefs, attitudes, and orientations in any political system. (6)

Political efficacy. The feeling that one has political influence and that one's political participation can make an impact. (6)

Political equality. An element in the definition of democracy that entails the principle of "one person–one vote," that is, every citizen has a vote and each counts equally. (6)

Political freedom. An element in the definition of democracy that entails freedom of speech, press, assembly, association, etc., such that people can organize and advocate in order to influence election results and public policy. (6)

Political party. An organized group that makes nominations and contests elections in the hope of influencing the policy and personnel of government. (1, 9)

Political patronage. Making appointments to public offices or awarding government contracts on a partisan basis. (14, 16)

Political socialization. The process whereby individuals acquire their political values, attitudes, beliefs, information, and opinions. (6)

Politics. The activity in which conflicting interests struggle for advantage or dominance in the making and execution of public policies. (1)

Popular sovereignty. An element in the definition of democracy that entails periodically allowing the public at large to exert its will—to have the final say—normally through general elections. (6)

Popular vote. The percentage of all votes cast for a candidate or party, regardless of who was elected. (8)

Poverty line. An amount of income such that anyone who received less would be living in poverty. (2)

Power. The ability of one actor to impose its will on another, usually considered to be the essence of politics and government. (1)

Prerogative powers. That small number of residual powers of the Crown that remain from the era of an all-powerful monarch that the Queen or governor general can still exercise on rare occasions at his or her own discretion. (13)

Pressure group. *See* Advocacy group/interest group/pressure group.

Prime ministerial government. The notion that the prime minister is now so pre-eminent that the label "cabinet government" no longer accurately describes how decisions are made in the political executive. (13)

Prime Minister's Office (PMO). The office that supports and advises the prime minister in partisan terms. (13)

Private bill. A bill introduced in Parliament that affects only a specific individual, company, organization, or group. (15)

Private member's bill. A public bill introduced in Parliament by an MP who is not in the cabinet. (15)

Private sector. That part of the economy operated by individuals, corporations, and other nongovernmental groups. (1)

Privatization. Transferring a government program, agency, or Crown corporation to the private sector. (14)

Privy Council. A body established by the Constitution Act, 1867, to advise the governor general in the exercise of the powers of that office but effectively taken over by the prime minister and cabinet. (13)

Privy Council Office (PCO). The office that supports and advises the prime minister,

cabinet, and cabinet committees in nonpartisan terms. (13)

Public Accounts Committee. The House of Commons committee that examines the Public Accounts and the Auditor General's reports and criticizes government officials for illegal or unwise expenditures. (14, 15)

Public bill. A bill introduced in Parliament that affects society in general. (15)

Public opinion. The sum total of opinions held by members of the public on any subject. (7)

Public opinion poll. A survey conducted to ascertain the opinions of the public on assorted matters. (7)

Public policy. A course of action or inaction chosen by public authorities to address a given problem or interrelated set of problems. (13)

Public sector. That part of the economy operated or financed by government. (1)

Public Service Commission. The central personnel agency of government designed to police the merit system and ensure that partisanship is kept out of the regular public service. (14)

Quebec Act. The 1774 British law that provided for a system of government for the colony of Quebec that included certain privileges for the French-language, Roman Catholic majority. (3, 11)

Question Period. The daily 45-minute period in the House of Commons in which opposition members spar with the prime minister and cabinet ministers. (15)

Quiet Revolution. The dramatic change of values and attitudes, especially toward the state, the new collective self-confidence, and the new brand of nationalism in Quebec in the 1960s. (3)

Reasonable limits clause. Section 1 of the Charter of Rights and Freedoms, which allows the courts to uphold a law even if it violates a Charter right. (11)

Recall. A populist device in which the signing of a petition by a certain proportion of the local electorate to recall their legislative representative means that the representative must resign. (6)

Red Tories. A minority faction within the former Progressive Conservative Party that had collectivist leanings akin to many

British and European conservatives, stressing order, tradition, stability, and a paternalistic concern for the condition of the working class. (9)

Redistribution. The process of reallocating seats in the House of Commons among the provinces after each decennial census and then redrawing constituency boundaries within each province. (8)

Reference case. A case referred to the courts by a provincial or federal cabinet usually to obtain a ruling on the constitutionality of a law. (16)

Referendum. A populist device in which a public policy proposal is submitted directly to the electorate. (3, 6)

Regionalism. Strong feelings of attachment to the region or province where one lives that often generate political activity. (2)

Regulations. The detailed rules drafted by the bureaucracy under the authority of laws passed by Parliament that are too voluminous and technical to put into the legislation itself. (10, 13, 14)

Regulatory tribunal. A government agency established to regulate an area of public policy, such as transportation or communications, that operates at arm's length from the cabinet. (5, 14)

Representative bureaucracy. A public service that reflects the composition of the population, with the most usual concerns being gender, ethnicity, and region. (14)

Representative democracy. A system of government based on periodic election of representatives to Parliament, as opposed to more direct participation by voters in making public decisions. (6, 9)

Representative government. A form of government including an assembly elected by the citizens but not necessarily incorporating the principle of responsible government. (11)

Residual powers. Those powers not given to the provinces in the Constitution Act, 1867, that were assigned to the federal government under the POGG clause in section 91. (12)

Responsible government. A form of government in which the political executive must retain the confidence of the elected legislature and resign or call an election if and

when it is defeated on a vote of nonconfidence. (1, 11, 15)

Returning officer. The official in charge of running the election in each electoral district. (8)

Right. That part of the ideological spectrum that cherishes individualism and believes in leaving the private sector to operate with minimal government intervention. (9)

Royal commission. An elaborate investigation set up by the cabinet to research a significant policy problem, to listen to and educate the public, and to make recommendations to the government. (14)

Royal Proclamation of 1763. The British policy enunciated after conquering Quebec that in a large area called Indian Territory forbade the purchase or settlement of land without a treaty between the Crown and the Indian peoples concerned. (4, 11)

Rule of law. The constitutional principle that all government action must be based on law and that governments and government officials must obey the law. (11)

Safe seat. A constituency that a single party can be assured of winning, election after election. (15)

Sexual orientation. One's sexual preference, usually either heterosexual or homosexual; it now constitutes a ground on which discrimination is prohibited. (4)

Shared-cost programs. Government programs whose cost is shared by the federal and provincial governments. (12)

Social democracy. A moderate leftist ideology that emphasizes the principle of equality and usually prescribes a large role for government to intervene in society and the economy. (9)

Social movement. An informal network of organizations and individuals who on the basis of a collective identity and shared values engage in political struggle intended to expand the boundaries of the existing system, such as the women's and environmental movements. (1, 10)

Social Union Framework Agreement. An overall framework of federal–provincial relations agreed to in 1999 by all governments except Quebec that sought to end long-standing irritants on both sides. (12)

Sovereignty.   Ultimate control or independence, such as Canadian national sovereignty vis-à-vis that of other countries. (1, 5)

Sovereignty-association.   The Parti Québécois proposal in which Quebec would be sovereign while maintaining an economic association with the rest of Canada. (3)

Speaker.   The presiding officer of the House of Commons. (15)

Speech from the Throne.   The document prepared by the prime minister and cabinet and read by the governor general at the opening of each session of Parliament that outlines the government's legislative proposals for the session. (13, 15)

Spending power.   The unofficial power of the federal government to spend money in any field, including those within provincial jurisdiction. (12)

Spin doctors.   Party officials and ministerial aides who talk to the media and try to influence media coverage by putting the best face on an event from their party's point of view. (7, 8)

Standing committees.   Those committees of the House of Commons that are set up semi-permanently and that parallel government departments. (15)

Standing Orders.   The written rules of the House of Commons. (15)

Staples theory.   The notion that Canadian economic development has gone through a series of stages based on the exploitation of one natural resource or another and the export of such resources, without the development of a secondary or manufacturing sector. (2)

Stare decisis.   The legal principle that precedents are binding on similar subsequent cases, which forms the basis of the common law system. (16)

Statute of Westminster.   The 1931 British law that declared Canada and the other Dominions to be fully independent. (5, 11)

Supremacy of Parliament.   The principle that no other organ of government can overrule Parliament or its laws. (15)

Supreme Court of Canada.   The highest court in Canada and the final court of appeal since 1949. (16)

Terrorism.   An act or threat of violence perpetrated by an ideological group that is intended to produce fear or change. (5)

Third-party advertising.   Advertising by advocacy groups, as opposed to political parties, during an election campaign. (8, 10)

Transnational corporations.   Corporations operating simultaneously in many countries throughout the world that often take orders from company headquarters and that individual states find difficult to control. (5)

Treasury Board.   A cabinet committee whose primary responsibility is to restrain government spending. (13)

Treasury Board Secretariat.   The government department that advises the Treasury Board in its deliberations and that functions as a restraining influence on departmental spending. (13, 14)

Treaty rights.   Aboriginal rights based on treaties signed with the Crown. (4)

Triple-E Senate.   A proposal for Senate reform in which each province would have an equal number of senators who would be elected and who would be given effective powers. (15)

Two-party system.   A type of party system in which two main parties are of approximately equal strength and alternate in office. (9)

Two-plus party system.   A type of party system in which two main parties are of approximately equal strength and alternate in office but are accompanied by one or more minor parties of significant strength. (9)

Visible minorities.   Members of ethnic groups, other than Aboriginal peoples, whose skin colour is not white. (4)

War Measures Act.   The law invoked in both world wars and during the 1970 FLQ crisis under which the federal cabinet was given emergency powers to deal with the crisis. (3)

Western alienation.   The feeling shared by many Western Canadians that their interests are not taken seriously in the national policy-making process. (2)

Westminster model.   The model of government developed in Britain in which the political executive is given extensive power to provide effective leadership. (1, 15)

White Paper on Indians. The 1969 Trudeau–Chrétien policy proposal to do away with the Indian Act and treaties and to fully integrate Aboriginal peoples into Canadian society. (4)

Women's movement. The collection of women's groups that mushroomed across the country, starting around 1970, demanding complete equality for women. (4)

World Trade Organization (WTO). An international organization to which Canada and most other countries belong that has the power to disallow national policies and practices that it deems discriminatory against companies from other states. (5)

Notes

Chapter 2

1. See, for example, Pierre Berton, *The National Dream* and *The Last Spike* (Toronto: McClelland and Stewart, 1970 and 1971, respectively); Robert Chodos, *The CPR: A Century of Corporate Welfare* (Toronto: Lorimer, 1973).
2. Task Force on Canadian Unity, *A Future Together* (Ottawa: Supply and Services, 1979), 26–27.
3. Wallace Clement and Daniel Drache, *A Practical Guide to Canadian Political Economy* (Toronto: Lorimer, 1978), 9–14.
4. David Kilgour, *Uneasy Patriots: Western Canadians in Confederation* (Edmonton: Lone Pine Publishers, 1988) and *Inside Outer Canada* (Edmonton: Lone Pine Publishers, 1990); Don Braid and Sydney Sharpe, *Breakup: Why the West Feels Left Out of Canada* (Toronto: Key Porter Books, 1990); Roger Gibbins and Loleen Berdahl, *Western Visions, Western Futures* (Peterborough: Broadview Press, 2003).
5. Donald Smiley, *The Federal Condition in Canada* (Toronto: McGraw-Hill Ryerson, 1987), 159.
6. Roger Gibbins, *Prairie Politics and Society* (Toronto: Butterworths, 1980), 191.
7. "The Rich 100," *Canadian Business* (6 Dec. 2004).
8. "The CEO of Power Financial Received $52 Million, Including $45 Million in Stock Options," *The Globe and Mail* (30 April 2004), B8.
9. Linda McQuaig, *Behind Closed Doors* (Toronto: Penguin, 1987).
10. *Exposing the Facts of Corporate Rule: A Handbook on How to Challenge the Big Business Agenda* (Toronto: Centre for Social Justice, 1998).
11. Irving Abella, ed. *On Strike* (Toronto: James Lewis & Samuel, 1974); Walter Stewart, *Strike!* (Toronto: McClelland and Stewart, 1977), ch. 4.
12. Statistics Canada, "Unionization," *Perspectives on Labour and Income*, cat. no. 75-001-XPE (Autumn 2002), 73.
13. Human Resources Development, "Union Membership in Canada—2001," *Workplace Gazette* (Fall 2001).
14. Gad Horowitz, *Canadian Labour in Politics* (Toronto: University of Toronto Press, 1968).
15. Based on periodic reports by Statistics Canada on personal incomes, the National Council of Welfare, and the Canadian Council on Social Development. A newer, "market-basket measure" of poverty has a slightly lower number living below the poverty line.
16. *The Canadian Fact Book on Poverty—2000* (Canadian Council on Social Development: Ottawa, 2000), 2.
17. Armine Yalnizyan, *Canada's Great Divide: The Politics of the Growing Gap between Rich and Poor in the 1990s* (Toronto: Centre for Social Justice, 2000).
18. Campaign 2000, *Pathways to Progress: Structural Solutions to Address Child Poverty* (Toronto, May 2004).

Chapter 3

1. Dale Thomson, *Jean Lesage and the Quiet Revolution* (Toronto: Macmillan, 1984).
2. Kenneth McRoberts, *Misconceiving Canada: The Struggle for National Unity* (Toronto: Oxford University Press, 1997).
3. Graham Fraser, *René Lévesque and the Parti Québécois in Power* (Toronto: Macmillan, 1984).
4. Roy Romanow, J. Whyte, and H. Leeson, *Canada … Notwithstanding: The Making of the Constitution, 1976–1982* (Toronto: Methuen, 1984); Edward McWhinney, *Canada and the Constitution, 1979–82: Patriation and the Charter of Rights* (Toronto: University of Toronto Press, 1982).
5. Patrick J. Monahan, *Meech Lake: The Inside Story* (Toronto: University of Toronto Press, 1991).
6. Alan C. Cairns, *Constitution, Government, and Society in Canada* (Toronto: McClelland and Stewart, 1988); *Disruptions: Constitutional Struggles, from the Charter to Meech Lake* (Toronto: McClelland and Stewart, 1991).

7. Kenneth McRoberts and Patrick Monahan, eds., *The Charlottetown Accord, the Referendum and the Future of Canada* (Toronto: University of Toronto Press, 1993); Peter Russell, *Constitutional Odyssey: Can Canadians Become a Sovereign People?* 2nd ed. (Toronto: University of Toronto Press, 1993); 3rd ed., 2004.

8. Richard Johnston, *The Challenge of Direct Democracy: The 1992 Canadian Referendum* (Kingston: McGill-Queen's University Press, 1996).

9. *Reference re Secession of Quebec*, [1998] 2 S.C.R. 217.

10. McRoberts, *Misconceiving Canada*.

11. Thomas Courchene, "Market Nationalism," *Policy Options* (October 1968).

Chapter 4

1. Department of Indian Affairs and Northern Development, "Basic Departmental Data, 1999," http://www.ainc-inac.gc.ca/pr/sts/bdd99//index_e.htm (Retrieved 15 Sept. 2001).

2. Geoffrey York and Loreen Pindera, *People of the Pines: The Warriors and the Legacy of Oka* (Toronto: Little Brown, 1991); Craig MacLaine and Michael Baxendale, *This Land Is Our Land* (Toronto: Optimum, 1990).

3. It is virtually impossible to keep pace with the many Supreme Court decisions related to Aboriginal issues. Several are listed on the book's website, but two examples are *R. v. Marshall*, [1999] 3 S.C.R. 456 and *R. v. Marshall*, [1999] 3 S.C.R. 533. The key Métis case is *R. v. Powley*, [2003] 2 S.C.R. 207.

4. *Nisga'a Final Agreement*, http://www.ainc-inac.gc.ca/pr/agr/nsga/nisdex12_e.pdf (Retrieved 15 Nov. 2004).

5. Statistics Canada, *Aboriginal Peoples Survey 2001—Initial Findings: Well-Being of the Non-Reserve Aboriginal Population*, cat. no. 89-589-XIE (September 2003); Canada, *Auditor General Report* (April 2003), ch. 6: "Federal Government Support to First Nations—Housing on Reserves."

6. Yasmeen Abu-Laban and Christina Gabriel, *Selling Diversity: Immigration, Multiculturalism, Employment Equity, and Globalization* (Peterborough: Broadview Press, 2002); Will Kymlicka, *Finding Our Way: Rethinking Ethnocultural Relations in Canada* (Toronto: Oxford University Press, 1998).

7. Neil Bissoondath, *Selling Illusions: The Cult of Multiculturalism in Canada* (Toronto: Penguin, 1994).

8. Penney Kome, *Women of Influence* (Toronto: University of Toronto Press, 1985), 86.

9. Statistics Canada, "Average Earnings by Sex and Work Pattern," http://www.statcan.ca:80/english/Pgdb/People/Labour/labor01b.htm (Retrieved 15 Sept. 2001). Two other useful Statistics Canada sources are *Women in Canada 2000*, cat. no. 89-503-XPE, and *The Persistent Gap: New Evidence on the Canadian Gender Wage Gap*, cat. no. 11F0019MPE, no. 157.

10. Penney Kome, *The Taking of Twenty-Eight* (Toronto: Women's Educational Press, 1983); *Women of Influence*, ch. 10.

11. Janine Brodie et al., *The Politics of Abortion* (Toronto: Oxford University Press, 1992).

12. David P. Ross, Katherine J. Scott, and Peter J. Smith, *The Canadian Fact Book on Poverty—2000* (Ottawa: Canadian Council on Social Development, 2000).

Chapter 5

1. R. McGregor Dawson, *The Government of Canada*, 5th ed., rev. Norman Ward (Toronto: University of Toronto Press, 1970), 54.

2. Donald Creighton, *Canada's First Century* (Toronto: Macmillan, 1970); George Grant, *Lament for a Nation: The Defeat of Canadian Nationalism* (Toronto: McClelland and Stewart, 1965); J.L. Granatstein, *How Britain's Weakness Forced Canada into the Arms of the United States* (Toronto: University of Toronto Press, 1989).

3. Canada, *Foreign Direct Investment in Canada* (Ottawa: Supply and Services, 1972), 14.

4. The pioneer of this theme was Kari Levitt, *Silent Surrender: The Multinational Corporation in Canada* (Toronto: Macmillan, 1970).

5. See Environment Canada, "What Is the Kyoto Protocol?" http://www.ec.gc.ca/climate/Kyoto-e.html (Retrieved 24 May 2004).

6. Human Resources Development Canada, *Workplace Gazette* 4, no. 3 (Fall 2001).

7. Statistics Canada, "Television Viewing, Fall 2002," *The Daily* (21 Nov. 2003), http://www.statcan.ca/Daily/English/031121/d031121a.htm (Retrieved 24 May 2004).

8. Solid statistics are hard to come by, but see Victor Rabinovitch, "The Social and Economic Rationales for Canada's Domestic Cultural Policies," in Dennis Browne, ed., *The Culture/Trade Quandary: Canada's Policy Options* (Ottawa: Centre for Trade Policy and Law, 1998), 30.

9. G. Bruce Doern and Brian Tomlin, *Faith and Fear: The Free Trade Story* (Toronto: Stoddart, 1991).

10. Duncan Cameron and Mel Watkins, *Canada under Free Trade* (Toronto: Lorimer, 1993); John Warnock, *Free Trade and the New Right Agenda* (Vancouver: New Star Books, 1988).

11. Government of Canada, *The North American Free Trade Agreement at a Glance*, cat. no. E75-56/1-1993E; Jeffrey M. Ayres, *Defying Conventional Wisdom: Political Movements and Popular Contention against North American Free Trade* (Toronto: University of Toronto Press, 1998).

12. Stephen Clarkson, *Uncle Sam and Us: Globalization, Neoconservatism, and the Canadian State* (Toronto: University of Toronto Press, 2002).

13. G. Bruce Doern et al., eds., *Border Crossings: The Internationalization of Canadian Public Policy* (Toronto: Oxford University Press, 1996).

14. Stephen McBride and John Shields, *Dismantling a Nation: Canada and the New World Order* (Halifax: Fernwood Publishing, 1993); William Watson, *Globalization and the Meaning of Canadian Life* (Toronto: University of Toronto Press, 1998); Linda McQuaig, *The Cult of Impotence: Selling the Myth of Powerlessness in the Global Economy* (Toronto: Viking, 1998); Maude Barlow and Tony Clarke, *Global Showdown: How the New Activists Are Fighting Global Corporate Rule* (Toronto: Stoddart Publishing, 2000).

15. Andrew Jackson and Matthew Sanger, eds., *Dismantling Democracy: The Multilateral Agreement on Investment and Its Impact* (Toronto: Lorimer, 1998).

16. Department of Foreign Affairs and International Trade, "Canada's Actions against Terrorism since September 11," http://www.dfait-maeci.gc.ca/anti-terrorism/Canadaactions-en.asp (Retrieved 19 Nov. 2004).

Chapter 6

1. Henry B. Mayo, *An Introduction to Democratic Theory* (New York: Oxford University Press, 1960), ch. 4.

2. Seymour Martin Lipset, *Continental Divide* (New York: Routledge, 1990), 8.

3. Pierre Berton, *Why We Act Like Canadians* (Toronto: McClelland and Stewart, 1982).

4. *Maclean's* (1 July 1995), 15.

5. Will Kymlicka, *Finding Our Way: Rethinking Ethnocultural Relations in Canada* (Don Mills: Oxford University Press, 1998).

6. Canadian Information Office, *Government Communications Survey—Wave IV: Final Survey Findings* (Fall 1999), http://www.infocan.gc.ca/survey/pubop_e.html (Retrieved 15 Sept. 2001); Shawn McCarthy, "Albertans Embrace Federation," *The Globe and Mail* (14 Feb. 2001). See also Statistics Canada, *2003 General Social Survey on Social Engagement, Cycle 17: An Overview of Findings*," cat. no. 89-598-XWE (July 2004).

7. W. Wolfson and B. Murphy, "Income Inequality in North America: Does the 49th Parallel Still Matter?" *Canadian Economic Observer*, cat. no. 11-010-XPB (August 2000).

8. Organisation for Economic Cooperation and Development, *OECD in Figures, 2002*, http://www1.oecd.org/publications/e-book/0102071e.pdf (Retrieved 15 June 2004), 68.

9. Neil Nevitte, *The Decline of Deference* (Peterborough: Broadview Press, 1996).

10. Michael Adams, *Fire and Ice: The United States, Canada and the Myth of Converging Values* (Toronto: Penguin, 2003).

11. Marcel Trudel and Genevieve Jain, *Canadian History Textbooks: A Comparative Study* (Ottawa: Royal Commission on Bilingualism and Biculturalism, 1970).

12. Ronald Landes, "Political Education and Political Socialization," in Jon Pammett and Jean-Luc Pépin, eds., *Political Education in Canada* (Halifax: Institute for Research on Public Policy, 1988), 17.

13. Frederick Fletcher, "The Mass Media and Political Education," in Pammett and Pépin, 92.
14. Alan Frizzell et al., *The Canadian General Election of 1988* (Ottawa: Carleton University Press), 69.
15. William Mishler and Harold D. Clarke, "Political Participation in Canada," in Michael Whittington and Glen Williams, eds., *Canadian Politics in the 1990s*, 4th ed. (Scarborough: Nelson Canada, 1995), 130.
16. Jon H. Pammett and Lawrence LeDuc, "Explaining the Turnout Decline in Canadian Federal Elections: A New Survey of Non-Voters" (March 2003), http://www.elections.ca/loi/tur/tud/TurnoutDecline.pdf (Retrieved 22 Nov. 2004).
17. Mishler and Clarke, "Political Participation," 134, 143.
18. Paul Howe and David Northrup, "Strengthening Canadian Democracy: The Views of Canadians," *Policy Matters* 1, no. 5 (July 2000), 40.
19. Ronald D. Lambert et al., "The Social Sources of Political Knowledge," *Canadian Journal of Political Science* (June 1988): 359–74.
20. R. Kenneth Carty, *Canadian Political Parties in the Constituencies*, Royal Commission on Electoral Reform and Party Financing Research Studies 23, cat. no. 21-1989/2-41-23E.
21. Judy Torrance, *Public Violence in Canada* (Montreal: McGill-Queen's University Press, 1986).

Chapter 7

1. The website of the Canadian Newspaper Association provides an up-to-date account of such ownership; see http://www.cna-acj.ca.
2. Paul Nesbitt-Larking, *Politics, Society, and the Media: Canadian Perspectives* (Peterborough: Broadview Press, 2001); David Taras, *Power and Betrayal in the Canadian Media* (Peterborough: Broadview Press, 1999); James Winter, *Democracy's Oxygen: How Corporations Control the News in Canada* (Toronto: McClelland and Stewart, 1980); John Miller, *Yesterday's News: How Canada's Daily Newspapers Are Failing Us* (Halifax: Fernwood Publishing, 1998).
3. Frederick J. Fletcher and Daphne Gottlieb Taras, "Images and Issues: The Mass Media and Politics in Canada," in Michael Whittington and Glen Williams, eds., *Canadian Politics in the 1990s*, 3rd ed. (Scarborough: Nelson Canada, 1990), 229.
4. Edwin R. Black, *Politics and the News: The Political Functions of the Mass Media* (Toronto: Butterworths, 1982), 80.
5. Peter Trueman, *Smoke and Mirrors: The Inside Story of Television News in Canada* (Toronto: McClelland and Stewart, 1980), 161.
6. Taras, *Power and Betrayal*, ch. 3.
7. The general thrust of David Taras in *The Newsmakers* (Scarborough: Nelson Canada, 1990).
8. Ibid., 30–31.
9. Fletcher, *The Newspaper and Public Affairs* (Ottawa: Royal Commission on Newspapers, 1981), 16; Fletcher and Taras, "Images and Issues," 222; Black, *Politics and the News*, 183; Peter Desbarats, *Guide to Canadian News Media*, 2nd ed. (Toronto: Harcourt Brace Jovanovich, 1990), 149; Arthur Siegel, *Politics and the Media in Canada* (Toronto: McGraw-Hill Ryerson, 1983), 14. Of course, other players also have their agendas, especially the prime minister and the bureaucracy.
10. Taras, *The Newsmakers*, ch. 3; Allan Levine, *Scrum Wars: The Prime Ministers and the Media* (Toronto: Dundurn Press, 1993).
11. Environics Media Study (Environics Research Group, December 1986), cited by Desbarats, *Guide to Canadian News Media*, 28, and its *1991 Media Study*.
12. Taras, *The Newsmakers*, 102.
13. Alan Frizzell et al., *The Canadian General Election of 1988* (Ottawa: Carleton University Press, 1989), 33.
14. Taras, *The Newsmakers*, ch. 4; Knowlton Nash, *Trivia Pursuit: How Showbiz Values Are Corrupting the News* (Toronto: McClelland and Stewart, 1998).
15. Henry Milner, "Civic Literacy in Comparative Context," *Policy Matters* 2, no. 2 (2001).
16. Allan Fotheringham, *Birds of a Feather: The Press and the Politicians* (Toronto: Key Porter Books, 1989), 139.

17. Black, *Politics and the News*, 12; Taras, *The Newsmakers*, 234.
18. Desbarats, *Guide to Canadian News Media*, 41.
19. Black, *Politics and the News*, 168.
20. Frizzell, 1988, 91.
21. John Turner's success in Vancouver Quadra in the 1984 election is often cited as an example of the underdog effect, given that all polls in the constituency indicated that he would lose. Joe Clark's personal victory in 2000 might be another such example.
22. Taras, *The Newsmakers*, 187, 192–94; Desbarats, *Guide to Canadian News Media*, 138.
23. Claire Hoy, *Margin of Error* (Toronto: Key Porter Books, 1989), 1–5.
24. Howard R. Penniman, ed., *Canada at the Polls, 1984* (Durham, N.C.: Duke University Press, 1988), 131.

Chapter 8

1. Three hundred and eight constituencies distributed purely on the basis of the 2001 population would have given Ontario 117 seats, British Columbia, 40, and Alberta, 30.
2. Alan Frizzell and Jon Pammett, eds., *The Canadian General Election of 1997* (Toronto: Dundurn Press, 1997); Jon H. Pammett and Christopher Dornan, eds., *The Canadian General Election of 2000* (Toronto: Dundurn Press, 2001).
3. Stephen Clarkson, "Yesterday's Man and His Blue Grits: Backward into the Future," in Alan Frizzell, *The Canadian General Election of 1993* (Ottawa: Carleton University Press, 1994), 33.
4. Lawrence LeDuc and Richard Price, "Great Debates: The Televised Leadership Debates of 1979," *Canadian Journal of Political Science* (March 1985).
5. *Maclean's* (5 December 1988).
6. Alan C. Cairns, "The Electoral System and the Party System in Canada," *Canadian Journal of Political Science* (March 1968): 55–80.
7. Henry Milner, ed., *Making Every Vote Count: Reassessing Canada's Electoral System* (Peterborough: Broadview Press, 1999); Law Commission of Canada, *Voting Counts: Electoral Reform for Canada* (Ottawa, 2004).
8. *Harper v. Canada (Attorney General)*, [2004] 1 S.C.R. 827.
9. Jon H. Pammett, "Elections," in M. Whittington and G. Williams, eds., *Canadian Politics in the 1990s*, 4th ed. (Scarborough: Nelson Canada, 1995), 242.
10. Jon Pammett, "Class Voting and Class Consciousness in Canada," *Canadian Review of Sociology and Anthropology* 24, no. 2 (1987): 269–90; Keith Archer, "The Failure of the New Democratic Party: Unions, Unionists, and Politics in Canada," *Canadian Journal of Political Science* (June 1985): 353–66.
11. See the section on class-based parties in Chapter 9 of this book; Janine Brodie and Jane Jenson, *Crisis, Challenge and Change: Party and Class in Canada Revisited* (Ottawa: Carleton University Press, 1988); Pammett, "Class Voting;" and Archer, "The Failure."
12. André Blais, et al., *Anatomy of a Liberal Victory: Making Sense of the Vote in the 2000 Canadian Election* (Peterborough: Broadview Press, 2002), ch. 7.
13. Harold D. Clarke, et al., *Absent Mandate: Canadian Electoral Politics in an Era of Restructuring*, 3rd ed. (Toronto: Gage, 1996).
14. John H. Pammett and Christopher Dornan, eds., *The Canadian General Election of 2004* (Toronto: Dundurm Press, 2004).

Chapter 9

1. In traditional European terms, a multiparty system implies that no party has a majority, leading to coalition governments. That was not the case in Canada between 1993 and 2004.
2. H.G. Thorburn, "Interpretations of the Canadian Party System," in H.G. Thorburn, ed., *Party Politics in Canada*, 6th ed. (Scarborough: Prentice-Hall Canada, 1991).
3. Janine Brodie and Jane Jenson, *Crisis, Challenge and Change: Party and Class in Canada Revisited* (Ottawa: Carleton University Press, 1988); Charles Taylor, *The Pattern of Politics* (Toronto:

McClelland and Stewart, 1970); Gad Horowitz, "Toward the Democratic Class Struggle," in Trevor Lloyd and Jack McLeod, eds., *Agenda 1970* (Toronto: University of Toronto Press, 1968).

4. Jon Pammett, "Class Voting and Class Consciousness in Canada," *Canadian Review of Sociology and Anthropology* 24, no. 2 (1987), 269–90; Keith Archer, "The Failure of the New Democratic Party: Unions, Unionists, and Politics in Canada," *Canadian Journal of Political Science* (June 1985), 353–66.

5. Horowitz, "Toward the Democratic Class Struggle," 254.

6. Thorburn, "Interpretations of the Canadian Party System"; Reginald Whitaker, *The Government Party: Organizing and Financing the Liberal Party of Canada, 1930–58* (Toronto: University of Toronto Press, 1977); George Perlin, *The Tory Syndrome: Leadership Politics in the Progressive Conservative Party* (Montreal: McGill-Queen's University Press, 1980).

7. John Meisel, "Decline of Party in Canada," in Thorburn, *Party Politics*; John Meisel, "The Dysfunctions of Canadian Parties: An Exploratory Mapping," in Thorburn, *Party Politics*; John Meisel and Matthew Mendelsohn, "Meteor? Phoenix? Chameleon? The Decline and Transformation of Party in Canada," in H.G. Thorburn and Alan Whitehorn, eds. *Party Politics in Canada*, 8th ed. (Toronto: Prentice-Hall, 2001).

8. Paul Howe and David Northrup, "Strengthening Canadian Democracy: The Views of Canadians," *Policy Matters* 1, no. 5 (July 2000).

9. John C. Courtney, *Do Conventions Matter? Choosing National Party Leaders in Canada* (Montreal: McGill-Queen's University Press, 1995); Maureen Mancuso et al., eds., *Leaders and Leadership in Canada* (Toronto: Oxford University Press, 1994).

10. Louis Hartz, *The Founding of New Societies* (New York: Harcourt, Brace and World, 1964); Gad Horowitz, "Conservatism, Liberalism and Socialism in Canada: An Interpretation," *Canadian Journal of Economics and Political Science* (May 1966), 143–71; Colin Campbell and William Christian, *Parties, Leaders, and Ideologies in Canada* (Toronto: McGraw-Hill Ryerson, 1996).

Chapter 10

1. Paul Pross, *Group Politics and Public Policy* (Toronto: Oxford University Press, 1986).

2. Ibid., esp. ch. 11.

3. William D. Coleman, *Business and Politics: A Study of Collective Action* (Montreal: McGill-Queen's University Press, 1988), and Stephen Brooks and Andrew Stritch, *Business and Government in Canada* (Scarborough: Prentice-Hall Canada, 1991), ch. 7.

4. William D. Coleman, "One Step Ahead: Business in the Policy Process in Canada," in Mark Charlton and Paul Barker, eds., *Crosscurrents: Contemporary Political Issues*, 2nd ed. (Scarborough: Nelson Canada, 1994).

5. Pross, *Group Politics*, ch. 5.

6. Susan Phillips, "Competing, Connecting, and Complementing: Parties, Interest Groups, and New Social Movements," in A. Brian Tanguay and Alain-G. Gagnon, eds., *Canadian Parties in Transition*, 2nd ed. (Scarborough: Nelson Canada, 1996).

7. Jeffrey M. Ayers, *Defying Conventional Wisdom: Political Movements and Popular Contention against North American Free Trade* (Toronto: University of Toronto Press, 1998).

8. Leslie Pal, *Interests of State: The Politics of Language, Multiculturalism, and Feminism in Canada* (Montreal: McGill-Queen's University Press, 1993).

9. Pross, *Group Politics*, ch. 6.

10. Robert Presthus, *Elite Accommodation in Canada* (Toronto: Macmillan, 1973). Presthus calls this phenomenon "elite accommodation."

11. Colin Campbell, *The Canadian Senate: A Lobby from Within* (Toronto: Methuen, 1983); John McMenemy, "The Senate as an Instrument of Business and Party," in Paul Fox and Graham White, eds., *Politics: Canada*, 7th ed. (Toronto: McGraw-Hill Ryerson, 1991).

12. Malcolm Taylor, "The Role of the Medical Profession in the Formulation of Public Policy," *Canadian Journal of Economics and Political Science* (February 1960), 108–27.

13. Ian Greene, "Conflict of Interest and the Canadian Constitution: An Analysis of Conflict of Interest Rules for Canadian Cabinet Ministers," *Canadian Journal of Political Science* (June 1990), 233–56.
14. Brooks and Stritch, *Business and Government*, 240; John Sawatsky, *The Insiders: Government, Business, and the Lobbyists* (Toronto: McClelland and Stewart, 1987), Epilogue.
15. Sawatsky, *The Insiders*, 315–16.
16. John A. Chenier, ed., *The Federal Lobbyists, 1995* (Ottawa: ARC Publications, 1995), ii.
17. Democracy Watch, "Join Our Coalition of Groups Pushing for Stronger Lobbying and Ethics Rules and Ethics Enforcement in Canada," press release issued 22 July 2002.

Chapter 11

1. Bayard Reesor, *The Canadian Constitution in Historical Perspective* (Scarborough: Prentice-Hall Canada, 1992).
2. Lord Durham, *Report of the Affairs of British North America*, ed. Gerald M. Craig (Toronto: McClelland and Stewart, 1963).
3. P.B. Waite, *The Confederation Debates in the Province of Canada, 1865* (Toronto: McClelland and Stewart, 1963); Donald Creighton, *The Road to Confederation* (Toronto: Macmillan, 1964).
4. Alan C. Cairns, *Constitution, Government, and Society in Canada* (Toronto: McClelland and Stewart, 1988), 31.
5. Andrew Heard, *Canadian Constitutional Conventions: The Marriage of Law and Politics* (Toronto: Oxford University Press, 1991). The author's definition is an amalgam of those Heard cites.
6. Reesor, *The Canadian Constitution*, ch. 4.
7. *Harper v. Canada (Attorney General)*, [2004] 1 S.C.R. 827.
8. Ian Greene, *The Charter of Rights* (Toronto: Lorimer, 1989), 172.
9. The leading cases in this respect are *Egan v. Canada*, [1995] 2 S.C.R. 513; *Vriend v. Alberta*, [1998] 1 S.C.R. 493; and *M. v. H.*, [1999] 2 S.C.R. 3.
10. F.L. Morton and Rainer Knopff, *The Charter Revolution and the Court Party* (Peterborough: Broadview Press, 2000).
11. Peter Russell, "The Political Purposes of the Canadian Charter of Rights and Freedoms," *Canadian Bar Review* (March 1983).
12. Michael Mandel, *The Charter of Rights and the Legalization of Politics in Canada*, rev. ed. (Toronto: Wall and Thompson, 1994).
13. Morton and Knopff, *The Charter Revolution*.
14. Seymour Martin Lipset, *Continental Divide* (New York: Routledge, 1990).
15. Greg Hein, "Interest Group Litigation and Canadian Democracy," *Choices* 6, no. 2 (March 2000).
16. Janet Hiebert, *Charter Conflicts: What Is Parliament's Role?* (Montreal: McGill-Queen's University Press, 2002).

Chapter 12

1. Donald Smiley, *The Canadian Political Nationality* (Toronto: Methuen, 1967).
2. Provincial representation within the institutions of the national government is sometimes called "intrastate federalism," as opposed to relations between federal and provincial governments, or "interstate federalism."
3. Peter Russell et al., *Federalism and the Charter* (Ottawa: Carleton University Press, 1989); Peter Hogg, *Constitutional Law of Canada*, 4th ed. (Toronto: Carswell, 1997).
4. V.C. MacDonald, "Judicial Interpretation of the Canadian Constitution," *University of Toronto Law Journal* 1 (1935–36), 260–85; *O'Connor Report*, Senate of Canada, 1939. It is ironic that judicial interpretation contributed to decentralizing a centralized Canadian federation but centralized a decentralized federation in the United States. See Roger Gibbins, *Regionalism* (Toronto: Butterworths, 1982), ch. 4.

5. Alan C. Cairns, "The Governments and Societies of Canadian Federalism," *Canadian Journal of Political Science* (December 1977), 695–725; Cairns, "The Judicial Committee and Its Critics," *Canadian Journal of Political Science* (September 1971), 301–45.

6. Direct taxes are derived from the very people who are intended to pay them, while indirect taxes are extracted from one person with the expectation that they will be passed on to someone else.

7. Donald Smiley, *Canada in Question: Federalism in the Seventies* (Toronto: McGraw-Hill Ryerson, 1972), 56.

8. Ibid.

9. Harvey Lazar, ed., *Canada: The State of the Federation, 1997*; Harvey Lazar and Tom McIntosh, eds., *Canada: The State of the Federation, 1998/99*; and Harvey Lazar, ed., *Canada: The State of the Federation, 1999/2000* (Kingston: Queen's University Institute of Intergovernmental Relations).

10. Herman Bakvis and Grace Skogstad, eds., *Canadian Federalism: Performance, Effectiveness, and Legitimacy* (Toronto: Oxford University Press, 2002).

11. J. Peter Meekison, Hamish Telford, and Harvey Lazar, eds., *Canada: The State of the Federation, 2002: Reconsidering the Institutions of Canadian Federalism* (Kingston: Institute of Intergovernmental Relations, 2002). The authors report that relations among line ministries remain highly interdependent, but that greater financial coordination and improved leadership from first ministers are required.

12. Ibid., esp. chs. 11 and 14.

Chapter 13

1. Leslie A. Pal, *Public Policy Analysis: An Introduction* (Toronto: Methuen, 1987), 4.

2. Samuel A. Bottomley, "Locked and Loaded: Gun Control Policy in Canada," in Robert M. Campbell, et al., eds., *Real Worlds of Canadian Politics: Cases in Process and Policy*, 4th ed. (Peterborough: Broadview Press, 2004).

3. David E. Smith, *The Invisible Crown* (Toronto: University of Toronto Press, 1996).

4. Frank McKinnon, *The Crown in Canada* (Calgary: McClelland and Stewart West, 1976), 124.

5. Andrew Heard, *Canadian Constitutional Conventions: The Marriage of Law and Politics* (Toronto: Oxford University Press, 1991), 47, 123.

6. In the case where no party wins a majority of seats, the convention is that the incumbent prime minister has a right to stay in office until defeated in a nonconfidence vote in the House of Commons.

7. Kenneth Kernaghan and David Siegel, *Public Administration in Canada: A Text*, 2nd ed. (Scarborough: Nelson Canada, 1991), 379–85.

8. Donald J. Savoie, *Governing from the Centre: The Concentration of Power in Canada* (Toronto: University of Toronto Press, 1999); Gordon Robertson, *Memoirs of a Very Civil Servant: Mackenzie King to Pierre Trudeau* (Toronto: University of Toronto Press, 2000); Jeffrey Simpson, *The Friendly Dictatorship* (Toronto: McClelland and Stewart, 2001).

9. Leslie Pal and David Taras, eds., *Prime Ministers and Premiers: Political Leadership and Public Policy in Canada* (Scarborough: Prentice-Hall Canada, 1988); Peter Aucoin, "Prime Ministerial Leadership: Position, Power, and Politics," in Maureen Mancuso et al., *Leaders and Leadership in Canada* (Toronto: Oxford University Press, 1994).

10. Savoie, *Governing from the Centre*, 137–39, 343.

11. Leslie Pal, "Hands at the Helm? Leadership and Public Policy," in Pal and Taras, *Prime Ministers and Premiers*, 25.

12. Frederick Fletcher, "The Prime Minister as Public Persuader," in Thomas A. Hockin, ed., *Apex of Power*, 2nd ed. (Scarborough: Prentice-Hall Canada, 1977).

13. David Taras, "Prime Ministers and the Media," in Pal and Taras, *Prime Ministers and Premiers*.

14. Denis Smith, "President and Parliament: The Transformation of Parliamentary Government in Canada," in Hockin, *Apex of Power*, 315.

15. Herman Bakvis, *Regional Ministers* (Toronto: University of Toronto Press, 1991); "Cabinet Ministers: Leaders or Followers," in Mancuso, *Leaders and Leadership*.

16. W.A. Matheson, *The Prime Minister and the Cabinet* (Toronto: Methuen, 1976), ix, 22–23.

17. S.L. Sutherland, "Responsible Government and Ministerial Responsibility: Every Reform Is Its Own Problem," *Canadian Journal of Political Science* (March 1991), 101.

18. Donald Smiley, *The Federal Condition in Canada* (Toronto: McGraw-Hill Ryerson, 1987), 88.

19. Bruce Doern and Peter Aucoin, eds., *Public Policy in Canada* (Toronto: Macmillan, 1979).

20. J. Stefan Dupré, "Reflections on the Workability of Executive Federalism," in Richard Simeon, ed., *Intergovernmental Relations* (Toronto: University of Toronto Press, 1985). Christopher Dunn suggests the best label would be "prime minister–centred cabinet" in Dunn, ed., *The Handbook of Canadian Public Administration* (Toronto: Oxford University Press, 2002).

21. Glen Milne, *Making Policy: A Guide to the Federal Government's Policy Process* (Ottawa: Glen Milne, 2000), 44.

22. On the Chrétien changes, see *The New Face of Government: A Guide to the New Federal Government Structure*, 2nd ed. (Ottawa: Canada Communication Group, 1994). He later appointed a cabinet committee on Public Security and Anti-terrorism.

23. Edward Greenspon and Anthony Wilson-Smith, *Double Vision: The Inside Story of the Liberals in Power* (Toronto: Doubleday Canada, 1996).

Chapter 14

1. Glen Milne, *Making Policy: A Guide to the Federal Government's Policy Process* (Ottawa: Glen Milne, 2000), 4.

2. Kenneth Kernaghan and David Siegel, *Public Administration in Canada: A Text*, 2nd ed. (Scarborough: Nelson Canada, 1991), 137.

3. S.L. Sutherland, "Responsible Government and Ministerial Responsibility: Every Reform Is Its Own Problem," *Canadian Journal of Political Science* (March 1991), 91–120.

4. Kernaghan and Siegel, *Public Administration in Canada*, 379–85; S.L. Sutherland, "The Al-Mashat Affair: Administrative Responsibility in Parliamentary Institutions," *Canadian Public Administration* (Winter 1991), 573–603.

5. Auditor General, *Reflections on a Decade of Serving Parliament*, Report of the Auditor General of Canada (February 2001), http://www.oag-bvg.gc.ca/domino/reports.nsf/html/01cap_e.html (Retrieved 6 Dec. 2004).

6. Donald J. Savoie, *Breaking the Bargain: Public Servants, Ministers, and Parliament* (Toronto: University of Toronto Press, 2003).

7. Gordon Osbaldeston, *Keeping Deputy Ministers Accountable* (Toronto: McGraw-Hill Ryerson, 1990); Savoie, *Breaking the Bargain*.

8. Linda McQuaig, *The Cult of Impotence* (Toronto: Penguin, 1998).

9. Milne, *Making Policy*, 43.

10. Jeffrey Simpson, *Spoils of Power* (Toronto: Collins, 1988).

11. J.L. Granatstein, *The Ottawa Men: The Civil Service Mandarins, 1935–1957* (Toronto: Oxford University Press, 1982).

12. See, for example, *The Globe and Mail* (December 10, 1997), A4.

13. Treasury Board of Canada Secretariat, *Annual Report on Official Languages, 2002–03*, http://www.tbs.sct.gc.ca/report/OfLang/2003/arol-ralo2_e.asp (Retrieved 30 June 2004).

14. Kathleen Archibald, *Sex and the Public Service* (Ottawa: Queen's Printer, 1970); Task Force on Barriers to Women in the Public Service, *Beneath the Veneer* 1 (Ottawa: Supply and Services, 1990).

15. Rand Dyck, "The Canada Assistance Plan: The Ultimate in Cooperative Federalism," *Canadian Public Administration* (Winter 1976), 587–602.

16. S.L. Sutherland, "On the Audit Trail of the Auditor General: Parliament's Servant, 1973–80," *Canadian Public Administration* (Winter 1980), 616–44; S.L. Sutherland, "The Politics of Audit: The Federal Office of the Auditor General in Comparative Perspective," *Canadian Public Administration* (Spring 1986), 118–48.

17. Kernaghan and Siegel, *Public Administration in Canada*, 498–502.

18. Leslie A. Pal, *Beyond Policy Analysis: Public Issue Management in Turbulent Times* (Scarborough: ITP Nelson, 1997); Guy B. Peters and Donald Savoie, *Taking Stock* (Montreal: McGill-Queen's University Press, 1998).

19. Jocelyn Bourgon, *Third Annual Report to the Prime Minister of Canada* (1995), http://www.pco-bcp.gc.ca/default.asp?Page=Publications&Language=E&doc=3rept95/cover_e.htm (Retrieved 6 Dec. 2004); Treasury Board, *Getting Government Right: Governing for Canadians* (February 1997), http://www.tbs-sct.gc.ca/report/govrev/Gfce.asp (Retrieved 6 Dec. 2004).
20. Kernaghan and Seigel, *Public Administration in Canada*, 4th ed., 302.

Chapter 15

1. C.E.S. Franks, *The Parliament of Canada* (Toronto: University of Toronto Press, 1987); John B. Stewart, *The Canadian House of Commons: Procedure and Reform* (Montreal: McGill-Queen's University Press, 1977).
2. John Bejermi, *Canadian Parliamentary Handbook* (Ottawa: Borealis Press, annual).
3. This and much more interesting and useful information about the House of Commons can be found on the Parliament's website at http://www.parl.gc.ca; click on "About Parliament" and go to the "A to Z Index."
4. Franks, *The Parliament of Canada*, 142.
5. Ibid., 6, 29, 96, 268.
6. Paul Thomas, "The Role of National Party Caucuses," in Peter Aucoin, ed., *Party Government and Regional Representation in Canada* (Toronto: University of Toronto Press, 1985).
7. Most of the others that passed dealt with changes to the name of an MP's constituency. Andrew Heard, *Canadian Constitutional Conventions: The Marriage of Law and Politics* (Toronto: Oxford University Press, 1991), 78.
8. *Standing Orders of the House of Commons* (2004), http://www.parl.gc.ca/information/about/process/house/standingorders/toc-e.htm (Retrieved 6 Dec. 2004); *Précis of Procedure* (2003), http://www.parl.gc.ca/information/about/process/house/precis/titpg-e.htm (Retrieved 6 Dec. 2004); *Glossary of Parliamentary Procedure* (2004), http://www.parl.gc.ca/information/about/process/house/glossary/gloss-e.htm (Retrieved 6 Dec. 2004).
9. Martin Westmacott, "Whips and Party Cohesion," *Canadian Parliamentary Review* 6, no. 3 (Autumn 1983).
10. The Research Branch of the Library of Parliament regularly publishes excellent summaries of political issues for the benefit of MPs and senators. These summaries are also found in many postsecondary libraries as *Background Papers* and *Current Issue Review* or at http://www.parl.gc.ca/common/Library.asp?Language=E.
11. Other defeats that did not cause much fanfare are noted in Franks, *The Parliament of Canada*, 139.
12. R.A. MacKay, *The Unreformed Senate of Canada*, rev. ed. (Toronto: McClelland and Stewart, 1967).
13. MacKay, *The Unreformed Senate*, 91–95; F.A. Kunz, *The Modern Senate of Canada, 1925–1963: A Re-Appraisal* (Toronto: University of Toronto Press, 1965), 337–47. Andrew Heard argues that a constitutional convention is emerging that the Senate may not insist on altering the financial provisions of money bills. See *Canadian Constitutional Conventions*, 94.
14. Kunz, *The Modern Senate*, 53–56. The case was officially referred to as *Edwards v. Att. Gen. of Can.*, [1930] A.C. 124.
15. MacKay, *The Unreformed Senate*, 110; Kunz, *The Modern Senate*, 186.
16. Colin Campbell, *The Canadian Senate: A Lobby from Within* (Toronto: Macmillan, 1978), 12–19, 147.
17. MacKay, *The Unreformed Senate*, 96–112.
18. In 1873, Alexander Mackenzie had asked the British government to summon additional senators but was refused on the ground that this was not necessary at the time.
19. Peter McCormick, "Canada Needs a Triple E Senate," in Paul Fox and Graham White, eds., *Politics: Canada*, 7th ed. (Toronto: McGraw-Hill Ryerson, 1991), 435–39; H. McConnell, "The Case for a 'Triple E' Senate," *Queen's Quarterly* (Autumn 1988), 683–98.
20. Serge Joyal, *Protecting Democracy: The Senate You Never Knew* (Montreal: McGill-Queen's University Press, 2003).

Chapter 16

1. Peter Russell, *The Judiciary in Canada: The Third Branch of Government* (Toronto: McGraw-Hill Ryerson, 1987), 5.
2. Ibid., 14.
3. Peter Russell, "The Effect of a Charter of Rights on the Policy-Making Role of the Canadian Courts," *Canadian Public Administration* (Spring 1982), 2.
4. Peter McCormick, *Canada's Courts* (Toronto: Lorimer, 1994), 3.
5. Russell, *The Judiciary in Canada*, 6.
6. Gerald L. Gall, *The Canadian Legal System*, 3rd ed. (Toronto: Carswell, 1990), 23–28.
7. Ibid., 30.
8. McCormick, *Canada's Courts*, 23.
9. Ibid., 56.
10. Russell, *The Judiciary in Canada*, 290.
11. Ibid., 313, 319–27; Peter Hogg, *Constitutional Law of Canada*, 2nd ed. (Toronto: Carswell, 1985), 142–48.
12. James G. Snell and Frederick Vaughan, *The Supreme Court of Canada: History of the Institution* (Toronto: The Osgoode Society, 1985); Russell, *The Judiciary in Canada*, 337.
13. Recent insights about its operation can be gleaned from biographies of two key players in Robert J. Sharpe and Kent Roach's *Brian Dickson: A Judge's Journey* (Toronto: University of Toronto Press, 2003) and Ellen Anderson's *Judging Bertha Wilson: Law as Large as Life* (Toronto: University of Toronto Press, 2002).
14. Carl Baar quotes an oft-repeated maxim that "to become a judge in the United States, you must be elected; to become a judge in Canada, you must be defeated," in "The Structure and Personnel of the Canadian Judiciary," in Paul Fox and Graham White, eds., *Politics: Canada*, 7th ed. (Toronto: McGraw-Hill Ryerson, 1991), 513.
15. Andrew Heard, *Canadian Constitutional Conventions: The Marriage of Law and Politics* (Toronto: Oxford University Press, 1991), 135.
16. During the Mulroney government's first term, 48 percent of all judges appointed were known Conservative supporters compared to 7 percent who supported opposition parties. Peter Russell and Jacob Ziegel, "Federal Judicial Appointments: An Appraisal of the First Mulroney Government's Appointments and the New Judiciary Advisory Committees," *University of Toronto Law Journal* 41 (1991), 4–37.
17. Commissioner for Federal Judicial Affairs, *Judicial Appointments: Information Guide and a New Judicial Appointments Process* (Ottawa: Supply and Services, 1988).
18. McCormick, *Canada's Courts*, 112.
19. Jacob S. Ziegel, *Merit Selection and Democratization of Appointments to the Supreme Court of Canada* (Montreal: Institute for Research on Public Policy, 1999); Standing Committee on Justice, Human Rights, Public Safety and Emergency Preparedness, "Improving the Supreme Court of Canada Appointments Process" (May 2004), http://www.parl.gc.ca/committee/CommitteePublication.aspx?SourceId=84157 (Retrieved 6 Dec. 2004).
20. Dennis Olsen, *The State Elite* (Toronto: McClelland and Stewart, 1980), ch. 3; Russell, *The Judiciary in Canada*, 164–65.
21. Heard, *Canadian Constitutional Conventions*, 124; Russell, *The Judiciary in Canada*, 176; Gall, *The Canadian Legal System*, 227–39.
22. *Valente v. the Queen*, [1985] 2 S.C.R. 673; Perry S. Millar and Carl Baar, *Judicial Administration in Canada* (Montreal: McGill-Queen's University Press, 1981).
23. Heard, *Canadian Constitutional Conventions*, 131; Russell, *The Judiciary in Canada*, 85–89; Gall, *The Canadian Legal System*, 236–38; McCormick, *Canada's Courts*, 130–31.

Index